Henry Brougham Guppy

The Solomon Islands And Their Natives

Henry Brougham Guppy

The Solomon Islands And Their Natives

ISBN/EAN: 9783744731843

Printed in Europe, USA, Canada, Australia, Japan

Cover: Foto ©Andreas Hilbeck / pixelio.de

More available books at **www.hansebooks.com**

THE

SOLOMON ISLANDS

AND

Their Natives.

BY

H. B. GUPPY, M.B., F.G.S.

LATE SURGEON, R.N.

LONDON:

SWAN SONNENSCHEIN, LOWREY & CO.,

PATERNOSTER SQUARE,

1887.

PREFACE.

WHEN, in the beginning of 1881, H.M.S. "Lark" was being prepared for her commission as a surveying ship in the Western Pacific, I was selected by Sir John Watt Reid, the Medical Director-General of the Navy, to be appointed as Surgeon. For this selection I was also in some measure indebted to the late Sir Frederick Evans, then Hydrographer, who was desirous that a person possessing tastes for natural history should be chosen. I subsequently received some instructions from Dr. Günther, Keeper of Zoology in the British Museum, to whom I may take this opportunity of expressing my sincere thanks for the encouragement he gave to me during the commission. Unfortunately there were no public funds from which I could be assisted; and, as a matter of fact, I may state that all expenses had to come out of my pay as a naval surgeon. At the close of the commission I received, mainly through the influence of Dr. Günther, a promise of a grant of £150 from the Royal Society of London for the exploration of the interior of the large island of Guadalcanar; but a very serious illness prevented me from carrying out my intention, and thus an expedition, which I had looked forward to as a fitting completion of my work in these islands, was never undertaken. However, my disappointment was in some measure diminished on my arrival in England, after being invalided, by the important results arising from the examination by Dr. John Murray, Director of the Challenger Commission, of that portion of my geological collection which threw light on the formation of coral reefs, and which exhibited the deep-sea deposits of the Challenger Expedition as rocks composing islands in the Solomon Group. To Dr. Murray I am indebted for much kindness in many ways, and I gladly take this opportunity of expressing my sincerest thanks.

In this volume I have chiefly confined myself to my observations on the anthropology, natural history, botany, and meteorology of the group, having originally reserved my account of the geology and of the coral reefs, together with my special descriptions of the islands, for another volume, which I hoped to publish shortly, if my first undertaking proved a success. My reasons for thus acting were to be found in a lack of funds and in the necessity of not over-lading my first venture, which, like a ship carrying a heavy though perhaps a valuable cargo, might founder within sight of the port of departure. This difficulty has been met by a generous arrangement of my publishers, in consequence of which both volumes will be brought out together. All my notes relating to these islands are there embodied, with the exception of my coral reef observations, which have been recently published by the Royal Society of Edinburgh in their Proceedings (1885-1886). However, to make this volume more complete, I have added a short introductory chapter containing a general description of the islands.

It is necessary that I should here briefly allude to the circumstances under which my observations and collections were made. Had I been previously aware of the difficulties and discomforts that would attend me, I should have hesitated to have performed more than a tithe of what I finally accomplished "per varios casus per tot discrimina rerum." Inexperienced and deprived of any official support or recognition of other than my professional duties, I was only urged on by the consciousness of the importance of the work I had voluntarily undertaken. At length my health began to give way, and it was with mixed feelings of satisfaction and apprehension that I returned to the islands for the third and last year. One cause of continual worry lay in the fact that for two-thirds of the time spent in this region, I had only my cabin for the disposal of my collections, the size of the ship (a schooner of about 150 tons), and the arrange-ments made before leaving England, not permitting of any other plan.

Under these circumstances I received the greatest assist-ance from Lieut.-Commander C. F. Oldham, who, notwith-standing that he had received no instructions concerning myself, smoothed the way for me and gave me the oppor-tunities I desired, often, it should be added, at the expense of much anxiety to himself. To the officers, Lieut. C. F. de M. Malan, Lieut. T. H. Heming, and Lieut. A. Leeper, I am lastingly indebted, not only for their constant aid, but also for the sympathy they evinced towards myself and my pursuits. From the petty-officers and crew I received much voluntary help, and I was often indebted to the services of Mr. Samuel Redman and Mr. Albert Rowe. My right-hand man was Mr. William Isabell who had been sent to the ship as Leading-Stoker to take charge of the condenser. Without his aid in the packing away of my collections and his cheerful readiness to assist me in every way throughout the commission, I should have broken down long before I did. To his careful attendance during my illness I owe my life.

With reference to the different sections of this work, I should remark that the anthropological notes are for the most part now published for the first time. The translation of Gallego's Journal and the historical sketch of the re-discovery of the group will, I hope, have a general as well as a special interest. In my natural history notes it will be seen that I am greatly indebted to the papers on my collections of shells and reptiles by Mr. Edgar Smith and Mr. G. A. Boulenger. For the identification of the greater part of my botanical collection, I am indebted to the courtesy of the officials at Kew and particularly to that of Prof. Oliver. I take this opportunity of acknowledging the kind assistance I received at Melbourne from Baron Ferd. von Mueller. My inexperience in botanical collecting considerably diminished the value of my collections, which have further suffered from the fact that I have been unable after repeated application to learn anything of a collection of ferns that I presented to the British Museum. During the commission I profited greatly by Lieut. Malan's previous experiences of the Pacific Islands. To Lieut. Leeper I am greatly indebted, as shown in the chapters on the vocabulary of Bougainville Straits and on the meteorology of the group. The enumeration of the many disinterested services I have received would carry me far beyond the limits of a preface. Of all of them I shall retain a lasting remembrance.

HENRY BROUGHAM GUPPY.

17 Woodlane, Falmouth.

INTRODUCTION.

THE Solomon Islands cover an area 600 miles in length. They include seven or eight large mountainous islands attaining an extreme height, as in the case of Guadalcanar and Bougainville, of from 8,000 to 10,000 feet, and possessing a length varying from 70 to 100 miles, and a breadth varying between 20 and 30 miles. In addition, there are a great number of smaller islands which range in size from those 15 to 20 miles in length to the tiny coral island only half a mile across. The islands fall naturally into two divisions, those mainly or entirely of volcanic formations and those mainly or entirely of recent calcareous formations.

In the first division, St. Christoval may be taken as a type of the large mountainous islands possessing massive profiles, such as Guadalcanar, Malaita, Isabel, etc. St. Christoval, which rises to a height of 4,100 feet above the sea, is composed in the mass of much altered and sometimes highly crystalline volcanic rocks (such as, in their order of frequency, dolerites, diabases, diorites, gabbros, serpentines, and saussuritic felspar-rock) which, as I learn from Mr. T. Davies, have been both formed and altered at considerable depths and indicate great geological age and extensive denudation. Recent calcareous rocks, such as will be subsequently referred to in the description of the second division of islands, flank the lower slopes at the sea-border up to an elevation of 500 feet. Fragments of similar diorites, dolerites, and other dense basic rocks, all much altered and often schistose, have been transported by trees to the coral islets off the coasts of Guadalcanar and afford evidence of the geological structure of that island. Serpentines were obtained by Dr Hombron in 1838[1] from St. George's Island, which is " ipso facto " a portion of Isabel. Bougainville and New Georgia are largely of more recent origin, as is indicated by their numerous symmetrical vol-

---

[1] " Voyage au Pole Sud et dans L'Oceanie," (D'Urville). Geologie : part ii., p. 211.

canic cones. However, the geological evidence at present at our disposal points generally to the great antiquity of the larger islands. The significance of this fact will be subsequently referred to. There can be little doubt that some of the mountainous islands will be found to yield in quantity the ores of tin and copper. A resident trader, Captain John Macdonald, has discovered arsenical pyrites and stream tin at the head of the Keibeck River in the interior of St. Christoval. A sample of stream tin from the southeast part of Bougainville was given to me by the Shortland chief. Copper will not improbably be found in association with the serpentine rocks of these islands.

The smaller islands of volcanic formation group themselves into two classes :

(1.) Those which, like Fauro and some of the Florida Islands, are composed partly of modern rocks, such as hornblende and augite-andesites with their tuffs and agglomerates, and partly of ancient and often highly crystalline rocks such as, as I am informed by Prof. Judd and Mr. T. Davies, quartz-diorites, quartz-porphyries, altered dacites and dolerites, serpentines, saussuritic felspar-rock, etc.

(2.) Those that are composed entirely or in the main of recently erupted rocks, islands which preserve the volcanic profile, possess craters, and sometimes exhibit signs of latent activity. Eddystone Island, which I examined, is probably typical of the majority of the islands of this class, such as Savo, Murray Island, and many others. It is composed of andesitic lavas of the augite type, is pierced by many fumaroles, and has a crater in the solfatara stage. Savo, though quiescent in the present day, has been in eruption within the memory of living men, and was in a state of activity in 1567 when the Spaniards discovered the group. Fumaroles and sulphur-deposits occur in Vella-la-vella. It may, however, be generally stated that the volcanic forces in these regions are in a quiescent condition at the present day, there being only one vent in active eruption, viz., Mount Bagana in the interior of Bougainville. Many small islands with volcanic profiles show no evidence of a latent activity. Amongst them I may mention those of Bougainville Strait, which are composed of andesitic lavas of the hornblende type.

I now pass to those islands which are composed mainly or entirely of recent calcareous formations.[1] Excluding the

[1] *Vide* my paper on this subject (Trans. Roy. Soc. Edin. : vol. xxxii., p. 545), and my work on the geology of this group.

innumerable islets that have been formed on the coral reefs at the present sea-level, we come first to those small islands and islets less than 100 feet in height, such as the Three Sisters and Stirling Island, which are composed entirely of coral limestone. In the next place there are islands of larger size and greater height, such as Ugi, which are composed in bulk of partially consolidated bedded deposits containing numerous foraminifera, and possessing the characters of the muds which were found by the "Challenger" Expedition to be at present forming around oceanic volcanic islands in depths probably of from 150 to 500 fathoms. Coral limestones encrust the lower slopes of these islands and do not attain a greater thickness than 150 feet. The next type is to be found in Treasury Island which has a similar structure to that of Ugi, but possesses in its centre an ancient volcanic peak that was once submerged and is now covered over by these recent deposits. Then, there are islands, such as the principal island of the Shortlands, in which the volcanic mass has become an eccentric nucleus, from which line after line of barrier-reef has been advanced based on the soft deposits. These soft deposits contain amongst other organic remains, the shells of pteropods and the tests of foraminifera in great abundance. In such islands I did not find that the coral limestone had a thickness of as much as 100 feet. In this island the upraised reefs are based upon hard foraminiferal limestones. Lastly, we have the upraised atoll of Santa Anna which within the small compass of a height of 470 feet displays the several stages of its growth ; first, the originally submerged volcanic peak ; then, the investing soft deposit resembling in character a deep-sea clay and considered to have been formed in considerable depths, probably from 1500 to 2000 fathoms ; and over all, the ring of coral limestone that cannot far exceed 150 feet in thickness. The islands formed mainly of the soft foraminiferous deposits have long level summits free from peaks. Judging from their profiles, the islands of Ulaua and Ronongo will be found to possess the structure of Ugi and Treasury. The western end of Choiseul has a very significant profile, and I have little doubt from my examination of the lower slopes that this extremity of the island is mainly composed of the recent soft deposits.

I now proceed to refer very shortly to the coral reefs [1] of these islands. The three principal classes are to be found in

---

[1] *Vide* my paper on this subject. (Proc. Roy. Soc., Edin., 1885-86.)

this region ; but of these, the fringing and barrier-reefs are more commonly distributed, whilst the atolls are comparatively few in number and of small size. A line of barrier-reefs, probably not much under 60 miles in length and bearing innumerable islets on its surface, fronts the east coasts of the islands of New Georgia at a distance of from one to three miles from the shore. Extensive reefs of the same class, having a broad deep-water channel inside them, lie off the large island of Isabel and off the south-coast of Choiseul. Barrier-reefs, of smaller extent, also skirt the west end of Guadalcanar and the southern end of Bougainville. I have referred particularly to these reefs because at the time that Mr. Darwin wrote his work on "Coral Reefs," fringing-reefs were alone believed to exist in these islands.

The larger islands of the Solomon Group are often separated from each other by depths of several hundred fathoms. St. Christoval, for instance, is separated from the neighbouring islands of Guadalcanar and Malaita by straits in which casts of 200 fathoms fail to reach the bottom. On the other hand, the same 100 fathom line includes both Bougain-and Choiseul. Judging, however, from the soundings obtained by Lieut.-Commander Oldham between the islands lying off the north coast of St. Christoval, it would appear probable that depths of 400 fathoms commonly occur between the islands of the Solomon Group. Although the soundings hitherto made in this portion of the Western Pacific go to show that this archipelago, together with New Ireland and New Britain, are included within the same 1,000 fathom line, which extends as a loop from the adjacent borders of New Guinea, we can scarcely urge this fact as evidence of a former land connection, seeing that one of the most interesting features in the geological history of this region is that of the enormous elevation which these islands have experienced in recent and probably sub-recent times. Independently of the character of the deposits discovered by me in the Solomon Islands, I arrived at the conclusion that there had been a recent upheaval of at least 1,500 feet. The characters of some of the deposits, as examined by Dr. Murray in the light of the "Challenger" soundings, however, afford indications of an upheaval of a far more extensive nature. I am informed, in fact, by Mr. H. B. Brady, that the foraminifera of some of the Treasury Island rocks indicate depths of probably from 1500 to 2000 fathoms. Geologists may look forward with the greatest

interest to the results of the examination by Mr. Brady
of the foraminiferous deposits of the Western Pacific.
One of the most important results will be to establish the
great elevation which has occurred in this region during
Post-Tertiary times. We are therefore justified in regarding the island groups of the Western Pacific as having
always retained their insular condition, situated, as they are,
in a region of upheaval, and separated, as they are, from
each other and from the Australian continent by depths of
from 1,000 to 2,400 fathoms. I have already pointed out
that the volcanic rocks of the large islands of the Solomon
Group are geologically ancient. Their elevation and the
great subaerial denudation which they have experienced
afford indications of the insular condition having been preserved from remote ages. It is this prolonged isolation that
explains the occurrence of the peculiar forms of the am-
phibia which I discovered in Bougainville Straits, and that
accounts for many of the peculiarities of the fauna of this
archipelago.

Having thus briefly considered the leading geological and
hydrological features of this group, I pass on to consider
these islands in the point of view of an intending settler.
They are for the most part clothed with dense forest and
rank undergrowth, and it is only here and there, as in the
western portion of Guadalcanar and in limited localities in
St. Christoval, that the forest gives place to long grass and
ferns, a change often corresponding with the passage from a
clayey and calcareous to a dry porous and volcanic soil.
As a rule, the calcareous districts of a large island possess a
rich red argillaceous soil, often 5 or 6 feet in thickness, and
in such localities the streams are large and numerous. In
the districts of volcanic formation the soil is dry, friable,
and porous, whilst the streams are few in number and of no
great size. In the principal island of the Shortlands the
difference in the character of the soil between the volcanic
north-west part and the remaining calcareous portion is well
exhibited. In the smaller islands the soil varies in character
according to the formation, those of volcanic origin being
singularly destitute of streams.

In chapter XVII. I have dwelt with some detail on the
climate. The healthiest portion of the group would, as I think,
be found in the eastern islands, and the healthiest part of each
island would be that which is exposed to the blast of the
south-east trade during a large portion of the year. The ex-

cessive annual rainfall, the humid atmosphere, together with the enervating season of the north-west monsoon, are amongst the chief evils of the climate. Malarious districts can be readily avoided by shunning the low-lying damp districts on the lee sides of islands. Dysentery is rare on account of the general purity of the water. But, if we believe native testimony, which I have found most reliable and which in this instance agrees with my own, the streams draining calcareous regions are least liable to suspicion. Should an intending settler ask me whether the climate is suitable for the European, I would reply that with proper precautions as to his habits and the selection of a site, the white-man can here preserve his health as well as in most other tropical islands in these latitudes.

I will conclude this introduction with some remarks on the vexed question of making annexations and forming protectorates in the Western Pacific. From the eagerness of our Australian colonies to control them and of France and Germany to possess them, the presumption arises that the islands in this region are worth holding. Yet, how surprising have been the changes within the last four years! When in 1882 I was in the Solomon Islands, British influence was recognised as paramount in New Guinea and throughout the Western Pacific. At the present time the British flag has been almost squeezed out of the Western Pacific. In April of this year (1886), the British and German Governments came to an arrangement by which the northern side of New Guinea together with New Britain, New Ireland, and the adjacent western half of the Solomon Group passed under the protection, or in other words into the practical possession, of Germany; whilst Great Britain by this arrangement was to consider the remaining islands of the Western Pacific and the south coast of New Guinea as her sphere of action. It is only in New Guinea that Great Britain has exercised her right. Amongst the remaining islands of the Western Pacific she has little scope either for acquiring territory or for establishing a protectorate. France possesses New Caledonia and in a geographical sense she can claim not only the Loyalty Islands but the New Hebrides Group. There only remains then for Great Britain the Santa Cruz Islands and the adjacent eastern half of the Solomon Group, in which, if she chooses, she can exercise her rights without dispute.

England's wisest policy in the Western Pacific is to

recognise the existing condition of things, and to deal with France as generously as she has dealt with Germany. Stifling my own patriotic regrets, I cannot but think that the presence of Germany in these regions will be fraught with great advantage to the world of science. When we recall our spasmodic efforts to explore New Guinea and the comparatively small results obtained, when we remember to how great an extent such attempts have been supported by private enterprise and how little they have been due to government or even to semi-official aid, we have reason to be glad that the exploration of these regions will be conducted with that thoroughness which can only be obtained when, as in the case of Germany, geographical enterprises become the business of the State.

CONTENTS.

CHAPTER V.

CULTIVATION—FOOD, &c.

CHAPTER VI.

THE PHYSICAL CHARACTERS AND RACE—AFFINITIES OF THESE ISLANDERS.

CHAPTER VII.

DRESS—TATTOOING—SONGS, &c.

CHAPTER VIII.

CANOES—FISHING—HUNTING.

CHAPTER IX.

PREVALENT DISEASES

CHAPTER X.

A VOCABULARY OF BOUGAINVILLE STRAITS.

THE SOLOMON ISLANDS.

CHAPTER I.

INTRODUCTORY.

THOSE who have never been tempted "to seek strange truths in undiscovered lands," will perhaps find it difficult to appreciate the disappointments, inconveniences, and petty difficulties which beset the traveller, however favourably circumstanced he may be. Patience and perseverance enable him finally to disregard these lesser hindrances and to devote his undisturbed attention to the principal objects he has in view : and thus, when writing at some future time the narrative of his experiences, he gives but little prominence to matters which affected very materially at the moment both his personal comfort and his chances of success.

Amongst the Solomon Islands the student of nature may be compared to a man who, having found a mine of great wealth, is only allowed to carry away just so much of the precious ore as he can bear about his person. For there can be no region of the world where he experiences more tantalisation. Day after day he skirts the shores of islands of which science has no "ken." Month after month, he may scan, as I have done, lofty mountain-masses never yet explored, whose peaks rise through the clouds to heights of from 7,000 to 10,000 feet above the sea. He may discern on the mountain-slopes the columns of blue smoke which mark the abodes of men who have never beheld the white man. But he cannot land except accompanied by a strong party ; and he has therefore to be content usually with viewing such scenes from the deck of his vessel. Fortunately, however, there are some parts of the Solomon

A

Group where the hostility of the natives has been to a great extent overcome by the influence of the missionaries and of the traders; but the interiors of the larger islands are almost without exception inhabited by fierce and treacherous tribes who forbid all approach.

In this chapter I have endeavoured to give some idea of my experiences during my rambles in different islands of the group. When geologising in these islands, one labours under the very serious disadvantage of being unable to get any view or form any idea of the surroundings, on account of the dense forest-growth clothing both the slopes and summits of the hills, which is often impassable except by the rude native tracks that are completely hemmed in by trees on either side. Bush walking, where there is no native track, is a very tedious process and requires the constant use of the compass. In districts of coral limestone, such traverses are equally trying to the soles of one's boots and to the measure of one's temper. After being provokingly entangled in a thicket for some minutes, the persevering traveller walks briskly along through a comparatively clear space, when a creeper suddenly trips up his feet and over he goes to the ground. Picking himself up, he no sooner starts again when he finds his face in the middle of a strong web which some huge-bodied spider has been laboriously constructing. However, clearing away the web from his features, he struggles along until coming to the fallen trunk of some giant of the forest which obstructs his path, he with all confidence plants his foot firmly on it and sinks knee-deep into rotten wood. With resignation he lifts his foot out of the mess and proceeds on his way, when he feels an uncomfortable sensation inside his helmet, in which, on leisurely removing it from his head, he finds his old friend the spider, with body as big as a filbert, quite at its ease. Shaking it out in a hurry, he hastens along with his composure of mind somewhat ruffled. Going down a steep slope, he clasps a stout-looking areca palm to prevent himself falling, when down comes the rotten palm, and the long-suffering traveller finds himself once more on the ground. To these inconveniences must be added the peculiarly oppressive heat of a tropical forest, the continual perspiration in which the skin is bathed, and the frequent difficulty of getting water. There are therefore many drawbacks to the enjoyment of such excursions undertaken without an aim. But let there be some object to be gained, and it is astonishing how small a success amply repays the naturalist for all the toil. As an example of the tedious nature of bush walking in these regions, I may state that crossing the small island of Santa Anna from south to north—a distance of 2½ miles—occupied on one occasion five hours. For nearly the whole distance my path lay either through a dense forest-growth which had never been cleared since this little island first rose as a coral-atoll above the waves, or amongst tangled undergrowth which often succeeded effectually in barring the way. Rarely could I obtain a glimpse of my surroundings, and in consequence it was on my pocket-compass that I entirely depended. Coral-rock honeycombed into sharp tearing edges covered the slopes, my way lying between the large masses of this rock that lay about in strange confusion, the smaller blocks swaying about under my weight as if eager to rid themselves of their unusual burden. At one place the coral-limestone over a space of about a hundred yards was perforated like a sieve by numerous holes two to three feet across and five to ten feet deep: but now and then a deep fissure appeared at the bottom of one of these cavities—leading Heaven knows where—in all probability the swallow-hole of some stream that once became engulphed in the solid rock. The spreading roots of trees, together with ferns and shrubs, often nearly concealed these man-traps from my view; and I found it necessary to clear the way for every step, a very tedious process at the close of a tiresome day's excursion.

In many places that I visited, the ascent of the stream-courses afforded the only opportunity of learning anything of the geological structure on account of the thick forest and the depth of the soil on the hill-slopes. Only at times are the sun's rays able to penetrate the dusky ravines through which the streams flow, being usually intercepted by the matted foliage overhead. Even in the hottest day, such a walk is pleasantly cool, since the necessity of wading waist-deep and sometimes of swimming is not unfrequent in the deeper parts of the stream. However, I found on more than one occasion, after having been wading for several hours along one of the streams in the cool damp air of the ravine, that I experienced a sudden sensation of chilliness accompanied by lassitude and nausea, the thermometer at the time registering 80° in the shade. Probably the depressing effects of the gloom and damp air of the ravine, and the wading for several hours under these conditions, may explain these symptoms.

I should have before referred to another very frequent inconvenience which, in more senses than one, dampened the ardour with which I set out on many of my excursions amongst these islands. The annual rainfall in these regions is probably about five times as much as the average annual rainfall in England. The showers themselves are usually very heavy, and often rain falls at the rate of an inch in the hour, which means a thorough wetting in less than a minute. When in the eastern part of the group, I rarely used to return on board without having had half-an-inch, or an inch, of rain distributed over my person. Such wettings, however, do but little harm as long as a flannel suit is worn, since the weather generally clears up after each shower and the powerful rays of the sun dry the clothes in a very few minutes without there being the necessity of stopping to take them off.

In spite of the numerous drawbacks, my excursions never lost their interest. Although accustomed to traverse districts which have been upheaved in recent times to elevations of several hundred feet above the sea, the finding of an ancient coral-reef high up a densely-wooded hill-slope, or the picking up of sand and recent sea shells in the interior of an island now supporting a luxuriant vegetation, always excited the same feelings of wonder and interest that I experienced on first landing on one of the recently upheaved islands of the Solomon Group. My thirst, fatigue, and bruises, were forgotten, as whilst contemplating my surroundings over a pipe I attempted to picture to myself the stages in the history of the island on which I was standing, and reflected on the unwritten past of the natives sitting smoking on the ground around me.

I was rarely unaccompanied in my excursions, since with the prospect of getting tobacco and pipes at the close of the day, natives were always found eager to accompany me. Frequently the boys and lads of the village were only too glad to assist me in carrying my bags. The young imps were always full of fun and frolic, making themselves useful in all kinds of ways, and enlivening the time by their singing, laughing, and continual chattering. Many were the speculations made concerning the nature of my pursuits, and many were the questions to which I had to give some reply. Gorai, the chief of the Shortland Islands, was very desirous to know what I made with the rocks I collected; but I found it somewhat difficult to give him an explanation which he could understand. On one occasion I was the cause of much amusement and perplexity to the natives of the village of Sinasoro in Bougainville Straits.

Hitherto I had been known to them chiefly on account of my
rock-breaking propensities, but during that particular visit I was
making a collection of plants. The chief men of the village received me very civilly, made me sit down, and began at once to
speculate on the nature of my new pursuit, the botanical line
being a new object for wonder with them. " Patu, he finish ?" (patu
meaning stone) was the question put to me by more than one of
their number ; and on my telling them that I was going to turn my
attention to " bulu-bulu "—their general name for plants they have
no name for—I had to explain to further inquirers that a particular fern, named " sinimi" in the native tongue (a species of
Gleichenia), which flourished on the higher slopes of their island, was
one of the objects of my excursion.

My usual plan on arriving at a village, which I had never
visited before, was to distribute a little tobacco amongst the curious
throng that pressed around, and then to light my pipe and look
pleasant whilst my guides were endeavouring to explain the
character of my pursuits. A white man without tobacco in these
islands is worse off than a man without any money in his purse in
London : for very little is given for nothing by these natives, and
the acceptance of a gift binds you to give an equivalent in return.
I remember once when landing on the beach of a village where the
natives seemed a little uncertain as to what kind of reception
they should give me, what a rapid transformation was produced by
the gift of a little tobacco to the chief. Where there had been
scowls and sullen looks a few moments before, smiles and laughter
now prevailed. The chief led me into his house, introduced me
to his principal wife, and in another minute I was dangling his
little son of about two years old upon my knee. This pleasing
transformation had been effected by the expenditure of a half-
pennyworth of tobacco ; and I could not resist framing at the time
the following doggrel rhyme, the excuse for which must be the
occasion that gave rise to it.

> Shade of Exeter Hall ! emerge from thy pall,
> Learn the token of union 'twixt white man and black :
> Not a brisk cannonade, nor the attractions of trade,
> But the mysterious influence of the fragrant *tambak*.[1]

[1] This is the manner of pronouncing "tobacco" amongst these islanders. In the Malay
Archipelago it is pronounced " tambaku." ("Crawfurd's Malay Grammar and Dictionary.")

Although I was rarely absent from the ship more than a couple of days at a time, my excursions had occasionally, as regards the number of my attendants, somewhat of an imposing appearance. Being anxious to visit a district named Komalia, on the north-west side of Alu, the principal of the Shortland Islands, that being the locality from which the natives obtained their slabs of a hard, crystalline diorite, upon which they used to sharpen their knives and axes, Gorai, the chief, volunteered to take me there. Accordingly, he appeared alongside the ship the next morning in a large war-canoe, fifty feet long, and manned by eighteen paddle-men. We started, twenty-four all told, including Gorai, three of his sons, and myself. The chief and I sat beside each other, on the second bow thwart, the post, I believe, which is usually occupied by a chief. Leaving the Onua anchorage shortly before ten A.M., we proceeded easily along at about three miles an hour, coasting the north side of Alu and passing numerous islets on the way. The day was fine but very hot, and there was no protection from the glare of the sun on the water. About half-past one, we reached the north-west point of Alu, where we put into a small cove to get water. Here we saw the tracks of a crocodile on the sand; and on proceeding on our way we saw another on the beach, which, however, soon dived into the sea. Shortly after this, two-thirds of the crew of the canoe jumped overboard after a small turtle, which managed to evade them. The men in the water disturbed another crocodile, which rushed boldly through the line of swimmers, and, diving under our canoe, soon disappeared. Three dugongs came up to the surface close to us; and the old chief fired a shot with his snider at one of them, but without much apparent effect. About half-past two, we reached our destination, and we at once proceeded in search of the volcanic rocks, which we soon succeeded in finding. There was not the slightest reason to question on what errand we were employed, and I doubt if there was ever a more odd-looking party of geologists. The old chief, distinguished from the rest of his men by a shirt, his only article of apparel, led the way; and I followed with about a dozen of his natives. Taking the cue from me, the whole party immediately began breaking up the rocks, and I was in a very short time supplied with an abundance of material to select from. Courtesy, however, compelled me to take all the chief brought to me, which was somewhat inconvenient since the old man displayed much energy in using my geological hammer. On returning to the beach where the canoe had been drawn up, we found that some of the natives had captured a wild boar by the aid of their dogs and spears. The animal was already disembowelled and was being quartered. Whilst we were preparing our evening meal, some of the men made temporary couches for the chief, his three sons, and myself, these couches being merely a layer of poles resting at their ends on two logs and raised about six inches above the ground, the materials being quickly obtained in the adjoining wood. As night fell, we lay down on our couches and smoked, whilst the natives, who had lit about half-a-dozen fires, were waiting for their roast pig, the quarters of which had been placed on a large pile of burning logs, built up in layers to a height of three feet, with three poles placed like a tripod over the pile to draw the fire up. When it was quite dark, the numerous fires lit up the wood around, whilst the natives made the place resound with their singing and laughter. Over our pipes, Gorai and I had some conversation on his ideas of a future state, which he summed up concisely in the phrase "go ground." In the middle of the night heavy rain came on; and since there was no shelter, I had simply to lie still and let it come down. My companions, however, used their pandanus mats to cover themselves from head to foot, and did not appear to be, in the slightest degree, inconvenienced by the wet.

On another occasion, I spent a night on the summit of Treasury Island, in the company of four natives, one of whom, named Erosini, knew a little English. Leaving the anchorage in the early morning, a three hours' tramp brought us to the large stream named Tellatella, on the north-east side of the island. Another four hours were occupied in wading up the stream, when we commenced to ascend the hill-slopes, arriving at the summit late in the afternoon. From here we could see, at a distance of about sixty miles, the lofty peaks of Bougainville, and midway between us lay the white beaches of the Shortland Islands. As it was getting dusk, we began to look around for what Erosini had described to me as a house where we might pass the night. It turned out, however, to be a very dilapidated "lean-to," which had been temporarily occupied by a native who had come up to look after his sago palms a year or more before. My men immediately set to work to make it habitable for the night, and then they began to prepare their evening meal, consisting of a two-pound tin of beef, three opossums, and a large fresh-water eel which had been captured during the day. With the night-fall, the

concert of frogs, lizards, and insects began. One could readily distinguish amongst the notes of the various contributors in the evening
chorus, the "kooroo" of the lizard, and the "appa-appa" of the frog,
sounds from which the native names for these creatures are derived,
viz., "kurru-rupu" and "appa-appa." Numerous fire-flies lit up the
recesses of the forest, as if to disclose the hiding-places of the performers in the general discord, but to no purpose ; and soon, rather
fatigued by our day's exertions, we fell asleep. So little had my
companions been used to wander over their island, that I found
three out of the four had never been in that locality before.

Not unfrequently, after having carefully chosen my guides, I have
found it necessary to lead instead of to follow ; but as a rule my
men have been very willing to trust to the directions of the compass, which I have found absolutely necessary in crossing the
smaller islands with no track to guide the course. Some of my
pleasantest memories are associated with my traverses across those
smaller islands. After forcing my way during some hours through
a tangled forest, irritated by the numerous obstructions in my
course and sweltering under the oppressive heat, I have suddenly
emerged from the trees on the weather coast of the island, where
the invigorating blast of the trade in a few moments restores the
equilibrium of mind and body as one drinks in the healthful breeze.
After such an experience, I have found myself with my native companions standing on the brink of a bold line of coral-limestone
cliff with the surf breaking below us, which even in the calmest
weather sends up one continued roar, whilst away to seaward, across
the blue expanse of water, extended the horizon unbroken by any
distant land. On the edge of the cliff the pandanus and the
cycad competed with each other for the possession of the seaward
margin of the island. The scene was peculiarly Pacific ; and as we
sat alone on the brink of the cliffs enjoying a smoke and contemplating the scene spread out below us, I fancied even the minds of
my natives shared with me that feeling of awe with which one views
the grander of nature's forces in actual operation. . . . . Equally
pleasant are my recollections of numerous tramps during fine weather
along the sandy beaches on the windward coasts of coral islands.
On such occasions the sea itself seemed to revel in the glory of the
day. Wave after wave, white-tipped with foam and reflecting the
brightest of the sun's rays, pursued each other merrily over the
surface of its unfathomable blue. Against the edge of the reef

broke the surf unceasingly, sending its whitened spray high into the air, and joining its hoarse bass with the hum of insect life from the neighbouring wood.

During the greater portion of our sojourn in the Solomon Islands, I had a small Rob Roy canoe made for me by Mr. Oliver, boat-builder of Auckland, N.Z. It was built of kauri pine, and measured 8½ feet in length and 3 feet in beam, being intended to combine compactness with stability. This little craft turned out a great success and was extremely handy, as I could haul it up on the beach with ease, and its stowage capability was something surprising. Numerous and varied were my experiences in this small canoe, but the most enjoyable were those when in the loveliest of weather I paddled gently along from one coral islet to another, admiring the variety in form and colour of the groves of coral over which my little craft smoothly glided. At other times in the sleepy hours of the afternoon I would tie up my canoe to the overhanging branch of a tree, and would land to enjoy a cocoa-nut, a pipe, and perhaps a nap. When lazy, I would get a tow from my native companions in their larger canoe ; and in this manner I was towed for more than a mile up one of the large streams that empty into Choiseul Bay. I used to penetrate into all kinds of solitary inlets, now disturbing the siesta of some unsuspecting crocodile as I paddled through the dismal tract of the mangrove swamp, or surprising a turtle in the shallow water of the lagoons inside the coral-reefs. In the deeper water I have passed through a shoal of clumsy porpoises, some of which I could have touched with my paddle ; whilst occasionally some huge shark, twice the length of my canoe, would come almost within reach, and then, after satisfying its curiosity, dive down into the depths again. Now and then my little craft would be borne on the shoulders of natives to some inland lakelet which I was anxious to explore. In its lightness I found this great advantage, that I could sometimes considerably shorten my journey by what I may describe as terrestrial navigation. On more than one occasion I have crossed the weather edge of a coral-reef, watching for my chance between the breakers, and keeping warily clear of the numerous coral nobs, any one of which would have upset the canoe and its contents ; but these are experiments which I should not care to repeat. I was only twice upset, and on both occasions my canoe displayed two other serviceable qualities, shipping but little water and losing none of its contents although bottom upwards. One of

these upsets was rather ludicrous.   I was crossing Alu harbour in
tow of a large native canoe, setting out on a two days' excursion
with all my stores on board, when my scientific zeal induced me to
lean over to pick up a piece of floating pumice.   At that moment
the large canoe gave a sudden tug and I found myself in the water
with my canoe bottom upwards beside me.   The men in the other
canoe turned her over on her keel, and I got in over the bow, finding
very little water inside, but quite sufficient to soak our store of
biscuit.   However, nothing was lost, although my watch stopped
half-an-hour afterwards and refused duty during the rest of the
season, and my aneroid was never of any use again, both these
articles having been carried in my belt.

On the weather coasts of cliff-girt islands exposed to the continuous trade-swell, much caution is needed in skirting the shore, as every
ten minutes or more a huge roller suddenly rushes in, exposing rocks
covered usually by three or four fathoms of water, and rising up the
face of the cliffs to a height twice as high as the usual level reached
by the breakers.   From my foolhardy disregard of this circumstance,
I very nearly lost my life in July, 1884, on the weather coast of
Stirling Island.   Having stood for some moments on the edge of
the cliff admiring the magnificent breakers that broke at the foot,
there having been a strong south-easterly gale during the two preceding days, I commenced to clamber down the face of the cliff to
reach a ledge that rose about twenty feet above the usual level of
the breakers.   Whilst I was pausing in the descent to examine the
numerous embedded corals in the cliff-face, a huge wave rose over
the ledge, swept up the face of the cliff over my head, and carried
me off as if I had been a feather.   I thought my last moments had
come, knowing that if swept off the ledge into the breakers below, I
should be dashed by the next roller against the base of the cliff.
As I was being carried off, I clutched a projecting point of coral-
rock with all my energy, and in a few moments the wave had left
me lying flat on my face on the ledge within two yards of its brink.
The next roller was fortunately of much smaller size, and in less
than a minute I had clambered up the face of the cliff again to a
position of safety, pretty well bruised and scratched about the arms
and legs, but otherwise none the worse.   My compass and other
things had fallen out of the pouches in my belt, showing that I had
described a somersault during the immersion.   Whilst waiting to

dry my clothes in the sun, I noticed that another ten minutes elapsed before a breaker of similar size rolled in.

I will conclude this chapter with some observations on the nature of the work performed by the officers of the survey. The usual experiences of a nautical surveyor, when detached from his ship for periods varying from a few days to a fortnight or more, are little known outside the circle of those more immediately interested in the work of the Hydrographic Department of the Admiralty. They would afford, as I have often thought, materials for an interesting volume, the perusal of which would give the general reader some idea of what nautical surveying really is. It is a work often hazardous and tedious to those engaged in the boats, and frequently full of anxiety for the commander who has to direct the survey.

The work in the Solomon Islands had its peculiar, and none the less trying, features. To be detached in a boat for a week off a coast, on which it was not considered prudent to land, except on particular points selected for the establishment of theodolite-stations, was a net uncommon experience with the surveying parties. The alternation of heavy rain and scorching heat served to vary the experience, but not to increase the comfort of those employed from sunrise to sunset in mapping the intricacies of an unsurveyed coast; and the kindheartedness of the surveying officer was often sorely tried, when, after a tedious day's work under these conditions, he had to tell off his men to keep a look-out for canoes, and a sharp eye on the land, to see that the boat did not drag. There were, of course, other occasions when the detached parties were engaged in surveying islands, the natives of which were friendly disposed; and then, if the weather favoured them, the week's absence from the ship partook almost of the nature of a pleasant picnic. In the Solomon Islands, however, a considerable experience of the inhabitants of an island is required before a boat can be sent away with the certain assurance that its occupants will meet with no mishap. The unfortunate massacre of Lieutenant Bower of H.M.S. "Sandfly," and of most of his boat's crew in 1880, whilst employed in the survey of the Florida Islands in this group, is but an example of the uncertainty that there always will be in dealing with these races. Although similar disasters have been recently almost of monthly occurrence in these islands, during our intercourse of 21 months with the natives we did not fire a single shot in anger, and in our turn we never witnessed a spear hurled or an arrow discharged except in sport.

The navigation of a sailing ship, such as H.M.S. "Lark," whilst engaged in the survey of a passage dotted with unknown, sunken coral-reefs, and skirted by islands inhabited by a race of savages who have obtained a notorious reputation on account of the ferocity they display to the white man, cannot but tax to the uttermost the capacity and nerve of the officer in command. I can recall more than one anxious moment, and probably there were others known only to those concerned in the navigation of the ship, when on our suddenly getting soundings in the middle of the night in a place where we expected to find "a hundred fathoms and no bottom," I set about putting my journals together in order not to lose what I had been at so much pains to obtain. Towards the completion of the survey, however, it was ascertained by Lieutenant Oldham that the ship might have sailed without danger over any of the isolated reefs which were not indicated at the surface by either a sand-key or an islet ; but this was a character of the reefs that was only ascertained by a process more pleasing to talk about than to undergo.

Before quitting this subject, I should refer to an apparent injustice which exists in the apportioning of no extra pay to the men employed in detached boat-work in the surveying service. With the exception of an issue of clothing, gratis, the boats' crews receive little or nothing in the form of a reward. I am strongly inclined to believe that the recognition, even in a slight degree, of the arduous character of their work, which is of quite an exceptional character as compared with the routine-employment on board the ordinary man-of-war, would do much towards increasing the interest usually displayed by the men employed in such a service.

CHAPTER II.

THE following anthropological notes are the result of my own personal observation and research, and are necessarily of a somewhat fragmentary character. I had no intention when I first visited these islands of making any special observations on the habits and manners of their inhabitants. When, however, I saw the apparent want of interest displayed by those who had it in their power to enrich the world with their accumulated experiences, I determined to jot down in my diary the things which came in my way during my intercourse with the natives. I cannot of course lay claim to the accuracy and more intimate knowledge such as missionaries and traders resident in the group must possess ; and it is to be deplored that such valuable sources of materials for a comprehensive work on the anthropology of this region should be allowed to lie fallow. My lengthened intercourse with the natives of certain parts of the group removed to some extent the disadvantages under which the traveller must always labour when not actually resident among them. My field of observation, however, was limited to but a small area of the whole region: and the greater part has yet to be explored and described.

Commencing my remarks by referring to the system of government usually adopted in these islands, it should be observed that the form of hereditary chieftainship, which prevails throughout the Pacific, here predominates. Every island that supports a number of natives may possess as many distinct chiefs—each claiming independence of the others—as there are villages in the island ; and this statement holds equally good whether applied to a large island like St. Christoval or to those of small size as Santa Anna and Ugi. Yet there is not unfrequently to be met a chief who, by the power of his wealth or by the number of his fighting men, assumes a degree of suzerainty over the less powerful chiefs in his vicinity. Thus, the influence of Gorai, the Shortland chief, is not only dominant over the islands of Bougainville Straits, but extends to the adjacent coast of the large islands of Bougainville and Choiseul, and reaches even to Bouka, more than a hundred miles away. The small island of Simbo or Eddystone, the Narovo of the natives, is under the sway of a powerful chief who resides, together with nearly all his fighting men, on an islet bordering its south-east side. His influence extends to the neighbouring larger islands, and is probably as despotic as that of any of the numerous chiefs with whom I was brought into contact. I might mention other instances in this group where a comparatively small island becomes the political centre of a large district. Similar instances are familiar amongst the other Pacific archipelagos, and notably in the case of Bau in Fiji; and they may all be attributed to the fact that the coast-tribes are of more robust physique and of more enterprising character than the inhabitants of the interior of the larger island, or " bushmen " as they are often termed.

The large island of St. Christoval is divided amongst numerous tribes between which there are constant feuds, each tribe having its own chief. A wide distinction exists between the inhabitants of the interior and those of the coast; and an unceasing hostility prevails between the one and the other. The distinction often extends to language, a circumstance which points to a long continuation of these feuds; and from it we may infer that the isolation has continued during a considerable period. The bush-tribes find their best protection on the summits of the high hills and on the crests of the mountain-ridges which traverse the interior of the island. I passed one night in the bush-village of Lawa, which is situated on a hill-top about 1,400 feet above the sea near the north coast of St. Christoval. As I was in a locality where probably no white man had been before, the novelty of my situation kept me awake the greater part of the night; and very early the next morning I rose up from my mat in the tambu-house to view, undisturbed, the interior region of the island. It was a gloomy morning. Thin lines of mist were still encircling the loftier summits or lingering in the valleys below. Here and there on the crest of some distant hill a cluster of cocoa-nut palms marked the home of a bush-tribe effectually isolated by deep intervening valleys from the neighbouring tribes. I gazed upon a region which had for ages worn the same aspect, inhabited by the same savage races, the signs of whose existence played such an insignificant part in the panorama laid out before me. Standing alone on this hill-top, I reflected on the deeds of barbarity which these silent mountains must have witnessed "in the days of other years," deeds which are only too frequent in our own day when the hand of every tribe is against its neighbour, and when the butchery of some unsuspecting hamlet too often supplies the captors with the materials for the cannibal feast.

By the unusual success of their treachery and cunning—the two weapons most essential to savage warfare in St. Christoval as well as in the other islands—some chiefs have acquired a predominance over the neighbouring villages, and their name inspires terror throughout the island. Amongst them, I may mention Taki, the chief of the large village of Wano on the north coast of this island. He has obtained the double reputation of being a friend to the white man and of being the most accomplished head-hunter in St. Christoval; and, as may be readily imagined, the efforts of the Melanesian Mission, by whom a station has been for many years established in this village,[1] have been greatly retarded by the indifference of this powerful chief. The resident teacher in the village was his own son, who had been selected by Bishop Selwyn and had undergone the usual training of teachers in Norfolk Island. I regret to write that he greatly lapsed during our stay in the group, that he appears to have accompanied his father on a head-hunting foray, and that he finally met with an untimely fate, being so severely wounded by a shark when fishing on the reef that he died a few hours afterwards. Taki, although not a Christian convert, was fond of displaying his connection with the Mission. He showed me a certificate which he received from Bishop Patteson in July, 1866; and in fact he is always ready to do the honours of his village to the white man. Of his head-hunting propensities, Captain Macdonald, an American trader resident in Santa Anna, told us the following tale: Not long before the arrival of H.M.S. "Lark" in the Solomon Islands, he was sailing along the St. Christoval coast, when he met Taki in his war-canoe proceeding on one of these expeditions. He endeavoured to place hindrances in the chief's way by telling him that he had native-traders living at the

---

[1] The Rev. J. Atkin was resident at Wano in 1871, shortly before he met his death with Bishop Patteson in Santa Cruz.

different places on the coast where he intended to land. But it was to no purpose. Taki saw the ruse, and taking it in good part remarked to Captain Macdonald that he had apparently a large number of natives trading for him. Waiting patiently until some unfortunate bushmen ventured down on the reefs to fish, the Wano chief surprised them, slaughtered many and carried the living and the dead in triumph to his village. When Mr. Brenchley visited this village in H.M.S. "Curacoa" in 1865, he saw evidence of a head-hunting foray, in which probably Taki had taken part in his youthful days. The skulls of 25 bushmen were observed hanging up under the roof of the tambu-house, all showing the marks of the tomahawk.[1] In our time, this chief conducted his forays less openly, and I saw no evidence of his work in the tambu-houses of his village.

The practice of head-hunting, above referred to, prevails over a large extent of the Solomon Group. The chiefs of New Georgia or Rubiana extend their raids to Isabel, Florida, and Guadalcanar; and thus perform voyages over a hundred miles in length. Within the radius of these raids no native can be said to enjoy the security of his own existence for a single day. In the villages of Rubiana may be seen heaps of skulls testifying to the success of previous expeditions. Captain Cheyne, when visiting Simbo or Eddystone Island in 1844, found that the natives had just returned from a successful expedition, bringing with them 93 heads of men, women, and children. In these expeditions, he says, they sometimes reached as far as Murray Island which lies about 135 miles to the eastward.[2] Their reputation, however, had extended yet further, since D'Urville who visited Thousand Ships Bay in 1838, tells us that the Isabel natives knew the land of Simbo and pointed to the west to indicate its direction.[3] The Rev. Dr. Codrington, in referring to these head-hunting raids,[4] remarks that the people of the south-west part of Isabel have suffered very much from attacks made on them year after year by the inhabitants of the further coast of the same island and of neighbouring islands, the object of these attacks being to obtain heads, either for the honour of a dead or living chief or for the inauguration of new canoes. He observes that a new war canoe is not invested with due *mana*, *i.e.*, supernatural power, until

---

[1] " Cruise of H.M.S. 'Curacoa ' " (p. 267) ; by J. L. Brenchley, M.A.

[2] " A Description of Islands in the Western Pacific Ocean " (p. 66), by Andrew Cheyne, London, 1852.

[3] " Voyage au Pole Sud," Paris, 1843 ; tom. v., p. 31.

[4] Journal of Anthropological Institute, vol. x., p. 261.

some man has been killed by those on board her; and any unfortunate voyagers are hunted down for the purpose on the first trip or afterwards. The Rubiana natives are said to have introduced head-hunting and human sacrifices into the neighbouring islands. They carry off not only heads but living prisoners, whom they are believed to keep, till on the death of a chief, or launching of a canoe, or some great sacrifice, their lives are taken.

White men have sometimes been the victims of these head-hunting expeditions. As is well known, Lieutenant Bower, of H.M.S. "Sandfly," met his death, together with the greater number of his boat's crew, on the islet of Mandoleana, in 1880, at the hands of a similar expedition undertaken by the Florida natives. Kalikona, the most influential chief of the Florida Islands, was freed from implication in this tragedy mainly through the efforts of Bishop Selwyn, to whose influence the subsequent surrender of the five natives concerned in the raid was chiefly due. More often than not, these head-hunting forays are unconnected with cannibalism, the mere possession of skulls being the principal object of the expedition. In some islands, there is a rude idea of justice perceptible in this practice. It is the custom in the eastern islands of the group to place out head-money for the head of any man who may have rendered himself obnoxious to any particular village. The money—a considerable amount of native shell-money—may be offered by the friends of a murdered man for the head of the murderer. Months, sometimes years, may elapse before the deed is accomplished and the money paid. The task is generally undertaken by a professional head-hunter, such as we met in the person of Mai, the second chief of the village of Sapuna, in the island of Santa Anna. To make a thorough examination of the home and surroundings of his victim, and to insinuate himself into that intimacy which friendship alone can give him, are necessary initiatory steps which only the cunning head-hunter can know how to carry to a successful issue. Time is of no moment. The means employed are slow, but the end is none the less secure; and when the opportunity arrives, it is the friend of months, if not of years, who gives the fatal blow.

In the above description of the head-hunter, I have had before my mind some of the reminiscences of Captain Macdonald, to whom I have before alluded. By his judicious treatment of the natives in the eastern islands, he has acquired a powerful influence for good amongst them; and it is to his past discretion that many a white man, myself among the number, has owed his safety when landing on St. Christoval.

When this island was being surveyed by the officers of H.M.S. "Lark," in 1882, we learned that there was head-money out for a white man's head in a district on the north side and nearly opposite Ugi. It appeared that about a year before a fatal accident had occurred on board a trading-vessel through a revolver going off unexpectedly and killing a native belonging to the district. It was the current opinion of resident traders that sooner or later the required head would be obtained. As characteristic of a trader's experience in these islands, I may add that on one occasion when visiting Mr. Bateman, a trader residing then on the north coast of Ugi, I was told by him that about a month before a friendly Malaita chief had arrived in a large canoe at Ugi with the information that head-money had been offered by another Malaita chief for the head of a white man. The chief who brought the news advised Mr. Bateman to remove his residence to the interior of the island; and the natives in his vicinity were very solicitous that the warning should be heeded.

I learned from Mr. Stephens, who has resided on Ugi for several years, that on one occasion when he was resident on Guadalcanar, on returning from an excursion up the bed of one of the streams, a message was received from the chief of a village in the interior warning him not to make any more similar excursions or he would take his life. The chief of the village, under whose protection Mr. Stephens was residing, took up the matter as an insult to himself; and sent a reply to the effect that if the neighbouring chief wished to remain on terms of amity with him, he should at once send a head in atonement for the threats directed against the white man. A day or two afterwards, Mr. Stephens saw the head, which had been duly sent.

The little island of Santa Anna, although but $2\frac{1}{2}$ miles in length, supports two principal villages, Otagara and Sapuna, which are as often as not at war with each other, although only separated by the breadth of the island. Such was the state of affairs during one of our visits to Port Mary in this island; and the fact that the natives of the two villages were connected by inter-marriages did not act as a deterrent in the matter. Through the restless spirit of Mai, the head-hunter before referred to, some old grievance had been dug up, the murder, I believe, some years before of the brother of Mai by the Otagara natives. The outcome of it was that in the middle of the night all the fighting men of Sapuna assembled at the tambu-house of Mai, and started off along the coast to pounce upon their fellow islanders on the other side. The utmost that could have happened would have been the slaughter of some unsuspecting man or woman on the skirts of the village : but, as it chanced, a thunder-storm with heavy rain overtook the party when near their destination ; and thus dampened their courage to such a degree that they returned to their own village with the excuse that the rain, by running down their faces, would have hindered them in throwing their spears and avoiding those of their opponents. On the following day, Mai led a party of Sapuna men to make another attack, and on returning in the afternoon from one of my excursions into the interior of the island, I learned that the party had returned triumphant, having killed one of their neighbour's large pigs, an act which is regarded as a " casus belli " in native politics.

In the person of Mai, we have a typical example of a Solomon Island head-hunter. The cunning and ferocity which marked his dealings, were sufficiently indicated in his countenance and his mien. He had established for himself the position of war-chief in his village of Sapuna, the reigning chief being of a more peaceable disposition. During one of our visits to this island we found that this war-chief had been very recently displaying his heroism in the most approved native fashion. He had led a war-party across to Fanarite on the opposite coast of St. Christoval, to avenge the death of a fugitive from a labour vessel who, having escaped at Santa Anna, subse-quently found his way to Fanarite where he was killed. The excuse, although somewhat circuitous, was quite sufficient for Mai, who in his disinterestedness thought more of this chance of gaining new laurels than of the untimely end of the native whose death he was so eager to avenge. Having reached the part of the coast where this man had been killed, the war-party lay in ambush and slaugh-tered a chief and two women as they were returning from their yam patches ; whilst they severely wounded another woman who escaped into the bush with a spear through her back. Having dipped their weapons in the gore of their victims, Mai and his party returned to Santa Anna. I was sorry to learn that a native, named Pukka-pukka, who had served in the "Lark" as an interpreter during the previous year, had taken an active part in this expedition. It appeared that the chief had aimed at him, but his musket missed fire, when Pukka-pukka shot him through the back with his snider. The scene of the tragedy was familiar to me, as I had landed there the year before. Pukka-pukka, who is a sensible young man and of by no means a bloodthirsty disposition, did not like my taking him to task for the part he took in this raid; and he protested more than once in a somewhat injured tone that his people did not fight without good cause. In his case, I felt confident that he was not tempted by the mere love of bloodshedding, the truth being that through the able tutorship of Mai, all old feuds are kept alive in the minds of the young men of the village, who, in their desire to distinguish themselves, come to regard such grievances as fair grounds for war. We soon learned that the Fanarite natives would seize the first opportunity to retaliate; and that head-money to a large amount had been offered for the head of a native of Santa Anna, and particularly for the head of Pukka-pukka.

The chiefs of the islands of Bougainville Straits possess far greater power over their peoples than that which is wielded by most of the chiefs we encountered at the St. Christoval end of the group. At Santa Anna and at Ugi, the position of the chief is almost an empty honour; and some man of spirit, though not of principle, such as Mai in the former island and Rora at Ugi, usurps by his fighting prowess a large share of the power. On the St. Christoval coast I met several such chiefs, who possess no influence beyond their own district, and often very little in that. Occasionally, as I have before observed, a chief is found who, like Taki at Wano, exercises a powerful influence over the less pretentious chiefs of neighbouring islands and districts. Some of the Guadalcanar chiefs are very powerful; but with them I had no personal intercourse; and I prefer to confine my remarks to those portions of the group with which I became acquainted. Returning, then, to the chiefs of the islands of Bougainville Straits, I may enumerate them in their order of importance—Gorai in the Shortland Islands, Mule at Treasury, Kurra-kurra and Tominas in Faro or Fauro, and Krepas at Choiseul Bay. There is constant communication between the natives of these islands, more particularly between those of Treasury, the Shortlands, and Faro, the distances between the islands varying between 15 and 25 miles. Intermarriages are frequent between the natives of these islands. They all speak the same language; and not uncommonly a man shifts his home from one island to another

1. GORAI, HIS PRINCIPAL WIFE, AND HIS SON FERGUSON.
2. FOUR OF THE WIVES OF MULE.

[*To face page* 21.

The chiefs are all connected either by blood-relationship or by marriage, and together form as powerful an alliance as might be found in the whole group. Visits of condolence are exchanged in times of bereavement between the chiefs ; and presents are conveyed from one to another. On one occasion we carried a present of sago from Mule to Gorai ; and I have on more than one occasion during our passages between these islands been made the bearer of a message from chief to chief.

Gorai, the well-known Alu chief, Alu being the name of his principal island, exercises a kind of suzerainty over the neighbouring chiefs. But his reputation and influence extend far beyond the islands directly or indirectly under his rule. From Treasury northward and eastward, throughout the Shortlands, across the straits to Choiseul Bay, through Faro, and along the coast of Bougainville, extending even to Bouka, his influence is predominant. Masters of vessels, recruiting labour on the coast of Bougainville, have a sufficient guarantee for the good behaviour of the natives of the places they visit, if they have been fortunate enough to secure the presence on board of one of the sons of Gorai. This chief has been the trusted friend of the white man for many years. On our first visit to Alu we were therefore prepared to think favourably of him. We found him on the beach, surrounded by a considerable number of his people. Shaking hands with us, he told us in his imperfect English that he was a friend of the white man. Rather beyond middle age, and somewhat shorter than the average native, he has an honest, good-humoured expression of countenance, which at once prepossessed us in his favour. Whilst seated in the dingy interior of one of his houses, surrounded by several of his wives, Gorai related to us the story—well known to all acquainted with the Solomon Group—of his reprisal a few years before on the natives of Nouma-nouma, a village on the east coast of Bougainville, for the murder of Captain Ferguson of the trading steamer " Ripple." The master of the " Ripple " was an old friend of Gorai, and traded extensively with him. On hearing the news, the chief mustered his men and despatched them in canoes, under the command of his eldest son, to the scene of the massacre, about a hundred miles away. The natives of the offending village were surprised, and about twenty of them were killed, including men, women, and children— " all same man-of-war," as Gorai too truthfully observed. One of the chief's sons has received the name of the unfortunate master of

the " Ripple ; " and I may here refer to the good name which
Captain Ferguson has left behind him, not only amongst the natives
of the Solomon Islands, but also amongst his fellow-traders in those
seas. The inhabitants of the Shortland Islands, Gorai's immediate ·
rule, live in great awe of their chief ; and the number of natives
who gathered round us when we first met the chief showed
us by their manner that in the friendship of the chief the white
man possessed the goodwill of his subjects. We were unable to
see very much of the mode of exercising his power ; but I
suspect that Gorai, like other chiefs, places but little value on the
lives of his people. Punishment is summarily dealt by the spear or
the tomahawk ; and I learned from natives of the adjoining islands
that the offence may be of a very trivial nature.

On one occasion, Gorai took me in his war-canoe on a geological
excursion to the north-west side of Alu. During our return, the
sun set when we were about twelve miles from the ship, and left us
to pursue our way in the darkness. Seated alongside the chief on
the second bow thwart of the canoe, I could not help reflecting how
many times he must have occupied the same seat in his war-canoes
when engaged in those expeditions which have made his influence
dominant on this part of the group. On our way we skirted the
beach of an islet on which were squatting a party of Alu natives
who had gone there to fish. Although we passed a few yards from
these men, not a word of recognition was exchanged. The sight of
a large war-canoe with Gorai and a white man in the bow passing
them in the dusk of evening must have been a novel one to them, yet
neither they nor our men exchanged a word. There they sat squatting motionless on the beach, and we passed them in silence. Gorai
subsequently explained to me that the reason of this was that the men
were " too much fright," or rather awed, by the presence of their chief.

The chief of the Shortland Islands has two or more elderly men
who act as his ministers. Many years ago he was living at
Treasury, of which island he was chief ; but being unwilling to
take part in the hostility displayed by the Treasury natives towards
the white men, he left the island under the chieftainship of Mule,
the present chief, who still remained in some degree under the rule
of Gorai. The Alu chief takes a pleasure in asserting that he is
" all same white man," at the same time deprecating the inferior
position of his race with the remark, " White man, he savez too
much. Poor black man ! He no savez nothing."

I now come to Mule, the Treasury chief, who numbers amongst his wives a sister of Gorai, Bita by name; whilst the Alu chief has returned the compliment by making Mule's sister, Kai-ka, the principal amongst his hundred wives. Mule, also known as Mule-kopa, has rather the appearance and build of a chief of one of the more eastern Pacific groups. He has a sedate expression of countenance, a prominent chin, and strongly marked coarse features. A large bushy head of hair adds to the dignity of his appearance; and his powerful limbs, depth of chest, breadth of shoulders, and greater height distinguish him pre-eminently from his people. His rule is as despotic in Treasury as that of Gorai in the Shortlands; and he maintains his sway rather by the fear he inspires than by possessing any feeling of respect on the part of his subjects. On more than one occasion I have heard the natives use threatening language towards their chief, when he had made some arbitrary exercise of his power. He had a habit of sending away to the bush any native who from his superior knowledge of English seemed to be supplanting him in the intercourse with the ships that visited the harbour. Even his right-hand man, who prided himself on his name of Billy, experienced his wrath on one occasion in this manner. Like other chiefs, Mule is grasping and covetous, shortcomings which are rather those of the race than of the individual. Although of the chiefs of Bougainville Straits I liked him the least, the contrast was rather due to the exceptionally good estimate we had formed of his fellow chiefs. The visits of H.M.S. "Lark" to this island have been the means of removing the very bad reputation which the natives had deservedly possessed: and I would especially invite the attention of my readers to the history of this change in the attitude of these natives towards the white man.

Captain C. H. Simpson, who visited this island in H.M.S. "Blanche" in 1872, described its people in his report to the Admiralty,[1] as being "the most treacherous and blood-thirsty of any known savages;" and the officers employed in making a sketch of the harbour had ample evidence of their ferocity. About seven years before, the natives had cut out a barque and had murdered her crew of 33 men. Previously they had captured several boats of whalers visiting the islands, and had massacred the crews. The Treasury natives were always very reticent to us when we tried to learn something more of the fate of the barque; but we learned

[1] "Hydrographic Notices, Pacific Ocean," 1856 to 1873 (p. 106).

little except that she was American, and was named "Superior."
The captain, whose name the natives pronounced "Hoody," was
carried away into the interior of the island and killed, and the
scene of his murder was once pointed out to Lieutenant Oldham
when crossing the island. As Captain Simpson charges the natives
with cannibalism, there can be little doubt of the ultimate fate of
the crew of the American barque. In the interval between the
occurrence of this event and the arrival of the "Blanche," no vessel
had anchored in the harbour, the ships always heaving-to off the
north coast, where the natives resided when Captain Simpson
visited the island. Treasury retained its bad reputation up to
the date of our visit; and but few traders had much knowledge
of the place, as they generally gave the island a wide berth.
We met but one man who spoke well of these natives, and he was
Captain Walsch of the trading schooner "Venture." All others
gave them the worst of characters : and led me to believe that my
acquaintance with Treasury would not extend beyond the deck of
H.M.S. "Lark." When Lieutenant Oldham first visited this island
in May, 1882, he had every reason to place but little confidence in
the natives; and in truth we all thought that the appearance and
behaviour of the natives justified the treacherous reputation which
they had obtained. Only two days were spent there, but no landing was effected : the chief made no response to the invitations to
visit the ship; and we left the harbour without much feeling of
regret. In June of the following year we again visited this island ;
and if the same procedure had been followed we should have been
a very long time in gaining the confidence of the natives. Lieutenant Oldham, however, paid an official visit to the chief, accompanied by Lieutenant Malan and myself. Mule and one of his sons
returned the visit within a couple of hours. Presents were exchanged; and the foundation of mutual confidence was thus laid.
The result may be briefly stated. In a few days I was rambling all
over the island, usually accompanied by a lively gathering of men
and boys. An intimacy was established with the natives, which
lasted until we bade farewell to the group in the following year ;
and the return of the "Lark" from her cruises was always a cause
of rejoicing amongst the natives. The men of the ship were known
by name to most of the people of the island : whilst Mr. Isabell, our
leading-stoker, made a deep impression upon them by his readiness
to employ his mechanical skill for their various wants, so much so

that Mule offered, if he would remain, to make him a chief with the
usual perquisite as to the number of his wives. For my own part,
I reaped the full benefit of our amicable relations with the natives;
and for the proof of this statement I must refer the reader to the
remarks on my intercourse with them, and to my observations on
the geology, botany, and other characteristics of the island.

Coming now to the chiefs of Faro or Fauro Island, I must
mention more particularly Kurra-kurra the chief of Toma, and
Tomimas the chief of Sinasoro, Toma and Sinasoro being the two
principal villages of the island. Kurra-kurra is, I believe, a half-
brother of Gorai. He has not, however, the same dignity of
manner, and has resigned most of his power into the hands of his
son Gorishwa, a fine strapping young man. Both father and son
are friends of the white man. Tomimas, the Sinasoro chief, also
related to Gorai, is somewhat taciturn even with his own people,
but a chief to be thoroughly trusted. On one occasion whilst assisting Lieutenant Heming and myself in demolishing our dinners
in a tambu-house at his village, Tomimas broke a long silence by
informing us through a native interpreter that the men of Sinasoro
were very good people, that they did not kill white men, and that
their chief was like Gorai. It is needless to write that we appreciated the good intention, though hardly the elegance of the chief's
solitary remark. In the following year, when I was returning from
a botanical excursion to the peak of Faro, I received an invitation
from Tomimas to visit him on the side of the harbour opposite to
the village. The chief, who awaited me on the beach, received me
cordially, telling me through one of the natives, who could speak a
little English, that he had collected for me the fruits and leaves of
the " anumi "—a tree of the genus *Cerbera*—which he had heard I
had been anxious to find. The kindly manner of the old chief
attracted me towards him, and I sat down, as he wished me, by his
side on the log of a tree, having first presented him with a large
knife which greatly pleased him. Close by, stood his four wives, to
whom he introduced me, pointing out to me the mother of his
eldest son Kopana, an intelligent young man of about twenty-two.
A bunch of ripe bananas was laid beside me, of which I was bidden
to partake. This was followed in a short time by a savoury vegetable
broth, which the chief brought with his own hands in a cooking-pot.
It was especially prepared for me on their learning that I had found
the plant (an aroid, *Schizmatoglottis*) in my excursions. There was

the spirit of true politeness displayed in the manner of the chief
and his wives, as they endeavoured to show that in the exercise of
their simple hospitality they were receiving, instead of conferring,
an honour. I felt that I was in the presence of good breeding,
although sitting attired in a dirty flannel suit in the midst of a
number of almost naked savages. My own party of Sinasoro
natives, who had been fasting for many hours, politely asked me
to partake of their meal which the generosity of the chief had prepared, before they thought of touching it themselves. I of course
complied with their request by tasting a cooked banana, when, this
piece of etiquette having been duly observed, they attacked the
victuals without ceremony.

Such was my pleasing experience of this Faro chief. During
the survey of this island, the natives showed every disposition to be
friendly towards us. In my numerous excursions I always met
with civility, and frequently with unexpected acts of kindness; and
I soon became known to them by the name given to me by the
Treasury natives, " Rŏkus " or " Dŏkus."

The principal chief of the district, immediately north of Choiseul
Bay, is named " Krepas." Several years before he had been living
at Faro, which he left on account of the death of all his wives.
When we first visited Choiseul Bay in September, 1883, we found
the natives very coy in approaching us, on account of the reprisal
of H.M.S. " Emerald," two years before, on the people of the neighbouring village of Kangopassa for the cutting out of the trading-
vessel " Zephyr," and the murder of a portion of her crew. After
two days, however, Lieutenant Oldham succeeded in removing their
suspicions, and the chief came on board. Subsequently Krepas and
his son, Kiliusi, accompanied me in a canoe during my ascent of one
of the rivers that empty themselves into this bay. I found the
chief and his son very useful guides, and was prepossessed in their
favour. On our return to Treasury, I was surprised to learn
from Billy, Mule's prime minister, as we termed him, that Krepas
was a practised cannibal, and would not think much of killing a
white man. Billy was deeply impressed by the circumstance of
my having shared my lunch with the chief of Choiseul Bay, about
two miles up one of the rivers. It was in this bay that the French
navigator, Bougainville, intended to anchor his ships in 1768, being
opposed by the hostility of the natives. The boats, which had been
sent in to find an anchorage, were attacked by 150 men in ten

canoes, who were only routed after the second discharge of fire-arms. Two canoes were captured, in one of which was found the jaw of a man half-broiled. The number of shoals, and the irregularity of the currents prevented the ships coming up to the anchorage before night fell ; and Bougainville, abandoning his design, continued his course through the Straits.[1] The description which the French navigator gave of these natives in 1768, applies equally well to those of the present day. When H.M.S. " Lark " revisited Choiseul Bay in October, 1884, not a single native was seen; so that it would behove future visitors to be very cautious in their dealings with these natives. Whilst off the coast north of this bay, a fishing-party of half-a-dozen men came off to the ship from the village of Kandelai; but they showed great suspicion of us. They would not come alongside for some time ; and when a present of calico was flung to them at the end of a line, they were divided amongst themselves whether to come and take it, some paddling one way and some another. At length they took the present and came alongside, but did not stay long, and soon paddled towards the shore, their suspicions by no means allayed. What had happened to cause this change of attitude, we could not learn. Evidently, the good impression which we had left behind us a year before, had borne no fruit. Probably, some inconsiderate action on the part of the crew of a trading-vessel had undone our work.

The professional head-hunter of the eastern islands of the group does not appear to be represented amongst the islands of Bougainville Straits. Raids are occasionally made on the villages of the adjoining Bougainville coast, but more, I believe, for the purpose of procuring slaves, than from the mere desire of fighting. There is, however, frequent friendly communication between the natives of the islands of the Straits and those of certain Bougainville villages, the former usually exchanging articles of trade for spears and tortoise-shell, and acting as middle-men in the traffic with the white men. It is however singular that the natives of the Straits trade with different villages on the Bougainville coast; and that, although on usually such friendly terms with each other, they are often on terms of hostility with the particular Bougainville village with which their neighbours trade. Thus, Mule, the Treasury chief, trades with the people of the village of Suwai, over which his brother Kopana is chief. Gorai, the Alu chief, on the other hand, is

[1] " Voyage autour du Monde," 2nd edit. augm. vol. II., Paris, 1772.

at war with the natives of Suwai, but maintains friendly communication with Daku, the chief of the village of Takura, and with Magasa the chief of the harbour of Tonali. Whilst spending a night at Sinasoro with Lieutenant Heming and his party, I with the rest had to share the tambu-house with a party of ten natives from Takura. They had come across for pigs and taro. The natives of the adjoining coast of Bougainville, possessing a different language, are not able to make themselves understood by the people of the Straits except by interpreters. I have seen one of these natives just as little able to make himself understood by the natives of Faro, as if he had been suddenly removed to some very distant country instead of only 30 miles away.

I have previously referred to the close friendship which usually prevails between the inhabitants of the islands of Bougainville Straits, linked together as they are by inter-marriages and by the possession of a common language. But in the calmest seas there are occasional storms ; and I will proceed to relate an extraordinary chain of events which came more or less under our observation whilst in this portion of the group. Shortly before our return to Treasury in April, 1884, there had been a terrible domestic tragedy, which at one time threatened to embroil all the chiefs of the Straits in actual war. It appeared that Kopana, the eldest son of Gorai, had, in a fit of temporary madness, shot one of his wives dead with his rifle, the unfortunate woman being a daughter of Mule, the Treasury chief. On hearing the news, Mule at once crossed over to Alu to exact vengeance on Kopana ; but Gorai would not permit him to harm his son ; and it was arranged between the two chiefs that Mule should be allowed to shoot one of the other wives of Kopana, as the price of blood. Early one morning the Treasury chief, armed with his snider rifle, took his way in a canoe up a passage I had often traversed in my Rob Roy, and surprising his selected victim at work in a taro patch, he shot her dead. At the same time he wounded her male attendant, an elderly native named Malakolo, the bullet passing through the left shoulder-joint from behind. When I saw this man six or seven weeks afterwards, he was fast recovering from the injury, although with a useless limb. Kopana, who is a headstrong son and beyond his father's control, naturally resented this act of Mule, and appears to have meditated a descent on Treasury. Collecting his followers and the remainder of his wives, he disappeared on what was given out as a tortoise-shell expedition. We found the Treasury people in a great dread of the daily arrival of Kopana ; and I had some difficulty in getting natives to accompany me in my excursions about the island. They did not care to leave the vicinity of the village ; and I found many of the bush-paths familiar to me in the previous year partly over-grown. Apparently through a sense of shame, Mule and his natives avoided telling us anything about the act of retaliation ; they were, however, loud in their endeavours to cast aspersions on Kopana. On our arrival at Alu, we learned the truth from Gorai to whom Mule had sent a native, who took a passage with us, asking him not to be too communicative in case we made inquiries. As it happened, however, the Treasury native was kept on board, and Lieutenant Oldham, on landing, learned the part Mule had played. Kopana was apparently quite conscious of his own responsibility in the matter, as he had left a present with Gorai to be given to the captain of any man-of-war who should come to punish him. Thus closed the first scene of this tragedy.

Whilst we lay at anchor off Gorai's village, it was evident that there was trouble brewing. The natives accompanying me in my geological excursions carried arms contrary to their usual practice. On the same day the two principal villages were found deserted ; and Gorai shifted his residence to another islet. Rumours became rife that the Treasury and Shortland natives had met with blood-shed; but the men we questioned made so many wilful misstatements that it was impossible to learn what had really happened. At length the truth came out. Being in Gorai's house one morning, I was told by the chief that his son had been attacked five days be-fore by the Treasury natives on the islet of Tuluba, off the west coast of Alu, that Kopana's canoe had returned without his master, bringing a man and a woman badly wounded, and that he shortly ex-pected the return of two large war-canoes which he had sent to the scene of the encounter. These two canoes returned whilst I was talking to the chief on the beach, bringing a few more survivors but without Kopana. The old chief then took it for granted that his eldest son was dead, and in telling me so showed no emotion whatever. In the evening, however, we learned, to our astonish-ment, that Kopana had returned, having not been engaged in the fray. It seemed that at the time of the encounter he was on a neighbouring islet. After some difficulty, I was able to get an ac-count of the affair.

Two Treasury war-canoes, it appears, attempted to land at Tuluba Islet one evening, where the crews were going to encamp for the night. Ostensibly the Treasury men were on their way to Bougainville to buy spears ; but since they were led by Olega, the brother of Mule and the fighting-chief of the island, it is probable that they were intending a descent on Alu from this islet of Tuluba. When the Treasury men discovered Kopana's party were already there, the fighting at once began. During the conflict, for which the Alu natives were ill-prepared, seeing that they were largely composed of Kopana's wives, one of the Treasury canoes was dashed to pieces on a reef and all the occupants were thrown into the water. In this unequal contest, the Alu natives had a man and a woman killed and a man and a woman wounded, both the women being wives of Kopana. In addition four other of Kopana's wives were captured by the Treasury men, who returned to their own island in the remaining canoe with a loss of four men wounded, of whom one subsequently died.

The unfortunate wives of Kopana had indeed borne the brunt from the very beginning. Within two months, three of them had suffered violent death, one of them was wounded apparently beyond recovery, and four had been carried off prisoners to Treasury. The singular feature of this breach between the Treasury and Alu natives, was that the animosity of the former was directed against Gorai's eldest son and not against the old chief, his father, who did not think it incumbent on him to interfere except for the purpose of pacifying the two parties.

I visited the two wounded brought back to Alu. Five days had already elapsed since the fight, and I found the wounds of both in a horrible condition. The wife of Kopana had a severe tomahawk wound of the thigh just above the knee, smashing the bone and im-plicating the joint. The man had a rifle-bullet wound through the fleshy part of the thigh and a pistol-bullet wound in the opposite groin. Nothing had been done in either case, and after the lapse of five days in a tropical climate, the condition of the wounds could be scarcely described. I was allowed to do but little, and considered recovery in either case most improbable. Both, however, recovered to my great astonishment. I found afterwards, on visiting the wounded at Treasury, that one man had been shot through the elbow-joint by one of his own party.

The subsequent events in connection with this outbreak of

·hostilities in the Straits may be soon related Although there was now open war between Alu and Treasury, it assumed a passive character, each side awaiting or expecting an attack from the other. Gorai was much concerned at this turn of events, seeing that, as he told me, he thought he had come to an amicable arrangement with Mule when he allowed him to take the life of one of his son's wives. The canoe-houses at Alu were usually filled during the day by a number of natives, all carrying their tomahawks and debating on the topic of the day. In the midst of them I once found Gorai talking in his quiet way to an attentive circle of armed natives. In the meanwhile the Treasury natives held a feast in celebration of their success ; and the four wives of Kopana were distributed about the village, but they experienced no ill treatment. In a few weeks the animosity displayed between the peoples of the two islands began to cool down ; and it soon became evident that the war was one only in name. At length peace was once more restored. In the beginning of October a number of Treasury natives came over to the west coast of Alu where Gorai was then residing, bringing with them Mule's principal wife, Bita, the sister of the Alu chief, together with a large present of bananas, taro, and other vegetables; and lastly, what was the most significant act of all, they brought with them the four wives of Kopana who had been captured on the islet of Tuluba. Gorai told me that amity was now perfectly restored, and that he was going to exchange visits with the Treasury chief to confirm the compact. Fortunately for the happiness of the natives of Bougainville Straits, war rarely disturbs the peaceful atmosphere in which they live.

I cannot doubt that, in the lives of the natives of these straits, we have the brighter side of the existence of the Solomon Islander ; and this result may, I think, be attributed in the main to the influence of Gorai, the Alu chief, who in his intercourse with white men, not always the best fitted to represent their colour, as I need scarcely remark, has learned some lessons in his own crude way which he could hardly have learned under any other conditions. Natives of the islands of the Straits can count with some confidence on the tenure of their lives, but this is simply due to the influence of the name of the Alu chief. And yet, however secure the surroundings of a native may be, he will never be entirely off his guard. Suspicion is a quality inherent in his mind, and it shows itself in most of the actions of his life. Even of those natives, who, in the capacity of interpreters, lived on board the ship for weeks together, one was always keeping watch over his comrades during the long hours of the night whenever we were at any anchorage away from their own island; and I have been told by the officers in charge of the detached surveying parties, that even after a hard day's work in the boat, they have found their natives keeping a self-imposed watch during the night.

I pass on now to the subject of the power of the "tambu," or "taboo" as it is more usually termed. The tambu ban constitutes the real authority of a petty chief in times of peace. In the eastern islands, the tambu sign is often two sticks crossed and placed in the ground. In such a manner, the St. Christoval native secures his patch of ground from intrusion. In the islands of Bougainville Straits, posts six to eight feet in height, rudely carved in the form of the head and face, are erected facing sea-ward on the beach of a village to keep off enemies and sickness. Similar posts are erected on the skirts of a plantation of cocoa-nut palms to warn off intruders. On one occasion, whilst ascending the higher part of a stream in Treasury, my natives unexpectedly came upon the faint footprint of a bushman; and my sheath-knife was at once borrowed by the chief's eldest son, who happened to be one of the party, to cut out a face in the soft rock as a tambu mark for the bushman, or in other words to preserve the stream. I have only touched on the exercise of the right of tambu in its narrowest sense. Scattered about in the pages of this work will be found numerous allusions to customs which would be comprised under this head in its widest meaning: for the power of the tambu is but the power of a code which usually prohibits and rarely commands; and in enumerating its restrictions and defining its limits, one would be in reality describing a negative system of public and private etiquette. It is worthy of note, that the term "tambu" is not included in the vocabulary of the language of the natives of Bougainville Straits, its equivalent being "olatu."

It may be here apposite to make some observations on the slavery which is practised in connection with the bush-tribes of these islands. As already remarked, a wide distinction usually prevails in the Solomon Group between the inhabitants of the coast and those of the interior; and although this distinction is most evident in the case of the larger islands, it also prevails, but to a less degree, in those of smaller size. It is a noteworthy fact that the bushmen are always looked down upon by their brethren of the coast. "Man-bush" is with the latter a term of reproach, implying stupidity and crass ignorance. I have frequently heard this epithet applied to natives who handled their canoes in an awkward manner or who stumbled in their walk whilst accompanying me in my excursions. On one occasion, when trying to obtain stone axes from the natives of Alu, I was referred with a smile to the bushmen of the neighbouring island of Bougainville, who still employ these tools. In the larger islands the bush-tribes and the coast natives wage an unceasing warfare, in which the latter are usually the aggressors and the victors—the bushmen captured during these raids either affording materials for the cannibal feast or being detained in servitude by their captors. But there prevails in the group a recognized system of slave-traffic, in which a human being becomes a marketable commodity—the equivalent being represented in goods either of native or of foreign manufacture. This custom which came under the notice of the officers of Surville's expedition, during their visit to Port Praslin in Isabel, in 1769,[1] obtains under the same conditions at the present time. These natives were in the habit of making voyages of ten and twelve days' duration with the object of exchanging men for "fine cloths covered with designs," articles which were manufactured by a race of people much fairer than their own, who were in all probability the inhabitants of Ontong Java.

The servitude to which the victims of this traffic are doomed is not usually an arduous one. But there is one grave contingency attached to his thraldom which must be always before the mind of the captive, however lightly his chains of service may lie upon him. When a head is required to satisfy the offended honour of a neighbouring chief, or when a life has to be sacrificed on the completion of a tambu-house or at the launching of a new war-canoe, the victim chosen is usually the man who is not a free-born native of the village. He may have been bought as a child and have lived amongst them from his boyhood up, a slave only in name, and enjoying all the rights of his fellow natives. But no feelings of compassion can save him from his doom; and the only consideration which he receives at the hands of those with whom he may have lived on terms of equality for many years is to be found in the circumstance that he gets no warning of his fate

[1] "Discoveries to the south-east of New Guinea," by M. Fleurieu, p. 143, Eng. edit.

There are in Treasury several men and women who, originally bought as slaves from the people of Bouka and Bougainville, now enjoy apparently the same privileges and freedom of action as their fellow islanders. It is sometimes not a matter of much difficulty to single out the slaves amongst a crowd of natives. On one occasion I engaged a canoe of Faro men to take me to a distant part of their island: and very soon after we started I became aware from the cowed and sullen condition of one of the crew that he was a slave. On inquiry I learned that this man had been captured when a boy in the island of Bougainville, and I was informed that if he was to return to his native place—a bush village named Kiata—he would undoubtedly be killed. Although in fact a slave, I concluded from the bearing of the other men towards him that his bondage was not a very hard one ; and he evidently appeared to enjoy most of the rights of a native of the common class. Sukai, however, for such was his name, had to make himself generally useful in the course of the day ; and when at the close of the excursion we were seated inside the house of a man who provided us with a meal of boiled taro, sweet potatoes, and bananas, he was served with his repast on the beach outside.

Mule, the Treasury chief, had adopted a little Bougainville bush-boy, named Sapeku, who was purchased when very young from his friends. In 1883 he was six or seven years old, and was the constant companion of the sons of the chief. He was a fat chubby little urchin, with woolly hair, and was known on board under the name of "Tubby." His wild excitable disposition full of suspicion showed to great contrast with the calmer and more confident demeanour of his companions. He was, however, a general favourite with us, although I should add he did not possess half the pluck of his associates. Mule also possessed, at the time of our visit, a young girl, twelve or thirteen years old, who had been not long before purchased from the Bougainville natives.

I have previously referred to the existence of bushmen on some of the smaller islands. In the interior of Treasury there are a few hamlets containing each two or three families of bushmen, who live quite apart from the other natives of the island. On more than one occasion I experienced the hospitality of these bush families, who in matters of dress are even less observant than the harbour natives. They are probably the remnants of the original bushmen who occupied this island. Over our pipes, I used frequently to converse with the natives on the subject of the past history of their island; and I gleaned from them that the enterprising race at present dominant in the Bougainville Straits came originally from the islands immediately to the eastward, using Treasury as a stepping-stone to the Shortlands and Faro, and ousting or exterminating the bushmen they found in the possession of these islands.

I will turn for a moment to the subject of slavery in the eastern islands of the group. In Ugi it is the practice of infanticide which has given rise to a slave-commerce regularly conducted with the natives of the interior of St. Christoval. Three-fourths of the men of this island were originally bought as youths to supply the place of the natural offspring killed in infancy. But such natives when they attain manhood virtually acquire their independence, and their original purchaser has but little control over them. On page 42, I have made further reference to this subject.

Connected in the manner above shown with the subject of slavery is the practice of cannibalism. The completion of a new tambu-house is frequently celebrated among the St. Christoval natives by a cannibal feast. Residents in that part of the group tell me that if the victim is not procured in a raid amongst the neighbouring tribes of the interior, some man is usually selected from those men in the village who were originally purchased by the chief. The doomed man is not enlightened as to the fate which awaits him, and may, perhaps, have been engaged in the erection of the very building at the completion of which his life is forfeited. The late Mr. Louis Nixon,[1] one of those traders whose name should not be forgotten amongst the pioneers who, in working for themselves, have worked indirectly for the good of their successors in the Solomon Group, once recounted to me a tragical incident of this kind on the island of Guadalcanar, of which he was an unwilling spectator. Whilst looking out of the window of his house one afternoon, he observed a native walk up to another standing close to the window and engage him in conversation. A man then stole up unperceived, and raising his heavy club above his head, struck the intended victim lifeless to the ground. Knowing too well the nature and purpose of the deed, Mr. Nixon turned away quite sickened by the sight.

The natives of the small island of Santa Anna enjoy the reputation of being abstainers from human flesh: but, inasmuch, as Mai the war-chief has acquired a considerable fortune, in a native's point of

---

[1] Mr. Nixon died at Santa Anna in the end of 1882.

view, by following the profitable calling of purveyor of human flesh to the man-eaters of the adjacent coasts of St. Christoval—a trade in which he is ably assisted by those who accompany him on his foraging expeditions—we can hardly preserve this nice distinction between the parts taken by the contractor and his customers in this extraordinary traffic. I learned from Captain Macdonald that in their abstinence from human flesh, the Santa Anna natives are not actuated by any dislike of anthropophagy in itself; but that the custom has fallen into abeyance since the chief laid the tambu-ban on human flesh several years ago, on account of a severe epidemic of sickness having followed a cannibal feast. On one occasion through the instrumentality of this resident, Lieutenant Oldham had the satisfaction of rescuing two St. Christoval natives whom Mai was carefully keeping in anticipation of the wants of the man-eaters of Cape Surville. As the result of an interview held with this chief, the two prisoners were sent on board the " Lark ; " but Mai gave them up with a very bad grace, protesting that he was being robbed of his own property. It is difficult to speculate on the reflections of the victim as he lives on from day to day in constant expectation of his fate. I am told that there is a faint gleam of tender feeling shown in the case of a man who, by long residence in the village, has almost come to be looked upon as one of themselves. He is allowed to remain in ignorance of the dreaded moment until the last: and, perhaps, he may be standing on the beach assisting in the launching of the very canoe in which he is destined to take his final journey, when suddenly he is laid hold of, and in a few moments more he is being ferried across to the man-eaters of the opposite coast. All persons whom I have met that have had a lengthened experience of the St. Christoval natives confirm these cannibal practices. They may sometimes be observed with all the horrible preliminaries which have been described in the cases of other Pacific groups ; whilst, on the other hand, it may be the habit to purchase and partake of human flesh as an extra dainty in the daily fare.

Captain Redlich, master of the schooner "Franz," who visited Makira on the south side of St. Christoval in 1872, states that he found a dead body in a war-canoe dressed and cooked whole. He was informed by Mr. Perry, a resident, that he had seen as many as twenty bodies lying on the beach dressed and cooked.[1] In 1865, Mr. Brenchley noticed at Wano, on the north coast of this island, the

[1] Journal of the Royal Geographical Society for 1874 (vol. 44), p. 31.

skulls of twenty-five bushmen hanging up under the roof of the
tambu-house, all of which showed the effects of the tomahawk and
all had been eaten.[1] At the present time it is not an easy matter
for any person not resident in the group to obtain ocular evidence of
cannibalism, since the natives have become aware of the white man's
aversion to the custom. I have, however, frequently seen the arm
and leg bones of the victim consumed at the opening of a new
tambu-house, as they are usually hung up over the entrance or in
some other part of the building. The natives, however, are generally reluctant to talk much about these matters; and I believe the
residents, in such matters, prefer to trust more to the testimony of
their own eyes than to the statements of the natives.

I have previously referred to the death of the son of Taki the
Wano chief, who was attacked by a shark whilst fishing on the St.
Christoval reefs. When we arrived at Ugi in April, 1883, shortly
after this event, we learned that his death would probably lead to a
further sacrifice of life, and that a human victim from some neighbouring hill-tribe would be required to remove the tambu-ban, or in
other words to propitiate the shark-god. At the completion of the
time of mourning, a gathering of the tribes of the district known as
a *béa* was to be held at Wano; and I obtained from Mr. Stephens
of Ugi the following particulars of this singular custom. From a
raised staging some fifteen feet in height, each of the warriors of any
renown addresses in turn the assembled people. The gathering is
composed not only of his own tribesmen but also of parties of fighting men from all the neighbouring villages, each party standing
aloof from the others. The orator, declaiming on the valour of his
own people and on his individual prowess, soon works himself into
a condition of excitement, and should any tribe be there represented
with whom there may have been some recent cause of ill-feeling, it
is probably made the object of the taunts of the speaker. The assembled natives, who are all armed, soon participate in the excitement. The people of the village support their champion, and openly
display their ill will against those at whom the diatribes of the
orator have been directed. The suspected strangers return the
taunts; and the feeling of irritation reaches its acme when a
threatening gesture or the throwing of a spear sets ablaze the suppressed passions. Every man darts into the bush and the village is
empty in a moment. A desultory contest then ensues in which the

[1] " Cruise of H.M.S. Curaçoa,'" by J. L. Brenchley.

people of the village, who have generally the best of it, pursue their visitors to the outskirts of their district; and from henceforth a long period of hostility begins.

Such is not an uncommon sequence of a *béa*, and I am told that the natives of the district, in which such a gathering is to be held, look forward to it with considerable apprehension. A human body is usually procured for these occasions; and the payment of the persons who procured it is made from contributions collected at the *béa*. Each leading chief endeavours to surpass his rival in the sum he gives; and flinging his string of shell money down from the stage on which he stands, he looks contemptuously at his rival's party. The body is apportioned out after the gathering is over; and if no contention has arisen, all assembled partake of the feast. Taki told Mr. Stephens that in order to obtain a body for his son's *béa*, he would have to start on another man-hunting expedition. A *béa* was also soon to be held in Ugi by Rora, the fighting chief of the village of Ete-ete, on behalf of his brother who had died about two years before. Cannibalism is however dying out in Ugi; and in this case a pig was to supply the place of a human body.

Whilst the ship was anchored at Sulagina Bay on the north coast of St. Christoval, I visited the village of that name and saw the chief who is named Toro. He received me civilly and shook hands. Outside the front of his house five skulls were hanging which belonged to some unfortunate bushmen who had fallen at his hands. On inquiring of a native who spoke a little English, I ascertained that their bodies had been "kaied-kaied," *i.e.*, eaten, although it was with a little hesitation that he admitted the fact. Numerous spears were thrust in among the pole overhead which supported the roof, one or two of them being broken at the point with some suspicious-looking dried-up substance still adherent. The same native explained to me, in a matter-of-fact way, that the points had broken off in the bellies of the victims.

Cannibalism is rarely if ever practised at the present day in the islands of Bougainville Straits. The people of the western extremity of Choiseul Island in the vicinity of Choiseul Bay are reputed by the Treasury Islanders to be still cannibals. During our stay in this bay we had no opportunity of satisfying ourselves in this matter. Bougainville, however, who visited this bay in 1768, records, as I have previously observed, that a human jaw, half-broiled, was found in one of the canoes which had been deserted by the natives after the repulse of their attack upon the French boats.[1] The Shortland natives accredit the Bougainville people who live around the active volcano of Bagana with the regular practice of cannibalism; and there can be little doubt that this custom is extensively practised amongst the scarcely known bush-tribes in the interior of this large island. Of the natives of New Georgia or Rubiana, Captain Cheyne avers that human flesh forms their chief article of diet; they were in his opinion, when he visited this part of the group in 1844, the most treacherous and bloodthirsty race in the Western Pacific.[2] These natives have of late years come more under the direct influence of the traders and probably would merit now a better name.

I will close this chapter with a short account, to some extent recapitulative, of the history of three natives of St. Christoval after they were recruited by the boats of the Fiji labour-vessel "Redcoat" in 1882. It will serve to illustrate some points already alluded to. Amongst the occupants of a tambu-house in which I slept on one occasion in the village of Lawa, in the interior of St. Christoval, were five men who were intending to offer themselves as recruits to the government-agent of the "Redcoat." Three of these men, one of whom was the chief's son, came under my observation again not many weeks after they had been received on board the labour-vessel. They escaped from the ship at Santa Anna, and seizing a canoe reached the adjoining coast of St. Christoval. Here they were pursued by Mai, in his capacity of purveyor of human flesh to the Cape Surville natives. Two of them were captured; but the third, who was the chief's son, had died at the hands of a local chief, who, wishing to remove the tambu-ban arising from the recent death of his wife, had effected his object by spearing his guest. Mai returned to Santa Anna with his two captives, and immediately became imbued with the idea that he had been insulted by the chief who, in successfully removing the tambu-ban from the shade of his departed spouse, had deprived him of one of his victims. Then the raid was carried out, which I have already described, as having resulted in the slaughter of three women and the chief of Fanarite. Mai now devoted his attention to preparing his two prisoners for the market on the opposite coast, and was thus employed when H.M.S. "Lark" arrived at Port Mary and rescued the prisoners

---

[1] "Voyage autour du Monde"; 2nd edit. augment; vol. ii., Paris, 1772.

[2] "A Description of Islands in the Western Pacific Ocean," by A. Cheyne (London, 1852).

When these two natives were brought on board, I at once recognised
my tambu-house companions in the village of Lawa; and I learned
to my regret that the chief's son, who had been killed, was the
sprightly young native who had on one occasion carried my geological bag. It is but just to remark that under Mai's care the condition of the two prisoners had considerably improved since I last
saw them. However, their troubles were not all over. They were
landed at Ugi; but the older of the two, on hearing that his life
would be probably required by the people of his own village to
atone for the death of the chief's son, preferred to remain at Ugi.
A report reached me in the following year, whether true or not I
was unable to ascertain, that he had been killed on returning to his
village.

CHAPTER III

THE FEMALE SEX—POLYGAMY—MODES OF BURIAL, ETC.

THE position of the female sex amongst the natives of the eastern islands of the Solomon Group would appear to differ but little from the position which it holds amongst races in a similar savage state. The women are without doubt the drudges of the men, and pitiable examples of this often came under my observation. On one occasion, when I was returning to the coast from an excursion into the interior of St. Christoval, I was accompanied by some half-a-dozen natives of both sexes who were bringing down yams to sell to the traders on the beach. The men were content with carrying their tomahawks; whilst the women followed up with heavy loads of yams on their heads. When a feast is in preparation, it is the work of the women to bring in the yams and taro from the "patches," which may be one or two miles away. In my excursions, I frequently used to see at work in their "patches" these poor creatures, whom drudgery had prematurely deprived of all their comeliness.

Women are excluded from the tambu-house. They are not permitted to remain in the presence of a chief at his meal; and even the wife after preparing her husband's meal leaves her lord alone, returning to partake of what remains after he has finished his repast. In the island of Santa Catalina we found that we had temporarily received the rank of chief when a bevy of young girls, who had been following us all the morning, walked solemnly away as we began our lunch; but no sooner had we lit our pipes than back came the little troop with smiling faces. In Ugi, a man will never, if he can help it, pass under a tree that has fallen across the path, for the reason that a woman may have stepped over it before him. On one occasion, in the village of Sapuna, in Santa Anna, I saw a man, whilst lighting his pipe, throw the piece of smouldering wood contemptuously on the ground, when a woman, in order to light her own pipe, stretched out her hand to take it from him.

The custom of infanticide throws a shade over not a few of these islands. During my frequent walks over the island of Ugi, where one may pass through a village without seeing a single child in arms, I often experienced a feeling of relief in leaving behind such a village where the prattle of children is but rarely heard. In Ugi, infanticide is the prevailing custom. When a man needs assistance in his declining years, his props are not his own sons but youths obtained by purchase from the St. Christoval natives, who, as they attain to manhood, acquire a virtual independence, passing almost beyond the control of their original owner. It is from this cause that but a small proportion of the Ugi natives have been born on the island, three-fourths of them having been brought as youths to supply the place of offspring killed in infancy. Yet some bright experiences, brighter, perhaps, in the contrast, recur to my mind. In the small island of Orika (Santa Catalina) the visitor will be followed about by a little train of children, of both sexes, with smiling, intelligent faces, and clad only in the garb which nature gave them. Whilst having an evening pipe in front of the house of Haununo, the young chief, Mr. W. Macdonald and I were surrounded by a varied throng of the natives of the village, both old and young. Numerous young children, from babes in arms to those three or four years old, formed no inconsiderable proportion of the number around us. Bright-looking lads, eight or nine years of age, stood smoking their pipes as gravely as Haununo himself; and even the smallest babe in its father's arms caught hold of his pipe and began to suck instinctively. The chief's son, a little shapeless mass of flesh, a few months old, was handed about from man to man with as much care as if he had been composed of something brittle. It would have taken many ship-loads of "trade," as Mr. Macdonald remarked to me, to have purchased the hopeful heir of the chief of Orika.

But to return to the subject of the position held by the women. When away with a recruiting party from the labour-ship "Redcoat," on the St. Christoval coast, I was present at the parting on the beach of six natives, who had elected to proceed to Fiji to work for a term of three years on the plantations. But little regret was observable in the faces of those whose friends were leaving them. Son parted with father, and brother with brother with apparently as little concern as if they were merely parting for the hour. The mother or sister played no part in this scene, a characteristic negative feature of the social life of these natives. However, amongst the six natives was an elderly woman who was following her husband to Fiji; and her departure was evidently keenly felt by a small knot of female companions on the beach. One poor creature stood at the edge of the water, looking wistfully towards the boat as it was being pulled away, and crying more after the manner of a fretful child. It was the bond of a true affection that knit together the heart of these poor women. In this episode I saw, to employ those beautiful lines of Milton,

" The sable cloud
Turn forth her silver lining on the night."

In it was evinced the only sign of the tenderer feelings which was displayed in the whole of that day's proceedings.

It is necessary for me to touch lightly on a subject, which, although less pleasing, is none the less essential to the short sketch which I have presented to my readers of the domestic relations of the natives in the eastern islands. Female chastity is a virtue that would sound strangely in the ear of the native. Amongst their many customs which when narrated strike with such a discordant note on the ears of the European reader, the inhabitants of St. Christoval and the adjacent islands have a usage which sufficiently enlightens us as to the unrestrained character of their code of morality. For two or three years after a girl has become eligible for marriage, she distributes her favours amongst all the young men of the village. Should she be unwilling to accept the addresses of anyone, it is but necessary for her admirer to make her parents some present. Fathers offer their daughters to the white man in the hope of a remunerative return ; and the white men, sometimes less scrupulous in their advances, provoke the hostility of the natives, and not unfrequently a lamentable massacre results. Conjugal fidelity is usually preserved in the limits of the same community ; but the men of Santa Anna, when they exchange their wives for those of the men of the adjoining St. Christoval coast, see in such a transaction no loosening of the marriage-tie, and restore their wives to their original position on their return to their homes.

In considering the domestic relations of the inhabitants of Bougainville Straits, we enter upon a more agreeable topic. The white man on first visiting these islands is struck with the shyness of the women as compared with those of St. Christoval and its adjacent islands. The unmarried girls are rarely seen; whilst, on the other hand, in Santa Anna and Santa Catalina there appears to be no restriction placed on their movements. The following incident in the island of Faro will serve to illustrate this shyness. Whilst following a path in the interior of the island, unattended by any companion, I suddenly surprised a woman sitting on a log with a child in her lap. She bolted away into the wood leaving the child, a little boy three or four years of age, on the ground in the middle of the path. The little urchin at once set up a terrific yell; but a present of a gilt necklace softened the tone of his distress, although it did not remove his fears. However, I passed along and soon had the satisfaction of hearing the mother returning to her child.

This fear of the white man is soon dispelled by kindly treatment. When I first visited Treasury Island my entrance into the village was the signal for every woman to rush into her house, and I could only catch a glimpse of their retreating figures. This shyness soon wore away during the lengthened visits of the "Lark;" and in a short time when I walked through the village I was surrounded by a troop of young boys shouting out my name of "Dokus" or "Rokasy" at the top of their voices. This was the signal for all who were indoors to turn out to greet me. The old people would hobble out to the door; and the married women with their babes in their arms would walk up to me calling me by name and holding up their little ones for me to see, as if only too proud to show me the confidence the visit of the "Lark" had inspired.

The females in these islands of the Straits perform most of the work in the "patches" or plantations. Towards the evening, they may usually be seen returning in their canoes from the more distant "patches" bringing home a goodly quantity of taro, bananas, and other vegetables. There is generally a man in the stern who steers with a paddle; whilst the crew of eight or ten women, sitting in pairs, paddle briskly along with their light paddles.

The powerful chiefs of the islands of Bougainville Straits usually possess a large number of wives of whom only the few that retain their youth and comeliness enjoy much of the society of their lord. The majority, having been supplanted in the esteem of their common husband, have sunk into a condition of drudgery, finding their employment and their livelihood in toiling for the master whose affections they once possessed. I learned from Gorai, the Shortland chief, who has between eighty and a hundred wives, that the main objection he has against missionaries settling on his islands is, that they would insist on his giving up nearly all his wives, thereby depriving him of those by whose labour his plantations are cultivated and his household supplied with food. A great chief, he remarked, required a large staff of workers to cultivate his extensive lands; or, in other words, numerous women to work in his plantations and to bring the produce home. Such a plea for polygamy is in this condition of society somewhat plausible. The domestic establishment of such a chief may be compared in its internal economy to a social community of bees. The head of the society is, in this case, a male who, whilst living on the fat produce of his lands and increasing his species, performs no active office for the good of the community. The workers consist of his numerous cast-off wives, who having been supplanted in their lord's affections as their personal attractions diminished in the course of years, have at length subsided into the position of drudges to procure food for the king and his progeny.

Mule's marital establishment is on a smaller scale than that of the more powerful Shortland chief. This Treasury chief possesses between twenty-five and thirty wives, and has numerous young sons who were my frequent companions during my excursions in this island. In both establishments there is a favourite wife who exercises some authority over the others, and is known among white men as the queen. The principal wives are generally distinguished from the others by a more dignified deportment, a slim graceful figure, and more delicate features. The coarser features, bigger limbs, and more ungainly persons of many of the wives at once mark the women of more common origin. The chief secures the fidelity of his wives by the summary punishment of death, suspicion being tantamount to proof, and an unwary action being held presumptive of guilt. Many of their wives are obtained by purchase from the Bougainville natives ; whilst others represent the tribute owed by some of the smaller chiefs.

The majority of the Treasury men have two wives who are usually widely separated by age. They are originally obtained by making a handsome present to the parents. Each wife in working on her husband's land has her own patch allotted to her to which she confines her labours. My association with the natives of Treasury gave me some insight into their social life, in which, I should add, the women occupy a somewhat better position than in the islands we visited to the eastward. Men have introduced me to their wives with an air of politeness which supplied an index of the social status of their helpmates : and to show that the position of authority may be reversed—although from the absence of clothing one cannot employ the expressive phrase applied to those women who rule their husbands in more civilized lands—I may here observe that on one occasion an able-bodied man complained to me that his wife chastised him on the previous night.

I had one very pleasing experience of the domestic establishment of the Treasury chief. Having informed Mule that I was desirous to witness the manufacture of the cooking-pots employed by the natives, he despatched four of his wives into the interior of the island to get the clay ; and in due time I was summoned to his house where I found myself in the midst of a dozen of his wives who were already hard at work, for the women are the potters here as in other parts of "savagedom." Mule's wives received me with much politeness, and made me sit down on a mat to watch the proceedings, being evidently much pleased with the idea of exhibiting their skill. For about five minutes there was but little work done as my curiosity led me to look more closely into the different steps of the process, a proceeding which caused much hilarity and elicited frequent exclamations of " tion drakono," often preceded by " Dokus," which implied that the doctor was a very good man. At last, after I had smiled on them to the best of my ability, and had gained their further approbation by taking on my knee a little well-scrubbed urchin that could hardly toddle, who in the most matter-of-fact manner made a vigorous onslaught on my chin and then went tooth-and-nail at my shirt-cuff, all in the best of humour and seemingly in an absent-minded kind of fashion as though its little mind was already occupied by far weightier matters—after all this, the more serious part of the entertainment became fairly under way. At its conclusion, I gave the principal wife a quantity of beads and a number of jews-harps to be distributed among her companions.

The marital establishment of Tomimas, one of the principal Faro chiefs, is small as compared with those of Gorai and Mule. He has only four wives who are named respectively, Domari, Duia, Bose, and Omakau, the first being the mother of the chief's eldest son, Kopana, an intelligent young man about twenty-two years of age.

In connection with the names of the women of Bougainville Straits, I should observe that there was always some reluctance on the part of the men to give me such names; and that when they did so, they usually uttered them in a low tone as though it was not the proper thing to speak of the women by name to others. This is especially noticeable when a man of the common class is asked the name of one of the chief's wives. ' On more than one occasion, when referring by name to the chief's principal wife in the course of a conversation with a native, I learned from the look of surprise, which the mention of the name elicited, that I had, unwittingly, been guilty of a breach of etiquette.

During the surveying season of 1883, which we passed among the islands of Bougainville Straits, we were witnesses of the mourning ceremonials that were observed in connection with the death of Kaika, the principal wife of the Shortland chief, or the queen as Gorai was pleased to call her. It was in the beginning of July that I first made the acquaintance of Kaika, Gorai having asked me to visit her as she was suffering from some indisposition. A month passed away before I again saw my royal patient, and on this occasion the chief accompanied me to his house. Here I found Kaika quite recovered from her illness, a result which she attributed to some medicine which I had given her. She was reclining in a broken down easy-chair, the gift of a trader, engaged in working an armlet of beads, and clad only in the usual " sulu " or waist-handkerchief. In age Kaika was probably between 25 and 30, her general appearance being that of a woman superior in caste to most of her fellow-wives. For a native, her features were good and regular, her figure slim but well proportioned, her carriage graceful. Her clean skin and bushy head of hair, dyed a magenta hue by the use of red ochreous earth, added to the general effect of her appearance.

Whilst sitting down beside Gorai and his spouse, the. latter showed me her little boy who was nearly blind. I was much struck with the tenderness displayed in the manner of both the parents towards their little son, who, seated on his mother's lap, placed his hand in that of his father, when he was directed to raise his eyes towards the light for my inspection.

The work of the ship took us away from Alu; and when we returned after an absence of five weeks, we learned that Kaika was dying. Landing on the ensuing day to see if I could be of any service, I was told that Kaika was dead; and as I stepped out of my Rob Roy, I received a message from Gorai to come and visit him. I found the old chief seated on the ground in front of his house,

looking very dismal. Near by, there were nine or ten of his wives
all well past the prime of life, withered and haggish, with heads
shaven and faces plastered with lime as a token of mourning. They
were squatting on the ground, and were engaged in droning out a
dismal chant, reminding me of a group of witches. Accompanying
Gorai into his house, I found there a numerous gathering of his
wives all with their faces plastered with lime; their dead-white
features, peering strangely at us through the gloom of the building,
gave the whole scene quite an uncanny look. The old chief appeared
to feel the loss of his favourite wife and broke down more than once
when talking to me of her. He told me that the end came when
we dropped our anchor in the bay, and he excused himself on account
of his grief from coming off to the ship—"too much cry," as he remarked of himself to me. When I was leaving him, he asked me
on the arrival of the ship at Treasury to inform Mule of his loss,
Kaika being the sister of the Treasury chief, and to request that his
own sister, Bita, who was Mule's principal wife, should come and
visit him. Returning to my canoe I passed some of Gorai's headmen who had plastered their foreheads and a part of their cheeks
with lime, an observance, however, which was not followed by either
the chief or his sons.

The next morning most of the men of the village were engaged
in fishing on the reef to obtain material for a great funeral feast that
was to be held in the afternoon. When I landed with Lieutenant
Leeper in the latter part of the day, we found ourselves on the beach
in the midst of about a hundred men carrying their tomahawks, and
assembled together on the occasion of the queen's demise. On entering the chief's grounds, which are tabooed to all the men of the
village except those on the staff of the chief, we came upon about
eighty women performing a funeral dance. Some of them were
Gorai's wives; whilst others were the principal women of the neighbouring villages. With their faces white with lime they formed a
large circle, in the centre of which were four posts placed erect in
the ground, each about ten feet high, charred on one side and rudely
carved in imitation of the human head, two of them painted red and
two white. Enclosed in the ring and grouped around the posts were
six women bearing in their hands the personal belongings of the
deceased, such as her basket, cushion, &c. To the slow and measured time of the beats of a wooden drum, a hollowed log struck by
a man outside the circle, the dancers of the ring adapted their move

ments, which consisted merely in raising the feet in turns and gently stamping on the ground. The central group of women danced around the posts, partly skipping, partly hopping, each woman holding up before her the article she bore, and regulating her steps to the beats of the drum. Now and then the man at the drum quickened his time, and the movements of the women of the ring became more spirited; whilst the central group of dancers skipped more actively around, the foremost woman sprinkling at each bound handfuls of lime over the dancers of the ring. As the weather was rainy, many of the women—all of whom wore a "sulu" reaching down to the knees—had their shoulders covered by their mats of pandanus leaves. This dance was repeated on the following day but with a smaller number of dancers. I was anxious to ascertain the manner in which the body had been disposed; but beyond the fact that interment had taken place in the ground some distance away, I could learn but little. It is, however, very probable that the body was first burned between the charred posts, around which the dance was performed, which would have served as supports for the funeral pyre. Further reference to this custom will be found on page 51.

In making inquiries as to the obsequies paid to the dead queen, I was much struck with the reluctance of the natives to refer to the event. They mentioned the name of the deceased in a low subdued tone as if it were wrong to utter the names of the dead. This mysterious dread which is associated with the mention of the names of the dead is found, as Dr. Tylor points out in his "Early History of Mankind" (3rd edit., p. 143), amongst many races of men. The example of the Australian native who *refuses* to utter them may be here cited as an extreme instance of this superstition.

Three days after the death of Kaika, all the men of Alu, with the exception of the chief and his sons, cut off their hair close to the scalp as a symbol of mourning for the deceased, an observance which produced a surprising change in the appearance of men whom I had been familiar with as the owners of luxuriant bushy periwigs. A similar custom of either shaving the scalp or of cutting the hair close prevailed in other islands of the group which we visited, as at Simbo and Ugi. In the latter island the shaving is restricted to the posterior half of the scalp. With this digression I will continue my account of the mourning ceremonials observed at the death of Kaika.

The news of the death of the principal wife of the Alu chief was

D

soon carried to the other islands of Bougainville Straits. Visits of condolence were paid to Gorai by Tomimas and Kurra-kurra, the two Faro chiefs; and parties of the women of Faro went to display in person their sympathy with the Alu chief on the occasion of his bereavement. We were the first to convey the news to Treasury; and as Mulo stepped on deck shortly after the ship had come to an anchor in Blanche Harbour, I informed him of his sister's death and of Gorai's request that his own sister Bita should go and visit him at Alu. The news of Kaika's death was received by her brother with much composure. Several weeks passed away before Bita could accomplish the long canoe voyage to her brother's island, as it is only practicable for a canoe in settled weather. There was a sudden demand for pairs of scissors in Treasury when the news of the death of Gorai's wife became generally known. Mule, his sons, and several of the men of the island showed their regard for the deceased by neatly trimming their bush / periwigs, not cropping their hair close as in the case of the Alu natives; and in accordance with custom the wives of the chief plastered their faces with lime.

A week after our arrival at Treasury feasts were prepared as offerings to the Evil Spirit—the *nito paitena* of the natives—to appease the wrath of that deity. For to his anger, as I was informed by an intelligent native named Erosini, the death of Kaika was attributed. Whilst walking through the village one evening, I came upon the "remains" of one of these feasts. The essence of the viands had doubtless been extracted by this direful spirit, inasmuch as I learned on the authority of Erosini that the "devilo," as he termed him, had already satiated his appetite; but to the eyes of ordinary mortals like myself, the dishes had not been touched. However, it was not long before numerous natives were helping themselves freely to the roasted opossums, boiled fish, taro, bananas, etc., which formed the feast. Although pressed to join in the banquet, I did not take to the idea of eating a vicarious meal for his infernal majesty; and I resisted the persuasion of one of my would-be hosts who, having scooped up with his hands a mixture of mashed taro and cocoa-nut scrapings, licked his fingers well and remarked it was very good "kai-kai." On the following day an old rudely carved tambu-post that had been erected on the beach was used as a target, at which, from a distance of about fifteen paces, the natives fired their muskets and discharged their arrows. This proceeding, so we learned, was to intimidate the "devilo" in case the feasts of the previous day had not propitiated him.

The mode of burial employed by the natives of the islands of Bougainville Straits varies according to the position of the deceased. The bodies of the chiefs and of any members of their families are usually burned; and the ashes are deposited together with the skull and sometimes the thigh-bones in a cairn on some sacred islet, or are placed in charge of the reigning chief. The natives were always reticent on this subject, a circumstance which prevented my ascertaining how the skull and thigh-bones were preserved from the flames. In the village of Treasury there are some memorials of departed chiefs, one of which is shown in the accompanying engraving. The one in best condition is that of the late chief, whose skull and thigh-bones were deposited on one of the islets in the harbour. They evidently mark the site of the funeral pyres. A wooden frame of the dimensions of a large coffin is placed on the ground and contains some young plants and the club of the deceased chief. Four posts charred on their inner sides and decorated on their outer sides with patterns in red, white, and black, are placed one at each corner of the frame. They are rudely carved at the top in the form of a face, and in all respects resemble those around which the funeral dance was performed at Alu, as described on page 49. A sprouting cocoa-nut is placed at one end of the frame, and a club is placed erect in the ground at the other end.

In the vicinity of Gorai's house, I noticed three small enclosures, apparently graves, two of them round and one oblong, and all fenced in by a paling of sticks. Lying on the ground within each enclosure were such articles as strings of trade-beads, clay-pipes, betel-nuts long since dried up, and dishes of palm leaves such as the natives use for serving up their food. A communicative old man informed me that a few months before a woman and a girl belonging to the chief's household had died, and that their bodies had been first burned between four posts and the ashes had been placed in the oblong enclosure. They bore, so he told me, the pretty names of Événu and Siali. On my asking the reason of placing articles such as beads and betel-nuts on the grave, he told me that in addition cocoa-nuts and other food had been placed there previously in accordance with the native custom, which the old man endeavoured to explain by pointing his fingers towards the skies. I should here mention that on the spot, where the body of Kaika had been burned some months before, there was placed a wooden framework in the form of a long box, the materials being obtained from a ship's fittings. Inside it were placed some beads and coloured calico.

The custom of depositing skulls in cairns on the points of islands, which is prevalent in the eastern portion of the Solomon Group, is not generally practised amongst the islands of Bougainville Straits: and I rarely came upon them in my excursions. However, on an islet in Choiseul Bay, I found two cairns, one of which was tenanted only by hermit-crabs with their cast-off shells, and the other contained two skulls that had apparently lain for years in their resting-place to which they were attached by the tendrils of creeping plants. On the summit of Oima, I came upon a heap of stones under which was supposed to be the remains of a Bougainville native killed in a fight, but I failed to find any of his bones after examining the heap. The sea is generally chosen as the last resting-place for the natives below the rank of chief in the islands of Bougainville Straits. Lieutenant Malan, whilst engaged in sounding at the entrance of the Alu anchorage, passed two large canoes in one of which were being conveyed, for burial in deep water, the remains of a woman who had died during the previous night. The relatives of the deceased accompanied the corpse, but took no share in the paddling, being employed in wailing and bemoaning their loss after the conventional manner of the Chinese. A peculiar style of paddling was adopted by the funeral party ; each man, pausing after every stroke, partially arrested the motion of the canoe by a back-water movement of his paddle.

In Simbo or Eddystone Island, the bodies of the dead are sometimes placed amongst the large masses of rock which lie at the base of Middle Hill on the west coast of the island. My attention was first attracted to this custom by the stench that came from this spot as I passed it in a canoe. Some human bones were observed on the reef which lies off the anchorage. In the eastern islands the dead are often buried at sea. In Ugi and in Florida the skulls are sometimes preserved in a cairn of stones built on the edge of a sea cliff, or at the extremity of a point, or in some remote islet. A dwarf cocoa-nut, which attains a height of from eight to twelve feet, frequently marks the grave of the chief in the island of Ugi. In one of the villages of this island I was shown the shrine of a chief, a small house in which suspended from the roof in a basket were the skulls of the chief and his wife concealed from view by a screen of palm leaves. Some articles of food, including a portion of an opossum, together with a large wooden bowl, were hung up before the screen.

The burial place for men in the village of Sapuna in Santa Anna is an oblong enclosure in the midst of the village which measures 24 by 18 feet, and is surrounded by a low wall of fragments of coral limestone. In this space all the bodies are buried at a depth of five or six feet; and after some time the skulls are exhumed and placed inside the wooden figure of a shark about three feet in length, which is deposited in the tambu-house. One of these wooden fish, which lay on the surface of the burial ground at the time of my visit, had recently been removed from the tambu-house on account of its being rotten through age, and the skull was to be re-interred. The body of a chief is placed at once in the tambu-house in a wooden shark of sufficient size. Women are buried in another ground, and the wooden sharks containing their skulls are deposited in a small house by the side of the tambu-house.

Into the subject of the superstitions and religious beliefs which are held by the natives of the Solomon Islands I shall barely enter, as only those who have become familiar with the natives by long residence among them, and who have acquired an intimate knowledge of their language, can hope to avoid the numerous pitfalls into which the unwary observer is so likely to fall. I would, therefore, refer the reader for information on this subject to a paper by the Rev. R. H. Codrington, entitled "Religious Beliefs and Practices in Melanesia," which was published in the Journal of the Anthropological Institute (vol. x., p. 261). Through Lieutenant Malan's knowledge of the Fijian tongue, a language understood by the men who had served their term on the Fiji plantations, I learned that the natives of Treasury and the Shortlands believe in a Good Spirit (*nito drekona*) who lives in a pleasant land whither all men who have lived good lives go after death, and that all the bad men are transported to the crater of Bagana, the burning volcano of Bougainville, which is the home of the Evil Spirit (*nito paitena*) and his companion spirits. That the natives of the Shortlands really believe in some future state is shown in the following singular superstition which came under my notice at Alu. I was returning one night in Gorai's war canoe from one of my excursions, when I noticed that the chief and his men were looking towards the coral island of Balalai which lies a few miles distant from the anchorage. They told me they were looking for a bright light which was sometimes to be seen shining at night in this island in the winter months of the year. This light they believed to be the spirit of Captain Ferguson of the "Ripple," who had been killed some years before by the natives of Nouma-nouma on the Bougainville coast. I suggested that it might be the watch-fire of a party of the Faro natives who had gone there to fish, or to hunt turtle; but my suggestion was pooh-poohed Balalai was evidently a haunted island in the minds of my companions, and I desisted from making any further remarks which would be likely to disabuse them of this idea. Often and often when we were anchored within sight of this island I remembered the story, but never saw the light.

The natives of Ugi believe that the souls of the dead pass into fireflies: and should one of these insects enter a house, those inside quickly leave it. The spirits of the dead in human shape are believed to frequent certain islets in Treasury Harbour, where they are occasionally seen by the women. Certain spirits, who are usually accredited with the power of sending sickness or other calamities, are said to take up their abodes in particular districts. Such a spirit haunts the picturesque glen of Tetabau on the northern slope of the summit of Treasury, if we may accept the statement of one of the islanders; and any native who is bold enough to enter this glen will, according to the general belief, provoke the anger of its invisible occupant. The party of natives who accompanied me to the summit of Tarawei Hill in the island of Faro refused to go further than the brink of the hill, because, as they said, there dwelt on the top some evil spirits who would send sickness and death on any intruder. I had therefore to walk along the crest of the hill alone. The echoes which the shouts of my men awakened as we descended the steep slopes to the west were, as I was told, but the voices of the spirits who haunted the summit of the hill.

In the island of Ugi the superstition of "ill-wishing" is very prevalent. When a man cuts off his hair, as in mourning, he buries it unobserved so that it may not fall into the hands of any one who may by sorcery bring sickness or some other calamity upon him; and he adopts the same precaution with reference to the husks of betel-nuts and similar refuse. Whilst I was obtaining some samples of hair from the natives of this island, I was told that if in the immediate future any sickness should befall those who had parted with their hair, they would assign the cause to me; yet, native-like, they allowed me to take a sample with their free consent, for it is their custom never to refuse to each other anything that is asked. The professions of the sorcerer and medicine-man are usually combined in the same individual. These men in the Shortlands have a great reputation in the minds of the natives, being accredited by them with a knowledge almost universal; and the precincts of their dwellings are tabooed even to the chief. One of them named Kikila, a sinister-looking individual with but one eye, had obtained much repute in the practice of his profession. When on one occasion Lieutenant Oldham complained to the chief that some of the calico had been removed by the natives from the surveying-marks, the services of Kikila were employed to bring about the death of the unknown culprit. The sorcerer was not himself aware who the man was; but we were told that for one of so much repute this was quite unnecessary. We never learned the result of his incantation; but in all probability they effected their purpose soon enough by working on the fears of the unfortunate offender. How it was to be done we could not satisfactorily ascertain; but there was no doubt as to the efficacy of the means employed in the minds of the natives.

Amongst the powers of the sorcerers are those of influencing the weather. But such powers are not confined to men of this class alone. In Ugi, different natives are accredited with being able to bring wind and rain; and I knew one man who had earned for himself a considerable reputation as a "wind-prophet." These powers are claimed by Mule, the Treasury chief, amongst his other prerogatives.

As far as I could ascertain, these natives keep no record, even in the memory, of the lapse of years. Nor are they acquainted with their own age. More than once when trying to obtain the date of particular events, I received the wildest replies. The safest method to employ in making such inquiries is to get the native to refer a recent event to some epoch in his own life, or in the case of earlier occurrences to associate them with his boyhood, manhood, or marriage. When he asserts that a certain event occurred whilst his father was a child, he is probably to be trusted; but when he goes back to the time of his grandfather, no further reliance can be placed on his statements, except as implying an indefinite number of years. I have observed elsewhere (page 76) that a grandfather is deemed a personage of such a high antiquity that these islanders, when referring to past events, seldom care to go beyond.

The only method of reckoning that came under my notice was in the instance of a Treasury native, who, whilst serving as interpreter on board the "Lark," kept a register of the time he was away from his island by tying a knot daily on a cord and marking Sunday by a piece of paper, the knots being about an inch apart. I learned from a Faro man that this is the method of recording days which is commonly employed by the inhabitants of Bougainville Straits, the "moons" or months being alone distinguished by a piece of native tobacco tied in the knot. Such a practice, however, would appear to be followed only during the temporary absences from their islands, as when they are away on canoe expeditions. A native, captured in 1769 by Surville, whilst at Port Praslin, in Isabel, kept count of the days of absence from his country by tying knots in a "lacet."[1] It is scarcely necessary for me to point out that in the "knotted cord" of the Solomon Islanders we have the elementary form of the "quipu" of the Incas.

Amongst the constellations, the Pleiades and Orion's Belt seem to be those which are most familiar to the natives of Bougainville Straits. The former, which they speak of as possessing six stars, they name "Vuhu;" the latter, "Matatala." They have also names for a few other stars. As in the case of many other savage races, the Pleiades is a constellation of great significance with the inhabitants of these straits. The Treasury Islanders hold a great feast towards the end of October, to celebrate, as far as I could learn, the approaching appearance of this constellation above the eastern horizon soon after sunset. Probably, as in many of the Pacific Islands, this event marks the beginning of their year. I learned from Mr. Stephens that, in Ugi, where of all the constellations the Pleiades alone receives a name, the natives are guided by it in selecting the times for planting and taking up their yams.

[1] From an extract of this voyage given in "Voyage de Marion." Paris, 1783: p. 274, circd.

VILLAGE OF SUENNA IN UGI.

To face page 57.

THE villages in the eastern islands of the group vary much in size. They usually contain between 25 and 40 houses, and between one and two hundred inhabitants. There are however some much larger, as in the case of Wano on the north coast of St. Christoval, which probably does not possess a population much under five hundred. In the larger villages the houses are generally built in double rows with a common thoroughfare between; and the tambu-house occupies usually a central position. In the village of Suenna, as shown in the engraving, which is one of the largest villages in Ugi, the houses are built around a large open space free of buildings. The usual dimensions of the dwelling-houses are as follows: length 25 to 30 feet, breadth 15 to 20 feet, height 8 to 10 feet. The gable-roof, which is made of a framework of bamboos thatched with the leaves of pandanus trees, or of cocoa-nut or areca palms, is supported on a central row of posts. The sides are low and made of the same materials as the roof. The only entrance is by an oblong aperture in the front of the building, which is removed $2\frac{1}{2}$ to 3 feet above the ground, so that one has literally to dive into the interior, which from the absence of any other openings, is kept very dark. Such are the dimensions and mode of structure of an ordinary dwelling-house in the eastern islands. The chiefs, however, have larger buildings, which in some instances, as in those of the more powerful chiefs, rival in size and in style the tambu-houses themselves. Many houses have a staging in front, which is on a level with the lower edge of the aperture that serves as the entrance. On this staging, protected by the projecting roof, the inmates are wont to sit and lie about during the day; and the men occasionally pass the night there. In the houses of the chiefs and principal men, there are generally spaces partitioned off for sleeping and containing

a raised stage for the mats; but in the dwelling-house of an
ordinary man no such partitions usually occur. Single men sleep
on the ground on a mat, which may be nothing more than the leaves
of two branches of the cocoa-nut palm rudely plaited together. Each
man lays his mat by the side of a little smouldering wood-fire, which
he endeavours to keep up during the night, and for this purpose he
gets up at all hours to fan it into a flame.

There is but little attempt made to please the eye in the way of
external or internal decoration in the ordinary dwelling-house of a
native in the eastern islands. Rows of the lower jaws of pigs with
the skeletons of fishes and the dried skins of the flying-fox are to
be seen suspended from the roof over the entrance; whilst the
spears, clubs, and fishing implements are either thrust between the
bamboos of the roof or slung in a bundle over the entrance. Of
furniture there is but little except the large cooking-bowls, the
mats, and a circle of cooking-stones forming a rude hearth in the
centre of the floor. I have seen in temporary sheds or "lean-tos,"
erected by fishing parties on the southern island of the "Three
Sisters," fire-places formed of a circle two to three feet across of
medium-sized *Tridacna* shells, the enclosed space being strewn with
small stones.

The houses of the chiefs usually display more decoration.
Amongst others I recall to my mind the brightly-coloured front of
the residence of Haununo, the intelligent young chief of Santa Catalina. I am not aware how long a native house will last. The
white residents, however, tell me that houses built for their own
use, which are more substantial than the ordinary native dwellings,
will stand some five or six years; and that, notwithstanding
the heavy rainfall of this region, the thatch remains admirably
waterproof.

I now come to the description of the houses in the islands of
Bougainville Straits. In the villages of Treasury and the Shortlands, the houses are arranged in a long straggling row; and although
close to the beach they are for the most part concealed by the trees
from the view of those on board the ships in the anchorage. In the
materials used, in their style, and in their general size, these houses
resemble those of St. Christoval and the adjacent smaller islands.
A thatch made of the leaves of the sago-palm or of the pandanus,
covers the gable-roof and the framework of the walls. The usual
dimensions of a dwelling-house are: length 25 to 30 feet, breadth

12 to 15 feet, height 10 to 12 feet. Since there are no means of admitting light except by the door, the interiors are very dark, insomuch that on entering one of these houses from the bright sunlight the eyes require some time before they can see at all. In the out-lying hamlets in the interior of these islands, the houses are often smaller and more rudely constructed; and the owner supplies the place of a door by placing a couple of large plantain leaves or a branch of a cocoa-nut palm before the entrance. Many of these small hamlets are only occupied during the planting season.

There is a far greater difference in size between the dwellings of the chiefs and those of the ordinary natives than exists in the eastern islands of the group, a distinction which might have been expected on account of the greater power of the chiefs of Bougainville Straits. Gorai, the powerful Shortland chief, has appropriated to himself more than an acre of ground on which stand the several buildings required for the accommodation of his numerous wives, children, and dependents. Its precincts are tabooed to the ordinary native; but the old chief is always ready to extend to the white man a privilege which he denies to his own people. His own residence, when we first met him, had no great pretensions in size or appearance, measuring 40 by 20 feet in length and breadth, and possessing a very dingy interior from the absence of any opening except the entrance to admit light. There was, however, a larger and better constructed building situated near his own for the accommodation of his female establishment. It measured 60 by 30 by 20 feet in length, breadth, and height; and was subsequently appropriated by the chief for his own use.

The residence of Mule, the Treasury chief, was one of the largest native edifices that I saw in the Solomon Group. It is a gable-roofed building, measuring about 80 feet in length, 50 feet in breadth, and 25 to 30 feet in height. The front of the house, which is at one of the ends of the building, has a singular appearance from the central part or body of the building, being advanced several feet beyond the sides, a style which is imitated in some of the smaller houses of the village. Its interior is very imperfectly lighted by small apertures in the walls. I should here refer to the large and neatly built house of the powerful chief of Simbo, who, contrary to the usual practice, prefers light to darkness in his residence.

In the two principal villages of Faro or Fauro which are named Toma and Sinasoro, a number of the houses are built on piles and raised from 5 to 8 feet above the ground, as shown in the accompanying plate. But this custom is by no means universal in the same village, and depends, as far as I could learn, on the personal fancy of the owner. Both these villages are situated on low level tracts bordering the sea; but their sites are free from moist and swampy ground, to the existence of which one might have attributed this practice. The houses built on the ground are about 30 feet long, 20 feet wide, and 12 or 13 feet high; whilst those raised on piles are considerably smaller, measuring 22 by 15 feet in length and breadth, the building itself being supported on a framework of stout poles lashed on the tops of the piles by broad stripes of rattan. These pile-dwellings are reached by rudely constructed steps made after the style of our own ladders. The roofs of the houses in these villages have a higher pitch than I have observed in houses of the other islands of the Straits. Their eaves project considerably beyond the walls, and the roof is often prolonged at the front end of the building forming a kind of portico. A neat thatch of the leaves of the sago palm covers the sides and roof of each building.

After remarking that the houses in the Florida Islands are often similarly built on piles not only at the coast, but also on the hill-slopes some distance from the sea, I pass on to briefly refer to the purpose of these pile-dwellings on land. It seemed to me probable that in previous years, when the natives of Faro were not on such friendly terms with their neighbours, the houses were built on piles for purposes of defence against a surprise; and that when comparative peace and order reigned, some persons preferred the more commodious house on a ground site to the smaller and less convenient building on piles. Various explanations have been advanced with reference to this custom of building pile-dwellings on dry land, some of which I will enumerate. It is held by some that this custom is but the survival of "the once purposeful habit of building them in the water." The exclusion of pigs and goats and the protection against wild animals have been suggested as probable objects of this practice; whilst by others it is urged that the purpose of these pile-dwellings is to obviate the effects of excessive rain and to guard against damp exhalations from a tropical soil. Whatever may be the cause or causes of this custom, it is one which is widely spread,

PILE-DWELLINGS IN FAURO ISLAND.

To face page 84.

being found in New Guinea, in the Philippines, amongst the tribes on the north-eastern frontier of India, and in Guiana.[1]

With regard to the internal arrangements of the houses in this part of the Solomon Group, but little remains to be said. In many houses a portion of a space is partitioned off for sleeping purposes, usually one of the corners; in others, again, the interior is divided into two halves by a cross-partition. More attention is here paid to the comfort of repose than in the eastern islands. In the place of the single mat laid on the ground, they have low couches, raised a foot to eighteen inches above the floor, on which they lay their mats; whilst a round cylinder of wood serves them as a pillow. These couches, which the natives can improvise in the bush in a few minutes, are usually nothing more than a layer of stout poles, such as the slender trunks of the areca palms, resting at their ends on two logs.

Mat-making is one of the occupations of the women of the Straits, the material employed being the thick leaves of a species of *Pandanus* which is known by the natives as the *pota*. The leaves are first deprived of their thin polished epidermis by being rubbed over with the leaves of a plant, named *sansuti*, which have a rough surface giving a sensation like that caused by fine emery paper when passed over the skin. The pandanus leaves are then dried in the sun, when they become whitened and leathery, and are then sewn together into mats. These mats are not only used to lie upon, but are also worn by the women over their shoulders as a protection in wet weather. They are especially useful, as I have myself found, when sleeping out in the open in wet weather. They are sufficiently long to cover the whole length of a native; and when he is sleeping out in the bush, he lies down on his couch formed, as above described, from the slender trunks of areca palms ready at his hand, and covering himself completely with his mat, he may sleep through a deluge of rain without being touched by the wet. The mat has a crease along the middle of its length, so that when placed over the body it resembles a "tente d'abri;" and the rain runs off as from the roof of a house. To intending travellers in these islands, I strongly recommend this form of couch. A native mat and a blanket are all he requires to carry. Almost anywhere in the bush he can find the areca palms,

---

[1] Those of my readers who desire further information on this subject should refer to the works of Tylor, Mosely, etc., and to " Nature " for the last few years.

the slender trunks of which, when placed as a layer of poles on two logs, will serve him as an excellent couch.

With regard to the domestic utensils in use amongst the natives of Bougainville Straits, I should observe that cocoa-nut shells pierced by a hole of about the size of a florin, are employed as drinking-vessels. The outer surface of the shell is usually coated over with a kind of red cement formed of a mixture of red ochreous earth and the resinous material, obtained from the fruit of the "tita" (*Parinarium laurinum*), which is employed for caulking the seams of the canoes. The exterior of these vessels is frequently ornamented by double chevron-lines of native shell-beads. Sometimes a tube of bamboo is fitted into the orifice of the vessel to form a neck, the whole being plastered over with the red cement and looking like some antique earthen jar. Both of these kinds of drinking-vessels are shown in the accompanying plate. Drinking water is always kept at hand in a house in a number of these cocoa-nut shells which, being hung up overhead, keep the water pleasantly cool, a plug of leaves being used as a stopper. The native, in drinking, never puts the vessel to his mouth, but throwing his head well back, he holds the vessel a few inches above his lips and allows the water to run into his mouth. The milk of the cocoa-nut is drunk in the same manner. The scoops or scrapers used in eating the white kernels of the cocoa-nuts are generally either of bone or of pearl-shell. Sometimes for this purpose a large *Cardium* shell is lashed to a handle, a small hole being made in the shell for this purpose. . . . . Wooden hooks of clumsy size, though showing some skill in their design and workmanship, are employed as hanging-pegs in the houses.

The cooking-vessels in use in the islands of Bougainville Straits are circular pots of a rough clay ware, usually measuring about nine inches in depth and breadth, but sometimes more than double this size. Cleansing these vessels out between the meals is deemed an unnecessary refinement. These cooking-pots, one of which is shown in the accompanying plate, are made by the women in the following manner: A handful of the clay, which is dark-reddish in colour and would make a good brick-clay, is first worked together in the hands into a plastic lump; and this is fashioned rudely into a kind of saucer to form the bottom of the vessel by basting the mass against a flat smooth pebble, three or four inches across, held in the left hand, with a kind of wooden trowel or beater

1

2

1. MODEL CANOE MADE BY A ST. CHRISTOVAL NATIVE.
2. PAN-PIPES. COCOANUT DRINKING VESSELS. COOKING-POT WITH
   CUSHION AND TROWEL. FAN.
   (All these Articles are from Treasury Island.)

[To face page 63.

held in the right hand. (One of these wooden trowels is figured in
the plate.) Whilst one woman is thus engaged, a couple of her companions are occupied in flattening out, by means of a flat-sided stick,
strips of the clay six to twelve inches in length and an inch in
breadth, their length increasing as the making of the vessel pro-
gresses. One of these strips is then placed around the upper edge
of the saucer ; and the potter welds or batters it into position, employing the same tools in a similar manner, the pebble being held
inside. The cooking vessel is thus built up strip by strip ; and to
enable the worker to give symmetry to the upper part of the pot, a
fillet of broad grass is tied around as a guide. An even edge is given
to the lip by drawing along the rim a fibre from the cocoa-nut husk,
and the interior and neck are finished off by the fingers well mois-
tened. Whilst being made, the cooking-pot is rested on a ring-
cushion of palm leaves, as shown in the same engraving. The time
occupied in making one of the ordinary sized pots is about three-
quarters of an hour. Thus made, they are kept in the shade for
three or four days to become firm ; and they are finally hardened by
being placed in a wood-fire. No glaze appears to be used, and the
vessels themselves show no signs of its employment. Their outer
surfaces are indistinctly marked by odd-looking patterns in relief,
reminding one somewhat of hieroglyphics, which are produced by the
same patterns cut into one of the surfaces of the wooden beater (as
shown in the engraving) for the purpose of giving the tool a
better hold on the clay. Some cooking-pots, as in the case of the one
illustrated, are ornamented with a chevron-line in relief below the
neck and partly surrounding the vessel.[1] This ware compares but
poorly with the finish and variety of design displayed by the glazed
pottery of Fiji. The Fijian women, however, employ similar tools
and accessories, namely, a flat mallet, a small round flat stone, and a
ring-like cushion of palm leaves ; but they do not appear from the
accounts given of the process by Commodore Wilkes,[2] Messrs.
Williams and Calvert,[3] and Miss Gordon Cumming,[4] to fashion the
clay in the first place into strips. I may here refer the reader to the
illustration, given by Commodore Wilkes in his narrative (vol. iii. p.

[1] Specimens of the pots, the implements, the clay, and the other accessories, have been placed in the Ethnographical Collection of the British Museum.

[2] " Narrative of the U.S. Explor. Exped. : " vol. iii., p. 348.

[3] " Fiji and the Fijians : " 3rd edit., 1870, p. 60.

[4] " A Lady's Cruise in a French Man-of-War : " London, 1882, p. 247.

348), of pottery-making in Fiji, as it exactly suits my description of pottery-making in these islands of Bougainville Straits.

It will be interesting, perhaps, to briefly notice some of the grada-tions in the art of pottery manufacture amongst the savage races in this quarter of the globe. A very simple method, as recorded by Captain Forrest [1] more than a century ago, was employed by the women of Dory Harbour, New Guinea. They formed "pieces of clay into earthen pots; with a pebble in one hand to put into it, whilst they held in the other hand, also a pebble, with which they knocked, to enlarge and smooth it." The natives of the Andaman Islands [2] advance another step in the process. We learn from Mr. Man that the only implements employed are, an *Arca* shell, a short pointed stick, and a board. The clay is rolled out into strips with the hand. One of these strips is twisted to form the cup-like base ; and the pot is then built up strip by strip. The method employed by the natives of Bougainville Straits in the Solomon Group, may be considered to be an improvement on the plan adopted by the Anda-man Islanders. As already described, they also fashion the clay into strips and build up the vessel in a similar manner, but in the employment of a special implement as the wooden beater, in the use of the ring-cushion, and probably in the more artistic details of the process, they make a nearer approach than do the Andaman Islanders to the pottery-making of the Fijians. Then we come in the ascending scale to the method employed by the women of the Motu tribe around Port Moresby, New Guinea. By the Rev. Dr. W. Turner,[3] we are informed that they use a round smooth stone and a wooden beater but no cushion, the vessel being made without the aid of strips of clay into two pieces, the body and the mouth, which are moulded together. This method, as employed by the Motu women, may not be superior to that followed amongst the women of Bou-gainville Straits ; but inasmuch as the former manufacture three kinds of vessels, one for holding water, another for cooking, and a third to be used as a plate, whilst the latter confine their art to the cooking-pot, I have assigned the first place to the former. [4] From

[1] " A Voyage to New Guinea and the Moluccas," by Captain T. Forrest : London, 1779, p. 96.

[2] Journal of the Anthropological Institute : vol. xii., p. 69.

[3] Ibid : vol. vii., p. 470.

[4] In the Ethnological Collection of the British Museum there are specimens from this quarter of New Guinea of the wooden beaters employed in the pottery making. They are highly carved and much more finished than those of Bougainville Straits, being labelled "blocks " in the collection, as if their chief use was for imprinting patterns on the clay. It

the work of the Motu women to the pottery of the Fijians, and between the different processes employed, there is a considerable advance in the art of pottery manufacture, as already described in the case of Fiji. There, a glaze is for the first time employed; whilst in their finish, their comparative elegance of design, in their multiplicity of pattern, and in the various purposes for which they are employed from the cooking-pot up to the ornamental jar, these Fijian vessels are greatly superior to all I have referred to, whether the work of a woman of Port Dory, of an Andaman Islander, of a woman of Bougainville Straits, or of a woman of the Motu tribe in New Guinea.[1]

The Polynesian plan of producing fire, which is known as the "stick-and-groove" method, was that which was occasionally employed by my native guides during my excursions in St. Christoval and in the island of Simbo. At the risk of being charged with undue prolixity, I will briefly describe it as I saw it performed. A dry piece of wood is first taken, and one side of it is sliced so as to form a flat surface. A small bit of the same wood is then pointed at one end and worked briskly along a groove which it soon forms in the flat surface. The friction in some three or four minutes produces smoke; and finally a fine powder, which has been collecting in a small heap at the end of the groove, begins to smoulder. After being carefully nursed by the breath of the operator, the tiny flame is transferred to a piece of touch-wood, and the object is attained. In most native houses in districts not often visited by the trader, pieces of the wood used for this purpose are left lying about on the floor. Wax matches, however, form an important item in the large quantities of trade-articles which pass into the hands of the natives of some of the islands; and in such islands any other method of producing fire is not generally employed. In most cases, when I had omitted to take matches with me in my excursions, my natives, although very desirous of getting a light for their pipes, were too lazy to obtain it by making use of the more laborious method of the "stick-and-groove." When making their own journeys in the bush, they carry along with them a piece of smouldering wood, a pre-

seems to me, however, that their principal purpose is as beaters, the simply cut patterns of the beater of Bougainville Straits, which serve to give the tool a better hold on the clay, being elaborated in the case of the New Guinea beater into ornamental patterns which have the same purpose.

[1] Two kinds of earthen pots from the Admiralty Islands are figured in the official narrative of the cruise of the "Challenger" (figs. 242 and 213). They differ in shape from those of Bougainville Straits and are probably made in a different manner.

E

caution which I used to encourage them to adopt when accompanying me, in order to save myself being pestered every few minutes for a light for their pipes.

Burning-glasses are in common use amongst the natives of some of the islands, as at Simbo. The reason of their being not always favourite articles of trade in other islands, I was at a loss to understand. The numerous fumaroles varying in temperature between 160° and 200° Fahr. which pierce the hill-sides of the volcanic island of Simbo, are employed by the natives for the purposes of cooking, as I have elsewhere observed (p. 86).

Fans serve the double purpose of nursing a fire and of cooling the person. Those in use in Treasury are made of the extremities of two branches of the cocoa-nut palm, the midribs forming the handle, whilst the long "pinnæ" are neatly plaited together to form the fan. One of these fans is figured in the pottery engraving. Although more coarsely made, they are of a pattern similar to the fans of Fiji and Samoa. The shape appears to have originated from the nature of the materials employed; and I suspect that in Fiji and Samoa, where different materials are used, the original shape which depended on the plaiting of the cocoa-nut leaves has been retained, whilst the material itself has been discarded.

The natives of Bougainville Straits burn torches during their fishing excursions at night and during festivals. For this purpose they use resins obtained from the "anoga,"[1] probably a species of *Canarium*, and the "katari," a species of *Calophyllum*, two tall trees which rank among the giants of the forest in this region. The resin of the "anoga" should be more properly described as a resinous balsam. It is white, is easily pulverised, and has a powerful odour, as if of camphor and sandal-wood combined. It concretes in mass inside the bark and in tears on the outer surface of the tree, and is usually obtained by climbing up and knocking it off the bark; but sometimes the tree is ringed at a height of four feet from the ground, a process which drains it of its resin but causes its death. The torch of this material is simply prepared by wrapping up compactly the powdered resin in a palm-leaf, which although outside answers the purpose of a wick. . . . The "katari" resin, which is less frequently used, is a dark-coloured material that burns with a tarry

---

[1] From Surville's description of his visit to Port Praslin in Isabel in 1769, it would appear that the natives burned torches made of this resin. ("Voyage de Marion." Paris, 1783; p. 274.)

and somewhat fragrant odour. Other resins and gums are yielded
by the trees, one of which somewhat resembles the "kauri" gum of
New Zealand, and occurs in a similar situation beneath the soil; but
I was unable to find the tree.

In the tambu-houses of St. Christoval and the adjoining islands
we have a style of building on which all the mechanical skill of
which the natives are possessed has been brought to bear. These
sacred buildings have many and varied uses. Women are forbidden
to enter their walls; and in some coast villages, as at Sapuna in the
island of Santa Anna, where the tambu-house overlooks the beach,
women are not even permitted to cross the beach in front. The
tambu-houses of the coast villages are employed chiefly for keeping
the war-canoes, each chief being allowed, as an honourable mark of
his position, the privilege of there placing his own war-canoe;[1] but
in the inland villages, these buildings are of course no longer employed for this purpose. Another use to which these buildings may
be put is described on page 53, in connection with the tambu-house
of Sapuna in Santa Anna, in which are deposited, enclosed in the
wooden figure of a shark, the skulls of ordinary men and the entire
bodies of the chiefs.

The front of the tambu-house in his native village is, for the
Solomon Islander, a common place of resort, more especially towards
the close of the afternoon. There he meets his fellows and listens
to the news of his own little world; and it is to this spot that any
native who may be a stranger to the village first directs his steps,
and on arriving states his errand or particular business. In my
numerous excursions, when thirsty or tired, I always used to follow
the native custom in this matter, being always treated hospitably
and never with any rudeness. The interior of these buildings is free
to any man to lie down in and sleep. On one occasion, when passing
a night in an island village of St. Christoval, I slept in the tambu-
house, the only white man amongst a dozen natives. Bloodshed, I
believe, rarely occurs in these buildings; and they are for this reason
viewed somewhat in the light of a sanctuary.

The completion of a new tambu-house is always an occasion of a
festival in a village. The festival is often accompanied by the
sacrifice of a human life; and the leg and arm bones of the victim

---

[1] Mr. C. F. Wood, in his "Yachting in the South Seas" (London, 1875), gives, as the
frontispiece of his book, an autotype photograph of the tambu-house of Makira in St.
Christoval, in which the war-canoes are well shown.

may be sometimes seen suspended to the roof overhead.✗ In the tambu-house of the village of Makia, on the east coast of Ugi, I observed hanging from the roof the two temporal bones, the right femur, and the left humerus of the victim who had been killed and eaten at the opening of the building; and similarly suspended in the tambu-house of the hill-village of Lawa on the north side of St. Christoval, in which I passed the night, I noticed over my head as I lay on my mat the left femur, tibia, and fibula, and the left humerus of the unfortunate man who had been killed and eaten on the completion of the building twelve months before. ✗ At these feasts there is a great slaughter of pigs that have been confined for some previous time in an enclosure of strong wooden stakes, which may be allowed to remain long after the occasion for its use has passed away. After the feast, the lower jaws of all the pigs consumed are hung in rows from the roof of the building. In one tambu-house I remember counting as many as sixty jaws thus strung up. ✗

The style of building and the size and relative dimensions of the tambu-houses are very similar in all the coast-villages of the eastern islands, a correspondence which may be explained from the necessity of the structure being long enough to hold the large war-canoes. As a type of these buildings, I will describe somewhat in detail the tambu-house of the large village of Wano, on the north coast of St. Christoval. Its length is about 60 feet and its breadth between 20 and 25 feet. The gable roof is supported by five rows of posts, the height of the central row being some 14 or 15 feet from the ground; whilst on account of its high pitch the two outer lateral rows of posts are only 3 or 4 feet high. The principal weight of the roof is borne by the central and two next rows, each of which supports a long, bulky ridge-pole. The two outer lateral rows of posts are much smaller and support much lighter ridge-poles. In each row there are four posts, two in the middle and one at each gable-end. These posts, more particularly those of the central row, are grotesquely carved, and evidently by no unskilled hand, the lower part representing the body of a shark with its head upwards and mouth agape, supporting in various postures a rude imitation of the human figure which formed the upper part of the post. In one instance, a man was represented seated on the upper lip or snout of the shark, with his legs dangling in its mouth, and wearing a hat on his head, the crown of which supported the ridge-pole. In another case the man was inverted; and whilst the soles of his feet supported the ridge-

pole, his head and chest were resting in the mouth of the shark.[1]
Long after the tambu-house has disappeared, the carved posts
remain in their position and form a not uncommon feature in a
village scene as shown in the engraving of a village in Ugi.
. . . The roof of the Wano tambu-house is formed of a framework of bamboo poles covered with palm-leaf thatch, the poles being
of equal size, whether serving as rafters or cross-battens, the latter
affording attachment for the thatch. The same materials are used
in the sides of the building. . . . . With reference to tambu-houses
generally in this part of the group, I should remark that they are
open at both ends, with usually a staging at the front end raised
about four feet from the ground, which may be aptly termed "the
village lounge."

The tambu-house of the interesting little island of Santa Catalina or Orika—the Yoriki of the Admiralty chart—is worthy of a
few special remarks. Its dimensions are similar to those of like
buildings in this part of the group, the length being between 60 and
70 feet. Placed in front of each of its ends are three circles of large
wooden posts driven into the earth, each circle of posts being 4 or 5
feet in height and enclosing a space of ground a few feet across, into
which are thrown cocoa-nuts and other articles of food to appease
the hunger of the presiding deity or devil-god. The ridge-poles and
posts are painted with numerous grotesque representations in outline of war-canoes and fishing-parties, of natives in full fighting
equipment, of sharks, and of the devil-god himself, with a long, lank
body and a tail besides. On a ridge-pole there was drawn in paint
the outline of some waggon or other vehicle with the horses in the
shafts: whether this was a reminiscence of some native who had
been to the colonies, or was merely a copy from a picture, I did not
learn. Some of the representations on the ridge-poles were of an
obscene character. The central row of posts were defaced by
chipping, which I was informed was a token of mourning for the
late chief of the island, who had died not many months before. Mr.
C. F. Wood met with a similar custom in 1873 in the case of a
native of a village at the west end of St. Christoval, who on the
death of his son broke and damaged the carved figures of birds and
fish in his house.[2] I am inclined to think that this house was a

---

[1] Mr. Brenchley, who visited Wano, or Wanga as he names it, in 1865, refers briefly in
his "Cruise of H.M.S. 'Curacoa'" to these carved posts (p. 267).

[2] "A Yachting Cruise in the South Seas:" London, 1875 (p. 133).

sacred building of some kind. . . . . Mr. William Macdonald,
through whose kindness I had the opportunity of visiting this
island, pointed out to me that two or three of the posts of the building had been carved into the figures of women, an innovation in the
interior of a tambu-house which I observed in no other building of
this kind.

The tambu-house of the village of Sapuna in Santa Anna, which
is shown in the accompanying plate, is higher, broader, and more
massive in structure than the other buildings which I have visited
in the adjacent islands. As in other tambu-houses, the forms of the
shark and of the human figure are given to parts of the posts ; and
in the hollow cavities of wooden representations of the shark on the
sides of the interior of the building are enclosed the entire bodies of
departed chiefs and the skulls of ordinary men. The carved central
post, which is seen in the accompanying engraving, affords a superior
specimen of native workmanship. It was originally brought, as I
was informed by one of the natives of Santa Anna, from Guadalcanar. The walls of this building are made more rain-proof by long
slabs, measuring 36 by 6 by 2 inches, which are cut out from the
dense matted growth of fibres and rootlets that invests the base of
the bole of the cocoa-nut palm.

The principal tambu-house in the village of Ete-ete, on the west
side of Ugi, is between 60 and 70 feet in length, from 25 to 30 feet
broad, and 11 or 12 feet in height. Here also the sculptured posts
represent the body of a shark with its head uppermost and supporting in the gape of its mouth the figure of a man, on whose
head rests the ridge-pole of the roof. The front of the building is
decorated with red and black bands, some straight, some wavy, and
others of the chevron pattern. Mr. Brenchley in his account of the
" Cruise of the ' Curacoa ' " gives a sketch of this tambu-house, which
he visited in 1865 (p. 258). Forming the frontispiece of his work is
a chromo-lithograph showing the two sides of an ornamental tie-
beam from the roof of a " public hall " at Ugi, which he presented to
the Maidstone Museum. It represents on one side sharks, bonitos,
and sea-birds supposed to be frigate-birds, and on the other side four
canoes with sharks attacking the crew of one of them, which is
bottom upwards.

The deification of the shark appears to arise from the superstitious
dread which this fish inspires. Its good-will may be obtained by
leaving offerings of food on the rocks before undertaking a long

TAMBU-HOUSE IN THE ISLAND OF SANTA ANNA

(Preparations for a Feast)

journey in a canoe. The natives of the neighbouring island of Ulaua, or Ulawa, propitiate the shark with offerings of their own shell-money and of porpoise teeth, which they prize even more than money; and, if a sacred shark has attempted to seize a man who has been able to finally escape from its jaws, they are so much afraid that they will throw him back into the sea to be devoured.[1] We learn from Mr. Ellis[2] and from Messrs. Tyerman and Bennet,[3] that in the Society Islands sharks were deified, that temples were erected for their worship in which the fisherman propitiated the favour of the shark-god, and that almost every family had its particular shark as its tutelary deity to which it bowed and made oblations.

At Alu and Treasury in Bougainville Straits, the tambu-house, which is such a prominent feature in the villages of the eastern islands, is represented by a mere open canoe-shed, for the most part destitute of ornament, and apparently held in but little veneration. Rows of the lower jaws of pigs, which are strung up inside the buildings, signify, as in the eastward islands, the number of animals slaughtered for the feast that was held to celebrate the completion of the canoe-shed. In the island of Faro, the canoe-houses are only temporary sheds built over the large war-canoes, and can have no sacred character in the mind of the native, the tambu-houses in the two principal villages of Toma and Sinasoro having no connection with the war-canoes. The tambu-house of the village of Toma is a neat-looking building about 18 feet high, 45 feet long, and 25 feet broad. It is open at the ends and partly open at the sides, and is built of much the same materials as the dwelling-houses. The roof, which is neatly thatched with the leaves of the sago-palm, is supported on stout ridge-poles by a central and two lateral rows of posts. There is no carving and but little decoration about the building; and from the circumstance of its being sometimes converted into a temporary drying-house for copra, we may draw some infer-ence as to the degree of sanctity in which such a building is held.

The weapons in common use in these islands are spears, clubs, bows and arrows, and tomahawks. An indication of the disposition of the natives may be usually obtained by observing whether arms

<hr/>

[1] "Religious Beliefs and Practices in Melanesia," by the Rev. R. H. Codrington, M.A. "Journal of the Anthropological Institute." Vol. x.

[2] "Polynesian Researches:" London, 1853. Vol. i., pp. 167, 329.

[3] "Voyages and Travels of the Rev. D. Tyerman and George Bennet, Esq.:" London, 1831. Vol. i., p. 247.

are habitually carried. In islands where the men go unarmed, the white man, from the absence of intertribal conflicts, has an additional guarantee for his own safety. On the other hand, amongst natives who never leave the vicinity of their villages without a spear or a club, he will require to be very cautious in all that concerns his safety.

The spears are usually 8 to 9 feet in length, with no foreshaft, and are made of a hard palm wood. Those of the natives of Bougainville Straits are very formidable weapons. They are armed with long points or barbs of bone, some of them 4 or 5 inches in length, and they are coloured white and red, are curiously carved, and are ornamented with bands of the same plaited material of which the armlets are made. The barbs and bands are imitated in the colouring of the head of the spear. These spears are made by the natives of Bougainville, and are exchanged with the people of the Straits for European articles of trade. I have seen them in the hands of the men of Simbo. In St. Christoval and the adjacent islands at the other end of the group, the spears are of dark wood, with carved heads and blunt wooden points and are uncoloured. As compared with those of Bougainville Straits, they are not very formidable weapons. They are only armed with blunt barbs cut out of the wood, which are rather more ornamental than useful.

In throwing a spear, the men of Bougainville Straits, whilst poising the weapon, extend the left arm in the direction of the object and often point the forefinger as well. None of the contrivances for assisting the flight of the spear, such as the throwing-stick or the amentum, were employed by the natives of the islands we visited. These weapons are used both as hand-weapons and as missiles. The natives of St. Christoval spear their victims through the abdomen, and as a mark of their prowess they often allow the gore to dry on the point of the weapon. A man in this island usually keeps his spears slung in a bundle under the projecting eaves of the roof in front of the entrance to his house.

Bows and arrows are much more commonly employed by the natives of Bougainville Straits than by the St. Christoval natives. The bows are stoutly made, and are from 6 to 7 feet in length. The string is of a strong cord. The arrows used in the first-mentioned locality are usually $4\frac{1}{2}$ to $4\frac{3}{4}$ feet in length. They have a long reed shaft, with a pointed foreshaft of a hard heavy palm wood inserted into the end, and measuring about one-fourth the length of the arrow

Although most of the arrows have simple pointed foreshafts, destitute of barbs, a few terminate in arrow-heads carved out of the hard wood. A kind of dart, much shorter than the arrow and armed with points of bone, is also used. About nine out of every ten arrows are notched for the bowstring. Feathers are not used; but the hinder shaft of each arrow is decorated with etchings as if in imitation of plumes. These arrows are essentially Melanesian in character, and much resemble those in the British Museum Collection from New Guinea and the New Hebrides.[1] At short distances of 25 or 30 yards, the natives make good shooting with the bow and arrow; but on account of the length of the arrow it is not to be depended on at greater ranges. For shooting fish and pigeons, the natives of these Straits sometimes employ small arrows fashioned out of the large leaf of a kind of reed. The midrib serves as the shaft, and a narrow strip of the blade of the leaf, which is left attached on each side of the shaft, serves the purpose of the plume. The end is pointed and hardened by fire. Such arrows are easily made, and are not generally sought for after they have been shot away.[2] On one occasion I observed a boy of Alu shooting a pigeon with an arrow terminating in fine points like a miniature fish-spear.

Poisoned spears and arrows are rarely employed by the natives of the Solomon Group.' They did not come under our observation in any of the islands that we visited. In the island of Savo, however, the natives are said to poison their spears and arrows by thrusting them into a decomposing corpse, where they are allowed to remain for some days.

The clubs vary in form in different parts of the group. In St. Christoval, they have flat recurved blades cut out of the flange-like buttresses of a tree having very hard wood which bears a polish like that of mahogany. In other islands, as in those of Florida, they

[1] To those who have never had their interest specially engaged in the subject of savage weapons, the above detailed description of these arrows may seem unnecessary; but, as Colonel Lane Fox originally pointed out, it is in the absence or presence of the feather and notch, in the length and formation of the shaft and its point, and in other characters, that the arrows of different races are distinguished from each other. Thus, in many parts of New Guinea in Melanesia generally, and throughout the Pacific, the arrows are destitute of feathers; while those from Europe and Asia are always feathered. (*Vide* "Catalogue of the original Lane Fox Collection," pp. 87-95; also, paper on "Primitive Warfare." "Journ. Unit. Ser. Inst.," 1867-68, for a general treatment of the subject.) Prof. Morse has shown that in the different methods of releasing the arrow from the bow, important race-distinctions are to be found. An abstract of his interesting paper is given in "Nature," Nov. 4th, 1886.

[2] Mr. Mosely in his "Notes by a Naturalist," p. 381, describes and figures very similar arrows which are used by the Ke Islanders for the same purposes.

have flattened oval blades like that of a paddle. Other clubs again,
like those of Guadalcanar, are more cylindrical, and have their ends
but slighty enlarged ; they are often ornamented with the so-called
" dyed grass." No weapons of the character of maces came under
my observation. Most clubs are pointed at the butt-end to enable
them to be stuck upright in the ground. These weapons are rarely
seen in the hands of the natives of Bougainville Straits, if I may
except an ornamental club which is carried at the dances.[1] The St.
Christoval club is also a defensive weapon. Its flat recurved blade
is used to turn aside a spear or an arrow just as the bat is employed
to slip a cricket-ball. Some have considered that these weapons are
merely paddles. I never saw them put to this use, and I should
add that they are most unsuited for such a purpose, being very
heavy and sinking in water. I have frequently met natives, when
away from the coast, carrying them on their shoulder ; and I often
learned from them of the true character of the weapon. Traders,
who had been years in this part of the group, spoke of them to me
as war-clubs. Together with their spears, the St. Christoval natives
carry them during their hostile incursions against the bushmen·
A singular W pattern that occurs on the flat blades of these St.
Christoval clubs was for a long time a puzzle to me. However
a very probable explanation of its origin has been given by Major-
General Pitt-Rivers.[2] It is one which goes to show that these
curved flat-bladed clubs originated as paddles, and that in proportion
as they came to be employed also for purposes of defence, their form
and material were in time changed, until their original use was
either lost or forgotten. In the early forms of this paddle-club, the
swell of the blade suggested the shape of the body of a fish ; and
the profile of a fish's head with the jaws agape was added to complete the resemblance. In course of time the blade lost its fish-like
form, but the outline of the snout with jaws agape was still retained
as an ornament. In this manner the W pattern of the present clubs
originated. The steps in the production of this pattern may be
illustrated in a series of clubs from those with most marked fish-like
form to those where the profile of the fish's snout in the form of a
W alone remains ; and this again by the omission of the mouth is
often replaced by a triangular nob.

[1] These ornamental clubs exactly resemble, both in form and decoration, some clubs from
New Ireland in the British Museum.

[2] " Nature," July 14th, 1881. I differ from the writer in considering these articles as
clubs, not paddles.

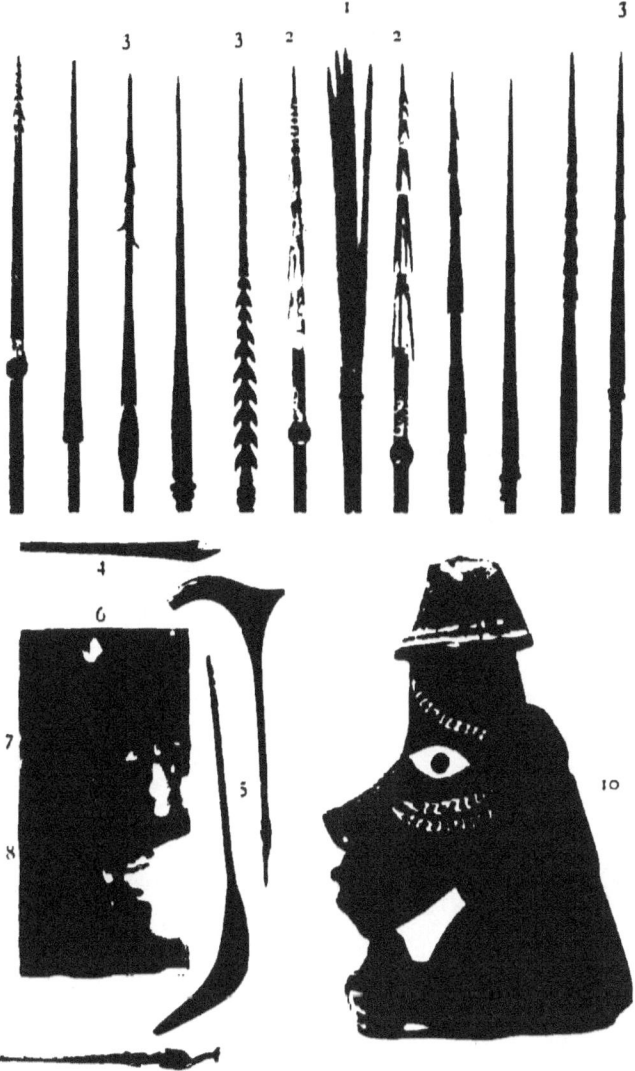

1. Fish-Spear.
2. Spears from Bougainville Straits.
3. St. Christoval Spears.
4. Head of a Florida Club.
5. St. Christoval Clubs.
6. Dance-Club of Treasury.
7. Canoe-Ornament, placed on the prow.
8. Hanging-Hook (Treasury I.).
9. Fish-Float.
10. Canoe-God, lashed to the stem.

[To face page 74.

Tomahawks and muskets, which have been introduced by the trader, are frequently possessed by natives of the coast. The owner of the tomahawk fits it with a long straight handle which he often decorates with inlaid pearl-shell. It is a formidable weapon in the hands of a native, and it is one which he usually employs very effectively, whether against his fellow islanders or against the white man. The muskets are often of little use on account of the lack of percussion caps and powder.

The defensive arm carried by these islanders is usually a narrow shield measuring 3 feet in length by 9 or 10 inches in breadth. With the exception apparently of St. Christoval, these shields are to be observed amongst the natives of most of the larger islands of the group. They appear usually to be made of a layer of light reeds or canes lashed together by rattan. In some islands, as in Florida and in Guadalcanar, they are worked over with fine wicker-work, and are ornamented with beads in the case of a chief. In other islands, as in Isabel and Choiseul, they are often more rudely constructed and have no wicker-work. In the two last islands they are rectangular in form. In Florida and Guadalcanar they are more oval and are slightly contracted in the middle. Mr. Brenchley figures one of the Florida shields in his " Cruise of H.M.S. 'Curacoa,'" (p. 281); whilst a sketch of a shield of the Port Praslin (Isabel) natives is to be found in the narrative of Surville's visit to this group.[1] The Port Praslin shield is deeply notched at one end. I did not observe these shields amongst the inhabitants of St. Christoval and the adjacent islands, a circumstance which may be explained by the fact that spears, and not bows and arrows, are the offensive weapons usually carried by these islanders. Yet we learn that three centuries ago it was with their bows and arrows that the St. Christoval natives usually assailed the Spaniards (vide pages 228, 231. It should be remembered that the flat-bladed curved clubs of these natives also serve the purpose of a defensive weapon.

The tactics employed in war are those which treachery and cunning suggest. Very rarely, I believe, does a fair, open fight occur. In their sham fights, one of which we witnessed on the beach at Santa Anna, two parties confront each other in open and irregular order and hurl their spears with all the excitement of a real contest. Every man keeps constantly on the move as in dancing a jig, in order to be able to more easily avoid the missiles hurled at him.

[1] Fleurieu's " Discoveries of the French in 1768 and 1769."

The boys of Treasury sometimes amuse themselves with a game of the same character, when they use as their weapons the stalk and bulb of the large taro. I was on one occasion much surprised at their skill in aiming apparently at one boy and hitting the one next to him.

The polished stone implements of their fathers have been to a large extent discarded by the natives of the coasts; but the natives of the interiors of the large islands, such as Bougainville, who may have been rarely, if ever, in communication with the trader, are said to be still in a large degree dependent on their stone axes and adzes. On account of the extensive introduction of trade axes, adzes, and knives, it was often difficult to obtain the polished stone implements from the people of a coast village, and natives were wont to express their surprise at my wanting such inefficient and old-fashioned tools. My inquiries as to when these stone implements were used usually received some such reply as the following: "Father, belong father, belong me, he all same"—the purport of which was that they were in use a long time ago, the native's grandfather being deemed a person of so high antiquity, that in referring to past events he seldom cares to go beyond. These stone axes and adzes are generally made of the hard volcanic rocks of this region. A few are fashioned out of the thick portion of the shell of *Tridacna gigas*.

The upper surface of a large mushroom-coral (*Fungidæ*), serves as an effective rasp for scraping canoes; and the large shell of a *Cyrena* and the sharper edge of a boar's tusk are similarly used for scraping spears and bows, which are ultimately rubbed smooth with powdered pumice.

The "bow-drill," armed with a steel point, was employed by Mule, the Treasury chief, in piercing the holes for the rattan-like thongs in the planks of his canoes. This was the only "bow-drill" that came under my notice, and I could not tempt its owner to part with it. In the British Museum Collection, however, there are two smaller tools of this kind from other islands of the group. Without describing it, I may remark that a similar "bow-drill" is figured in Commodore Wilkes' account of the Bowditch Islanders,[1] by Dr. G. Turner[2] in his account of the Samoans, and by Signor D'Albertis in his book on New Guinea.[3] The history of the "bow-drill," as we

---

[1] "Narr. U. S. Expl. Exped.," vol. v., p. 17.
[2] "Nintcen years in Polynesia," p. 273.
[3] Vol. ii., p. 378.

learn from Dr. Tylor,[1] is an interesting one. It originated with the
"fire-drill," which is simply a pointed piece of wood that is twirled
between the hands. This was then made more efficacious by winding a cord around it, when it became a "cord-drill." By substituting
for the cord a bow with a loose string, a still more useful tool
was obtained : and from this simple form of "bow-drill" the Pacific
islanders have obtained the improved boring-tool they now employ.

I should here allude to the round stones, rather larger than a
cricket-ball, which are employed as "cooking-stones" and for cracking the hard kanary-nuts. They are to be seen in the majority of
the dwellings in the eastern islands ; and they often mark the sites
of old villages and the temporary homes of fishing-parties.

The grinding slabs and blocks of rock, which were used for
rubbing down the stone axes, are still to be seen in the coast villages,
their surfaces being sometimes worn into a hollow. At present
these blocks are used for grinding down the shell bead-money and
for sharpening the iron tools. I have sometimes come upon them
marking the position of an old village, the site of which had been
long concealed by the growth of trees and scrub. In some islands
where it is not possible to obtain stones of a sufficient hardness, these
blocks have been transported from considerable distances. A large
block of a crystalline trap-rock, more than a third of a ton in weight,
which now lies on the reef-flat in the vicinity of the village of
Vanatoga on the east side of Santa Anna, was originally brought
down from the summit of the island to be used as a grinding block.
Slabs of a quartz-diorite, which is found in the north-west part of
Alu, and which is much valued for its hardness, have been transported
in canoes to Treasury Island more than twenty miles away and to
the other islands of the Straits. From their size, they would weigh
usually five or six hundredweight.

Amongst the interesting discoveries which I have made in the
Solomon Group, I should refer to that of the occurrence of worked
flints, which are commonly found in the soil when it is disturbed
for purposes of cultivation, and are frequently exposed after heavy
rains. My attention was first directed to this matter on noticing a
specimen of flint in the possession of Mr. Howard at Ugi, and I
soon obtained a number of specimens from this island, and from the
adjacent large island of St. Christoval. The majority of them were
of common flint, but fragments of chalcedony and cornelian were

1 "Early History of Mankind:" pp. 237-246.

frequent, and a jasper also occurred. The largest specimen, which was nearly 4 lbs. in weight, clearly showed traces of artificial working, and, as I am informed by Professor Liversidge, was evidently a large, stone axe or tomahawk. Of the rest, some were cores, others were flakes, resembling in their form, and often in their white colour, the flakes of the post-tertiary gravels; whilst one specimen possessed the shape of an arrow-head. Some of these flints presented the appearance of having been re-fashioned after lying disused for ages. In such specimens, there were two sets of facets or fractured surfaces, the one whitened by weathering or exposure, the other displaying the natural colour of recently broken flint. All were, in fact, of the palæolithic type. The specimens, that I obtained in the islands of Treasury and Alu in Bougainville Straits, were usually of chalcedonic flint, and possessed the form of hammer-stones, scrapers, etc. Worked flints will probably be found in most of the islands of the Solomon Group, except, perhaps, in those of purely volcanic formation (vide page 80). They are said to occur in Santa Anna, and I had a specimen given to me from Ulaua.

There are two interesting circumstances in connection with these flints to which I should allude. In the first place, the inhabitants of these islands are ignorant of their nature and their source. I was gravely informed by the natives of Treasury-Island, that the flints which they brought me from the disturbed soil of their plantations had tumbled from the sky, a superstition which reminds one of a similar belief prevalent in some rural districts of our own country as to the origin of the polished stone implements or celts. In a similar way the men of the Shortland Islands explained to me the occurrence beneath the soil of lumps of gum, which, like the masses of the *kauri* gum of New Zealand, mark the original position of the trees from which they were derived.

Concerning these flint implements, we may fitly ask : Who were the race of men that formed and used them ? How long a period has elapsed since these men inhabited this region ? Whence did they come ? Where are their descendants to be sought ? Are they to be found amongst the present inhabitants of this group, who, having discarded the rude flint implements for polished stone tools of volcanic rock, regard, with ignorant contempt, the handiwork of their ancestors ? To these queries we may with some confidence reply that the original inhabitants of these islands belonged to the once widely spread Negrito race, of which we find the remnants in our own day in the aborigines of the Andaman and Philippine Islands, and that their characters, both physical and linguistic, have been fused with those of other races which have reached the Solomon Islands both from the Malay Archipelago to the west, and from the islands of Micronesia and Polynesia to the east. The present natives of this group may, in truth, be considered as the result of the fusion of the Negrito aborigines with the Malayan, Micronesian, and Polynesian intruders.

The second interesting point with reference to these ancient flint implements is concerned with their original source. Professor Liversidge, in drawing attention to my specimens, which he exhibited at a meeting of the Royal Society of New South Wales in December, 1883, remarked that this discovery of flints in these regions afforded a very strong proof of the probable presence of true chalk of cretaceous age in the South Sea Islands, and he alluded to a soft white limestone undistinguishable from chalk, which had been previously brought from New Ireland by Mr. Brown, the Wesleyan missionary.[1] Chalk-rocks came under my observation in the Solomon Islands; but in no case was I able to find embedded flints (vide Trans. Roy. Soc. Edin., Vol. 32, Part 3). I think it, however, highly probable that when the interior of one of the large islands such as Guadalcanar has been explored, older chalk formations containing flints will be discovered. The island of Ulaua, which I was unable to visit, would probably afford some clue as to the source of these flints. Although in all likelihood this island possesses the general geological structure of the neighbouring island of Ugi, which is described on page vii. yet it possesses one peculiar feature. Mr. Brenchley,[2] when landing on the beach of this island of Ulaua in 1865, picked up a great many pieces of flint scattered about among the broken-up coral, and he wondered where they came from. Captain Macdonald, a resident trader in this part of the group, informed me that flints are abundant on the beaches of this island, together with fragments of a white chalk-like rock.[3]

---

[1] "Journal of the Royal Society of New South Wales:" vol. xvii., p. 223; vide also "Geolog. Mag." Dec., 1877. Mr. H. B. Brady is at present engaged in working out the Foraminifera of this New Ireland rock. Its age, though still sub judice, is probably comparatively recent.

[2] "Cruise of the 'Curaçoa,'" p. 255.

[3] Should any of my readers in the Western Pacific have the opportunity of visiting the island of Ulaua, it would be well worth their while to pay careful attention to the mode of occurrence of these flints. I am of the opinion that imbedded flints will be found in the recent rocks of this island.

In the island of Faro, which is entirely of volcanic formation, flints are not known to the natives, and it would be interesting to ascertain whether they are similarly absent from other islands of the same character. When in search of the source of these flints, I was more than once led off on a false scent. It was on one such occasion, when accompanying Gorai, the Shortland chief, on an excursion in his war-canoe to the north-west part of the island of Alu, that I experienced a great disappointment. Learning from the chief that he could direct me to the place where the flints ("kilifela") were found, I was in great hope of at last finding them imbedded. The locality, however, proved to be of volcanic formation, and a pit or cave in which the flints were to be found, successfully eluded our efforts to discover it. I would, however, recommend future visitors to endeavour to find this pit which lies a little way in from the beach and close to the north-west point of Alu. Its examination might throw some fresh light on the aborigines of these regions.

The occurrence of flints on the south-east coast of New Guinea has been recorded by Mr. Stone.[1] He tells us that the small island of Tatana at the head of Port Moresby is " strewn with pieces of a cornelian-coloured flint, called by the natives *vesika* and used for boring holes through shell, bone, or other hard substances." In 1767, Captain Carteret found spears and arrows pointed with flint in use amongst the natives of the Santa Cruz Group and of Gower Island, one of the Solomon Islands.[2] M. Surville, when anchored in Port Praslin in the Solomon Group in 1769, observed that the natives employed " a sort of flint " as knives and razors and for obtaining fire.[3] In my own intercourse with these islanders I did not find flints in use among them ; but it is very probable that in some islands the ancient flint implements are occasionally employed for cutting purposes.[4]

[1] " A few months in New Guinea," by O. C. Stone. London, 1880, p. 72.

[2] Hawkesworth's " Voyages ": vol. i., pp. 296, 297.

[3] Fleurieu's " Discoveries of the French in 1768 and 1769," etc : p. 144.

[4] In Raffles' " History of Java " (1830 ; vol i., pp. 25, 33) it is stated that common flints, hornstone, chalcedony, jasper, cornelian, etc., are frequently found in the beds of the streams of this island. If not already inquired into, further information should be sought concerning the shape and the source of these flints

CHAPTER V.

THE inhabitants of the islands of Bougainville Straits display far more interest in the cultivation of the soil than do those of St. Christoval and its adjacent islands. Whether this circumstance may be attributed to the greater powers wielded by the chiefs of these islands, and to the consequent tranquillity which their peoples enjoy, or whether it is due to the comparatively isolated position of these islands of the Straits which has secured to their inhabitants a freedom from the attacks of neighbouring tribes, I can scarcely distinguish. It is, however, probable that the explanation of the extensive cultivated tracts with the consequent abundance of food in the one region, and of the meagre patches of cultivation with the resulting dearth of food in the other, lies more in the surroundings than in the individual character of the natives.

In the island of Treasury acres and acres of taro and banana plantations lie in the immediate vicinity of the village; and I passed through similarly cultivated tracts in the east and west districts of the island. The wide and level region, which constitutes the margin of the island, is covered with a deep productive soil. Cultivation is not confined, however, to the more level districts. Large cultivated patches lie on the hill-slopes behind the village; and in other places fire and the axe are constantly employed in the preliminary work of clearing the hill-side. The islands of the Shortlands exhibit a corresponding degree of industry on the part of their inhabitants. When crossing the eastern part of the island of Morgusaia, I traversed for nearly a mile one continuous tract of cultivation. In the midst of the taro and banana plantations stood groves of the stately sago palm and clumps of the betel-nut palm. An occasional bread-fruit tree towered over all; and now and then a lime tree was pointed out by my guides. This extensive tract belonged to the chief.

F

Some of the cultivated patches in the Shortlands are marked out by lines of poles laid flat on the ground into long, narrow divisions, about twenty feet in width, each wife of the owner of the patch confining her labours to her own division.

On the east side of the island of Fauro, the interval between the villages of Toma and Sinasoro is to a great extent under cultivation, and is occupied chiefly by banana and taro plantations. Similar indications of the prosperity of the inhabitants are displayed in the number of cocoa-nut palms and bread-fruit trees, with here and there a grove of sago palms, which occupy the low tract of land on which the village of Toma stands. In the planting season natives of the Straits spend weeks in their distant plantations in the interior of their islands; and in the instance of Fauro Island, many of them possess other plantations in the small outlying uninhabited islands which they visit in parties at the regular periods.

In the islands of Bougainville Straits, the banana, taro, and the sweet potato are the vegetables which are grown in greatest quantity. The yam does not appear to be such a favourite article of food as in the eastern islands. I observed in Treasury that the natives protect the short stems of the large taro against the depradations of the large frugivorous bats (*Pteropidæ*) by lashing them round with sticks.

Here, as in the eastern islands, the following method of climbing the cocoa-nut palm and other trees prevailed. A lashing or thong around the ankles supports much of the weight of the body, and serves as a fulcrum for each effort of the climber towards the top. When the cocoa-nut palm is rather inclined to one side, I have seen a native adopt the mode of the West Indian negro, and walking up the trunk on all fours, after the style of monkeys . . . . . It is a singular circumstance, as residents in the group inform me, that natives never seem to be struck by a falling cocoa-nut, notwithstanding that they must be frequently exposed to injury from this cause. I have often, when sitting amongst a group of natives in a village under the shade of the cocoa-nut trees, been warned by those around me that the nuts might fall on us. On two occasions I have had heavy cocoa-nuts fall to the ground within reach of my arm, which, if they had struck my head with the momentum imparted by a drop of some fifty feet, would undoubtedly have stunned me.

I may here refer to the sago palm, which is grown in far greater numbers in the islands of Bougainville Straits than in St. Christoval and its vicinity. It furnishes not only the vegetable-ivory nut of these islands and the sago, which is an important item in the native dietary, but its leaves supply the thatch for the roofs and sides of the houses. Although belonging to the same genus, *Sagus*, it is evidently distinct in species from the sago palm of Fiji (*Sagus vitiensis*), which, according to Mr. Horne, grows on the low-lying swampy land, and attains a height of about 35 feet.[1] In the Solomon Islands, the height of full-grown sago palms varies between 60 and 70 feet; whilst the situations in which they are usually found, lie on the hill-slopes and in the drier districts of the islands. In the islands of Fauro and Treasury groves of sago palms occur both on the lower slopes and in the higher districts. They occur on the summit of Treasury at a height of a thousand feet above the sea; and I observed a few at Fauro at a height of 1400 feet. I found them in the middle of the breadth of St. Christoval, between Wano and Makira . . . . . The sago palm in these islands is the finest specimen of the *Palmaceæ*. I often used to admire its heavy bole terminating above in its handsome crown of massive branches.[2]

In the extraction and preparation of the sago, the natives of Bougainville Straits employ the following method. After the palm has been felled and all the pith removed, either by scooping it out or splitting the trunk, the pith is then torn up into small pieces and placed in a trough extemporised from the broad sheathing base of one of the branches of the felled tree. The trough is then tilted up and is kept filled with water, which running away at the lower end passes through a kind of strainer, made of a fold of the vegetable matting that invests the bases of the branches of the cocoa-nut tree, and is then received in another trough of similar material. The fibrous portion of the pith is thus left behind, and the sago is deposited as a sediment in the lower trough. When this trough is full of sago, the superfluous water is poured off, and the whole is placed over a fire so as to get rid of the remaining moisture. This method of sago-washing is similar to that which is employed in the islands of the Malay Archipelago. The sago is now fit for consumption, and is wrapped up in the leaves in the form of cylindrical packages 1½ to 2 feet in length. For the convenience of the water-supply, sago-washing is carried out usually on the side of a stream. The refuse

[1] "A Year in Fiji," by John Horne, F.L.S. London, 1881, p. 68.

[2] Although this palm, when full grown, has the appearance of great age and durability, it does not live for more than 20 years, when it flowers, bears, and dies.

is afterwards allowed to decay on the banks, and the water of the
stream is contaminated for a long time after, whilst the air in the
vicinity is impregnated with the unpleasant sour odour of the decaying debris.

The diet of these islanders is essentially a vegetable one, and
most of the common articles of food have already been referred to.
Yams, sweet potatoes, two kinds of taro,[1] cocoa-nuts, plantains, and
sugar-cane form the staple substances of their diet. In St. Christoval
and the adjacent islands the yam is more extensively cultivated;
whilst in the islands of Bougainville Straits the taro and the sago-
palm are more usually grown and the yam is less preferred. The
bread-fruit appears to be but an occasional article of food; and it
was only now and then, as in the vicinity of the village of Toma in
Fauro Island, that I observed the tree in any numbers. In Bougainville Straits there appears to be but one variety of the bread-
fruit tree (*Artocarpus incisa*) which ripens in August. Its leaves
are deeply lobed *(pinnatisect)* and have an even surface; and the
fruit are stalked, seedless, rough, and of a somewhat oval shape. In
Santa Anna there is another variety of the *Artocarpus incisa*, the
fruit of which has seeds and ripens in October. In the plantations
of Treasury Island I came upon a tree which is apparently a variety
of the Jack-fruit tree *(Artocarpus integrifolia)*; it is known to the
natives as the "tafati," whilst the bread-fruit tree is known in this
part of the group as the "balia." Two cucurbitaceous fruits are
commonly grown in the islands of Bougainville Straits. One is a
large pumpkin, and the other is an oval "pepo," about six inches
long, known to the natives as the "kusiwura;" it is a variety of
Cucumis melo, and is a very good substitute for the ordinary cucum-
ber. Amongst other vegetables grown in the cultivated patches of
this region are two varieties of a species of *Solanum*, probably
repandum, which are known to the natives as "kobureki" and
"kirkami;" and a second species of yam, *Dioscorea sativa* ("alapa").[2]

Amongst the fruit-trees grown by the natives of Bougainville
Straits in their plantations are the Papaw-tree (*Carica Papaya*): a

---

[1] The small taro, which also grows wild on the sides of the streams and is called "koko"
in Bougainville Straits, is apparently *Colocasia esculenta*. The large taro, which grows to a
height of 7 or 8 feet, and is known as the "kalafai," may be the same as the "via kana" of
Fiji (*Cyrtosperma edulis*). I cannot, however, speak with any authority on this subject, as I
collected no specimens.

[2] Traders occasionally introduce foreign vegetables. Gorai, the Shortland chief, grows a
litt'e maize in one of his plantations.

species of Lime which the Alu chief grows in his extensive cultivated
patches; a Mango, probably *Mangifera indica* ("faise"); the "foro-
long," a species of *Barringtonia* (probably *B. edulis*) which, when in
flower, is at once known by its handsome pendent yellow spikes
2½ feet in length; the kernel of the fruit is eaten, but it is not equal
in flavour to the similar kernels of the "saori" (*Terminalia catappa*)
and the "ka-i" (*Canarium* sp.); the "sioko," is apparently another
species of *Barringtonia*, the fruit of which ripens in May; the "usi,"
a tall tree 60 or 70 feet high (not determined), the fruits of which
are juicy, seedless, and have a pleasant flavour; the leaves have an
acid taste and are eaten by the natives.

Such are the principal fruits and vegetables cultivated by the
natives of this part of the group; but before proceeding to the
methods of cooking and of serving them up, I should refer to the
white kernels of the "ka-i," a species of *Canarium*, which form one
of the staple articles of vegetable food throughout the Solomon
Group. My specimens sent to Kew were only sufficient for generic
identification. It is, however, probable that this tree is identical
with, or closely allied to, *Canarium commune*, which is the familiar
"kanarie" of the Malay Archipelago, and the "kengar" of the
Maclay-Coast, New Guinea.[1] This tree is mainly indebted to the
fruit pigeon for its wide dispersal. The fruit is of a dark purple
colour, oval in shape, and 2 to 2½ inches in length. Its fleshy covering, which is also eaten by the natives, invests a triangular stony
nut inclosing the white kernel which sometimes rivals the almond
in delicacy of flavour. It requires a little practice to crack the nut
readily. For this purpose the natives employ a rounded stone of
the size of a cricket ball, the nut being placed in a little hollow on
the surface of a flat stone. The fruit-pigeons are very fond of the
fleshy covering of this fruit; and it is their disgorgement of the
hard nuts which collect at the foot of the trees, that often saves the
native the necessity of climbing up and picking the fruit for himself. This nut, which is familiarly known in this group as the Solomon Island Almond, and in the Malay Archipelago as the Kanary
Nut, is in fact an article of considerable importance in the dietary
of the inhabitants of these regions, and it is often stored up in large
quantities. In order to keep them, the natives of Treasury Island
hang the nuts up in leaf-packages from the branches of the cocoa-
nut palms. The Spanish discoverers of the Solomon Islands under

[1] "Proceedings, Linnean Society, N.S.W." Vol. x., p. 349.

Mendana, seized and carried off to their ships the stores of these almonds, as they called them, which they found in the houses of the unfortunate natives. According to Miklouho-Maclay, the inhabitants of the Maclay Coast of New Guinea store up the nuts of the *Canarium commune* between May and July.[1] Labillardiére, writing at the end of last century, tells us that the natives of Amboina lay in a large stock of the kernels of the *Canarium* for their voyages.[2]

With reference to the mode of cooking employed, I should remark that it varies in different parts of the group. In St. Christoval and the adjacent islands very palatable cakes are produced by mashing together the taro, cocoa-nut, plantain, and kanary-nut. Portions of the paste are placed between leaves in a pit in the ground in the midst of hot ashes and heated cooking-stones, and the whole is covered over with earth and left undisturbed for some time. The vegetables may be also cooked entire in this manner. Stone-boiling is also employed in this part of the group in cooking vegetables and fish. A large wooden bowl, about two feet long and containing water, is filled with yams, breadfruit, and other vegetables. Red hot cooking-stones of the size of the two fists are then taken out of the fire and dropped into the bowl until the water begins to boil. The top is then covered over with several layers of large leaves which are weighed down by stones placed on them. The heat is thus retained in the bowl, and after an hour the leaves are removed when the contents are found to be daintily cooked.[3] In volcanic islands, such as Simbo, the natives utilise the steam-holes or fumaroles for cooking their food. Whilst I was examining a solfatara in this island, I found that I had unconsciously trespassed within the precincts of a public cooking-place; and in order to silence the clamour of the native women, I had to distribute necklaces to all.

In the islands of Bougainville Straits, where the art of pottery is known, the vegetables are usually boiled in the cooking-pots which are not cleaned out after use. The leaves of the small taro are thus cooked and make an excellent substitute for spinach. The plan-

---

[1] "Proc. Lin. Soc , N.S.W.," Vol. x., p. 340.

[2] "Account of a Voyage in Search of La Pérouse." London. 1800 (Vol. i., p. 377).

[3] This method of cooking, aptly termed "stone-boiling" by Dr. Tylor ("Early History of Mankind:" 3rd edit., p. 263), which is often employed by savage races unacquainted with the art of pottery, is represented in our own day by the old-fashioned tea-urn. As late as 1600, the wild Irish are said to have warmed their milk with a stone first cast into the fire. ("Tylor's Primitive Culture:" vol. i., p. 40.)

tains are boiled in their skins, and are to the European palate when thus cooked most insipid. The sago, which is a common article of food in this part of the group, is not sufficiently dried during its preparation and it soon turns sour; but this is no objection with the native who devours it with the same eagerness whether it is rancid or sweet. It is usually only half-cooked in a little packet of leaves; but when required for keeping, it is well baked, and in the form of cakes is a favourite food with children. The Solomon Islander, however, has not the forethought of the inhabitants of the Malay Archipelago in laying by a store of sago for future use. When a sago palm is felled, there is usually no lack of friends to assist the owner in consuming the sago. The native of Bougainville Straits serves up the cooked vegetables in trays made of plaited palm leaves or of the sheathing base of the branch of the "kisu" palm. A pleasantly flavoured dish is made of mashed taro,[1] covered with cocoa-nut scrapings; and in such mixed dishes the kanary-nut ("ka-i") often occurs.

Although the native of Bougainville Straits to a great extent subsists on the produce of his plantations, there are a great number of edible wild fruits and vegetables which he also employs as food, and which in times of scarcity would supply him with ample sustenance. I have already referred to the kanary-nut, the fruit of the *Canarium*, as forming a staple article in his diet. The nuts of the "saori" (*Terminalia catappa*) have a small edible kernel which has an almond-like flavour and is much appreciated by the natives. It is the "country almond" of India and, as Mr. Horne tells us, it is extensively eaten in Fiji where the tree is known as the Fijian almond tree.[2] In Tanna in the New Hebrides, as we learn from Mr. Forster, it is also eaten.[3] The fruit of the common littoral tree *Ochrosia parviflora* ("pokosola") contains an edible flat kernel. The three common littoral species of *Pandanus* also furnish sustenance in times of dearth; the seeds of the drupes of the "sararang" and the "pota" contain small edible kernels, and the pulpy base of the "darashi" is also eaten. The pulpy kernels of the fruit of *Nipa fruticans* are occasionally eaten as in the Malay Archipelago; but the natives of Bougainville Straits do not seem to be acquainted with the alcoholic liquor which this palm yields to the inhabitants

---

[1] The taro and other vegetables are often pounded in a mortar made from the hollowed trunk of a small tree and pointed at its lower end so that it can be implanted in the ground.

[2] "A Year in Fiji." London, 1881: (p. 88).

[3] "Observations made during a Voyage round the World." London, 1773.

of the Philippines. The fruit of the "aligesi" (*Aleurites ?*), a stout climber common in the woods of Treasury, has a pleasantly flavoured kernel like that of the kanary-nut; and on one occasion my party and I lunched on these kernels; the outer pulp of the fruit has a dry scented but by no means unpleasant flavour. The kernels of the fruit of a stout tree that grows on the verge of the mangrove-swamps in Fauro Island, and which is probably *Sapium indicum*, are said to be edible by the natives; my natives and I partook of them on one occasion when one man became very sick for some time, and I afterwards found that it was an euphorbiaceous tree, a circumstance which explained his illness; I should therefore doubt the edibility of these nuts. This tree is known by the same native name ("aligesi") as the preceding, which apparently belongs to the same order. The white kernels of the "kunuka," a species of *Gnetum*, are cooked and eaten by the inhabitants of Fauro; this tree grows to a height of sixty feet and has a cylindrical prominently ringed trunk.

The growing tops of several species of palms are much appreciated by the natives of Bougainville Straits; and on several occasions I have largely made my lunch off them. They are usually eaten uncooked. The top of the common *Caryota* palm ("eala") is often preferred. Mr. Marsden[1] and Mr. Crawfurd[2] inform us that in the Malay Archipelago the growing top of the same or of an allied species of *Caryota (C. urens)* is a favourite article of food. It is there known as the true "mountain cabbage," and Mr. Marsden tells us that in Sumatra it is preferred to the cocoa-nut. Amongst other palms which in Bougainville Straits supply in their growing tops the so-called cabbage are the "momo," a species of *Areca*, the "sensisi," a species of *Cyrtostachys*, and the "kisu."

I have already referred to the fact that the small taro grows wild in the ravines and on the banks of the streams in this region. A very savoury vegetable soup is made from the leaves and unopened spathe of a small arum that grows wild on the banks of the streams in Fauro Island. It is a species of *Schizmatoglottis* and is known to the natives as the "kuraka." I should here allude to a wild yam which I found during one of my excursions in this island. The mountain-plantain, which grows on the sides of the valleys, and in moist, sheltered situations as high as a thousand feet above the sea,

---

[1] "History of Sumatra." London, 1811 : p. 89.
[2] "History of the Indian Archipelago." Edinburgh, 1820 : vol. i., p. 447.

furnishes in its small seeded fruits, when cooked, an occasional substitute for those of the cultivated plantain ; it grows to a height of 35 feet, and on account of its striking appearance it often forms a conspicuous feature in the vegetation at the heads of the valleys. It is known as the " kallula."

Amongst the wild fruits which are eaten by the natives in this part of the group, are those of two trees named the " natu" and the " finoa." As my specimens were insufficient for the determination at Kew of the characters of these trees, I may add that the "natu" grows to a height of a hundred feet, its fruit being of the size of a small melon and having a pleasant flavour. The " finoa" grows to a height of fifty feet ; it is occasionally found in the plantations.

The natives of the Shortland Islands informed me that the neighbouring people of Rubiana were accustomed to eat the fruits of the common littoral tree *Morinda citrifolia* ("urati"), but that they did not themselves eat it. The shoots of a tree named " poporoko,' which belongs probably to the *Olacineæ*, are eaten by the inhabitants of Fauro, who also consider as edible the tiara-like cones (?) of the *Gnetum Gnemon* (" meriwa").

The fronds of ferns are in some species edible ; amongst them, I may particularly refer to the " quaheli" (unfortunately not identified), which is eaten by the natives of Treasury Island. Fungi, which are generally known in this part of the group as " magu," are often cooked and eaten ; but through inadvertence I am now unable to refer particularly to the edible species. A delicacy with the natives of Treasury is an alga, a species of *Caulerpa*, which grows in the sheltered waters just below the low-tide level at the western end of the harbour. They eat it with keen relish, when freshly picked from the rocks, holding it over the mouth and munching at it just as if it were a bunch of grapes, which it somewhat resembles in appearance. There is another non-edible species of *Caulerpa* which grows in the broken water on the weather or outer side of the reef-flats.[1]

Tacca pinnatifida (" mamago"), commonly known as the South Sea or Tahiti Arrowroot, is often seen on the coral islets in Bougainville Straits. The natives, though acquainted with the nutritious qualities of the plant, make little if any use of it. Mr. Horne,[2] writing of it in Fiji, says that the arrowroot obtained from the

[1] I am indebted to Mr. Moore of Sydney, for the identification of the genus.
[2] " A Year in Fiji," p. 104.

roots of this and another species of *Tacca* (*T. sativa*) is even more
nutritive than the ordinary arrowroot which is obtained from a very
different plant (*Maranta arundinacea*). This leads me to remark
on the singular fact that the inhabitants of one Pacific group are
often unacquainted with, or make but little use of, sources of vegetable food which in other groups afford a staple diet. Whilst the
Fijians and the Society Islanders make use of the arrowroot obtained
from *Tacca pinnatifida*, the inhabitants of the Radack Archipelago,
as Chamisso informs us,[1] seldom use it, although the plant is very
frequent on the islands; and I have already remarked that the
natives of Bougainville Straits make little if any use of the same
plant. The Fijians were unacquainted with the nutritious qualities
of their sago palm (*Sagus vitiensis*) until Mr. Pritchard and Dr.
Seemann extracted the sago.[2] On the other hand we have seen
that the natives of Bougainville Straits largely consume the sago of
their palm which belongs to another species of *Sagus* growing not
in the swamps as in Fiji, but in more elevated and drier situations.
In the instance of *Cycas circinalis*, one of the common littoral trees
in the Pacific, we find considerable variation in the knowledge
possessed by the inhabitants of different regions of its value as a source
of food. Its growing top produces a cabbage which, as we learn from
Mr. Marsden, is much esteemed by the people of Sumatra.[3] Its
fruits, when their noxious qualities have been removed by macera-
tion or by cooking, are largely consumed in seasons of scarcity by the
inhabitants of the Moluccas, New Ireland,[4] south-east part of New
Guinea, and North Queensland.[5] Its central pith yields an inferior
kind of sago to the inhabitants of some of the islands of the Eastern
Archipelago ; and a gummy exudation resembling tragacanth, which
is yielded by this tree, has probably a medicinal value. The
natives of Bougainville Straits are not acquainted with the sago-
producing character of this tree nor with the fact that its fruits are
edible ; they, however, prepare an application for the ulcers from
which they often suffer by macerating the fruits in question. Mr.
Horne observes that the Fijians do not make use of the *Cycas*

---

[1] "A Voyage of Discovery into the South Sea," by Otto von Kotzebue : London, 1821 :
vol. III., pp. 15 }, 154.

[2] "A Mission to Viti," by Dr. Berthold Seemann ; p. 291.

[3] "History of Sumatra," p. 89.

[4] Labillardière's "Voyage in search of La Pérouse :" London, 180} : vol. I., p. 254.

[5] "Work and Adventure in New Guinea," by Messrs. Chalmers and Gill ; p. 310.

circinalis as a sago-yielding plant :[1] we learn, however, from Dr. Seemann, that its sago is reserved for the use of the chiefs.[2] . . . . I may here refer to the fact that the Treasury Islanders, although acquainted with the common *Caryota* palm ("cala") as yielding a kind of sago, do not often avail themselves of it.

Fish,[3] opossums (*Cuscus*), and pigs supply the natives of Bougainville Straits with the more nitrogenous elements of food. But as with vegetable so with animal food, the term "kai-kai"[4] is a very comprehensive one with the Solomon Islander. Shellfish furnish occasional sustenance. Amongst them I may mention *Tridacna gigas*, and species of *Hippopus, Cardium, Turbo*, and of many other marine genera. The *Cyrenæ*, that lie sunk in the black mud of the mangrove swamps, are much esteemed : and those natives who have their homes in these gloomy and unwholesome regions employ as food *Pyrazus palustris* which thrives in little clusters on the mud, and in the puddles around the mangrove roots. The Unios and the freshwater Nerites are also eaten. The flesh of the large monitor-lizard, *Varanus indicus*, is much prized. The crocodile is not rejected ; and, as the following anecdote will show, the past misdeeds of all its tribe are heaped upon it, whilst the victors at the same time satisfy their sense of hunger, and glut their feelings of revenge. . . . . The freshwater lake of Wailava in Santa Anna is frequented by crocodiles which occasionally attack natives fishing on the banks. At the end of 1882, one of these animals was shot by Mr. Charles Sproul, an American resident. The news of its death caused great rejoicing amongst the people of the village ; and Mr. Sproul, who was looked upon as a great hero, received presents of yams as an acknowledgment of his prowess. After he had skinned it, he gave the carcase to the village, and a feast was held. One old man, who had been nearly carried off by a crocodile at the lake a few years before and had had his leg broken, was positive that this was the identical animal, and he was so delighted at its death, that, as Mr. Sproul told me, there was nothing he would not have done for him. The old man claimed as his share the portion of the head attached

---

[1] Horne's "Fiji," p. 104.

[2] Seemann's "Viti," p. 289.

[3] I came upon some bushmen from the interior of Bougainville, who, although they were staying some time at a village on the coast of Fauro, would not eat fish : and I learned from the Fauro natives that the Bougainville bushmen abstained from fish, even when they were able to get it.

[4] "Kai-kai" is a term for "food" : but, like "tambu," it has been introduced by traders.

to the carcase, and bones and all were eaten with that additional relish which the sensation of feasting on his enemy would naturally produce.

The Solomon Islanders are very fond of fatty food. They have been observed to drink the liquid fat of pigs with the same gusto with which a white man would quaff an iced drink on a hot day. They much appreciate the fat in the abdomen of the Cocoa-nut Crab (*Birgus latro*); and, without much regard for the feelings of the crab, they may throw it alive on the hot cinders of a fire in order to cook its fat.

A depraved taste for decaying flesh would appear not to be peculiar to the upper classes of civilized nations. Mr. Stephens of Ugi tells me that he has known natives of Ontong-Java, which lies off the Solomon Group, to allow the carcase of a pig to remain buried in the ground until it was rotten, when they dug up their treasure and enjoyed their feast under cover of the night as though conscious of the depravity of the act. It was the strong odour which penetrated his dwelling that attracted the attention of Mr. Stephens to their proceedings.

The methods of cooking animal food may be here referred to. In the eastern islands of the group, it may be boiled in a wooden bowl by means of hot-stones as described on page 86. In Bougainville Straits, when a fishing-party returns towards nightfall with their capture of fish, they erect on posts a large framework or grating of sticks, which is raised about three feet from the ground. On this the fish is placed, a large fire is kindled beneath, and, by a combined process of scorching and smoking, the fish is cooked. As the portion of the grating on which the fish lies is usually almost burned away, the framework is made some ten feet in length by five feet in breadth, and the next fish to be cooked is placed on a fresh part of it. On a framework of this size a considerable number of fish may be thus cooked. Fish such as eels are cut up into pieces, and each piece after being compactly wrapped around with leaves is kept on the wood-fire for about half an hour. When an opossum is to be cooked, it is first placed for a short time on the fire in order to singe the hair off. It is then cut open, and the viscera are removed: of these, the intestines are subsequently cleaned and eaten. The body is then placed, without any further process, on top of the fire; and there it remains until, after being well scorched as well as roasted, it is considered to be cooked: when thus prepared, the flesh is juicy and tender, but has a strong flavour. Pigs are first quartered, and then placed on a pile of logs built up in layers to a height of about three feet, over which three poles are placed like a tripod about six feet in height, in order to draw the fire up. When thus roasted, the flesh of the wild pig is very good eating, and may be thought by some white men to be superior in flavour to the flesh of our farm-bred pigs.

There are usually two meals in the day (viz., at its commencement and at its close) in the case of those who are working in the cultivated patches; whilst those who remain in the village may indulge in a mid-day repast. Often during my excursions I have been glad to take advantage of the simple hospitality of the natives; and I have found a light meal of boiled bananas or of partly cooked sago, when taken in the middle of the day, a convenient, though not a palatable, form of nourishment for a hard day's work in these islands.

I was once present at a feast in the village of Sapuna in Santa Anna. Each man's contribution was added to the general store. Heaped up in large black wooden bowls, such as are in common use in St. Christoval and the adjacent islands, the materials for the feast were first placed in front of the tambu-house, and then carried to the house of the chief, where they were distributed. For several days before, the women had been engaged in bringing in the yams and other vegetables from the "patches" in the interior of the island, whilst their indolent spouses had been lounging about with empty pipes in the village. The feast was held at night, and was accompanied by much shouting. The natives gave vent to the exuberance of their spirits, and mingled the most demoniacal yells with their peals of laughter. The feast may be fitly described as a "gorge." When it was concluded at an early morning hour, silence came over the village, and everyone retired to their homes, where they remained in a torpid condition during the rest of the day; and, in fact, for some days afterwards the men were incapacitated for active labour.

I should have previously referred to a kind of wild honey ("manofi"), the work of a bee about the size of the ordinary house-fly, which is much esteemed by the natives of Bougainville Straits. It is more fluid than our own honey, and has a scented flavour. It is drunk off like water by these natives. The honeycomb is merely a collection of bags of brown wax of the size of a walnut and aggre-

gated together in an irregular mass, which is often found in a hollow
in the lower part of the trunk of a tree. The inhabitants of this
region have apparently no acquaintance with the uses of wax, and
thus differ from the Andaman Islanders, who employ it for caulking
the leaks in their canoes and for waxing their bowstrings.[1]

The Solomon Islanders are inordinarily fond of tobacco-smoking,
a habit which prevails with both sexes and almost at all ages.
Tobacco has in fact established itself as the principal currency
between the trader and the native; and without it a white man
would be as destitute in these islands as the beggar is in more
civilized lands. In a village the visitor will sometimes be followed
by a knot of little urchins five or six years of age who have slipped
down from their mothers' backs to pester him for tobacco; and I
have seen a child in its mother's arms allowed to take the pipe from
its parent's lips and puff away with apparent enjoyment. Should
there be a scarcity of tobacco in a village when a ship arrives, the
trader may drive a cheap bargain, and the curiosity-seeker may
readily purchase anything he desires. We were able on such occasions to obtain, for a piece of tobacco of the size of the thumb-nail,
articles, such as fish-hooks, which required for their manufacture
days of tedious labour. In the waste-ground of villages a few
tobacco plants are often grown. This is very frequently the case in
the villages of the islands of Bougainville Straits, where native-
grown tobacco is often preferred to the trade-tobacco. This home-
grown tobacco is there known as " brubush." The leaves are never
cut up for smoking, but are usually rolled roughly into twists; and
when the native is going to smoke, he stuffs two or three large
pieces into his pipe. Claypipes obtained from the traders are always
used. These islanders very rarely make wood pipes for themselves,
although they must often see them in the mouths of white men. I
never met with a native who, having broken or lost his clay pipe,
had the energy to manufacture a pipe of wood. There is, however,
such a specimen of native work in the British Museum collection.
I could not ascertain any information relative to the introduction of
tobacco-smoking. It was, however, probably introduced from the
West independently of the influence of the trader. The natives of
the Maclay Coast and of the South Coast of New Guinea allege that
the habit was unknown two generations ago, and that the seeds of
the plant, with the knowledge of tobacco-smoking, have been intro-

[1] Journ. Anthrop. Inst., vol. VII., p. 463.

duced from the West. In the Louisinde Archipelago and in South-
East New Guinea, tobacco was unknown until the last few years.[1]

The practice of chewing the betel-nut is prevalent through the
group, and is accompanied by the usual accessories, the lime and the
betel-pepper (*Piper Betel*). In St. Christoval and the neighbouring
small islands, the lime is carried in bamboo boxes, which are
decorated with patterns scratched on their surface. In the islands
of Bougainville Straits, gourds are employed for this purpose, the
stoppers of which are ingeniously made of narrow bands of the leaf
of the sago palm wound round and round in the form of a disc and
bound together at the margin by fine strips of the vascular tissue of
the "sinimi" fern (*Gleichenia* sp.). Plain wooden sticks, like a
Chinese chop-stick, are used for conveying the lime to the mouth ;
but frequently the stick is dispensed with, when the fingers are used
or the betel-nut is dipped into the lime.

The Piper Betel, which is known in Bougainville Straits as the
"kolu," is grown in the plantations, where it is trailed around the
stems of bananas and the trunks of trees. In these straits, as on the
Maclay Coast of New Guinea,[2] the female spike, or so-called fruit, is
more usually chewed with the betel-nut. Around St. Christoval the
leaves are generally preferred.

The betel palm, the "olega" of the natives, which is apparently
identical with, or closely allied to, *Areca catechu*, the common betel-
nut tree, is grown in clumps and groves in the vicinity of villages.
The fruits of other species of *Areca*, which grow wild, are occasionally used as substitutes for the ordinary betel-nut ; in Bougainville Straits the fruits of the "niga-solu," "niga-torulo," and "poamau" are thus employed, those of the "poamau" being appropriated
by the women.

Betel-chewing is practised by both sexes. It has a marked
stimulant effect ; but the natives allege that no harm results from its
constant use. The betel-pepper gives the betel-juice the "bite" of
a glass of grog : by the natives it is considered to remove the taint

---

[1] Miklouho-Maclay in Proc. Lin. Soc., N. S. W., vol. X., p. 352.

Crawfurd makes some interesting remarks on the introduction of tobacco into the Malay
Archipelago, whence, as I have shown above, the plant has been evidently introduced into
the Western Pacific. The Java annals affirm that tobacco was introduced in 1601 ; and, as
supporting this statement, Crawfurd observes that the plant is not mentioned by European
travellers in this region before the beginning of the 17th century. (Malay Grammar and
Dictionary, vol. I., p. 191.)

[2] Miklouho-Maclay : Proc. Lin. Soc., N. S. W., vol. X., p. 350.

of the breath. The betel-juice is the active agent in the production of the red colour which stains the saliva and the mouth of the betel-chewer. I satisfied myself that the saliva was not necessary for producing this colour, which may be readily obtained by mixing the betel-nut and lime in rain water.

When away on an occasion with a party of natives, I once was tempted by curiosity to chew a betel-nut which I afterwards swallowed in order to experience its full effect. Very shortly afterwards my head began to feel heavy, and I had an inclination to lie down, whilst my sight was sensibly dimmed. These effects passed away in about twenty minutes. In my cabin I tried the effect on my circulation of merely chewing a single nut. Five minutes afterwards I found my pulse had increased in force and in frequency from 62 to 92 beats per minute. There was a sensation of fulness in the head and temples, but no perceptible effect on the vision. The pulse retained this frequency for another five minutes; but it did not resume its previous rate until more than half-an-hour had elapsed since the beginning of the experiment. Subsequently I tried the effect of chewing two betel-nuts. The first increased the pulse by twenty beats per minute, and gave rise to restlessness and a feeling of fulness in the head. The second sustained, but did not increase the frequency of the pulse. On account of nausea I chewed the second nut with difficulty. No effect was produced on locomotion by these two nuts; but my sight was sensibly dimmed. On turning-in for the night soon afterwards, I experienced during the first hour rather vivid dreams characterised by rapid shifting of the scene and change in the "dramatis personæ." Some of the crew who, at my desire, tried the effect of chewing a single nut, informed me that it affected them much the same as a glass of spirit would. The natives themselves are usually content with chewing one nut at a time. two nuts, as they told me, produced unpleasant symptoms, and a bad head.

The betel-nut, in truth, possesses far greater stimulating properties than I had previously suspected. A single nut had much the same effect on me as a glass of sherry would have had. I believe that the extent of its intoxicating qualities is not generally known.

I may here remark that I did not come upon the custom of kava-drinking in these islands. According to the Rev. Mr. Lawes, the kava plant (*Piper methysticum*) grows wild in the forests of the

South-Coast of New Guinea, but its use is unknown. It may similarly be found in the Solomon Islands. On the Maclay Coast, as we are informed by Miklouho-Maclay, the custom of kava-drinking has been introduced not very long ago.[1]

1 Proc. Lin. Soc., N S.W., vol. X., pp. 350, 351.

CHAPTER VI.

I WILL in the first place briefly refer to the position assigned to
these islanders in the classification of the different races of man.
Professor Flower, in a recent address,[2] divided the different varieties
of the human species into three principal divisions, the Ethiopian,
the Mongolian, and the Caucasian, a system of classification which,
although often advanced and as often disputed, has now been preferred to other more complicated methods of classifying the different
varieties of man. Around or between these three types all existing
varieties can be ranged.

The Solomon Island natives are usually referred to the
Melanesian group of the Ethiopian division, a group which includes
the Papuans of New Guinea and the majority of the inhabitants of
the islands of the Western Pacific; but my observations on the
physical characters of these natives have shown that the type of a
Solomon Island native varies considerably in different parts of the
group, in some islands approaching the pure Papuan, in others
possessing Polynesian affinities, and in others showing traces of
the Malay. The *prevailing characters*, however, are distinctly
Melanesian or Papuan. The Melanesians, who, according to Professor Flower, are chiefly distinguished from the African negroes by
the well developed *glabella* and supra-orbital ridges in the male,
greatly excel the true African negroes, the Hottentots and Bushmen,
and the Negritos of the Andaman and Philippine Islands, who are
included in the Ethiopian division, in all that affects their social
condition. In their usuages, their rites, their dwellings, their agri-

---

[1] My observations on the physical characters of these islanders were embodied in a paper
read before the Anthropological Institute in July, 1885. They were to be published in the
Journal of that society.

[2] The President's Anniversary Address to the Anthropological Institute, Jan. 27th, 1885.

culture, their canoes, and in many other respects, the Melanesian or Papuan peoples display a far greater intellectual capacity than we find exhibited by the other members of the Ethiopian division.

I cannot here enter at length into the question of the peopling of the various groups of islands in the Pacific. It is a question on which conclusions drawn from the linguistic and physical characters of the inhabitants of these islands do not always agree. Professor Keane[1] holds that the three principal divisions of the varieties of man are represented in this region: the *Caucasian* in the Polynesians inhabiting the islands of the south-central Pacific (Marquesas, Samoa, Tonga, &c.); the *Mongolian* in the Micronesians of the islands of the north-central Pacific (Gilbert, Marshall, Caroline, Ladrone Islands); and the *Ethiopian*, or as he terms it the Dark Type, in the Papuans of the Western Pacific (to whom he restricts the name Melanesian), New Guinea, and the adjacent islands of the Indian Archipelago. It is to the different mingling of these three principal types, that the widely varying characters of the peoples dwelling in the several regions of the Pacific are attributed. According to Professor Keane, the Polynesians of the south-central Pacific are almost purely Caucasian, without a trace of Mongolian blood. This view, however, is not supported by Professor Flower who contends that the combination of the Mongolo-Malayan and Melanesian characters, in varying proportions and under varying conditions, would probably account for all the modifications observed among the inhabitants of the Pacific Islands.

The theory advanced by Professor Keane with reference to the peopling of the Pacific Islands, is one on which some of my observations in the Solomon Islands, although not directly connected with the subject, have some bearing. The primitive Negrito race, as now exhibited in the Andaman Islander, according to this view is the original stock of all the dark races. From its home in the Indian Archipelago, it extended westwards to Africa across the now lost continent of Lemuria, and eastwards " across a continent of which the South Sea Islands are a remnant—to become slowly differentiated into the present Papuan or Melanesian peoples of those islands." Subsequently, the Caucasians of southern Asia, impelled before the southerly migration of the Mongols from higher Asia, occupied the islands of the Indian Archipelago and extended eastwards to their

[1] *Vide* a series of three papers in vol. XXIII. of " Nature " on the Indo-Chinese and Oceanic Races.

present homes in the south-central Pacific (Samoa, Tonga, the
Marquesas, Society Islands, &c).   The Mongols following close upon
them, finally reached the groups of islands together known as
Micronesia in the north-central Pacific (Ladrone, Caroline, Marshall,
Gilbert Islands, &c.).

The reference to the supposed sunken continents in the Indian
and Pacific Oceans, which served as stepping-stones in these
migrations, merits my attention.   From our most recent knowledge
of the geological structure of tropical islands, to which my observations in the Solomon Islands have in some measure contributed, it
may be inferred that there is but little geological evidence to support the view of the existence of these submerged continents.   The
theory of subsidence, on which Mr. Darwin's explanations of atolls
was based, cannot now be urged in support of prolonged periods of
subsidence in the tropical regions of the Indian and Pacific Oceans.
The groups of atolls, which there occur, were formed, as shown by
recent investigations, around and over oceanic peaks of volcanic
formation, and independently of any movement of subsidence.[1]

With reference to the migration eastwards of the Eastern Polynesians, I would allude to a piece of evidence which was advanced
by Mr. Hale in support of the view that the island of Bouro in the
Malay Archipelago was the starting-point of the migration.   Quiros,
the Spanish navigator, was informed in 1606 by a native captured
at Taumaco, near the Santa Cruz Group, that there was a large
country named Pouro in the vicinity of that region.   This *Pouro*,
however, was without doubt the neighbouring island of St. Christoval (one of the Solomon Group) which retains the native name of
Bauro at the present day, and as we learn from Gallego's journal,[2]
was called by the natives *Paubro* rather over three centuries ago.
Mr. Hale, however, who of course was not acquainted with the
native name of St. Christoval, endeavours to identify this Pouro, of
which Quiros was informed, with the distant Bouro of the Indian
Archipelago.   (*Vide* note xv. of the Geographical Appendix) . . . .
The foregoing remarks have not been offered with any object of
criticising a view on which I am not competent to speak.   The
misconception having come under my notice, I considered it my
duty to refer to it.

[1] *Vide* the writings of Murray, Agassiz, Geikie, and others.   In my volume of geological
observations, to be shortly published, I have referred at length to this subject.

[2] *Vide* page 229 of this work.

In the course of my researches I came upon a circumstance which appears to point in an unmistakeable manner to the Indian Archipelago as being the highway by which the Eastern Poly-nesians have reached the Pacific. The circumstance, to which I refer, is that it is possible to trace the native names of some of the common littoral trees, such as the *Pandanus, Barringtonia speciosa*, &c., from the Indian Archipelago across the central Pacific to the Austral and Society Islands. In illustration, I will take *Barring-tonia speciosa*, referring the reader, however, for the other trees to page 186, of this work. In the Indian Archipelago, I find the native names of this tree to be *Boewa boeton* and *Poetoen*.[1] In the islands of Bougainville Straits in the Solomon Group, it is known as *Puputu*. In Fiji, it is known as *Vutu*;[2] in the Tongan Group, as *Futu*;[3] and in the Hervey and Society Islands as *E-Hoodu*[4] or *Utu*.[5] It is interesting to notice the modifications which the name of this tree undergoes, as one follows it eastward from the Indian Archipelago to the centre of the Pacific Ocean, a distance of between 4,000 and 5,000 miles; and it is equally instructive to reflect that without the intermediate changes, intermediate it should be added in a geogra-phical as well as in an etymological sense, the names at the end of the series would scarcely seem to be related. The Indian Archi-pelago would appear to be the home of this littoral tree, which on account of the buoyancy of its fruits has not only been spread over Polynesia, but has reached Ceylon and Madagascar.[6] From its home in the Indian Archipelago, it has therefore extended to the eastward as far as the central Pacific, and to the westward nearly across the Indian Ocean. . . . It is obvious that much informa-tion of this kind might be collected which would be of considerable value to philologists; and even in the case of this single tree I have only, so to speak, broken the ground. The tedious character of the research necessary to collect the scanty information I have obtained on this subject, will be amply compensated for, if my remarks should prove suggestive to residents in the different islands of the Indian and Pacific Oceans.

[1] "De Inlandsche Plantennamen," by G. J. Filet (*vide* reference on page 185).

[2] "Year in Fiji," by J. Horne : p. 70. (1881.)

[3] "Ten years in South-Central Polynesia," by the Rev. T. West : p. 146. (1865.)

[4] "Observations made during a Voyage round the World," by J. R. Forster. (1778.)

[5] "Jottings from the Pacific," by Wyatt Gill : p. 198. (1885.)

[6] "Report on the Botany of the Challenger," by W. Botting Hemsley : vol. I., part iii.. p. 152.

The physical characters of a typical Solomon Islander.—Notwith-standing the variety in some of the characters of these natives, it is not a difficult matter to describe a typical individual who combines their most prominent and most prevalent characteristics. Such a man would have a well-proportioned physique, a good carriage, and well-rounded limbs. His height would be about 5 feet 4 inches; his chest-girth between 34 and 35 inches; and his weight between 125 and 130 pounds. The colour of his skin would be a deep brown, corresponding with number 35 of the colour-types of M. Broca;[1] and he would wear his hair in the style of a bushy periwig in which all the hairs are entangled independently into a loose frizzled mass. His face would have a moderate degree of subnasal prognathism, with projecting brows, deeply sunk orbits, short, straight nose, much depressed at the root but sometimes arched, lips of moderate thickness and rather prominent, chin somewhat reced-ing. His hairless face would have an expression of good humour, which is in accord with the cheerful temperament of these islanders. The form of his skull would be probably mesocephalic. The pro-portion of the length of the span of the extended arms to the height of the body, taking the latter as 100, would be represented by the index 106·7. The length of the upper limb would be exactly one-third the height of the body; and the tip of his middle finger would reach down to a point about $3\frac{1}{3}$ inches above the patella. The length of the lower limb would be slightly under one-half ($\frac{49}{100}$) of the height of the body; and the relations of the lengths of the upper and lower limbs to each other would be represented by the intermembral index 68. I was only able to obtain the measurement of six women who belonged to the small islands of Ugi and Santa Anna, off the St. Christoval coast. Their average height was 4 feet 10½ inches, which corresponds with the rule given by Topinard in his "Anthropology," that for a race of this stature 7 per cent. of the height of the man (5 feet 3½ inches, in this part of the group) must be subtracted to obtain the true proportional height of the woman. The hair of the women has the same characters as that of the men. Their figures have not usually that breadth of hip which the European model would possess. The general appearance of the younger women is not unattractive, but they soon lose their good looks after marriage. In Bougainville Straits, it was often possible

[1] The colour types employed were those given in the "Anthropological Notes and Queries," published by the British Association in 1874.

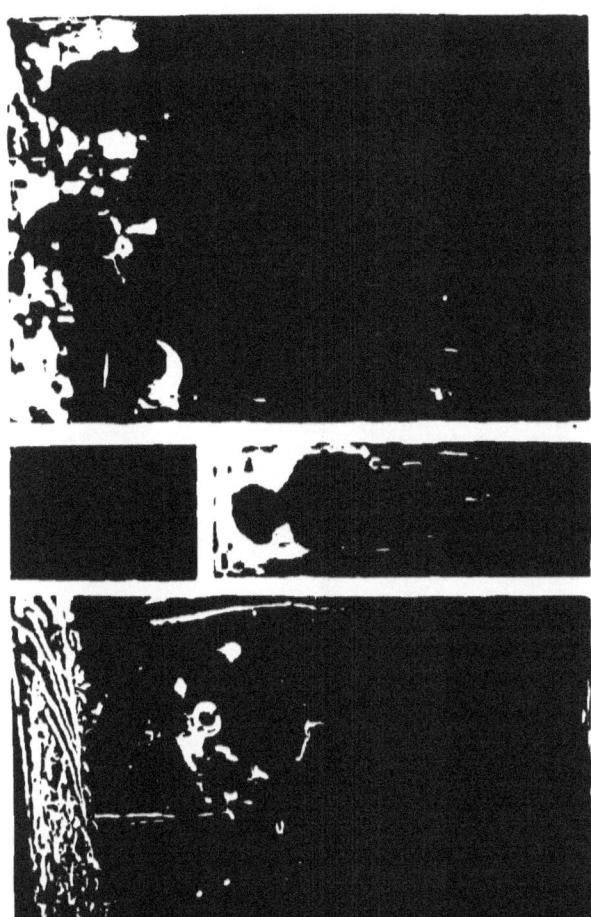

1. WOMEN OF SANTA ANNA
2. MEN OF UGI WEARING SUNSHADES
3. MAN OF UGI
4. MAN OF UGI

to notice amongst the wives of the chiefs two castes of women of very different appearance, the one with elegant figure and carriage, slim limbs and more delicately cut features, the other more clumsily proportioned with stout ungainly limbs and a coarse type of features.

I found that two constant variations in the type of the Solomon Island native are presented by the natives of the islands of Bougainville Straits (including Choiseul Bay), and the natives of St. Christoval and its adjoining islands at the opposite end of the group. In the former region there exists a taller, darker, more robust, and more brachycephalic race; whilst in the latter locality the average native is shorter, less vigorous, of a lighter hue, and his skull has a more dolichocephalic index. From 35 to 40 natives were examined in each region, and some of the principal distinctions may be thus tabulated :

	Average Height.	Colour of Skin.	Cephalic Index of living subject.
St. Christoval, ...	5 ft. 3½ in.	Colour-types, 35 & 28	76
Bougainville Straits,...	5 „ 4¼ „	„ „ 35 & 42	80·7

In the districts of Urasi and the Uta Pass on the north coast of Malaita,[1] there would appear to exist an almost brachycephalic race, of a lighter hue than is possessed by the natives of Bougainville Straits. Differences are in fact constant in their localities throughout the group, the most marked that came under my observation being between the natives of Bougainville Straits and those of St. Christoval at the opposite end of the group, as already alluded to. D'Urville, the French navigator, who visited this group in 1838, contrasts in a similar way the natives of St. Christoval and Isabel with those of Bougainville. The former appeared to him small and feeble in comparison with the more vigorous, sturdier, and much blacker natives of the latter island. He was particularly struck with the diminutive and wretched appearance of the natives of Isabel around "Thousand-Ships Bay," as compared with the vigorous well-made natives of Bougainville.[2] . . . . . In some islands of small size, we find the natives markedly different from those around them. In the small island of Santa Catalina, off the eastern end of St.

[1] I was indebted to the Hon. Curzon Howe, Government Agent of the labour schooner "Lavina," for the opportunity of examining these Malaita natives.

[2] "Voyage au Pole Sud et dans l'Oceanie," (Tome V., p. 105, hist. du voyage.)

Christoval, the natives are distinguished from all others in this part of the group, by their finer physique, lighter colour, and greater height. They do not appear to intermarry much with the surrounding tribes; but they are, strange to relate, in friendly communication with the natives of some district on the coast of Malaita, with whom they probably intermarry. On the coasts of Guadalcanar there would appear to be some of the finest types of the Solomon Islander. Unfortunately, I had but little opportunity of observing them.

Having briefly referred to some of the general facts resulting from my observations on the physical characters of these islanders, I now come to refer to the observations themselves. They were confined for the most part to the natives of the opposite extremities of the group—at the eastern extremity to the natives of St. Christoval and of the adjoining small islands of Ugi, Santa Anna, and Santa Catalina; and towards the opposite extremity to the natives of the islands of Bougainville Straits, which include Treasury Island, the Shortland Islands, Faro Island, together with Choiseul Bay. Observations, although fewer in number, were also made on the natives of the following intermediate islands, viz., Malaita, the Florida Islands, and Simbo or Eddystone Island.

All the measurements, unless otherwise stated, refer to male adults.

STATURE.

Height in feet and inches.	Number of Measurements.
4 feet 11½ inches to 5 feet 0 inches.	2
5 „ 0 „ — 5 „ 1 „	5
5 „ 1 „ — 5 „ 2 „	6
5 „ 2 „ — 5 „ 3 „	13
5 „ 3 „ — 5 „ 4 „	18
5 „ 4 „ — 5 „ 5 „	9
5 „ 5 „ — 5 „ 6 „	10
5 „ 6 „ — 5 „ 7 „	6
5 „ 7 „ — 5 „ 8 „	2
5 „ 8 — 5 „ 8½ „	1

Total, 72

The foregoing table includes all the measurements of height which I obtained in the various parts of the group. The range of these 72 measurements is 4 feet 11¼ inches to 5 feet 8½ inches.

Fifty of these are gathered together between 5 feet 2 inches and 5 feet 6 inches. Arranging the whole series in order, I find that the value of the central number (36th) is 5 feet 4 inches; of the quarter-points, the value of the 18th is 5 feet 3 inches, and of the 54th, 5 feet 5¼ inches; and the values of the 9th and 63rd in the scale are 5 feet 1¼ inches, and 5 feet 6 inches respectively. There is a disturbing element in this series, which is probably the result of combining in the same series the natives of the Bougainville Straits islands and those of St. Christoval, the latter being rather shorter, as noticed below. We may, however, take the value of the median as representing the average height of a native of the Solomon Islands, viz., 5 feet 4 inches, or 1·625 mètres, which is somewhat below the medium height of the human race, as stated by Topinard at 1·65 mètres. It is, however, in a marked degree in excess of the height which Mayer gives for the Papuans, viz., 1·536 mètres (*vide* Topinard's Anthropology).

Deviations of a constant character are found in different parts of the group, and often in different districts of the same island. The natives of the islands of Bougainville Straits, for instance, are noticeably taller than those of St. Christoval at the opposite end of the group, the averages of about thirty measurements in each region, differing by from one half to three quarters of an inch. This difference of height in these two localities is accompanied by other important changes in the physical characters which will be subsequently referred to.

The range of my measurements may be contrasted with those obtained by Miklouho-Maclay on the coast of New Guinea (*vide* "Nature," Dec. 7th, 1882).

Papua-Koviay coast,	...	...	1·75 to 1·48 mètres.
Maclay coast,	...	...	... 1·74 to 1·42 „
Solomon Islands,	...	...	... 1·74 to 1·51 „

CHEST-GIRTH.

The range of the eighteen measurements given in the subjoined table is 31½ to 37 inches : and since half of these are included between 34 and 35 inches, we may consider these as the limits of the average chest-girth of the natives in the portions of the group in which the measurements were made, viz., the islands of Bougainville Straits and St. Christoval, with its adjoining islands.

Girth in inches.	Number of Measurements	Stature taken as 100.
		50...1
31¼ to 32	1	52-53...3
32 to 33	3	53-54...7
33 to 34	3	54-55...3
34 to 35	9	55-56...2
35 to 36	0	56-57...1
36 to 37	2	57·2 ...1
	Total, 18	Total, 18

Taking the average height (5 feet 4 inches) as 100, the proportion, which a chest girth of 34½ inches would bear, would be 53·9. This very closely corresponds with the values of the median of the accompanying series, which itself agrees with the value of the average of the indices. This index of chest-girth may be compared with results given by Topinard :

Englishmen,	...	...	54·0
Negroes, ...	..	...	52·3
New Zealanders, ...	...	...	51·4
Solomon Islanders,	...	...	53·9

WEIGHT OF BODY.[1]

Twelve natives of the Shortland Islands were taken promiscuously and weighed, the following being the results, stated in pounds :—100, 103, 116, 117, 120, 120, 123, 130, 148, 148, 150, 154. The mean of these numbers is 127 ; and the average weight would probably vary between 125 and 130 pounds, or between 57 and 59 kilogrammes. This probable average weight is quite in accordance with the size and build of a typical Solomon Island native ; and agrees with the general rule that the weight in pounds ought to be about twice the height in inches ; the average height being 64 inches, and the average weight 125 to 130 lbs.

LENGTH OF LIMBS.

The points of measurement employed were :—

(a) *For the upper extremity* : (1) a point half an inch outside, and on the level with the apex of the coracoid process of the scapula ; (2) the centre of the hollow of the elbow on a line drawn from the interspace between the head of the radius and the external condyle of the humerus (indicated by a dimple when the fore-arm is extended) to immediately below the internal condyle; (3) the centre of a line joining the apices of the styloid processes of the radius and ulna on the front of the wrist.

(b) *For the lower extremity* : (1) a point on the middle of the front of the thigh on a level with another point midway between the anterior superior spinous process of the ilium and the upper edge of the great trochanter ; (2) a point on the "ligamentum patellœ " on a level with the upper edge of the external tuberosity of the tibia ; (3) the centre of the front of the ankle on a level with the base of the internal malleolus.

(1) *The intermembral index*, or the ratio between the length of the upper and lower limbs, taking the latter as 100. From the table subjoined, it will be seen that the range of 26 indices is 64 to 73.

---

[1] Mr. Evered, ships-steward assistant, obtained these weights for me.

Eleven of these lie between 67 and 68: and since the average of my numbers, which is 68, corresponds with the value of the median of the series, we will take this index of 68 as representing the average ratio of the lengths of the two limbs compared together.

Intermembral index.	Number of measurements.
64	1
65	2
66	3
67	6
68	5
69	3
70	1
71	3
72	1
73	1
	Total, 26

(2) *The index of the fore-arm and arm*, or the ratio between the lengths of the fore-arm and arm, taking the latter as 100. The range of 27 indices is 79 to 100. Of these 16 are included between 87 and 91 ; and the average of the numbers is 88.

Indices.	Number of Measurements.
79	1
80	1
82	2
83	2
84	1
86	1
87	6
88	2
89	1
91	7
95	1
100	2
	Total, 27

(3) *The index of the leg and thigh*, or the ratio between the lengths of the leg and thigh, taking the latter as 100. The range of 27 indices, as shown in the subjoined table, is 68 to 97. Of these, two-thirds are included between 74 and 83 : and since the value of the median, which is 80, corresponds nearly with the average of the numbers, we may take it as representing the average proportion which the leg bears to the thigh amongst these natives.

Indices.	Number of Measurements.
68	1
69	1
70	1
72	1
	Carry forward, 4

Indices.	Number of Measurements.
	Brought forward, 4
73	1
74	2
75	2
78	1
79	1
80	3
81	2
82	2
83	4
88	3
92	1
97	1
	Total, 27

(4) *The index of the arm and thigh,* or the ratio between the lengths of the arm and thigh, taking the latter as 100. The range of 27 indices is 56 to 73. Of these, three-fourths are grouped between 61 and 69. The average of the figures is 65, and the median of the series is 66.

Indices.	Number of Measurements.
56	1
57	1
60	1
61	2
62	2
63	3
64	2
65	1
66	3
67	4
69	3
70	1
71	1
73	2
	Total, 27

(5) *The proportion of the length of the upper limb to the height of the body,* taking the latter as 100.

Indices.	Number of Measurements.
32	1
32-33	10
33-34	10
34-35	4
35-36	2
	Total, 27

These 27 indices range between 32 and 36: three-fourths of them are included between 32 and 34. Since the average of the numbers, which is 33·3, nearly corresponds with the value of the median, we may take it as representing the proportion which the length of the upper limb bears to the height of the body amongst these natives.

(6) *The proportion of the length of the lower limb to the height of the body*, taking the latter as 100. The range of these 27 indices is 46·9 to 51·6. Two-thirds of the total number are included between 48 and 50; and since the average of the numbers, which is 49·1, corresponds nearly with the value of the middle index of the series, we may take it as representing the proportion that the lower limb usually bears to the height of the body amongst these natives.

Indices.	Number of Measurements.
46-9	1
47-48	4
48-49	8
49-50	10
50-51	3
51·6	1
	Total, 27

(7) *The span of the outstretched arms.*—The following indices—69 in all—show the ratio of the span of the arms to the height of the body, taking the latter as 100 :—

Indices.	Number of Measurements.
100	1
101-102	4
102-103	2
103-104	4
104-105	5
105-106	5
106-107	18
107-108	11
108-109	6
109-110	9
110-111	3
112·6	1
	Total, 69

The range of these indices is 100 to 112·6; and the indices of greatest frequency are those included between 106 and 107. Placing all the indices in their order, I find that the value of the central of the series is 106·7, and of the quarter-points 105·2 and 108·6 respectively. Taking 106·7 as representing the average proportion which the span of the arms bears to the stature amongst these natives, I may compare it with similar results given for other races in Topinard's Anthropology :—

American soldiers (10,876),	...	...	...	104·3
Solomon Islanders (69),	...	...	...	106·7
Negroes (2020),	...	...	...	108·1

(8) *Distance of the tip of the middle finger from the upper edge of the patella.*

Distance.	Number of Measurements.
2 inches.	2
2 to 3 ,,	6
3 to 4 ,,	11 (9 of these at $3\frac{1}{2}$ inches).
4 to 5 ,,	2
Total,	21

From this table it will be seen that amongst 21 natives the tip of the finger never approached the patella nearer than two inches, and was never farther removed than five inches. The value of greatest frequency is $3\frac{1}{2}$ inches, and it may be taken as approximating to the average distance. Comparing it with the average stature (64 inches) taken as 100, we obtain the index 5·46; but by comparing the distance of the middle finger above the patella with the stature as 100 in each individual measurement, we obtain a more reliable average index somewhat smaller than the preceding

Indices.	Number.
3·12-4·00	4
4·00-5·00	5
5·00-6·00	9
6·00-7·00	1
7·00-7·94	2
Total,	21

In this table the indices range between 3·12 and 7·94: nearly half are included between 5·00 and 6·00; the value of the median is 5·24, and the average of the numbers is 5·19. Accepting the value of the median as our average index for these natives, it may be compared with similar results for other races given in Topinard's Anthropology :

American soldiers (10,876),...7·49
Negroes (2020)..................4·37
Solomon Islanders (21),........5·24

I will conclude my remarks on the length of the limbs by giving from the preceding "data" the limb measurements of a Solomon Island native of average height :

Height of body, ...64 in. ⎫ Index of height, and length
⎧ Length of upper limb, $21\frac{1}{4}$,, ⎭ of upper limb, 33·3.
Intermembral ⎪ Length of arm, ...$11\frac{1}{3}$,, ⎫ Index of arm and fore-arm,
index, 68. ⎨ Length of fore-arm, ...10 ,, ⎭ 88.
⎩ Length of lower limb $31\frac{1}{3}$,, ...Index of height, and length
of lower limb, 49.

Length of thigh ......$17\frac{1}{3}$,, ⎫ Index of thigh and leg, 80.
Length of leg ....14 ,, ⎭

The form of the skull as indicated by the relation to each other of its

length and breadth.—A hundred measurements, which I made of the heads of natives in this group,[1] in order to obtain their proportional breadth, taking the length as 100, gave indices varying between 69·2 and 86·2. The whole series, however, displays a tendency to grouping around different medians, and thus points to the important inference that we cannot accept one type of the skull as a distinctive character of the Solomon Islander. As shown in the subjoined table, which gives the indices corrected to actual skull-measurements by subtracting two units as proposed by M. Broca, there would appear to be a marked preponderance of mesocephaly; but from my measurements being limited both in number and locality, the safest conclusion to draw will be the most general one, viz., that all types of skulls. brachycephalic, mesocephalic, and dolichocephalic, are to be found prevailing amongst the islands of the Solomon Group, the particular type being often constant in the same locality.[2] If my measurements had been five times as numerous. and had been spread equally over the group, I might somewhat narrow my conclusions; and in truth brachycephaly might have formed a more important factor in the series, if I had measured the heads of the same number of natives from the north coast of Malaita which I measured in the districts of St. Christoval and of Bougainville Straits. In the subjoined table I have accepted all indices below 75 as dolichocephalic, those between 75 and 80 as mesocephalic, and those above 80 as brachycephalic.

Cephalic indices which have been reduced to actual skull-measurements by the subtraction of two units.

Dolichocephalic indices	...	...	29
Mesocephalic	...	...	52
Brachycephalic	...	...	19
			—
			100

I now come to consider more in detail the series of measurements

[1] The localities were—St. Christoval and the adjoining islands of Ugi and Santa Anna, Florida Islands, north coast of Malaita (Urasi and Uta Pass), Simbo or Eddystone Island, the islands of Bougainville Straits, including the west end of Choiseul)

[2] This conclusion is in accordance with the extensive observations of Miklouho-Maclay in New Guinea and in the Melanesian Islands. He found brachycephaly common in the New Hebrides, indices of 81, and even of 85, not being rare. The indices of several hundred measurements of New Guinea natives varied between 62 and 86. This eminent traveller therefore arrived at the conclusion that no classification of these natives can rest on the form of the skull. ("Nature," xxvii., pp. 137, 185. Proc. Lin. Soc., N.S.W., vol. VI., p. 171.'

given below. In this series, which ranges from 69·2 to 86·2, there is a want of uniformity arising from the fact that the numbers tend to gather together around three centres, one between the indices 75 and 76, another between the indices 80 and 81, and the third between the indices 82 and 83. We have thus in this series of· a hundred indices, obtained by measurement of the head of the living subject, evidence of different prevailing types of skull amongst the natives of the Solomon Group ; and it will be subsequently shown that each locality has usually one prevailing type.

Cephalic Indices (Living Subject.)	Number of Measurements.
69·2 to 70	2
70 „ 71	1
72 „ 73	3
73 „ 74	3
74 „ 75	6
75 „ 76	8
76 „ 77	6
77 „ 78	6
78 „ 79	11
79 „ 80	12
80 „ 81	16
81 „ 82	7
82 „ 83	10
83 „ 84	7
85 „ 86	1
86 „ 86·2	1
Total,	100

(1) *St. Christoval and the adjoining islands of Ugi, Santa Anna, and Santa Catalina.* As shown in the subjoined table, this series of 35 indices has a wide range between 69·2 and 86·2. The value of the median index of the series is 75·9 ; and the average of the numbers is 76·6. Out of the 35 indices, 11 are included between 74 and 76. On the whole, however, I should take 76 as representing the average cephalic index in this part of the group, although even here, as shown in the series, there is some disturbing element.

Cephalic Indices.	Number of Measurements.
69·2 to 70	2
70 „ 71	1
72 „ 73	2
73 „ 74	2
74 „ 75	6
75 „ 76	5
76 „ 77	3
77 „ 78	2
78 „ 79	4
79 „ 80	3
Carry forward,	30

Cephalic Indices.	Number of Measurements.
	Brought forward, 30
80 „ 81	1
82 „ 83	2
83 „ 84	1
86 „ 86·2	1
	Total, 35

(2.) *The Islands of Bougainville Straits,* which include Treasury Island, the Shortland Island, Faro Islands, and the western extremely of Choiseul. The range of the subjoined forty indices is 75·9 to 85·2. The contrast between this and the preceding St. Christoval series, as shown in the grouping in the indices, well illustrates the prevalence of distinct types in these twor egions of the group. The indices of greatest frequency are included between 80 and 81 : the average of the figures is 80·6, and the value of the median index is 80·7, which may be accepted as the typical index.

Cephalic Indices.	Number of Measurement.
75·9 to 76	2
76 „ 77	1
77 „ 78	2
78 „ 79	6
79 „ 80	3
80 „ 81	9
81 „ 82	5
82 „ 83	5
83 „ 84	6
85 „ 85·2	1
	Total, 40

(3.) *The North Coast of Malaita.*—Through the kindness of the Hon. Curzon-Howe, government-agent of the labour schooner "Lavina," I was enabled to measure ten natives who had been recruited from the districts of Urasi and the Uta Pass on the north coast of Malaita.

Cephalic Indices.	Number of Measurements.
79·3 to 80	2
80 „ 81	4
81 „ 82	1
82 „ 83	3
	Total, 10

This series, though small, is compact, its range being 79·3 to 83. The average of the numbers is 81·2, which I will take as typical of these localities.

(4.) *The Island of Simbo or Eddystone.*—From the head-measurements of nine natives I obtained the following cephalic indices—72·9, 73·8, 75·8, 76·6, 77·0, 78·0, 78·7, 79·3, 80·4—the average of which just falls short of 77, which however may be taken as an approximation of the prevailing index.

H

(5.) *The Florida Islands.*—Measurements of six natives of Mboli Harbour gave the following cephalic indices, ... 77·2, 79·3, 79·3, 80·0, 80·7, 81·4, ... the average of the numbers being 79·6.

I will now proceed to sum up briefly the results of the foregoing hundred measurements of the head of the living subject. It will first be necessary to reduce them to the form of measurements of the actual skull by subtracting two units from the index, as proposed by M. Broca. The effect of this correction in shown in the following table :

	Number of Measurements.	Living Subject.	Skull.
St. Christoval and adjoining islands,	35	76·0	74·0
The islands of Bougainville Straits, ...	40	80·7	78·7
The north coast of Malaita, ..	10	81·2	79·2
The island of Simbo or Eddystone, ...	9	77·0	75·0
The Florida Islands, ...	6	79·6	77·6

Accepting all indices below 75 as dolichocephalic, those between 75 and 80 as mesocephalic, and those above 80 as brachycephalic, we find therefore that mesocephaly, as represented by an average index of 78·7, prevails amongst the natives of the islands of Bougainville Straits ; whilst dolichocephaly, as represented by an average index of 74, prevails amongst the natives of St. Christoval and its adjoining islands at the opposite end of the group. On the north coast of Malaita exists a type of native with an almost brachycephalic index. The foregoing remarks refer only to the average in each locality. When we apply the same correction to the table of the hundred measurements as given on page 112, we find, as stated on a previous page, that 29 are dolichocephalic, 52 are mesocephalic, and 19 brachycephalic. It would, therefore, appear from these observations that, whilst brachycephaly is not uncommon, dolichocephaly is more frequent, and mesocephaly prevails. Although this result may give an indication of the truth, at present it would be safer, for reasons given on page 111, to accept the general conclusion that these three types of skulls prevail in the Solomon Group.

As confirmatory of the foregoing corrected measurements of the head of the living subject, I will add the indices of nine skulls procured amongst the eastern islands of the group.[1]

[1] I take this opportunity of expressing my indebtedness to my messmates Lieut. Leeper and Lieut. Heming, and to my friend Dr. Beaumont, staff-surgeon of H.M.S. "Diamond," for the majority of the skulls in this small collection. The officers of the survey, whilst away in their boats, had more opportunities than I had of obtaining these specimens. As I was usually accompanied by natives, I was often unable to take advantage of occasions.

74·1 } Rua Sura Islets, off north coast of Guadaleaner
74·1 }
74·1 Ugi Island.
74·5 Port Adam, Malaita.
75·5 ⎫
75·9 ⎬ Ugi Island.
80·0 ⎮
80·0 ⎭
84·9 Kwahkwahru, Malaita.

Measurements of Women.—I was only able to obtain measurements of six women, all of them from the small islands of Ugi and Santa Anna, off the St. Christoval coast.

Height.	Span of Arms. (Stature—100.)	Intermembral Index.	Distance between middle finger and patella.
4 ft. 8 in.	100·8	65	3¼ in.
4 „ 9 „	102·1	68	3½
4 „ 9¾ „	104·3	68	4
4 „ 10 „	104·7	71	—
5 „ 0 „	106·9	—	Average, 3⅝
5 „ 3 „	108·3 Average, 68		

Average, 4 ft. 10½ in.   Average, 104·5

Arm and Height Index.	Leg and Height Index.	Cephalic Index.
32·5	48·5	71
33	48·5	75
33	50	76·8
33·5	51·5	76·8
34·5	—	79·6
35·5	Average, 49·6	82·1

Average, 33·7

Considering the paucity of the observations, the average indices of the limb-measurements agree closely with those obtained for the men. The average height of the women would appear from these few measurements to be that which they ought to possess as compared with the height of the men. This conclusion is based on the rule given by Topinard in his " Anthropology " that for a race of this stature 7 per cent. of the man's height must be subtracted to obtain the proportional height of the woman.

The Features.

The facial angle taken was that between a line dropt from the forehead to the alveolar border of the upper jaw, and another line drawn from the external auditory meatus through the central axis of the orbit, the angle being taken with a goniometer. Amongst eighty natives from different parts of the group, the angle varied between 87° and 98°. Seventy-five of the natives had facial angles between 90° and 95°; and the average of the whole number of angles was 93°. On applying the method for obtaining the facial angle of Cloquet to two large photographs of the faces in profile of two typical natives, I find the angles to be 63° and 67° respectively. The common characters of the features may be thus described : face rather angular, with often a beetle-browed aspect from the deeply sunk orbits and projecting brows; forehead of moderate height and breadth, and somewhat flattened ; middle of face rather prominent on account of the chin receding ; moderate subnasal prognathism as indicated by Cloquet's facial angles of 63° and 67°; lips rather thick and often projecting; nose usually coarse, short, straight, and much depressed at the root, with broad nostrils and extended alæ ; in about one man out of five the nose is arched in a regular curve, giving a Jewish cast to the face.

The Hair, Colour of Skin, Powers of Vision, &c.

Amongst the natives of the Solomon Group, there are four common styles of wearing the hair, which I may term the woolly, the mop-like, the partially bushy, and the completely bushy : these prevail with both sexes, the fashion varying in different islands. From frequent observations of the different modes of wearing the hair, I am of the opinion that their variety is to be attributed more to individual caprice than to any difference in the character of the hair. According to his taste, a man may prefer to wear his hair close and uncombed, when the short matted curls with small spiral give it a woolly appearance,[1] somewhat resembling that of the hair of the African negro. Should he allow his hair to grow, making but little use of his comb, the hair will hang in narrow ringlets three to eight inches in length, a mode which is more common amongst the natives of the eastern islands of the group, and which is best described as the " mop-headed " style. More often, from a moderate amount of combing, the locks are loosely entangled, and the hair-mass assumes a somewhat bushy appearance, the arrangement into locks being still discernible, and the surface of the hair presenting a tufted aspect.[2] The majority of natives, however, pro-

[1] With the bushmen of the interior, the hair appears to be permanently woolly (vide p. 121).

[2] My experience, however, goes to prove that of Miklouho-Maclay that the hair grows uniformly over the scalp and not in little tufts separated by bald patches as described by Topinard.

duce by constant combing a large bushy periwig in which all the
hairs are entangled independently into a loose frizzled mass, the
separate locks being no longer discernible. Of these four styles of
wearing the hair, I am inclined to view the "mop-headed" style as
the result of the natural mode of growth, it being the one which
the hair would assume if allowed to grow uncombed and uncut.
The native of these islands unfortunately makes such a constant use
of his comb that one rarely sees his hair as nature intended it to
grow. When, however, a man with bushy hair has been diving for
some time, the hairs, disentangling themselves to a great extent,
gather together into long narrow ringlets, nature's "coiffure" of the
Solomon Islander. I was pleased to find that Mr. Earl[1] and Dr.
Barnard Davis,[2] in writing on the subject of the hair of the Papuans,
also consider that the hairs would naturally arrange themselves in
long narrow ringlets if left uncombed, and that the bushy frizzled
periwig is produced by teasing out the locks by means of the comb.
This bushy frizzled mass of hair is sometimes referred to, as if it
were one of the natural characters of the Papuans: but since it is
also characteristic of other dark races of Africa and South America,
and may be produced in Europeans, it has but little distinguishing
value.[3] Mr. Prichard in his "Physical History of Mankind" (vol.
v. p. 215), expresses himself to be in doubt whether the bushy
frizzled hair affords any racial distinction, but he seems to have lost
the point of the remarks of Mr. Earl (to whom he refers) concerning
the natural mode of growth of the hair in long narrow ringlets.
The term "mop-headed" is often applied to the Papuan with a
bushy frizzled periwig: but since a mop is neither bushy nor
frizzly, the term is more appropriately employed as I have used it,
and as I see Dr. Barnard Davis uses it, in connection with that style
in which the hair hangs in long drawn-out ringlets. The tendency
of the hair to roll itself into a spiral of small diameter is attributed
to the thin flattened form of the hair in section. According to Dr.
Pruner-Bey, the hair in the Papuan is implanted perpendicularly
and not obliquely, as in the great majority of the races of man.[4]

[1] "The Papuans" by G. W. Earl (page 2). London, 1853.
[2] Vide a paper by Dr. J. Barnard Davis in vol ii. (p. 95), of Journ. of Anthrop. Inst.
[3] These bushy periwigs are found also among the Kaffirs in Africa and among the Cafusos of South America. Dr. Pruner-Bey, who appears to view these bushy periwigs as resulting from the natural growth of the hair, remarks that he has met in Europe three individuals whose hair had the same aspect. I have seen a characteristic Papuan periwig produced in England in the case of a fair-haired girl. (Anthropological Review: Feb. 1864.)
[4] The Anthropological Review for February 1874 (p. 6).

The hue of the hair in adults varies usually in accordance with the changes in the colour of the skin. Amongst the St. Christoval natives it agrees with the numbers 35 and 42 of the colour-types of M. Broca ; whilst amongst the darker-hued natives of the islands of Bougainville Straits the hair is of a deeper hue, corresponding with the colour-types 34 and 49. The average thickness of eleven samples of hair from the former locality is from $\frac{1}{180}$ to $\frac{1}{210}$ of an inch ; whilst in the latter locality, where the hair is of a darker hue, the hairs are individually coarser, ten samples giving an average thickness of $\frac{1}{170}$ to $\frac{1}{120}$ of an inch. The diameter of the spiral, when measurable, varies between 5 and 10 millimètres,[1] its usual range throughout the group ; but on account of the practice of combing, it is often difficult to measure it with any degree of accuracy. These measurements, however, are double the size of the curl (2 to 4 mm.) which Miklouho-Maclay[2] has determined to be characteristic of the Papuan. The difference may be due to the greater intermingling of the eastern Polynesian element amongst the Solomon Islanders.

The natives of the eastern islands of this group frequently stain their hair a light-brown hue by the use of lime, a practice which frees the hair of vermin. The passing visitor might easily carry away with him the impression that such light-brown hair was a permanent character ; but on examining adults, he would usually find that the hair is much darker at the roots. The natives (women and boys) of the islands of Bougainville Straits, and according to Labillardiére,[3] those of the adjacent island of Bouka, stain the hair by the use of a red ochreous earth, the colour of which, blended with the deep colour of the hair, produces a striking magenta hue.

With regard to the amount of hair on the face, limbs, and trunk, great diversity is observed even amongst natives of the same village. Epilation is commonly employed, a bivalve shell being used as a pair of pincers ; but there can be no doubt that the development of the hair varies quite independently of such a custom. Out of ten men taken promiscuously from one of the villages on the north coast of St. Christoval, perhaps, five would have smooth

---

[1] In young boys in different parts of the group, the hair sometimes grows in larger flat spirals having a diameter of from 12 to 15 millimètres.

[2] "Nature." Dec. 21st, 1882.

[3] Labillardiére's "Voyage in search of La Pérouse," vol. i. p. 246. London 1800.

faces ; three would possess a small growth of hair on the chin and upper lip ; the ninth would possess a beard, a moustache, and whiskers of moderate growth ; whilst the tenth would present a shaggy beard, and a hairy visage. With the majority of the Solomon Islanders, the surfaces of the body and limbs are comparatively free from hair ; but hairy men are to be found in most villages, and in rare and exceptional cases, the hairy-bodied, hairy-visaged men are the rule. It would appear that in this group, the qualities of treachery and ferocity are possessed in a greater degree by those communities in which hairy men prevail. Hairy-visaged men are commonly found amongst the natives of the Florida Islands. In Bougainville Straits, the great majority of the men keep their faces and chins free from hair, which the chiefs and the older men usually permit to grow.

With age the hair generally assumes an iron-grey hue, as if the decoloration was incomplete. In one old man, however, who was the patriarch of Treasury Island, the hair was completely grey. Baldness usually commences over the fore-head ; and is not uncommonly observed beginning amongst middle-aged men. The old women apparently regard hair as an unnecessary encumbrance, the little that remains in later life being generally removed.

I have not yet referred to an almost straight-haired element which has been infused amongst the inhabitants of Bougainville Straits. The individuals, thus characterised, have very dark skins, the hair being even darker, and corresponding in hue with the colour-types 34 and 49. With such natives the face is flatter, and the nose is more *écrasé* than usual. The hair may be almost straight : and, if not very long, it is often erect, giving the person a shock-headed appearance ; whilst in some cases it tends to gather into curls of a large spiral. Other natives possess hair which combines the straight and frizzly characters, giving the whole mass, when combed out, an appearance partly wavy and partly bushy. Small boys in this part of the group have frequently curly heads of hair with large flattened spirals. Traders tell me that straight-haired individuals are found amongst the hill-tribes of St. Christoval at the opposite end of the group. I have seen two such natives, one a woman, and the other a man whom I met near Cape Keibeck on the north coast of the island.

A few remarks with reference to the prevailing hues of the skin may be here interesting. It would seem to be a general rule

that the darker-skinned natives occur in the western islands of the
group, such as New Georgia, Bougainville Straits, and Bougainville;
whilst the lighter-coloured natives are more restricted to the eastern
islands such as St. Christoval, Guadalcanar, &c.   In different parts
of the Solomon Group, the colour of the skin, as may have been
already inferred, varies considerably in shade from a very deep
brown, exemplified by colour-type 42 of M. Broca, to a copperish
hue, best typefied by colour-type 29.   The prevailing darker hue of
the western islands is represented by type 42, and the prevailing
lighter hue of the eastern islands by type 35.   Where there is no
means of comparison, the darker hues of the skin might be called
black.   The lightest hues, such as would appear to characterise
natives in isolated localities, as in Santa Catalina, and on the north
coast of Guadalcanar opposite the Rua Sura Islets, would be best
exemplified by colour-type 28.   The elderly natives are, as a rule,
more dark-skinned than those of younger years, the difference in
shade being attributable partly to a longer exposure by reason of
their age to the influence of sun and weather, and partly to those
structural changes in the skin which accompany advancing years.
The colour is usually fairly uniform over the person, but in the case
of the Malaita natives, before referred to, the colour of the face
and chest was of a lighter hue than that of the limbs and body, as
exemplified by contrasting the colour-types 28 and 35.[1]

I would draw attention to the circumstance that my observations were confined to the coast tribes of these islands.   The larger
islands, which may be compared in size to the county of Cornwall,
are but thinly populated in their interior by tribes of more puny
physique and less enterprising character, who are ill-suited to cope
with their more robust and more war-like fellow-islanders of the coast.
These " bushmen," as they are called, are accredited by the coast-
natives with inferior mental capabilities as compared with their
own.   To call a man of the coast a " bushman " is equivalent to
calling him a stupid or a fool, a taunt which is commonly employed
amongst the coast-natives.   The stone adzes and axes, which have
been discarded by the inhabitants of the coast, are said to be still
employed by the bushmen.   I was unable to make any measurements of these natives; but those I saw were usually of short
stature and of a more excitable and suspicious temperament.   The

---

[1] *Vide* page for remarks on the effect of the prevailing skin-disease, an inveterate form of
body-ringworm, on the colour of the skin.

hair is worn in the woolly style, is short like that of the African Negro, and its surface has often a peculiar appearance from the hairs arranging themselves in little knobs. I believe that these bushmen, and at the present time I am recalling to my mind those of the interior of Bougainville, have naturally shorter hair than those of the coast, and that the peculiar character of the hair just described is a permanent one.[1] These bushmen probably represent the original Negrito stock of these islands, which, at the coast, often loses many of its characters on account of the intermingling with Eastern Polynesian and Malayan intruders.

With the object of testing the powers of vision possessed by the natives of these islands, I examined the sight of twenty-two individuals who were in all cases either young adults or of an age not much beyond thirty. For this purpose I employed the square test-dots which are used in examining the sight of recruits for the British army, and I obtained the following results. Two natives could distinguish the dots clearly at 70 feet, one at 67 feet, two at 65 feet, three at 62 feet, four at 60 feet, two at 55 feet, three at 52 feet, four at 50 feet, and one at 35 feet. I roughly placed the average distance at which a native could count the dots at about 60 feet, which is a little beyond the standard distance for testing the normal vision of recruits, viz., 57 feet; but I laid no stress on this difference, and briefly noted in my journal that these natives possessed the normal powers of vision. The quickness of the natives in perceiving distant objects, such as ships at sea, was a matter of daily observation to us; and I was often much surprised by their facility in picking out pigeons and opossums, which were almost concealed in the dense foliage of the trees some 60 or 70 feet overhead. I was therefore impressed with the greater discriminating power possessed by these savages; but the results of my observations on their far-seeing powers were not such as would justify the conclusion that they excelled us very greatly in this respect.

Having read an interesting correspondence in " Nature " during February and March, 1885, on the subject of " civilisation and eye-sight," I forwarded the results of my observations to that journal (vide, April 2nd). A fortnight afterwards there appeared a communication from Mr. Charles Roberts, in which he added greatly to

---

[1] Mr. Earl, who well describes this knobby appearance of the surface of the hair of some Papuan tribes, also believes that these tribes may sometimes have naturally short hair. (" Papuans," p. 2.)

the value of my observations by comparing them with results obtained by the use of the army test-dots in the case of English agricultural and out-door labourers, results which were extracted from the Report for 1881 of the Anthropometric Committee of the British Association. After making this comparison Mr. Roberts remarked that *the figures gave no support to the belief that savages possess better sight than civilised peoples;* and he pointed out that my average of 60 feet, which, however, I had only roughly estimated, was somewhat excessive and should have been 57·5 feet, which is only half a foot more than the distance at which Professor Longmore has determined these test-dots ought to be seen by a recruit with normal powers of vision. My observations were comparatively few, but, as above shown, they give no support to the view that savages possess superior powers of vision as compared with civilised races.

In the correspondence in "Nature," above referred to, Mr. Brudenell Carter supported the "commonly received view" that the savage possesses greater acuteness of vision; but Lord Rayleigh held that it would be inconsistent with optical laws to hold that the eyes of savages, considered merely as optical instruments, are greatly superior to our own; and he observed that it appeared to him that the superiority of the savage is a question of attention and practice in the interpretation of minute indications. The same opinion was expressed by Mr. Roberts, when he referred to the common mistake of travellers in confounding acuteness of vision with the results of special training or education of the faculty of seeing, results which, as he remarked, are quite as much dependent on mental training as on the use of the eyes.

There is a circumstance which may influence the powers of vision possessed by these islanders; and it is this. With the object, I believe, of excluding flies and other insects from their dwellings, the natives keep the interiors dark, the door being usually the only aperture admitting light. Coming in from the direct sunlight, I have often had to wait a minute or two before my eyes became accustomed to the change; but the natives do not experience this inconvenience. Some hours of the day they commonly spend in their houses; whilst at night they use no artificial light except the fitful glare of a wood fire. It would seem probable that the influence of the opposite conditions presented by the darkness of their dwellings and the bright sunlight, would be found in the increased

rapidity of the contraction and dilation of the pupil with the
enlargement, perhaps, of the retinal receiving area. It is, however,
a noteworthy circumstance that these natives are able to pass from
the bright tropical glare outside their dwellings to the dark interiors, and *vice versá*, without showing that temporary derangement
of vision which the white man experiences whilst the iris is
adapting itself to the new condition.

My attention was not attracted by the size of the pupils; but I
paid no especial attention to this point. Mr. J. Rand Capron in the
correspondence in " Nature," above alluded to, refers to the circumstance that the pupil varies in size in individual cases; and he
instances the case of one of his assistants possessing unusually large
pupils who had a singularly "sharp" eye for picking up companions
to double stars, small satellites, &c., and who could read fine print
with a light much less bright than is usually required. "The
peculiarity affecting my assistant's eyes," as Mr. Capron writes,
"may be more common with the savages than with us." I am inclined myself to believe that, on a careful comparison being made,
the pupils of the savage will be generally found to be larger. If
such should be the case, we shall have a ready explanation of his
better discriminating powers of vision.

The eyes of these natives have usually a soft, fawn-like appearance with but little expression. Of the twenty-two individuals
whose sight I examined, I came upon only one whose powers of
vision seemed at all defective. In this instance—that of a man
about thirty years old—the nature of the cause was sufficiently
indicated by the prominence of the eyes and the nipping of the lids,
especially when the sight was strained by trying to count the test-
dots at a distance. The limit of distance at which this man could
count the test-dots was 35 feet. The question which presented
itself to my mind in this case was, whether a white man, who could
count the dots at the same limit of distance, would exhibit to the
same degree the external signs of myopia.

I also made some observations on the colour-sense of the inhabitants of Bougainville Straits. Although able to match the
seven colours of the spectrum, viz., red, orange, yellow, green,
Prussian blue, indigo, and violet, they have only, as far as I could
ascertain, distinctive names for white, red, yellow, and sometimes
blue; whilst all the other colours, including black, indigo, dark blue,
violet, green, &c., are included under one or more general names for

dark hues, as shown in the list below. Some of the names of the colours have been suggested by the colours of objects with which the natives are familiar. Thus, one of the names of dark hues is evidently taken from that of charcoal (*sibi*). Again, one of the names for red is but the native term for blood (*masini*); whilst the commonest word for yellow (*temuli*) is also the name of a scitamineous plant, the bulbous root of which possesses a yellow juice. Yellow must be a familiar colour to these natives, as they sometimes decorate their persons with the yellow juice that exudes from incisions into the fruits of *Thespesia populnea*, one of the commonest of littoral trees. They possess also the *Morinda citrifolia*, the roots of which supply a bright yellow dye that is employed in other Polynesian groups, such as in the Society Islands, for staining purposes. The circumstance that different men often applied different names to the same test-colour, shows that they have no recognised list of colour-names; and it would appear probable that all the names are of a suggestive nature, or in other words that they are derived from the names of objects with the conspicuous hues of which the natives are familiar.

NATIVE NAMES FOR COLOURS.

WHITE, ...	Anaa ; Ana-anaa.
RED, ORANGE, ...	Alec ; Masi-masini ; Loto.
YELLOW, ...	Temuli ; Samoi ; Latili.
BLUE, ...	Totono.
BLACK, INDIGO, VIOLET, GREEN (dark), BLUE (dark), ...	Söipa ; Kia ; Sivi-sivi ; Malai.

The pigments employed in decorating the posts of houses, canoe-ornaments, carved clubs, &c., are white, red, and black. Blue is a favourite colour with the natives of Bougainville Straits when choosing beads and other articles of trade; and, in fact, blue is the favourite colour for beads in most of the islands.

In the eastern islands, pigments of white, red, and black are also those which are commonly employed for decorative purposes. In the island of Ugi, as Mr. Stephens informed me, the same word is used to indicate all the dark colours. A native of this island cannot distinguish the different colours in the rainbow: and it should be here remarked that he views the appearance of a bow with a large arc as a warning of the approach of hostile canoes, and he retires accordingly to his house.

The following notes on the gestures and the expressions of the emotions of the Solomon Islanders, which I was led to make after a perusal of Mr. Darwin's well-known work on these subjects, occur scattered about the pages of my journals; and I must crave the indulgence of my reader if they are, from this reason, of a somewhat disconnected character.

The natives of Bougainville Straits and of other parts of the group *beckon* with the hand, in a manner almost the reverse of our own. Instead of holding out the hand with the palm uppermost and motioning with the forefinger, they beckon with the palm downwards, and motion with all the fingers. On several occasions, when motioning a native to approach by means of our own gesture, I have had to adopt his own mode of beckoning before he could understand me. . . . . Clapping the hands is a common means of evincing *astonishment* and *delight*, the hands being usually held up before the face as in the attitude of prayer, but little noise being made. Mule, the Treasury chief, clapped his hands before his face, when Lieutenant Leeper showed him some of his paintings; and surprise was exhibited in a similar manner by the men of Alu, whilst I was taking a sample of hair from the head of one of their number. Some young lads of Fauro clapped their hands noiselessly during their laughter when I gave them a tune on the Jews-harp: whilst a party of Treasury boys, who accompanied me on one of my rambles, thus evinced their pleasure when some matches for lighting our pipes were unexpectedly found in my bag.

The following mode of signifying *hunger* was often adopted by my youthful native companions in my excursions, when the sun was near its meridian altitude, in order to remind me of the biscuit I generally carried for them; and the little imps used to repeat the gesture in an exaggerated form for my amusement. The belly is drawn in to a surprising degree by the powerful contraction of the abdominal muscles; and, assuming a dismal expression of countenance, the hungry individual points with his finger to this unmistakeable sign of the apparently empty condition of his stomach, and says "kai-kai, muru" (food for stomach). Labillardière tells us that the natives of New Caledonia signified their hunger in a similar manner by pointing to their bellies, and contracting the abdominal muscles as much as they could.[1] . . . . The natives of Bougainville Straits make use of the exclamation, "Agai," to indicate *pain* and *suffering*, This cry often rang pitifully in my ears when, from the prejudices

---

[1] "Voyage in search of La Pérouse" (Eng. edit.: London 1800) vol. ii., p. 213.

of the natives, I was unable to render much surgical aid in the case of the severe gunshot injuries, which resulted from the conflicts between the Treasury and Shortland islanders.

Elevation of the eyebrows with a slight throwing backward of the head is the gesture of *assent.* A native sometimes raises his eyebrows slightly to indicate *caution* or *reticence* under circumstances in which we should employ a cough or a wink; and, by the same sign, a *question* may be asked, and as silently answered by a similar movement of the eyebrows, accompanied by a throwing up of the head. A native of Simbo, on one occasion, because I would not give him tobacco, signified his *contempt* for me by spitting on the ground. A woman of Alu informed me that she was the *mother* of two girls standing near, by first pointing to her daughters, and then touching her breasts. When *puzzled*, a native sometimes adopts our sign of perplexity by frowning, and scratching his head.

On one occasion, I was much amused by the behaviour of some of the Treasury boys, lively young imps who used frequently to accompany me on my excursions. One of their number had been offended by his companions, who immediately began to caper round him, distorting their faces in a peculiar manner by drawing the eyes and mouth towards each other with their fingers, and producing an appearance reminding me of the human faces on the dance-clubs of Bougainville Straits and New Ireland. Sometimes they would only go through the motions by scraping their fingers down their cheeks. The object was evidently to create terror, but only in a mimic fashion.

But little gesticulation is used in ordinary conversation. A native of Cape Keibeck, on the north coast of St. Christoval, who went through the motions of throwing a spear in time of battle, assumed a hideous expression of countenance with eyes starting and knitted brows, much as Mr. Mosely describes in the instance of a native of Humboldt Bay, New Guinea.[1] A native, who is planning the performance of an act of treachery, usually exhibits during his conversation an excited, restless manner, with a slight trembling of the limbs and a partial loss of control over the facial muscles. It is in this manner that white men, resident in the group, when approaching a village with which they are unacquainted, often find an indication of the hostility or friendliness of the inhabitants by observing the unconscious bearing of the first men they meet.

[1] "Naturalist on the Challenger," p, 441.

These islanders converse in a low, monotonous voice; and are unaccustomed to loud, stentorian tones, such as those in which words of command are given. I was told a story of a white man who had engaged some natives to take him out in a canoe to the site of a sunken rock, which he intended to blow up with dynamite as it obstructed the channel. Immediately on dropping the charge, he shouted out to his crew to paddle away as quickly as possible and at the same time gesticulated wildly. The men opened their eyes wide and stared at him with astonishment, but never moved; and before they could recover themselves, off went the charge, and the canoe and its occupants were blown into the air. However, but little damage was caused except to the canoe. My informant told me that if the men had been told quietly to paddle away, the accident would never have happened.

I now come to the subject of the disposition of these islanders. There is a generosity between man and man, which I often admired, although it was easy to perceive that there was a singular relation between the giver and the recipient. A native rarely refuses anything that is asked; but, on the other hand, he is not accustomed to offer anything spontaneously except when he expects an equivalent in return. His generosity is, in truth, constrained by the knowledge of the fact that by a refusal he will incur the enmity of the person who has made the request. Often when during my excursions I have come upon some man who was preparing a meal for himself and his family, I have been surprised at the open-handed way in which he dispensed the food to my party of hungry natives. No gratitude was shown towards the giver, who apparently expected none, and only mildly remonstrated when my men were unusually voracious. I was often amused at noticing how a native's friends would gather around when there was a sago palm to be felled.

But there is one occasion when the existence of friends must be very trying to a Solomon Islander, and that is when he returns to his island after his term of service in the plantations of Fiji or Queensland has expired. He brings with him his earnings of three years in the shape of a musket, a couple of American axes, and a large box filled with calico, coloured handkerchiefs, tobacco, pipes, knives, beads, &c. On landing at the beach, he is greeted by the greater portion of the village. The chief at once appropriates the musket, as his way of welcoming the wanderer on his return. His father selects, with due deliberation, the best tempered of the axes.

The chief's son relieves him of one of the largest knives. His numerous relations and friends assist themselves to some of the more valuable articles in the box; whilst the calico and beads are evenly appropriated by the different ladies of the village, as their manner of evincing their pleasure at his safe return. The unhappy man dares not refuse, and he finally leaves the beach for his own house with a very light box and a heavy heart. But his friends in the neighbourhood think it their duty to convey their congratulations in person; and in a few days the box alone remains, which it is very likely that the chief has already secured "in prospectu." The foregoing is by no means an exaggerated account of the reception which awaits a Solomon Islander when he returns from his term of service in the colonies.

The natives of this group have obtained for themselves the reputation of being the most treacherous and bloodthirsty of the Pacific Islanders. Here, however, as in other groups, the inhabitants have been judged according to the circumstances attending the visit of the navigator. If he has come into collision with them, he paints their conduct in the darkest colours; but if, as has rarely been the case, there has been nothing to interrupt the harmony of his intercourse, he is apt, in his description of the peaceful character of the natives, to reflect on the want of humanity which marked the dealings of his predecessors. But for us a middle course would seem preferable; and in approving the mild measures of the one, we must not forget that the harsh treatment of the other may have arisen in circumstances over which he had little control. The early intercourse between civilized and savage peoples must of necessity be fraught with peril, until the latter cease to look upon every stranger as a probable foe. It is not often that we have the pleasure of reading such accounts as are given by Kotzebue and Chamisso of their intercourse with the Radack Islanders; yet we must remember that the humane principles of La Pérouse led, unfortunately, to the massacre of M. de Langle and eleven others in the Navigator Islands. Here again the middle course is to be followed; and the traveller most successful in his dealings with these races will be he who obtains for himself their fear as well as their affection.

The early intercourse of the Solomon Islanders with the Spaniards, and with the first French navigators, was too often marked by bloodshed to enable us to form a correct estimation of the disposition of these natives. We therefore turn without regret to the more pleasing experience of a later voyager in these seas. In his account of his intercourse with the natives of Isabel in 1838, D'Urville thus refers to these islanders: "Nous sommes les premiers à inscrire dans l'histoire des habitants de ces îles, une page en faveur de leur caractère: ils auraient pu, presque sans dangers, massacrer ceux de nos officiers qui sont allés chercher l'hospitalité aux villages d'Opihi et Toitoi, et j'aime à croire qu'ils n'auraient pas résisté à la tentation, si dans leur caractère il n'y avait pas eu quelques sentiments d'affection ou de probité."[1]

In recalling my own experiences, I can scarcely remember a single instance in which I was aught but kindly treated by a race of savages who have been so often characterised as the most treacherous and bloodthirsty in the Pacific. I was constantly in their power, since, in my excursions, I very rarely had any other companions. I will, therefore, frame my estimate of their character in the words of the French navigator, that they would not have been able to resist the temptation of harming me, if there was not in their disposition something of the sense of honour and affection.

[1] "Voyage au Pole Sud," etc. Vol. V., p. 106.

CHAPTER VII

THE dress worn by the men of these islands is generally of the scantiest description. A narrow band of cloth, worn like a T bandage, often constitutes their only garment. In some islands visited by traders, waist-cloths are worn. Often, however, and especially amongst the bush tribes, the Solomon Islander presents himself as guiltless of clothing as did our original parents. The dress of the women varies considerably in different islands of the group. The married women of St. Christoval and the adjacent small islands wear the scantiest of fringes, which cannot be dignified by the name of dress : whilst the unmarried girls dispense with clothing altogether. In the Florida Islands, the women are more decorously clad, and wear a longer fringe. In the eastern islands, however, the influence of the missionary and the trader have caused a more general employment by the women of the "sulu" (a large coloured handkerchief), which is fastened around the waist, and is very becoming. The women of the islands of Bougainville Straits commonly wear the "sulu ;" but they frequently discard it for a time; as when they are wading on the reefs, and then they are content with an improvised apron of long leaves ("bassa"), the stalks of which are passed under a narrow waist-band. On one occasion at Alu, when arriving at the beach after one of my excursions into the interior of the island, I came upon a party of women who were bathing in the sea. They at once came out of the water, and began to interrogate my guides, having first provided themselves in the most unabashed manner with temporary aprons of fern fronds and the leaves of trees. They then gathered round me to learn where I had been, and what I had been doing ; and after I had satisfied their curiosity, I sent them away, highly pleased with some tobacco and beads.

The men of these islands are always very anxious to become the possessors of European articles of clothing, such as shirts, coats, hats, etc.; but the happy owners seldom don them except during the visit of a ship, when they strut about clad in some solitary garment, such as a shirt or a waistcoat, or often only a hat. I had often some difficulty in preserving my gravity when I met some sedate individual, as naked as on the day when he was born, wearing a round hat on his head, and carrying his shirt on his arm. The fortunate possessor of a shirt usually regards it as a kind of light overcoat, to be worn on especial occasions; and in some islands the possessors seem to prefer carrying their shirts on their arms wherever they go. A few men, who have these articles of clothing, never take them off after they have begun to wear them. Such a practice, however, is quite opposed to the usual cleanly habits of these islanders. Whilst we were in Bougainville Straits, three natives were employed on board as interpreters, who were dubbed by the men, Jacket, Waistcoat, and Trousers, as they used to wear a suit between them. On one occasion, when I had induced some Faro men to take me in their canoe to an island some distance away, I was amused at the appearance of my crew, to whom I had previously given shirts. We were, for all the world, like a party of nigger-minstrels. Following the waggish advice of the quarter-master, the natives turned up their large collars. Off we started, and the sight of their serious countenances, half buried in their collars, was too much for my gravity: but when we landed, and my men proceeded in a dignified manner to disembark, they looked so ludicrously sedate in their long-tailed shirts, that I roared with laughter.

The most picturesque of the personal ornaments of the natives of the eastern islands is a frontlet of the handsome white cowries (*Ovulum ovum*). About a dozen of these shells, rather small in size, are strung together, and bound across the forehead. A single shell is sometimes worn on the front of the leg just below the knee. Many men possess large crescent-shaped plates of the pearl shell found in these seas, and which they wear on the breast. Resident traders, such as Captain Macdonald at Santa Anna, have largely supplied the natives with these ornaments. Necklaces made of the teeth of dogs, porpoises, fruit-bats, and phalangers (*Cuscus*), are commonly worn. The seeds of the *Coix Lachryma* are also employed for this purpose. Various articles are used as necklace-pendants, such as *Bulla* shells, the pretty *Natica mamilla*, beans, the hard palate of a fish (probably a ray), and other things. One native was very proud of a fragment of a willow-pattern plate, which he had smoothed off and ground down to a convenient size for his necklace.

Shell armlets[1] are in general use, and their number and size frequently denote the rank of their owner. Those most prized are fashioned out of the thickest part of the shell of *Tridacna gigas* towards the hinge. On one occasion, in the island of Simbo, I had an opportunity of observing the tedious process of making these *Tridacna* armlets. A hole is first bored through the solid thickness of the shell, and in it is inserted a piece of hoop iron, with one edge roughly jagged, after the fashion of a saw. This is worked with the hands, and after much labour the ring is sawn out of the shell. It is then rubbed down and polished with sand. On account of the tedious nature of the process of making them, these *Tridacna* armlets are much prized by their possessors. Amongst the numerous articles employed in trading with these natives is a very good imitation of this armlet made of tough white porcelain, and valued at about half a dollar. Smaller armlets are also cut out of large shells belonging to the genera *Trochus* and *Turbo*. The shell armlets of these islanders are often first placed on during youth, or at the first attainment of manhood; and, as the wearer grows older these ornaments become too small to pass over the elbow, and are permanently worn. Armlets are also made of native shell-money worked into patterns. Sometimes a couple of curved boar's-tusks are joined together for this purpose. Excluding the shell armlets, those most frequently worn are made of what is commonly known as "dyed grass." This material, however, consists, for the most part, of the strips of the vascular tissue of ferns, belonging to *Gleichenia* and other genera, which are neatly plaited together in patterns (*vide* page281) The prettiest specimens of this work are to be obtained at Savo. The same plaited armlets are worn by the Admiralty Islanders.[2] In some parts of New Guinea, strips of rattan are worked in with this material.[3] . . . In the Solomon Islands, armlets are usually worn on the left arm. The native

---

[1] By "armlet," I mean an ornament encircling the arm above the elbow.

[2] There is a chromo-lithograph of these ornaments in the "Narrative of the Cruise of the 'Challenger.'"

[3] Specimens in British Museum collection.

usually carries his pipe or his tobacco tucked inside them. They are often worn very tight, especially in the case of the plaited armlets, which actually constrict the limb.

Nose ornaments are not commonly worn in the eastern islands, though the nasal septum is generally pierced by a hole for the appendage which may be of tortoise-shell, bone, shells, &c. Youths keep the hole patent by retaining in it a small piece of wood of the thickness of a lead pencil, and between one and two inches in length. The tip of the nose is frequently pierced by a small hole about half an inch deep, in which a small peg of wood is sometimes placed which projects beyond the nose and gives the face an odd appearance.

The lobes of the ears are perforated by holes, which by continual distension become of the size of a crown-piece and often larger. In some islands, as in Santa Anna, a disc of white wood 1½ to 2 inches in diameter is placed in these holes. Sometimes they are kept in shape by the insertion of a shaving of wood rolled into a spiral; but more frequently they are left empty. Singular uses are made of these holes in the lobes of the ear, pipes and matchboxes being sometimes placed in them. On one occasion, Taki, the Wano chief, came on board with a heavy bunch of native shell-money hanging from each ear, a sign of mourning, as he informed us, for a recently deceased wife. In some instances, more particularly amongst the elder men, the pendulous loop formed by the distended hole in the lobe becomes severed and hangs in two pieces. I am told that when these loops break, the two parts are readily joined by paring the torn surfaces obliquely and binding them together.

The natives of the islands of Bougainville Straits pay less attention to personal decoration than do those of St. Christoval and the adjacent islands. The large *Tridacna* armlets are not often worn, the small shell armlets being those generally preferred, and as in the case of those worn in the eastern islands, their number indicates the rank and wealth of the wearer. The plaited arm-bands described on page 132 are frequently worn. Armlets made of trade beads are favourite ornaments of the women: when visiting the houses of the chiefs, I have sometimes found their wives employed in this kind of fancy-work, small red, blue, and white beads being tastefully worked together in the common zig-zag pattern. Here, as in the eastern islands, the septum of the nose is pierced by a hole, but I rarely saw any ornament suspended from it. The women of Treasury Island, however, sometimes wear in this aperture a tusk-like ornament, 1½ to 2 inches long, which is made from the shell of the giant clam. Occasionally I have observed clay pipes carried in this perforation in the nasal septum. Here, also, the lobes of the ears are pierced by large holes, and in the older men they hang in loops 2 to 3 inches in length.

The men of Simbo (Narovo Island) streak their countenances with lime, whilst the boys of Treasury Islands sometimes paint their faces around the eyes with the red ochreous earth that they employ for staining the hair. The young lads of Faro occasionally adorn their faces with silvery strips of a fish's swimming-bladder which they plaster on their cheeks.

In the matter of personal decoration I should observe that the men usually wear the plumes, not that the women dislike decorations, but because they do not often have the opportunity of wearing them. If a trade necklace or some similar ornament is given to a woman, it will very soon be observed adorning the person of her husband. An incident of this sort particularly annoyed me on one occasion in the island of St. Christoval; but I might as well have tried to persuade a pig that it was a glutton as have attempted to convince a native that such a transaction was ungallant. In some islands it is the custom for the husband on the occasion of a festival to load his favourite wife with all his worldly wealth in the form of the native bead money; and, as at Santa Anna, the wives of the headmen parade about the village thus heavily attired and presenting such a picture of "portable property" as would have gladdened the heart of Mr. Wemmick himself. This shell-money, to which I have frequently referred in this work, and which is so often employed in personal decoration, consists of small pieces of shells of different colours shaped and strung together like beads. In the eastern islands, this money is largely derived from the natives of Malaita. Six fathoms of it are said to be sufficient for the purchase of a pig. The same kind of money is used by the inhabitants of the Admiralty Islands, New Ireland, New Guinea, and the New Hebrides. In the last two localities it is worked into armlets.[1]

The men of the Solomon Islands are very fond of placing in their hair a brightly-coloured flower such as that of *Hibiscus tiliaceus*, or a pretty sprig, or the frond of a fern. My native companions in my

[1] The natives of the Solomon Islands also occasionally employ as money the teeth of fish, porpoises, fruit-eating bats (*Pteropidæ*), and of other animals.

excursions rarely passed a pretty flower without plucking it and placing it in their bushy hair; and they were fond of decorating my helmet in a similar fashion. Sometimes one individual would adorn himself to such an extent with flowers, ferns, and scented leaves, that a botanist might have made an instructive capture in seizing his person. In addition to the flowers placed in his bushy mass of blackish-brown hair, he would tuck under his necklace and armlets sprigs and leaves of numerous scented plants, such as *Evodia hortensis* and *Ocymum sanctum*. He would take much pleasure in pointing out to me the plants whose scented leaves are employed in the native perfumery, most of which are of the labiate order, and are to be commonly found in the waste ground of the plantations. The women seldom decorate themselves in this manner. Those of Bougainville Straits make their scanty aprons of the leaves of a scitamineous plant named " bassa " which, when crushed in the fingers, have a pleasant scent.

The fondness for decorating the person with flowers and scented herbs has been frequently referred to by travellers in their accounts of the natives of other parts of the Western Pacific. Mr. George Forster tells us that the people of Tanna and Mallicolo in the New Hebrides place inside their shell armlets bunches of the odoriferous plant, *Evodia hortensis*, together with the leaves of crotons and other plants.[1] We learn from Mr. Macgillivray,[2] and from Mr. Stone,[3] that the natives of the south-east part of New Guinea are similarly fond of decorating themselves with flowers and scented leaves which they place in the hair and inside their armlets and necklaces.

Tattooing is practised amongst both sexes in many islands; but the process differs from that ordinarily employed in the circumstance that the pigment is frequently omitted, and for this reason the marks are often faint and only visible on a close inspection. In this manner the natives of St. Christoval and the adjacent islands have their cheeks marked by a number of shallow grooves arranged in a series of chevron-lines, and differing but little if at all from the general colour of the skin. On the trunk the lines are of a faint blue hue, and here a pigment is more frequently used. The process, as employed in the island of Santa Anna, consists in deeply abrading

[1] "A Voyage round the World," by George Forster, London, 1777; (page 276.)

[2] "Voyage of H.M.S. ' Rattlesnake,'" by John Macgillivray; London, 1852.

[3] "A few months in New Guinea," by O. C. Stone; London, 1880.

the skin with such instruments as a piece of a shell, the flinty edge of the bamboo, the tooth of a large fruit-eating bat (*Pteropidae*), or even by the long finger-nails. The older lads have to submit themselves to this operation before they obtain the rights of manhood; and I was informed that during its progress they are kept isolated in a house and fed on the blood of a certain fish (?) After it is completed, they are at liberty to marry, and they are allowed to take part in the fighting and in the fishing expeditions.

Tattooing is not generally practised amongst the people of the islands of Bougainville Straits. I only observed it in a few instances, more particularly amongst the women, when it resembles that which has been .above described. A party of men from the village of Takura on the coast of Bougainville, whom I met on one occasion, had their faces marked with shallow linear grooves of much the same colour as the skin, which commenced at the "alæ nostri.' and, curving over the cheek-bones, terminated above the eyebrows. These lines were more distinct than those which mark the faces of the natives in the eastward islands, although they were probably produced in a similar manner. Another pattern of tattooing, which may be described as a branching coil, is to be found in the representation of the head of a native of Isabel Island, which was obtained from a mould taken in D'Urville's expedition in 1838.[1] Some men of the districts of the Uta Pass and Urasi on the north coast of Malaita, whom I met on one occasion, had their faces marked with a double or a single row of blueish dots commencing on the cheek-bones and meeting on the forehead.

In the place of tattooing, the inhabitants of the islands of Bougainville Straits ornament their bodies with rows of circular and somewhat raised cicatrices which are usually about the size of a fourpenny piece and about a third of an inch apart. In the case of the men, the shoulders, upper arms, and chest are thus marked: a double row of cicatrices commences on the shoulder-blade of either side, and crossing the upper arms near the apex of the insertion of the deltoid muscle these rows arch over the armpits and meet at the lower part of the sternum. The chiefs and their sons often have an additional row of these marks. Although this is the common fashion, one sometimes meets men who have the cicatrices confined to the chest or to the shoulders, or to only one side of the body. Amongst the women, the shoulders, upper arms, and breasts are

[1] Plate vi. : Atlas Anthropologie ; "Voyage au Pole Sud et dans l'Oceanie."

similarly marked as shown in the engraving here given, and in addition they have these rows of cicatrices across the inside of the thigh. A triple row across the left breast distinguished the principal wife of the chief of Treasury Island. This method of ornamenting the body with raised cicatrices, which I also observed in the case of the party of Takura natives above referred to, would appear to be a sign of manhood and womanhood, as it is not to be found amongst the younger of either sex. With regard to the mode of producing these marks, I could only ascertain that they were made by placing the powdered dust of touchwood on the skin and then igniting it. To produce such a permanent and indelible cicatrix, I should think it probable that means were employed to convert the burn into a festering sore. The light colour of these scars would appear to indicate that no pigment is used in the process. I should remark that this custom of raising the skin in cicatrices, especially on the shoulders, breasts, and thighs, is very prevalent among the Papuans of the south and south-west coasts of New Guinea.[1] Mr. Mosely describes the same method of ornamenting the body as he observed it amongst the men of the Admiralty Islands.[2]

It may be here noticed, that the practice of circumcision is apparently not to be met with in these islands, except, as observed by Dr. Codrington, in the pure Polynesian settlements,[3] with which, however, I did not come into contact.

I have previously described the modes of wearing and of decorating the hair (pages 116, 134), and can only make a few remarks here. In some islands, as at Ugi, the young boys have the entire scalp shaven with the exception of two tufts on the top of the head. Then again, at the other extreme of life, it is often the custom for old women to assist the natural falling-off of the hair and remove it altogether. As a sign of mourning, the hair may be trimmed, cut close, or shaved off.

The Solomon Islander often carries his comb stuck in his bushy hair. As shown in the figure in this work, the comb in common use throughout this group resembles very much in pattern and mode of workmanship that which is in use in parts of New Guinea, the Admiralty Islands, the Tonga Group, and other islands of the

---

[1] "Papuans" by G. W. Earl; (p. 5.)
[2] Journ. Anthrop. Inst. vol. vi., p. 379.
[3] Ibid., vol. x; p. 261.

Western Pacific. The combs of different islands may vary somewhat in details, but they belong all to this pattern, being usually
made of a hard dark wood, the teeth consisting of separate pieces
either bound tightly or glued together by a kind of resin. The
handles and upper parts are often prettily decorated with the plaited
" dyed grass," so-called (*vide*, page 132). An excellent coloured
illustration of an Admiralty Island comb is to be found in the official
narrative of the cruise of the " Challenger." In the islands of Bougainville Straits, the native often carries in his hair an instrument
three prongs rudely fashioned out of bamboo, as shown in one of
the figures. It is used as much for scratching the head as for
combing the hair.

Head-coverings are rarely to be found in this group, except in
Bougainville and Bouka. A native of Treasury showed me a singular conical hat which he had brought from Bouka. It really was a
double hat, one inside the other, the inner hat being made of the
leaf of the " kiari," a species of *Heliconia*, and the outer of the fan-
shaped leaf of the " firo," a palm of the genus *Licuala*. A band of
the so-called plaited " dyed grass " encircles the base and keeps the
hat on the head. A similarly shaped hat but smaller and shorter,
and made of the leaf of the " kiari," was worn by some Bougainville
natives from the village of Takura, whom I met in Fauro Island.
It was placed towards the back of the head ; and as it covered
only a small portion of the crown, it was evidently more ornamental than useful. In addition, these natives wore a little bunch of
feathers on each temple. Their appearance in this grotesque head-
dress was rather ludicrous.

It is a remarkable circumstance that although the Solomon
Islanders, as a rule, wear no protective covering for the head, the
carved figures of their tambu-posts are usually represented with
very European-looking hats. These carved tambu-posts have various uses (*vide*, page 32). In a similar manner in Bougainville
Straits, the hat is to be noticed in the case of the little wooden
figures which are fastened on the stems of canoes as protective
deities. . . . . . .Where these islanders first obtained their
idea of a hat of this shape is a matter for speculation. It may have
been originally suggested by the hats of the Spanish soldiers three
centuries ago, who by means of their musketry seldom failed to make
a lasting impression of their visit during the six months spent by
the expedition in the group.

Hanging-hook.

Comb.

Fish-float.

Series of patterns, derived from the chevron or zig-zag line, which are used for decorative purposes by the Solomon Islanders. The principal steps in the series are alone indicated, the intermediary stages being often exemplified in the ornamental designs of these natives. (The dotted lines are my own).

Sunshades in the form of a peak of plaited grass bound to the forehead and projecting over the eyes are occasionally worn by the natives of Bougainville Straits, whilst fishing in canoes, in order to protect their eyes from the sun's glare on the water. In Ugi, these sunshades are sometimes worn on gala days. They did not, however, appear to be in constant use in any part of the group which we visited.

The common decorative pattern employed by the natives of the islands that we visited was the chevron line. It is the pattern used in tattooing the face in the eastern islands ; and it is represented in alternating hues of red, white, and black, on the fronts of tambu-houses. It is rudely cut on the outer border of the small shell armlets of St. Christoval, and ornaments the cooking-pots and drinking-vessels of Bougainville Straits. (*See Illustration.*) In some of the shell armlets a continuous lozenge or diamond-shaped design is produced by the arrangement of the chevron lines as shown in the woodcut. The advance from this design to the dis-connected lozenge pattern is then but an easy gradation. These chevron lines are often curiously transformed. The Z pattern of inlaid mother-of-pearl, which is shown in the illustration of the canoe-god, is apparently but a broken chevron line. On the heads of the Treasury spears fantastic patterns are cut out in which the chevron design is adapted to the human skeleton (*See illustration*). . . . . . I may here add that the bamboo boxes used for the betel lime are ornamented with rectilinear patterns (scratched on their surfaces) which resemble those used in ornamenting the similar lime boxes of New Guinea, Borneo, and Sumatra.[1] The ornamental dance-clubs of Bougainville Straits exactly resemble the clubs from New Ireland and possess those singular distorted representations of the human face which characterise New Ireland ornamentation.

Caution is required in studying the modes of ornamentation of these islanders. The remark made by the Rev. Mr. Lawes, in reference to the women of the Motu tribe in New Guinea,[2] that they are glad to get new tattooing patterns from the printed calicoes, is equally applicable to some of the Solomon Island natives. On one occasion I was gravely informed by a native, as a fact likely to add to their interest, that some designs I was copying had this origin.

The Solomon Island songs, although often monotonous to the

---

[1] Exhibited in the British Museum Ethnological collection.

[2] Journ. Anthrop. Inst. vol. VIII., p. 369.

cultivated ear, appeared to me to be in consonance with the wild character of these islanders Often when I have stopped to rest and enjoy a pipe in the midst of my excursions, it may have been beside a stream in the wood or on the edge of a tall cliff overlooking the sea, my native companions have sat down and commenced their monotonous chanting, which, discordant as it may have sometimes seemed to me, appeared to be in unison with my surroundings. Now raised to a high key, now sinking to a low, subdued drone, now hurried, now slow and measured, these rude notes recalled to my mind rather the sounds of the inanimate world around me, such as the sighing of the wind among the trees or the shrill whistle of the gale, the noise of the surf on the reef or the rippling of the waves on the beach, the rushing of a mountain torrent or the murmuring of a rivulet in its bed. My thoughts at such times recurred to those unpolished ages in the history of nations when the bard attuned his melody to the voices of the waves, the streams, and the wind, and found in the mist or in the cloud his expression for the shadowy unknown. At no time have the poems of Ossian appeared to my mind to be invested with greater beauty than when I have been standing in solitude in some inland dell or on some lofty hilltop in these regions. The song of the bard of Selma, despite its ruggedness, on such occasions, appealed more powerfully to my imagination than many more finished verses, and seemed more in keeping with scenes that owed to man nothing, remaining as they had been for ages, Nature's handiwork.

Frequently whilst descending some steep hill-slope or whilst following the downward course of a ravine, my natives were wont to make the woods echo with their shouts and their wild songs. The natural impulse to make use of the vocal organs whilst descending a mountain is worth a moment's remark. Often I found myself involuntarily shouting with my savage companions, when their loud peals of laughter attracted my attention. Some years ago, when visiting the Si-shan Mountains which lie behind the city of Kiukiang on the south bank of the Yang-tse, I remember listening to the cries of the Chinese wood-cutters as they returned in the evening down the narrow gorges that led to their homes. As their shouts died away in the higher parts of the mountain, the echo was caught by the wood-cutters below, and was answered back in such a manner that the men further down the gorges took up the cry.

The training of natives of these islands by the Melanesian

WAR DANCE and CANNIBAL SONG.

Mission at Norfolk Island has shown that the compass of their voices and their ear for music are capable of much cultivation. When staying with Bishop Selwyn at Gaeta in the Florida Islands, I heard familiar hymn-tunes sang with as true an appreciation of harmony as would be found in the Sunday School of an English village, and sung by a congregation of natives of both sexes, who, with the exception of their teachers, had never left their island.

During our lengthened sojourn in Bougainville Straits, we became very familiar with the popular tunes of the natives; and through the exertions of Mr. Isabell, I have been able to reproduce in this work three of the commonest airs.[1] The songs are usually sung in chorus, and a droning accompaniment is often introduced by some of the men which is especially well given in the second tune. There appear to be four or five common airs. All are short and most of them have refrains which are repeated over and over again. The first tune is a cannibal song and is sung at the war dances. Its words, as I learned from Gorai, the Shortland chief, are the address of a man to his enemy, in which he informs him of his intention to kill and eat him. The second tune, though not possessing words, is often sung or rather chanted by the men. When sung by a number of persons, its wild music is to an imaginative mind very suggestive of the savage life. I have heard it sung by about forty men whilst passing the night with them in the village of Sinasoro in Faro Island. The tambu-house, in which we were, was dimly lighted, and the natives were squatting around a wood-fire chanting their wild song in chorus, and terminating it in a fashion that sounded very abrupt to the white man's ear. The third tune is a pretty air which the men of the "Lark" used to play with the concertina in waltz time. The words, accompanying it, have a music of their own. I learned from the natives of Treasury Island that this tune was brought from Meoko (Duke of York Islands) not long since.

The Pandean pipe is the musical instrument in common use amongst the natives of the Islands of Bougainville Straits. I did not notice it in St. Christoval and the adjacent islands at the other end of the group, where it is either not known or but rarely used. The distribution of this instrument in the Pacific is interesting. It is figured by D'Albertis in his work on New Guinea, and there are specimens in the British Museum Collection from Brumer's Island

---

[1] Mr. Isabell was indebted for assistance to Mr. Tremaine of Auckland, N.Z.

off this coast, as well as from the Admiralty Islands, the New
Hebrides, the Tonga Group, and New Zealand. The instruments
from all these localities are distinguished from the Solomon Island
pan-pipe by the reeds being arranged in a single row and being of a
much smaller size. They are also more neatly made. Those used
by the Treasury and Shortland natives are composed of a double
row of from 6 to 8 reeds, the second row being merely added to give
support to the instrument. The longest reed is usually a foot in
length and three quarters of an inch in bore; whilst the shortest
reed is about 5 inches long and rather less than half an inch
in bore. Some natives prefer instruments having twice this
length. The Pandean pipes, played at the public dances of Alu,
are of very large size, the length of the longest reed of one
which I measured being between 3½ and 4 feet. At such perform-
ances, the air is given by the smaller pipes; whilst the bass notes of
the larger pipes form a droning but harmonious accompaniment. The
music of these instruments, being in the usual contracted compass,
is of a somewhat monotonous character. Those of Treasury Island
are said to be only adapted for playing one tune, which is the
second air given on the page. I learn from Mr. Isabell, who was
interested in this matter, that the natives vary the number of reeds
in the instrument according to the air it is intended to play. The
musician accompanies his melody with a nodding of the head and
a swaying of the body on the hips, movements which are anything
but expressive and are in fact rather ludicrous.

Jew's harps of foreign manufacture are much in demand amongst
persons of both sexes and all ages throughout the Solomon Group.
In the eastern islands they fashion them of bamboo, as in the
New Hebrides and New Guinea;[1] but I did not observe any native-
made instruments amongst the people of Bougainville Straits. The
women of Treasury Island produce a similar though softer kind of
music by playing, somewhat after the fashion of a Jew's harp,
on a lightly made fine-stringed bow about 15 inches long. This is
held to the lips and the string is gently struck with the fingers,
the cavity of the mouth serving as a resonator. . . . That
school-boy's delight, the "paper-and-comb instrument," finds its
counterpart in these islands. On one occasion, when I was enjoying
a pipe and watching the surf on the south coast of Stirling Island,

---

[1] Mr. Mosely in his "Notes by a Naturalist" gives an illustration of a Jew's harp from
the New Hebrides.

a young lad, who accompanied me, amused himself with some rude
music by holding in front of his lips, as he hummed a native air, a
thick leaf in which he had made a hole about half an inch wide,
leaving the thin transparent epidermis intact on one side ; the vib-
ration of this thin membrane gave a peculiar twang to his voice.

The drum in common use in the different islands we visited was
made of a portion of the trunk of a tree, 8 to 10 feet long, hollowed
out in its interior and possessing a slit in the middle. It is placed
lengthways on the ground, and is struck by two short sticks.
Similar drums are employed by the inhabitants of the New
Hebrides[1] and the Admiralty Islands.[2] This pattern may therefore
be described as the Melanesian· drum. A kind of sounding-board,
placed in a pit in the ground and struck by the feet of the dancers,
is described in my account of the dances of these islanders (*vide*
page 144).

As conches, the two large shells, *Triton* and *Cassis* are commonly
used. For this purpose, a hole is pierced for the lips on the side of
the spire.

Dancing is performed on very different occasions in these islands.
Besides the war, funeral, and festal dances, there are others which
partake of a lascivious character both in the words of the accompanying chant and in the movements of the hands and body.
Whilst visiting the small island of Santa Catalina, I saw one of these
dances performed by young girls from 10 to 14 years of age. An
explanation of their reluctance to commence, which at first from my
ignorance of what was to follow I was at a loss to understand, soon
offered itself in the character of the dance, and evidently arose from
a natural sense of modesty that appeared strange when associated
with their subsequent performance. There are, however, other
dances, purely sportive in their nature. Of such a kind were some
which were performed for my benefit at the village of Gaeta in the
Florida Islands. About twenty lads, having formed a ring around
a group of their companions squatting in the centre, began to walk
slowly round, tapping the ground with their left feet at every other
step, and keeping time with a dismal drone chanted by the central
group of boys. Every now and then the boys of the ring bent forward on one knee towards those in the middle, while at the same

[1] " A year in the New Hebrides " by F. A Campbell, p. 108. The drums are placed erect
in the earth.

[2] Mosely's "Notes by a Naturalist on the 'Challenger,'" p. 471.

time they clapped their hands and made a peculiar noise between a
hiss and a sneeze : the chant then became more enlivening and the
dancing more spirited. On the following day the women of the
village took part in a dance which was very similar to that of the
boys, except that there was no central group, and that they wore
bunches of large beans around the left ankle which made a rattling
noise when they tapped the ground at every other step with the
left foot. Bishop Selwyn, to whom I was indebted for the opportunity of witnessing these dances in the village of Gaeta, informed
me that in the Florida Islands, dancing is often more or less of a
profession, troupes of dancers making lengthened tours through the
different islands of this sub-group.

During a great feast that was held in the island of Treasury,
the following dance was performed. Between thirty and forty
women and girls stood in a ring around a semi-circular pit, 5 feet
across, which was sunk about 4 feet in the ground. A board, which
was fixed in the pit about half way down, covered it in with the
exception of a notch at its border. On this board stood two women,
and as they danced they stamped with their feet, producing a dull
hollow sound, to which the women of the circle timed their dancing,
which consisted in bending their bodies slightly forward, gently
swaying from side to side, and raising their feet alternately. All
the while, the dancers sang in a spirited style different native airs.
Now and then, a pair of women would dance slowly round outside
the circle, holding before them their folded pandanus mats which
all the performers carried.[1]

I was present at a dance given on one occasion at Alu, prepara-
tory to a great feast which was about to be held. Soon after sunset
the natives began to assemble on the beach, and when Gorai, the

---

[1] The employment of a hole in the ground as a resonator does not appear to be common.
Mr. Mosely in his "Notes by a Naturalist," p. 309, refers to a somewhat similar use of holes
in the ground by the Fijians who place a log-drum of light wood over three holes and strike
it with a wooden mallet.

chief, arrived on the scene, between thirty and forty men arranged
themselves in a circle, each carrying his pan-pipe. They began by
playing an air in slow time, accompanying the music by a slight
swaying motion of the body, and by alternately raising each foot.
Then the notes became more lively and the movements of the
dancers more brisk. The larger pipes took the part of the bass in
a rude but harmonious symphony, whilst the monotonous air was
repeated without much variation in the higher key of the smaller
instruments. At times one of the younger men stopped in the
centre of the ring, tomahawk in hand, and whilst he assumed a
half-stooping posture, with his face looking upwards, the musicians
dwelt on the same note which became gradually quicker and louder,
whilst the dancing became more brisk, until, when the tip-toe of
expectation was apparently reached, and one was beginning to feel
that something ought to happen, the man in the centre who had
been hitherto motionless, swung back a leg, stuck his tomahawk in
the ground, and one's feelings were relieved by the dull monotone
suddenly breaking off into a lively native air. . . On another occasion, I was present at a funeral or mourning dance, which was held
in connection with the death of the principal wife of the Alu chief.
It will be found described on page 48.

I will conclude this chapter by alluding to a favourite game of
the Treasury boys which reminded me somewhat of our English
game of peg-tops. An oval pebble about two inches long is placed
on a leaf on the ground. Each boy then takes a similar pebble,
around which a piece of twine is wound; and standing about eight
feet away, he endeavours in the following manner to throw it so as
to fall on the pebble on the ground. The end of the twine is held
between his fingers; and as the twine uncoils, he jerks it backwards
and brings his pebble with considerable force on top of the other.

CHAPTER VIII

IN the eastern islands of the Solomon Group there is a considerable uniformity in the construction of the canoe. " Dug-out " canoes are rarely to be seen, except in the sheltered waters of some such harbour as that of Makira, when they are provided with outriggers. In the case of the built canoes, outriggers are not employed, and, in truth, the general absence of outriggers is characteristic of this group. The small-sized canoe, which is in common use amongst the natives of St. Christoval and the adjacent islands, measures fifteen or sixteen feet in length and carries three men. The side is built of two planks; whilst two narrower planks form the rounded bottom. Both stem and stern are prolonged upwards into beaks which are rudely carved ; whilst the gunwale towards either end is ornamented with representations both of fishes, such as sharks and bonitos, and of sea-birds. The planks are sewn together, and the seams are covered over with a resinous substance that is obtained from the fruit of the *Parinarium laurinum* which is a common tree throughout the group. This resinous material takes some weeks to dry, when it becomes dark and hard.

Of the larger canoes, which are similarly constructed, I will take as the type the war-canoe. Its length is usually from 35 to 40 feet : its sides are of three planks ; and the keel is flat, the stem and stern being continued upwards in the form of beaks. Native decorative talent is brought into play in the decoration of the war-canoe. Its sides are inlaid with pieces, usually triangular in form, of the pearl-shell of commerce (*Meleagrina margaritifera*) ; and the small and large *opercula* belonging to shells of the *Turbinidæ* with flat spiral discs produced by grinding down ordinary Cone-shells (*Conidæ*) are similarly employed. Along the stem and beak there is usually attached a string of the handsome white cowries

(*Ovulum ovum*), or of the pretty white *Natica* (*Natica mamilla*). In the island of Simbo or Eddystone, where these shells are used in a similar manner to decorate the large canoes, the white cowry marks the canoes of the chiefs; whilst the *Natica* shell decorates those of the rest of the people.

The pretty little outrigger canoes of Makira on the St. Christoval coast are only nine inches across; and the native sits on a board, resting on the gunwales of his small craft. From one side there stretch out two slender poles four or five feet in length and supporting at their outer ends a long wooden float which runs parallel with the canoe.

The war-canoes have the reputation amongst resident traders of being good sea-boats. They frequently make the passage between Malaita and Ugi, traversing a distance of about thirty miles exposed to the full force of the Pacific swell. A similarly exposed but much longer passage of ninety miles is successfully accomplished by the war-canoes of Santa Catalina, when the natives of this small island pay their periodical visits to a friendly tribe on the coast of Malaita.

Skilfully managed, even the smaller canoes, which carry two or three persons, will behave well in a moderately heavy sea. I frequently used them and had practical experience of the dexterity with which they are handled. On one occasion I was coasting along the west side of the island of Simbo in an overladen canoe; and there was just enough " lop " and swell to make the chances even as to whether we should have to swim for it or not. It was astonishing to see the various manœuvres employed by my natives to keep our little craft afloat—now smoothing off with the blade of the paddle the top of the wave as it rose to the gunwale, now dodging the swell and taking full advantage of its onward roll, now putting a leg over each side to increase the stability of the canoe; by such devices, in addition to continuous baling, I managed to escape the unpleasantness of a ducking.

Although the larger canoes of the Solomon Islanders are apparently suited to the requirements of the natives, yet the want of an outrigger must be often felt, especially in making the unprotected sea passages from one island to another. The natives of Bougainville Straits who, as referred to below, occasionally fit their war-canoes, when heavy laden, with temporary outriggers of stout bamboo poles, must evidently be aware of the deficiencies of their canoes, unless thus provided: yet for some reason or other they make

no general use of this contrivance. Bishop Patteson in 1866 was
surprised to see on the St. Christoval coast an outrigger canoe which
had been built by the natives after the model of a canoe that had
been drifted over from Santa Cruz some years before.[1] He says that
the natives found it more serviceable than their own canoes for
catching large fish : yet in 1882 after a lapse of sixteen years, we
found no signs of this style of canoe having been adopted by the St.
Christoval natives. It seems to me that the explanation of the outrigger canoe not being generally employed by the natives of these
islands lies in the arrangement of the larger islands of this group in
a double line enclosing a comparatively sheltered sea 350 miles in
length, which is, to a great extent, protected from the ocean swell.
Thus, the head-hunting voyages of the New Georgia natives to the
eastward, which may extend to Malaita 150 miles distant, are
entirely confined to these sheltered waters. The passages between
Malaita and the eastern islands, which I have referred to above, are,
however, in great part exposed ; but they are only undertaken in
very settled weather.

On account of the frequent communication which is kept up
between the different islands of Bougainville Straits, where open-sea
passage of from 15 to 25 miles have to be performed, the larger
canoes are in more common use and in greater number than in the
eastern islands of the group. These large canoes vary in length between 40 and 50 feet, are between $3\frac{1}{2}$ and 4 feet in beam, can carry
from 18 to 25 men, and are paddled double-banked. They are stoutly
built with three lines of side-planking and two narrow planks forming the bottom of the canoe : all the planks are bevelled off at their
edges and are brought, or rather sewn, together by narrow strips of
the slender stems of a pretty climbing fern (*Lygonia* sp.), the
"asama" of the natives, which have the pliancy and strength of
rattan. The seams are caulked with the same resinous material that
is employed for this purpose in the eastern islands, and is obtained
from the brown nearly spherical fruits of the "tita" of the native,
the *Parinarium laurinum* of the botanist.[2]

The natives of Bougainville Straits do not decorate their canoes
to any great extent ; and in this they differ from those of St.
Christoval, who, as I have remarked, ornament the prows and gun-

---

[1] "Life of Bishop Patteson," p. 126 (S.P.C.K. pub.).

[2] The resin of this fruit is used for the same purpose in Isabel and probably throughout the
group. It is similarly used in the Admiralty Islands. Narrative of the "Challenger," page 719.

wales with carvings of fish and sea-birds, and inlay the sides with pearl-shell. The stems and sterns of the large canoes of Faro and of Choiseul Bay are continued up in the form of high beaks, which rise 12 to 15 feet above the water. I was at first at a loss to find the explanation of these high beaks, which give the canoes of Bougainville Straits such a singular appearance. In the narratives of the voyages of Bougainville and Surville who observed those high-beaked canoes, the former at Choiseul Bay in 1768,[1] and the latter at Port Praslin, in Isabel, in 1769,[2] we find the explanation required, which is, that these high prows, when the canoe is turned end on to the enemy, afford shelter against arrows and other missiles.

For sea-passages, greater stability is sometimes given to the large canoes of the Straits, by temporarily fitting them with an outrigger on each side, in the form of a bundle of stout bamboos lashed to the projecting ends of three bamboo poles placed across the gunwales of the canoe. The large canoes, in crossing from one island to the other in the Straits, employ often a couple of small lug-sails which are made from calico or light canvas obtained from the traders. I never saw any sails of native material: but it was worthy of remark that in 1792, when Dentrecasteaux approached close to the west coast of the Shortland Islands, he noticed "large canoes under sail," which, to quote directly from the narrative, "annonçoient une navigation active dans cet archipel d'Iles extrêmement petites."[3] Why the natives of these Straits no longer employ sails of their own manufacture, it is difficult to say. The very recent introduction of trade calico cannot have caused them to be set aside for those of the new material, since when a native wants to have a sail, and has no calico, he has no recourse to sails of his own manufacture. Rather, it would appear, that the canoes under sail, which navigated these Straits a century ago, belonged to a people more enterprising than the present inhabitants of these islands.

To the stem of the canoe, just above the water-line, is sometimes attached a small misshapen wooden figure, which is the little tutelar deity that sees the hidden rock, and gives warning of an approaching foe. One of these figures is shown in the accompanying illustration.

[1] "Voyage autour du Monde : " 2nd edit. augment. Paris, 1772 ; Vol. II., p. 187. In this work there is an engraving of one of these canoes.

[2] " Discoveries of the French to the South-East of New Guinea," by M. F eurieu. London, 1791 (p. 139).

[3] " Voyage de Dentrecasteaux," redigé par. M. de Rossel, Paris, 1808 : tom, 1, p. 117.

They are similarly employed by the natives of the adjacent island of Simbo, and of other islands in this part of the group. Often they are double-headed, so that the little deity may keep a watchful look-out astern as well as ahead ; and then they are placed on the tops of the high beaks of the Faro canoes. Probably the Chinese custom of painting eyes on the sides of the bows of the junks, and the similar practice of the Maltese, in the case of their boats, may date back to the little gods of wood that were attached to the bows and stems of the canoes of their barbarous predecessors. The origin of the figure-heads of our ships may perhaps be traced back to times of savagery when a similar superstitious practice prevailed.

" Dug-out" canoes are only to be found in the sheltered waters of Treasury Harbour. They are from 16 to 18 feet long, are provided with an outrigger, and are so narrow that the occupant sits on a board placed on the gunwales with only his feet and legs inside the canoe. In the quiet waters of the anchorage at Simbo, the natives make use of a raft of poles lashed together somewhat after the manner of a catamaran, such as I have seen on the coast of Formosa.

A few remarks on the mode of paddling, and on the paddles employed, may be here fitting. The long tapering blade,[1] which is in common use in the eastward islands, gives place in Bougainville Straits to the oval and sub-circular blades. All the paddles which I saw had cross-handles. Those used by the women of the Straits are unusually light, more finished, and are sometimes decorated with patterns in red and black. According to the length of the journey, one or other of two styles of progression is adopted. In short distances, they often proceed by a succession of spurts with a stroke of 60 and more to the minute, each spurt lasting a few minutes, and being followed by a short interval of rest. In longer distances they employ a slower stroke of from 40 to 50 to the minute, which is varied by occasional spurts. On one occasion when taking a journey of 12 miles in a war canoe, I was much struck with the different kinds of strokes by which my crew of eighteen men varied their exertions. They usually paddled along easily at about 50 strokes to the minute : but every ten or fifteen minutes they began a series of spurts, each spurt beginning with a short sharp stroke of about 60 to the minute, and passing into a slow strong stroke of about 28 to the minute. After a succession of these spurts, which occupied altogether about five minutes, they settled down again into their

[1] See illustration.

previous easy stroke of 50 to the minute. Frequent stoppages occur during the course of a long journey, either for enjoying a chew of the betel-nut or for smoking a pipe; and the average speed, from this reason, would not exceed three miles an hour, whilst a day's run, between daylight and dusk, in fine weather would be from 25 to 30 miles.

When a corpse is being transported in a canoe to its last resting-place in the sea by the natives of the Shortlands, they adopt a funeral stroke, pausing between each stroke of the paddle, and by a slight back-water movement partly arresting the progress of the canoe. I remember on one occasion, whilst watching a large canoe starting from Ugi to the opposite coast of St. Christoval, remarking their singular style of paddling. At every other stroke each man raised his arm and paddle much higher in the air, and gave a vigorous dig into the water, a very effective style as regards speed, and one likely to impress a timid enemy with fear. . . . Before leaving this subject, I should refer to the paddling-posture of these natives. All of them in the different islands we visited squat down with their legs crossed, facing the bow. The New Guinea practice of standing up to paddle a canoe did not come under my observation except in the case of outrigger canoes, and in such canoes it was not the rule. I should infer that the posture of sitting or standing to paddle a canoe varies in accordance with the use of or non-employment of an outrigger. If, as in the case of the Solomon Island canoes, outriggers are rarely used, then the sitting posture will be found to be the one adopted, since the unaided stability of the canoe does not permit of the standing posture. If, on the other hand, outriggers are usually employed, it follows that, as in certain parts of New Guinea, the more effective posture of standing is preferred.

As fish form a staple diet of a large proportion of these islanders, much ingenuity is shown in the methods devised for catching them. In the eastern part of the archipelago, kite-fishing is commonly employed. A kite[1] is flown in the air from the end of a canoe, and to it a fishing-line is attached in place of the usual tail. Whilst the man in the canoe paddles slowly ahead, the movement of the kite whisks the bait about on the surface of the water; and when the fish bites, the kite goes down. Instead of a hook and bait, the natives usually employ for this mode of fishing some stout spider-

---

[1] Some of these kites, which I saw, had a form rudely representing a bird with expanded wings. Others had a squarish form and were made of palm leaf.

web, which gets entangled around the teeth and snout of the fish, and can be used several times. The explanation of this plan of catching fish is probably as follows. The kite swaying in the air offers some resemblance to an aquatic bird hovering over the water where a shoal of small fish occurs. It thus attracts the larger fish, who are said to follow the movements of these birds, and are thus guided in the pursuit of the smaller fry. It is with this object that the natives of the Society Group tie bunches of feathers to the extremities of the long-curved poles which, projecting from the fore-part of the canoe, support the lines.[1] As bearing on this subject, I may remark that it is not uncommon in these seas to observe porpoises, large fish, and sea-birds joining together in the pursuit of small fry. On one occasion, when in my Rob Roy canoe, I got into the thick of the fray. A large number of sea-birds were hovering over the water, which was alive with fish, about a foot in length, which, in pursuit of small fry, were themselves pursued by a shoal of porpoises, and were pecked at by the birds as, in their endeavour to escape, they leapt out of the water. It was a lively spectacle. The fish jumped out of the water all around me, whilst the birds hovering within reach of my paddle swooped down on them ; and the huge porpoises, joining lazily in the sport, rose quietly to the surface within a few feet of the canoe, showed their dorsal fins, and dived again in pursuit of their prey. I stupidly fired three shots with my revolver into the hovering flock of birds ; but it was not until after the third report that they temporarily suspended the chase. . . . Another common method of fishing in the eastern islands, which resembles in its idea that of the kite-fishing, consists in the use of a float of wood about three feet in length and rather bigger than a walking-stick. It is weighted by a stone at one end, so that it floats upright in the water, a fishing-line with the spider-web bait being attached to its lower end. The upper end of the float, which is out of the water, is rudely cut in imitation of a wading-bird ; and here we have the same idea exhibited which I have described above in the case of kite-fishing, the figure of the bird being *supposed* to attract the larger fish. There is, however, this difference. A glance at one of these floats, one of which is figured elsewhere, will convince anyone that a fish is not likely to be deceived by such a sorry representation of a bird. Doubtless we have here an instance of the survival of a more effective method of fishing, in which the idea has

[1] Ellis's "Polynesian Researches," Vol. I., p. 149-50.

been retained, but the utility has been lost. This plan is in fact nothing more than the employment of a float, which is thrown into the water by the fisherman, who follows it up in his canoe and looks out for its bob.

In the eastern islands the fishing spear is frequently employed. With this weapon in his hand, the native wades in the shallow water on the flats of the reefs, and hurls it at any passing fish. The night-time is often chosen for this mode of fishing. A party of natives provided with torches, spread themselves along the edge of the reef and stand ready to throw their spears as the fish dart by them. During the day, when the reef-flats at low-tide are covered only by a small depth of water, the fishermen advance in a semicircle until a fish is observed, when the two wings close in, and the fish is sur-rounded. The kind of fish-spear which they use much resembles that which Mr. Ellis describes in his account of the Society Islands.[1] As shown in the engraving (p. 155), the head of the fish-spear is com-posed of five fore-shafts of hard wood, notched at their sides, and ar-ranged around a similar fore-shaft. These are bound together, and the whole is fitted into the end of a stout bamboo, giving the weapon a total length of about seven feet . . . . The fish-spear does not appear to be so commonly used by the natives of Bougainville Straits. There, its place is often taken by the bow and arrow, which are weapons that are not in use amongst the natives of St. Christoval and the adjacent islands at the eastern end of the group.

I should here remark that, when fishing on the reefs, natives are sometimes struck by the gar-fish with such force that they die from the wound. The possibility of this occurrence has recently been doubted. But that such is the case, we incidentally learned from the natives of the Shortlands. The people of Wano, on the north coast of St. Christoval, believe that the ghosts which haunt the sea, cause the flying-fish and the gar-fish to dart out of the water and to strike men in the canoes; and they hold that any man thus struck will die.[2] This superstitious belief could only have arisen from the circumstance of natives having met their death in this manner; and it is probable that in this respect the larger flying-fish would be quite as much to be feared as the gar-fish. Mr.

---

[1] " Polynesian Researches," vol. I., p. 143.
[2] " Religious Beliefs and Practices in Melanesia," by the Rev. R. H. Codrington, M.A. Journal of Anthropological Institute, vol. X.

Moseley, in his "Notes by a Naturalist," p. 480, refers to such
an event as not of uncommon occurrence in some of the Pacific
Islands.[1]

The material, from which the natives of Bougainville Straits
manufacture the twine for their fishing-nets and lines, is usually
supplied by the delicate fibres lining the bark of the young branches
of a stout climber, which is known to the natives as the "awi-sulu."
This climber, which is probably a species of *Lyonsia*, has a main
stem of the size of a man's leg, which embraces a tree, whilst it
sends its offshoots for a distance of some 40 or 50 feet along the
ground. It is the delicate fibres lining the inside of the skin of the
young procumbent branches that the native selects for his purpose.
By scraping the thin bark or skin with the edge of a pearl-shell,
the fibres are first cleared of other material : they are then dried in
the sun ; and when dry, they are arranged in small strands, three of
which are twisted together into a fine line by rolling them with the
palm of the hand on the thigh. The natives sometimes obtain the
material for their nets and lines from the common littoral tree, the
Hibiscus tiliaceus, which they name "dakatako."

In making their nets, our common netting-stitch is employed,
the needle being of plain wood, 18 inches long, and forked at each
end ; whilst the mesh employed is a piece of tortoise-shell, having
for a width of an inch a length of 2½ inches. The method of netting
familiar to ourselves appears to be generally employed amongst the
native races of this portion of the globe. We learn from the Rev.
George Turner that in Samoa the same stitch and the same form of
needle are employed which are in use in Europe.[2] The natives of
Port Moresby, in New Guinea, net "so precisely in our mode that
the seamen of H.M.S. "Basilisk" took up their shuttles and went on
with their work."[3] The needle employed at Redscar Bay, on the
coast of the same island, is more like our own, the mesh being of
tortoise-shell, two to three inches long.[4] When Captain Bowen, of
the ship "Albemarle," was visited in 1791 by some natives of the
Solomon Islands who came off to him in their canoes, he thought he
had found in the apparently European workmanship of their nets a

---

[1] *Vide* also "Nature," index of vol. XXVIII., for some further correspondence on this
subject.
[2] "Nineteen Years in Polynesia" (London, 1861), p. 272.
[3] Moresby's "New Guinea" (1876), p. 156.
[4] These specimens are in the British Museum Ethnological collection.

clue to the fate of La Pérouse, a very pardonable error which receives its explanation from the above facts.[1]

Fishing on the reef-flats with large hand-nets is a common occupation of the men in the islands of Bougainville Straits. Some five or six men form a party, each man carrying a pair of long hand-nets in which the netting is stretched on a long bamboo some 20 feet in length and bent like a bow, as shown in the accompanying figure. The fishing party wade about on the flat near the edge of the reef, each man being about 20 paces apart, and dragging behind him a pair of these clumsy-looking nets, one in each hand. When a fish is perceived they close round; and every man spreads out his nets, one on each side like a pair of wings, thus covering an extent of some 40 feet. By skilfully dropping his nets, when it makes a rush in his direction, the native secures the fish, which, dashing head first against one of the nets, gets its snout caught in the meshes; and a couple of blows on the head complete the capture. I have seen fish of the size of an ordinary bass caught in this manner. Smaller nets, 4 to 6 feet in length, with a finer mesh, are used for catching fish of less size. The large hand-net is known as the "sorau," and the small hand-net as the "saiaili." Such is one of the commonest methods of fishing in the Straits. For this purpose, fishing parties often visit the uninhabited small islands and coral islets that lie off the coasts. There they erect temporary sheds and remain for one or two weeks. In the numerous uninhabited islets and small islands which I visited, I frequently came on the temporary habitations erected by fishing parties; whilst propped up against the trees were the long bamboo poles on which the nets are stretched. The natives of St. Christoval and the adjacent islands employ a similar method in fishing on the reef-flats. Fishing parties often spend a week or two on the small islands and reefs which lie

[1] Dillon's "Discovery of the Fate of La Pérouse" (1829), vol I., p. lxix.

off the St. Christoval coast; thus the men of Wano visit for this
purpose the islet of Maoraha, about 12 miles down the coast;
whilst those of Sulagina cross over to the Three Sisters, which are
about the same distance away.

Dip-nets, such as I have seen in common use on the banks of
the Chinese rivers, are here employed, though on a smaller scale, for
catching small fish. They are usually 7 or 8 feet across, and are
stretched on two crossed bamboos. Seine-nets, much prized by the
natives on account of the labour expended in making them, and
buoyed up with floats of the square fruits of the *Barringtonia
speciosa*, are commonly employed. There are other modes of net-
fishing, of which I am ignorant, some of which probably came under
the notice of the officers of the survey: and I hope that in reading
these remarks they may be induced to supplement them with additional information.

The fish-hooks employed vary in form and workmanship in
different parts of the group. In the sheltered harbour of Makira,
the natives whiff in small outrigger-canoes for a small fish of the
size of a smelt, using very fine lines and small delicately made hooks
of mother-of-pearl. During our stay at the island of Simbo or
Eddystone, one of the principal articles of exchange between the
natives and ourselves was a somewhat clumsy kind of fish-hook
used for catching large fish. The shank is of pearl-shell cut in the
shape of the body of a small fish, 2 to 2½ inches long, and rather less
than half an inch wide. The hook itself, which is destitute of barbs
and is made of tortoise-shell, is bound by strong twine to the tail-
end of the shank. Considerable labour must be expended in making
one of these hooks : but so eager were the natives for tobacco, that
we were able to obtain them for small pieces of this article which
could not have been worth more than half a farthing. It is worthy
of note that in the island of Treasury, about 80 miles to the north-
west, these hooks are not made by the natives, who were anxious to
obtain from us those which we had brought from Simbo. Very
similar, though larger, hooks are used by the natives of other Pacific
groups; amongst them I may refer to those employed by the
Society Islanders[1] for catching dolphins, albicores, and bonitos.
These hooks, wherever they are used, as I need scarcely add, answer
the purpose of both hook and bait. The fish-hooks of European
manufacture, which are one of the articles used in trading with the

[1] Ellis's "Polynesian Researches," vol. I. p. 146.

natives, are in demand in many islands, though not in all. In some islands, in fact, the native fish-hook is preferred.

The various ingenious methods of ensnaring and decoying fish, which are employed by the natives of this archipelago, would alone afford, to a true enthusiast in the sport of fishing, materials for a small volume. A plan which I saw employed at Ugi consisted in tying a living fish to the end of a bamboo float and using it as a decoy for other fish. The fisherman repairs to the reef when it is covered by a depth of between 2 and 3 feet of water. Placing the fish and bamboo float in the water, he follows them up either in his canoe or on foot. The fish swims along, drawing the bamboo float after it: it soons decoys some other fish from its retreat, when the fisherman watches his opportunity and catches his fish in a hand-net which he carries with him.

A singular mode of fishing, which Mr. Stephens of Ugi described to me as being sometimes employed in that part of the group, may be here alluded to. A rock, where fish resort, which lies 3 or 4 feet below the surface, is first selected. On the surface of the water is placed a ring of some supple stem so as to include within its circumference the rock beneath. No fish on the rock will pass under this ring, which is gradually contracted in size until the fish become crowded together, when they are scooped up with a hand-net.

The following ingenious snare was employed on one occasion by my natives in Treasury, when I was anxious to obtain for Dr. Günther some small fish that frequented one of the streams on the north side of the island. I was very desirous to have some of these fish, and my natives were equally anxious to display their ingenuity in catching them. They first bent a pliant switch into an oval hoop, about a foot in length, over which they spread a covering of a stout spider-web which was found in the wood hard by. Having placed this hoop on the surface of the water, buoying it up on two light sticks, they shook over it a portion of a nest of ants, which formed a large kind of tumour on the trunk of a neighbouring tree, thus covering the web with a number of the struggling young insects. This snare was then allowed to float down the stream, when the little fish, which were between 2 and 3 inches long, commenced jumping up at the white bodies of the ants from underneath the hoop, apparently not seeing the intervening web on which they lay, as it appeared nearly transparent in the water. In a short time one of the small fish succeeded in getting its snout and gills entangled in the web, when a native at once waded in, and placing his hand under the entangled fish secured the prize. With two of these. web-hoops we caught nine or ten of these little fish in a quarter of an hour.

As in other Pacific groups, the natives sometimes catch fish by throwing small bits of some poisonous fruit on the water, when in a short time the fish rise dead to the surface. The crushed kernels of the fruits of the common littoral *Barringtonia* (*B. speciosa*) are thus employed by the natives. I tried them on one occasion in a fresh-water lake in Stirling Island, which abounded with fish, but after the lapse of two or three hours, no dead fish appeared at the surface.

The use of dynamite for destroying fish, by white men in the group, has led to its occasional employment for a similar purpose by the natives, whenever white men have been thoughtless enough to give them this substance. In August, 1882, I visited a village in the Bauro district on the north coast of St. Christoval, which had lost its chief, a few days before, from an injury to the hand, resulting from an accidental explosion of dynamite whilst fishing. Such occurrences must not be uncommon in these and other islands. In the previous April, we met with a native teacher at Mboli Harbour who had lost one of his hands from a similar cause.[1] At the end of May, 1884, I removed the left hand of Captain Smith, the master of the labour-schooner "Lavina," who had received a very serious injury of the hand whilst fishing with dynamite on the coast of Malaita. Some of the fresh-water fish which I sent to Dr. Günther were obtained in this way through the kindness of Mr. Curzon-Howe, the Government agent of the "Lavina;" and as I witnessed the operation, I am in a position to pronounce on the hazardous nature of the mode in which the dynamite was employed. . . . . With reference to the natives, there are two very obvious reasons why this explosive substance should not be permitted to get into their hands, even if we disregard the hazard that would attend its use. In the first place, they might employ it against white men and against their fellows; and in the next place, its employment for obtaining fish would tend to encourage the already too indolent habits of these islanders.

I pass on now to the subject of pig-hunting in these islands.

---

[1] Since writing the above, I have learned from my friend, Dr. Luther, late of H.M.S "Dart," that he had to amputate on two occasions in the cases of natives who had sustained severe injuries of the hand whilst fishing with dynamite.

Wild pigs occurred in most, if not all, of the islands which we visited. I was frequently warned by the natives, when undertaking a solitary excursion, to look out for the boars, who attain a ferocity which, on account of their powerful curved tusks, it would be dangerous to provoke unarmed. On more than one occasion when alone, I came unexpectedly in the bush on one of these boars, who are in appearance by no means despicable antagonists. When they stand their ground, it is necessary to be prepared for their onset; but as a rule they only indicate their presence by the noise which they make when scampering away. In the islands of Bougainville Straits, where there are numerous plantations of sago palms, the wild pigs are very fond of the fruit of this palm before the albumen of the seed attains its stony hardness. They often select as their retreats the hollow trunks of the palms which have been felled and emptied of the sago. Their habit of frequenting the plantations of sago palms, and of feasting on the remains of the palms that have been lately cut down and the pith removed, was observed by Captain Thomas Forrest in the island of Gilolo, in the Indian Archipelago.[1] On the approach of any special occasion of feasting, pig-hunting becomes a necessary sport with the natives; but in addition, they frequently take to it for the sake of replenishing their larders. With his spear and a couple of dogs, a man is usually successful in getting his pig. The dogs bring the animal to bay, when he is speared by the hunter, who, if alone, at once sets to work to quarter and roast his quarry, and thus considerably lightens the weight he has to carry back. During my excursions, my natives used to frequently leave me when their dogs had roused a pig in the bush; and on one occasion, when, much to my indignation, they had been absent for an hour, they came back triumphantly with two large boars. Captain Forrest, in his account of his voyage to New Guinea, gives an illustration of " Papua men in their canoes hunting wild hogs "[2] off the island of Morty, near the large island of Gilolo. These men are represented with the spear, bow, and arrow, and a dog. Such a method of hunting pigs never came under my notice in the Solomon Islands and must necessarily be rarely employed.

Wild dogs are numerous in the bush in the interior of Alu. They never attack the natives or the pigs and, as they always slink away when alarmed, they are not often seen. They subsist on the

---

[1] "A Voyage to New Guinea and the Moluccas." London, 1779 (p. 39).
[2] Ibid., Plate XI. of book of plates.

opossums (*Cuscus*), waiting to catch them at the foot of the trunks of the trees as they descend to the ground at nightfall. When I was away on an excursion with Gorai the Alu chief, the native dogs that were with us ran down a wild dog and worried it to death. I came in at the death, and was not very much pleased with the spectacle which afforded much amusement to Gorai and his men. The unfortunate dog was apparently of the native breed. How these animals have come to prefer this mode of life I could not learn.

My native companions during my excursions rarely returned to their homes without bringing back an opossum (*Cuscus*). Usually this animal was caught without much trouble, as it slumbers during the day and may be then surprised amongst the foliage of the tree where it finds its home. Sometimes, however, when the keen eyes of my natives discovered an opossum amongst the leafy branches overhead, we were enlivened by an exciting hunt. On such occasions, one man climbs the tree in which the animal is esconced whilst three or four other men climb the trees immediately around. By dint of shouting and shaking the branches, the opossum is started from its retreat, and then the sport commences. This clumsy looking creature displays great agility in springing from branch to branch, and even from tree to tree. Suspended by its prehensile tail to the branch above, the *Cuscus* first tests the firmness of the branch next below, before it finally intrusts its weight to its support. It runs up and down the stouter limbs of the tree like a squirrel; but its activity and cunning are most displayed in passing from the branches of one tree to those of another. At length, scared by the shaking of the branches, and by the cries of the natives who have clambered out on the limbs as far as they can get with safety, the opossum runs out towards the extremity of the limb, proceeding cautiously to the very terminal branchlets, until the weight of its body bends down the slender extremities of the branch, and it hangs suspended by its tail in mid-air about ten feet below. The gentle swaying of the branches in the wind, aided probably by its own movements, swings the opossum to and fro, until it approaches within grasp of the foliage of the adjoining tree. Then the clever creature, having first ascertained the strength of its new support, uncoils its tail. Up goes the branch with a swish when relieved of its weight; and in a similar manner the opossum swings by its tail from the slender branches of the tree to which it has now transferred its weight. Finally the opossum reaches the ground, where its awkward movements render it an easy capture. It is then tied to a stick and carried home alive on the shoulder of a native.

The *Cuscus* is a common article of food with these islanders; and in some islands, as in Simbo or Eddystone, it is kept as a pet by the natives. Out of seven opossums that were kept as pets on board the "Lark," all died within a few weeks, being apparently unable to withstand captivity. Most of them, however, were young. The cause of the death of one of them was rather singular. Immediately after its death the skin of the animal was literally covered with small ticks about the size of a pin's head and distended with blood, whilst the body presented the blanched appearance of an animal bled to death. It had been ailing for a day or two before and was incessantly drinking all liquids it could get, even its own urine: but the ticks had not been sufficiently numerous to be observed; and in fact they appeared to have covered the animal in the course of a single night. As I was informed by the natives of Simbo, these animals subsist on the shoots and young leaves of the trees: on board the "Lark" they cared for little else than bananas. They make a curious clicking noise when eating, and often hold the substance in their fore-paws. When taken out in the day-time from their boxes they were half asleep, and at once tried to get out of the bright light into the shade. In the night-time they were very restless in their prisons, making continual efforts to escape between the bars, and as soon as they were let out they moved about with much activity. The older animals are sometimes rather fierce. One of them which belonged to the men used to spend a considerable portion of its time up aloft; and, when in want of food, it would descend the rigging and go down to the lower deck. Their naked tails have a cold clammy feeling; and with them they were in the habit of swinging themselves from any object. When the *Cuscus* was about to be taken up by its master, it moored itself to the nearest object by means of its tail. It always descended a rope head first, but kept its tail twined round the rope during its descent so as to be able to withdraw itself at once if necessary, the tail supporting the greater portion of its weight.

Although the natives, who accompanied me in my various excursions, usually displayed their skill in following a straight course through a pathless wood where they could only see a few yards on either side of them, yet on more than one occasion they were, to use

a nautical phrase, completely out in their reckoning, and I had to
bring my compass into use and become the guide myself in order to
avoid passing the night in the bush. When in the interior of the
north-west part of Alu accompanied by Gorai, the chief, and a
number of his men, I was astonished at the readiness with which, in
the absence of any tracks, they found their way to the coast. Gorai
led the way; and on my asking him how he managed to know the
right direction in a thick forest with neither sun nor trade-wind to
guide him, he merely remarked that he " saveyed bush," and pointing with his hand in a particular direction, he informed me that
" Mono stopped there," Mono being the native name for Treasury.
There was a little uncertainty among the natives as to whether the
old chief was guiding us aright; but there was no hesitation on the
part of Gorai, whose course as tested by my compass was always in
the same direction; he, however, disdained the use of the compass
and ultimately brought us back to the coast. When passing
through a district with which he is but little acquainted, the native
frequently bends the branches of the bushes as he passes, in order
to strike the same path on the way back. He must be frequently
guided in his course through the forest by noticing the bearing of
the sun and the swaying of the upper branches of the trees in the
trade-wind, guides which were often employed by myself when
alone in the bush: but when, as not uncommonly happens, there is
such a dense screen of foliage overhead, that neither the sun nor the
upper branches of the trees can be seen, he must employ other
means of guidance. Rude tracks, usually traversed the least frequented districts of the islands which we visited; and their per-
sistence appeared to be sometimes due to the fact that they were
used by the wild pigs.

Fallen trees commonly obstruct the most frequented paths in the
vicinity of villages: and there they remain until decay removes
them, for the native has no idea of doing an act for the public
weal: with him, in such and kindred matters, what is everybody's
business is nobody's. Captain Macdonald, in his capacity as a chief
in Santa Anna, adopted the serviceable method of employing
natives, who had committed petty offences, in making good walks
in the vicinity of the houses of the white residents. The example
however was not followed by the natives for the approaches to their
own village of Sapuna. Being quite content with their narrow foot-
paths, they probably could not understand that whatever contributed
to the public good was also to the advantage of the individual.

CHAPTER IX

PREVALENT DISEASES.

I HAVE previously remarked that in these islands the duties of the sorcerer and the medicine-man are frequently combined. The same man, who can remove a disease by exorcism and by ill-wishing can bring sickness and death upon any obnoxious individual, may also be able in the estimation of the people to procure a fair wind for an intended voyage, or to bring about rain in a season of drought. I had more than one opportunity of satisfying myself of the fact that the medicine-man often trades upon the credulity of his patients, and that he is himself aware that all his charms and incantations are mere trickery. In Santa Anna his services are often employed to procure the recovery of a sick man, and by some form of incantation he pretends to appease the anger of the offended spirit to whom the illness is attributed. Captain Macdonald, who has long resided in this island, informed me that when on one occasion he had relieved by medicine the sufferings of a native who had in vain employed the exorcisms of the village physician to effect his cure, the success of his treatment did not detract in any way from the reputation of the medicine-man, who, having informed himself of the progress of the patient, after Captain Macdonald had given his remedy, foretold his recovery and took to himself the whole credit of the cure.

In the island of Ugi chunam (burnt lime) is one of the domestic remedies employed in sickness, being rubbed into the skin of the patient by his friends. The chunam of some men is supposed to be more efficacious than that of others, and messengers may be sent from one end of the island to the other to procure it. One of our Treasury natives, who was employed on board, had a reputation as medicine-man. His method of treatment in the case of one of his own comrades consisted in tying a particular leaf around the limbs and joints to localize the pain, and in striking the affected part with the same leaf. On one occasion this man was himself laid up with a large abscess in the buttock, which he attempted to cure by tying a strip of the leaf around the thigh and by placing another for a few moments over the seat of the abscess. He would not let me do much for him; and from absorption of the purulent matter into the blood, a number of abscesses began to form in other parts of the body which brought him into a serious hectic condition. The poor fellow's cries of "Agai" "Agai," corresponding to our exclamations of pain, made me feel acutely for him; but he placed little faith in our offices, his great desire, as intimated by his frequent cries of "Feli" (Fire), was to be placed beside a large wood fire. He was sent on shore and given in charge of his wife on our arrival off Treasury. When I landed to see him a few hours after, I found him with his wish at last gratified; there he lay beside a roasting fire, the very last condition that seemed likely to promote his recovery. However he slowly regained his health, and I did what I could for him in buying sago and other articles of food from his own people who were not very ready with their supplies for the sick man.

This brings me to the subject of the indifference often displayed towards the sick and invalids. The natives view these things in a very matter-of-fact way. On more than one occasion when in the house of sickness, the son or the brother of the sick man has remarked to me, in the coolest manner, "Him too much sick. I think by-and-by finish;" and it is astonishing to hear of the manner in which they allow the sick to shift for themselves. In the islands of Bougainville Straits the very aged, who are unable to get about or to be of any service to themselves, are placed in a house in which they are left alone although supplied with food; and there they remain until they die. Two old and decrepit men, who were both fast hastening to their ends, being the subjects of chronic lung affections, were placed together in a house in Treasury where they were supplied with food but rarely if ever visited. They were placed there to die as the relations informed us; and there they remained day after day until the end arrived. Mr. Stephens told me that in his island of Ugi, if a cocoa-nut is placed by the side of the sick man, his friends consider they have done all in their power. No attempt is made to alleviate pain, or to soothe by companionship the tedious hours of the sick. He lies deserted on his roughly plaited mat of palm-leaves, in his wretched home where the sunlight rarely enters; and there he awaits, perhaps without regret, his approaching death. When consciousness leaves him, his friends regard him as already dead, attributing the spasmodic breathing and the convulsive efforts of the dying man to the agency of some evil spirit.

The influence of superstition probably explains the indifference which prevails as to the welfare of the sick and aged. Those afflicted with such an infirmity as blindness are kindly treated by their fellows. I was particularly struck, whilst looking on at a feast in the village of Treasury, by the attention that was paid to the wants of a young blind man who sat aloof from the rest. He was blind from his birth, and I particularly pleased him by sitting down beside him and giving him a stick of tobacco.

In the case of those who have received some severe injury, such as a gunshot wound, considerable care is shown by the friends in their welfare. I saw much of the natives who were wounded during the hostilities carried on between the natives of Treasury and the Shortlands, and was astonished at the ease with which they recovered from apparently hopeless injuries. My experience goes to support the opinion laid down by Professor Waitz in his "Anthropology of Primitive Peoples,"[1] that the healing power of nature is greater among savage than among civilized races. The principle of non-interference was literally carried out in defiance of the laws of hygiene and of the experience of modern surgery. After the unfortunate conflict on the islet of Tuluba, off the west coast of Alu, I visited the wounded man and woman who had been brought back to their homes. I found the woman lying in a dingy little house in which I had to stand still for a few minutes before I could see my patient. Five days had elapsed since the fight; and the condition of a wound, which has been left alone for this period in a tropical climate, may be well imagined. She had received a severe tomahawk wound just above the right knee, smashing the bone and implicating the joint. The parts were much swollen and there was profuse suppuration. No attempt had been made to wash the wound, and in consequence it stunk horribly. A few pieces of split bamboo, less than a foot in length, were lashed in a slack fashion around the joint by means of rattan; but they could have given little or no support. Under the couch, which was merely a layer of poles raised about a foot from the ground,

[1] English edition: translated by J. F. Collingwood: London, 1863: p. 126.

were placed hot stones wrapped up in leaves, from which the warmth ascended to the injured limb which was left uncovered and exposed to the flies and other insects. The poor woman was moaning terribly; and her cries of "Agai" were painful to listen to, especially as I was permitted to do but little. They would neither wash nor cover the wound, and persisted in keeping up the hot air treatment by means of the hot stones wrapped in leaves, which were placed under the couch. I pronounced her recovery as hopeless ; and was after a time obliged to discontinue my visits, upon being told by one of the medicine-men that as he could make her well, my presence was not required. I never saw the woman again, but sometime after I learned that she was nearly well.

The man who was wounded at the same time had received a rifle-bullet through the thigh without injuring the bone, and another through the groin. I found his wounds in the same horrible condition, with the wound of exit in the thigh as large as my fist. Nothing whatever had been done except placing hot stones in leaves under the limb on the ground beneath ; and nothing more was done. There the man lay for several weeks with his wounds unwashed and exposed to the air. In course of time he recovered. One of the Treasury natives had been shot by one of his own party, the rifle-bullet passing through the right elbow from behind, and apparently disorganising the joint. I saw him a month after he had received the injury, lying in a very emaciated condition on his couch, with the wounded limb stretched out beside him quite unprotected and displaying an extensive flesh-wound in front of the joint. The hot-stone treatment had been the only one employed. In another month or five weeks he was up and about, but of course with a useless elbow. One of the Alu natives, who had been shot through the left shoulder from behind by the Treasury chief, had nearly recovered when I saw him six or seven weeks after, although the arm was useless.

Reflecting on the hot-stone treatment which the natives employed for these severe injuries, I came to think that it was really efficacious. They said themselves that the hot air eased the pain, and this was probably effected, as I hold, by the warmth relaxing the parts after suppuration had begun and thus assisting the escape of the purulent discharges. The surgeon of our own time may take a hint from this practice of the Solomon Islander. It would certainly scarcely accord with the principles of modern surgery if a

gunshot injury of one of the larger joints was to be treated in one
of our general hospitals by being constantly kept in a current of
heated air, uncovered and even unwashed. The experiment, however, would be worth a trial in cases where amputation is unpractic-
able and where death is the probable result.

It is a common saying amongst white men who have had to deal
with these natives, that when a man makes up his mind to die he
assuredly will, even although apparently in robust health. Such
cases are not unusual on board labour-ships on their way to the
Queensland and Fiji plantations, and they may be regarded as of
the nature of nostalgic melancholy or home-sickness. It is in truth
hard to imagine the train of thoughts which must pass through the
simple mind of a native when his island-home disappears below the
horizon, and he is borne away to a strange land from which, it may
be, some of his acquaintances have never returned. Even the
attractions of the box of trade that his servitude will earn may be
insufficient to keep down the undefined apprehensions which fill his
breast; and the knowledge of the impossibility of seeking his friends
or his island again for what must appear to him an indefinite
period may only serve to strengthen his longing for home. Here
we have that disease with which the army surgeons of Europe were
familiar, and which has been most recently exhibited amongst the
Italian troops stationed at Masowah on the coast of the Red Sea.
It is that "strange disease" which Dr. Livingstone so pathetically
describes in his "Last Journals," as affecting the victims of the
slave-trade in the lake region of Africa. I remember on one occasion, when visiting a labour-vessel that had arrived in Treasury
Harbour, my attention was drawn by the mate to a native of New
Ireland who had eaten little for some days and was looking over
the side of the ship towards the shore in a depressed and moody
manner. I saw that the thoughts of the poor fellow were in reality
far away ; and I passed on to see some of the other sick men. The
next morning this New Ireland native was missing, and in the
evening his body was found washed up on the beach. . . . I
would refer my readers to some interesting remarks on this subject
from the pen of Mr. Romilly,[1] whose official experience in the
Western Pacific enables him to write with authority. The Solomon
Islanders, according to this author, are less affected by this disease
than those of other groups ; whilst the New Hebrides natives

[1] "The Western Pacific and New Guinea." London, 1886: pp. 16, 177. .

appear to be most subject to it. Not only do natives often die of nostalgia before they are landed, but many die from this cause after their arrival in Fiji ; and the only way to cure those affected is the one least likely to be followed, that is, " to send them home."

In the eastern part of the Solomon Group, one commonly meets natives limping along with large ulcerous sores on the soles of the feet, seated usually near the base of the toes. They are often caused by stepping on the sharp corals when fishing on the reefs, or by splinters of wood piercing the skin of the soles of the feet when walking in the bush. As a rule, the native pays no attention to these sores, and from neglect the ulceration extends both on the surface and to the deeper tissues, exposing the tendons and the metatarsal bones. Ultimately some or all the toes may be lost, and an unshapely clubbed foot arises from the subsequent contraction of the cicatrised surface. At other times, where the ulceration has been superficial but has extended between the toes, adhesion and perfect union of the lateral surfaces of the toes ensue, and a continuous covering of skin bridges over the intervening spaces. Mr. Nisbet, the government agent of the labour-scooner " Redcoat " from Fiji, showed me a Solomon Island native with a foot of perfect form but with apparently no toes. A continuous covering of skin covered the whole foot like a thin sock, and the toes were only recognisable by the touch. The man appeared to be but little incommoded by this obliteration of the toes. Among the natives of New Britain, as we learn from Mr. Romilly,[1] " the toes are not unfrequently joined together by a tough membrane," a defect which does " not seem to impair their activity." This evidently results from superficial ulceration in the manner I have above described.

These ulcerous sores, if left exposed to the irritation of sand, dirt, and flies, may last for years and may ultimately cause death. Dr. Livingstone in his " Last Journals " (vol. ii. chaps. 2 and 3) speaks of the ulcers of the feet from which many of the slaves die in the region west of Tanganyika. They eat through everything, muscle, tendon, and bone, and often lame permanently. " The wailing of slaves tortured with these sores is one of the night sounds of a slave camp." These ulcers, however, as they affect the Solomon Islanders, have a natural tendency to heal. When staying with Bishop Selwyn at Gaeta in Florida, I accompanied him on his morning round of visits to his patients, most of them being the sub-

[1] "The Western Pacific and New Guinea." London, 1886, p. 21.

jects of these large ulcerous sores on the feet and legs. He tells me that with rest and cleanliness they soon take on a healing action. Carbolic oil was the application he used, and it seemed well suited for these discharging, loathsome sores. Several of the men of the " Lark " were laid up with these ulcers of the feet for many weeks. The ulcers in their case assumed a circular form with raised callous edges and an irritable inflamed surface, being attended by much pain in the surrounding parts. The free application of lunar caustic every two or three days followed by poulticing, I found to be the most effectual treatment. Dr. Livingstone, who was himself laid up with these sores for eighty days in the interior of Africa, found the best of all topical applications to be malachite rubbed down with water on a stone and applied with a feather. The natives of Treasury Island in the Solomon Group use an application prepared by pounding the fruit of the *Cycas circinalis*, which grows near the edge of the cliffs on the south coast of the adjacent Stirling Island.

There is a loathsome skin disease very prevalent amongst the inhabitants of this group, which is generally known as the Solomon Island or Tokelau ringworm. I should estimate that two-fifths of the total population of these islands are thus affected. We found it more prevalent in some islands than in others. In Treasury, for instance, four-fifths of the people are the subjects of this disease, and half of the chief's wives who number about thirty are almost covered with it. In the southern large island of the Florida Islands, it appears to affect quite one half of the population. It ranges from one end of the group to the other, neither sex nor age affording any immunity. The chiefs and their families, however, seem to be less liable to this disease. The skin of every man does not appear to afford a suitable nidus for the growth of the fungus which is the cause of the eruption ; and this is evident from the circumstance that one parent may be covered with the disease while the other is entirely free from it. This skin-eruption, although so repulsive in appearance in the eyes of the European when he first visits the group, is not viewed with any feelings of disgust by the natives ; and even the European after spending some time in the group learns to disregard its repulsiveness. Those affected show no anxiety to be quit of it and evince great indifference when any offer is made to them to cure it. It is to them only an inconvenience ; and apparently causes no irritation except when the skin is hot and perspiring, as after exertion.

When this disease first came under my notice in the early part of 1882, I was unacquainted with what had been previously written on the subject. I accordingly made a microscopical examination of the affected skin and arrived at the conclusion, previously formed by those far more competent to express an opinion than myself, that the eruption was an inveterate form of body-ringworm. As it is to be seen affecting the skin of young children in the form of limited circular patches, which usually commence on the belly, it displays all the essential characters of *Tinea circinata* or body-ringworm. Spreading all over the trunk and limbs, the eruption assumes a chronic character and its typical characters become obscured. The whole skin, with the exception of that of the face and scalp which are not attacked by the disease, is covered by a great number of wavy desquamating lines partly concentric in their arrangement; and on account of the intervals between the lines being of a paler hue, the whole skin obtains a singular marbled appearance.

To such a degree is the skin implicated in some cases of the disease that the rapid desiccation and desquamation of the epidermal cells lead to a partial decoloration of the deeper parts of the cuticle, as though the rate of the production of pigment was less rapid than the rate of its removal in the desquamative process. This disease, in other words, tends to decolorize the skin. From this cause, one occasionally meets with a native whose skin as compared with that of his fellows is of a pale sickly hue. The tendency to produce a lighter colour by the too rapid destruction of the pigment is especially noticeable in those cases where the body is only partially covered with the eruption, there being a marked contrast between the paleness of the affected surfaces and the dark hue of the healthy skin. The influence of this cutaneous disease on the colour was remarked by Commodore Wilkes amongst the natives of the Depeyster Islands in the Ellice Group. He refers to the skin of those affected as much lighter than in any Polynesian race he had hitherto met with.[1] The same effect of this disease was noticed by Mr. Wilfred Powell amongst the natives of New Britain.[2]

I have entered somewhat at length into the subject of the partial decoloration produced by this eruption, because it has a bearing on that "quæstio vexata," the causes of race-colour. Pathology, in fact, affords more than one instance of changes, almost of a perma-

1 " Narrative of the U.S. Exploring Expedition," London, 1845 ; vol. V. p. 40.
2 " Three years amongst the Cannibals of New Britain," London, 1883, p. 86.

nent character, produced in the colour of the skin through the influence of abnormal action. Dr. Tylor in one of his lectures[1] alludes to "the morbid appearance of race-character" produced by the bronzing of the skin in Addison's disease, which is shown to be immediately due to a deposit of pigment in the *rete mucosum* closely resembling that of the negro. "The importance of the comparison," he says, "lies in its bridging over the physiological differences of race, by showing that morbid action may bring about in one race results more or less analogous to the normal type in another." To the partial decoloration of the skin in Tokelau ringworm and to the bronzing of the skin in Addison's disease, these remarks equally apply.

This disease has been variously spoken of by different authors and travellers as Leprosy, Icthyosis, Psoriasis, Pityriasis versicolor, and Tokelau Ringworm, of which it is needless to remark that the last is the only name which is correct. The medical officers of the United States Exploring Expedition, under Commodore Wilkes in 1841, were the first to recognise the nature of the eruption in the case of the inhabitants of the Depeyster Islands in the Ellice Group.[2] In 1874 Dr. Tilbury Fox, after having examined some scrapings of the skin which had been sent to him from Samoa, published in the "Lancet" (August 29th) a paper on "Tokelau Ringworm and its Fungus," in which he established the true character of the disease, and disposed of a view held by the Rev. Dr. G. Turner of the Samoan Medical Mission and by Dr. Mullen, R.N. of H. M. S. "Cameleon," that its origin may have been connected with the occurrence of numerous dipterous insects found in scrapings of the skin after the use of sulphur ointment. This last he showed to be only an accidental feature of the eruption. Two years afterwards, Dr. Fox in connection with Dr. Farquhar wrote an account of "Certain Endemic Skin and other Diseases in India and Hot Climates generally" (London 1876), in which further reference was made to this disease. It was there shown that Tokelau ringworm, Burmese ringworm, Chinese ringworm, and the Indian ringworms known familiarly as "dhobie itch," "washerman's itch," "Malabar itch," etc., are all of them forms of *Tinea circinata tropica* variously modified by such circumstances as the personal habits, the nature of the

---

[1] Delivered at Oxford on Feb. 15th, 1883: ("Nature" vol. xxviii., p. 9). *Vide* also Topinard's "Eléments d'Anthropologie générale:" Paris 1885, p. 325.

[2] "Narrative of the U. S. Explor. Exped.": vol. v., p. 40.

apparel, and the character of the climate. A proof of the correctness of this conclusion came under my observation in the Solomon Islands, where the white men in taking this disease from the natives suffer from it frequently in the form of " dhobie itch." The parasitic disease *Tinea circinata tropica* to which, as above shown, all tropical ringworms should be referred is, as Dr. Fox remarks in his work on " Skin Diseases " (3rd edit., 1873, p. 451), " nothing more or less than ordinary ringworm of the body (*tinea circinata*), such as we have in Europe, determined in its occurrence to certain parts of the body by peculiar circumstances, and assuming characters somewhat different from those observed in the disease as it exists in colder climates, in consequence of the greater luxuriance of the parasite consequent upon the presence in one case of a greater amount of heat and moisture, which are favourable to the development and speed the growth of fungi."

The particular form of the disease to which the name Tokelau Ringworm should be applied has a very wide distribution. Mr. G. W. Earl in his work on "The Papuans" (London, 1853; p. 37) speaks of this disease under the name of "icthyosis " as being very prevalent amongst all the coast tribes of the Indian Archipelago: but I gather from some references made by Mr. Wallace to this affection in his account of the Malay Archipelago (3rd edit., 1872, p. 449) that it is not to be found so much amongst the pure Malays as amongst the tribes of mixed origin. Mr. Marsden in his "History of Sumatra" (London 1811, p. 190) refers to it as being very common amongst the inhabitants of Pulo Nias an island which lies off the west coast of Sumatra. His description of the disease leaves no doubt as to its true character, but he himself is uncertain as to whether it is an "impetigo " indicating a mild type of leprosy, or whether it is not ordinary "shingles " or a confirmed stage of ringworm. The same disease was recently observed by Mr. H. O. Forbes amongst the natives of Timor-laut and of the island of Buru, islands which lie at the opposite end of the Indian Archipelago.[1] Two centuries since, Dampier well described this disease in the case of the inhabitants of Mindanao in the Philippines and of those of Guam in the Ladrones.[2]

Coming to New Guinea, I find that this disease prevails all along its coasts and in many of the off-lying islands, such as the Ki and

[1] "A Naturalist's Wanderings in the Eastern Archipelago;" pp. 331, 402; London, 1885.
[2] "Voyage round the World." London 1729, vol. i., p. 334.

Aru Islands, Teste Island, Woodlark Island, etc. The authorities on which I have founded this general statement are numerous and include, Modera, Bruijn Kops, Wallace, Mosely, Miklouho-Maclay, Comrie, W. Turner, Chalmers, Wyatt Gill, Romilly, Lyne, and others, whose descriptions, though they often did not recognise the true character of the eruption, leave no reasonable doubt on the matter.

This disease was observed by Mr. Wilfred Powell to be very frequent amongst the natives of New Britain and the Duke of York Islands, where it is called "buckwar."[1] Dr. Comrie, R.N., when serving in H.M.S. "Dido," found it to be very frequent amongst the natives of New Ireland.[2] Through the islands of the Solomon Group it is widely spread, as I have already shown: and from them it has extended to the different groups to the eastward, reaching the Gilbert, Ellice, Tonga and Samoa Groups.

In the Western Pacific we are able in some instances to trace the eastward extension of this disease during the last half century. Dr. G. Turner in his annual report of the Samoan Medical Mission, dated October, 1869, refers to the recent introduction of the Tokelau Ringworm amongst the Samoan Islanders as the introduction of a new disease. It was brought to Samoa from Bowditch or Tokelau Island where it had been also unknown until about ten years before, when it was introduced by a native of the Gilbert Group who had been landed by a whaler. The Gilbert or Kingsmill Islanders, according to the narrative of Commodore Wilkes, believed that the disease came from the south-west, and called it the "south-west gune," the nearest islands in that direction being those of the Solomon and Santa Cruz groups, between 800 and 900 miles away. Commodore Wilkes, however, was of opinion that this disease had reached the Kingsmill Group from the Depeyster Islands in the Ellice Group to the south-south-east; and he refers to the circumstance that the disease was most prevalent in the southern islands of the Kingsmill Group, being apparently absent from Makin the northernmost island;[3] but this distribution of the disease may be also urged in support of the more probable view of the natives that it came from the south-west. We are thus able to trace one probable track of this disease from the Solomon Islands, or one of the

---

[1] "Three years among the Cannibals in New Britain," London, 1883, p. 54.

[2] Journal of the Anthropological Institute, vol. vi. p. 102.

[3] "Narrative of the U. S. Explor. Exped." vol. v. p. 105.

groups immediately adjacent to them, across a wide tract of sea to the Gilbert and Ellice Groups, and from there to Tokelau Island, and thence to Samoa. The French navigator, Dentrecasteaux,[1] found the same disease to be very prevalent amongst the inhabitants of the Tonga Islands towards the end of last century; and it seems strange that it did not reach the Samoa Group until about seventy years after. The Tonga natives, however, may have derived it by another and more direct course from the westward, namely through the New Hebrides and the Fiji Groups.

I may appear to have entered with unnecessary detail into this subject, but it is apparent that this fungoid skin disease, disseminated as it is by personal contact and other similar agencies, would have reached these sub-central Pacific Groups long ago if they had been occupied through ages by their present inhabitants. The same evidence, therefore, which can be brought forward to prove the recent appearance of this disease amongst the natives of these groups may also be advanced in support of the recent occupation of these islands by the eastern Polynesians.

From the previous remarks on the distribution of Tokelau Ringworm it may be inferred that in New Guinea and in the islands of the Malay Archipelago we have the home of the disease. From this region it has spread eastward towards the centre of the Pacific; and we may also infer that this eastward extension of the disease has occurred within the last three hundred years, since in the accounts which Gallego and Quiros give of the natives of the Solomon, Santa Cruz, and New Hebrides Groups at the time of their first discovery by the Spaniards, there is no reference to the prevalence of any cutaneous disease, which, if it had existed, would most certainly have attracted the notice of these early navigators.

I only had one opportunity of treating this affection, and that was in the person of a native of Guadalcanar, who was shipped on board as an interpreter, and who had been the subject of the disease for about five months. Partly from its obstinacy, and partly from the difficulty of ensuring that the remedies were regularly and thoroughly employed, my experience was not very satisfactory. Sulphur ointment, mercurial ointment, tincture of iodine, and a lotion of hyposulphite of soda (1 in 12) were severally used, and after about three weeks the skin was almost clean. Some weeks

---

[1] "Voyage de Dentrecasteaux," par M. de Rossel, tom. I. p. 323, Paris 1808.

afterwards, the eruption re-appeared on the forearms in the form of the characteristic small circumscribed patches of body-ringworm. The local remedy, which I found most rapid in its effect as a parasiticide in the treatment of this case, was the tincture of iodine of which two applications completely removed the disease from the fore-arms. The lotion of the hyposulphite of soda and the mercurial ointment had apparently but little influence on the disease. The sulphur ointment, however, had a gradual curative action. To ·many of the vessels which leave Queensland and Fiji to recruit labour in the Solomon and New Hebrides groups, sulphur ointment is supplied ; and the government-agents are instructed to use it in all cases of this disease amongst the natives recruited. I learned from some of these gentlemen that, when the remedy is applied thoroughly, and under superintendence, they usually succeed in thoroughly cleansing the skin from the eruption before the ships return to the colonies.

A pustular eruptive disease peculiar to children, which has been referred to by various authors as prevalent in the New Hebrides, Fiji, Tonga, and Samoa groups, affects many of the young children of the Solomon Islands, usually occurring about the age of five. A number of large papules, twice the size of a split pea, which subsequently become filled with a pustular fluid, appear on the face. These pustules by rupturing tend to unite and form unhealthy-looking sores of the size of a florin. The disease pursues a regular course of papule, pustule, and sore ; and is said never to recur. As far as I could learn, the natives interfere but little with its progress ; and, as in Fiji where it is known as *coko*,[1] they regard the disease as having a salutary influence on the future health of the child.

That peculiar spinal disease, which produces so many hunch-backs in the Society and Samoan groups, and which is so well described by Mr. Ellis in his " Polynesian Researches " (2nd edit., 1831, vol. iii. pp. 39, 40), does not prevail among the Solomon Islanders. I can only recall one instance of spinal deformity which came under my observation. It was in the person of a little boy about ten or eleven years old, who was the subject of lateral and posterior curvature of the spine. The little fellow, who was a native of Simbo, apparently experienced no inconvenience from the deformity, since a firm ankylosis had occurred. He was able to accompany me

---

[1] " Fiji and the Fijians," by Messrs T. Williams and J. Calvert. 3rd edit. 1870, p. 151.

in my ascents to the summit of his island, which is elevated about
1,100 feet above the sea.

An epidemic catarrhal disease, which is allied to influenza, is
very prevalent amongst the natives of these islands. It is commonly followed by lung-complications, which not infrequently cause
the death of the sufferer. Such an epidemic in running through a
village sometimes carries off several of the inhabitants. The elderly
natives are, in fact, very liable to pulmonary affections; such diseases usually terminate their lives.

From the occurrence of an epidemic of this catarrhal disease, a
village often obtains an unhealthy reputation; and the natives abandon
it for some other situation, which is selected rather for the convenience
of its position than for its freedom from unhealthy influences. A
generation ago, one of the principal villages in the island of Ugi was
situated on the level summit of a hill overlooking Selwyn Bay on
the west coast, a site which would have at once been chosen both
for its salubrity and for its capability of defence. However, a
number of deaths occurred in the village from epidemic catarrhal
disease; and the inhabitants shifted their homes to the low-lying
unhealthy situation where the village of Ete-ete now stands.

Epidemics of mumps occur occasionally amongst these islanders.
In October, 1882, whilst we were taking to Ugi the crew of the
"Pioneer," a schooner which had been wrecked off the coast of
Guadalcanar, some cases of this disease appeared among the
natives belonging to that ship, affecting ten out of the twenty on
board, and pursuing its usual course. It was evident that the
disease had been originally brought from Brisbane, as the ship
which was engaged in returning natives from the Queensland plantations, had had three cases previously, the first having occurred on
her arrival at Makira harbour, just a week after she left Brisbane.
That mumps is sometimes a fatal disease amongst these races, there
is no reason to doubt. Mr. Stephens of Ugi informed me that a
few years since, some natives of Lord Howe Islands, whom he was
employing on his premises, rapidly succumbed to this disease.

Men who were the subjects of *Elephantiasis arabum* were occasionally seen in the different islands we visited. Instances of "lymph-
scrotum" most frequently typify this disease, but now and then
cases of "swollen leg" occur. In the island of Faro or Fauro in
Bougainville Straits, the natives attribute this disease to the water
of particular streams. There is a stream on the west side of the

island, the water of which when drunk is said to produce "swollen legs." For this reason the water is never employed; and the ban is even extended to the cocoa-nut trees on its banks.

Natives, who are the subjects of such congenital deformities as " hare-lip," are rarely seen. Very probably in such cases life is destroyed by the parents soon after birth. I only observed one instance of " hare-lip " which occurred in the case of a man of Simbo. This malformation, which was of the single character, was associated with abnormal development of crisp hair on the body and more particularly on the back. As an instance of another kind of congenital deformity, which however came but rarely under my observation, I may refer to a man of Ugi who had six perfect toes on the right foot, both fifth and sixth toes being provided with nails and apparently arising from a common metatarsal bone. None of his family had the same deformity, which in his case was probably inconvenient in more ways than one, as the print of his foot was familiar to every native in the island.[1]

Strabismus is not uncommon amongst the natives of these islands, and appears to occur with the same relative frequency as amongst more civilised people.

Venereal diseases, both constitutional and local, are said by traders to be very frequent in certain islands, as in Ugi, which have had most intercourse with the outer world. I rarely however came upon unequivocal evidence of the constitutional form of these diseases, those cases which came under my immediate observation being of the non-constitutional types which, as in other tropical regions, are often of a rapidly destructive character. The natives of Ugi assert that these diseases have not been introduced within the memory of any living man, and no tradition prevails with reference to their origin. I shall scarcely enter into the question of the introduction of these diseases into the more central groups of the Pacific, a subject which is discussed in most of the narratives of the early expeditions to those regions, but in a spirit of unfairness and mutual recrimination which goes far to invalidate the conclusions arrived at. Negative evidence, however, must be of a very exhaustive character before it would warrant the inference that to the licence, so freely permitted to the crews of the English and French expeditions during the latter half of the last century, must be at-

---

[1] Mr. Romilly, in the work referred to on page 168, alludes to the strange prevalence of these congenital deformities of the hands and feet in New Britain.

tributed the presence of these diseases among the Polynesian races. M. Rollin, who, as surgeon of the frigate "Boussole," accompanied La Pérouse on his ill-fated voyage, adduces evidence to show the probability of these diseases having existed in the Pacific before the discoveries of the French and English navigators in that region ; [1] and La Pérouse himself approaches very near the truth when he suggests that the free intercourse, which prevailed between the natives and the crews during those expeditions, may have increased the activity and destructive tendency of the pre-existing diseases.[2] For, not only has M. Parrot of Paris demonstrated from an examination of the skulls of some South American aborigines the existence of Syphilis in the New World before Columbus set foot on its shores, but he affirms without hesitation, after examining three fragments of infant skulls from a dolmen in central France, that this disease existed in prehistoric times ("Lancet," May 10th, 1879). We are not therefore surprised at finding references to venereal diseases in the ancient literature of China, India, Arabia, Greece and Rome (Aitken's "Medicine," 6th edit, 1872, vol i. p. 859) ; and having regard to the ethnological past of the Pacific, we can with some confidence assume that the original stock, derived in the first place from the Asiatic continent, brought with them these diseases.

The susceptibility of these islanders to comparatively small falls of temperature is an element in their predisposition to disease which should not be disregarded. This susceptibility was strikingly shown to me on one occasion, at the end of August 1882, when I was following up the course of a stream at Sulagina on the north coast of St. Christoval. Accompanied by a party of natives, I was wading up the stream for several hours, the water often reaching the waist, whilst a steady deluge of rain completed the wetting. Although the air was merely comparatively cool for this latitude (10° 30′ S.), the thermometer in the shade standing at 80° Fahr, my natives were shivering with the cold ; whilst I myself felt only the inconvenience of having been soaked through for so many hours. As soon as we returned to the coast, all my party huddled themselves together around their wood-fires in a little hut and warmed their hands and feet as eagerly as we should in winter-time at home. As I stood in the hut looking comfortably on at my naked companions who,

---

[1] "Voyage round the World, by La Pérouse," edit. by Milet-Mureau : London : vol. iii., p. 180.

[2] Ibid. vol. ii. p. 52.

shivering and with their teeth chattering, were endeavouring to warm themselves around the fires, I recalled to my mind an incident which Mr. Darwin relates in his " *Journal of the Beagle* " (p. 220), which although analogous, illustrates the converse of these conditions. " A small family of Fuegians "—he writes—" soon joined our party round a blazing fire. We were well clothed, and though sitting close to the fire were far from too warm ; yet these naked savages, though further off, were observed, to our great surprise, to be streaming with perspiration at undergoing such a roasting."

Instances of mental weakness or of insanity amongst the natives of these islands rarely came under my notice. However, more than one of the chiefs whom we met had a half-witted individual on his staff, who made himself generally useful to his master. The chief's fool, as we called him, was frequently my guide in the island of Santa Anna. He was the general butt of the village ; and I was told the girls would sometimes seize hold of him and roll him about in the sand. Insanity would appear to be of uncommon occurrence amongst these islanders ; but I suspect that such individuals are not permitted to live. Whilst the " Lark " was engaged in the survey of Faro Island in Bougainville Straits, I learned that there was a madman, who was partially dumb, living in the bush in the interior of the island. Having murdered his wife about five months before our visit, he had taken to the forest where he led a solitary life at enmity with his fellow-islanders, who would have killed him as they told me, if they found him. He frequently used to steal from the plantations ; and during our stay in the island he was observed by a woman near one of the yam patches. The chief's son came up to me one afternoon, after I had returned to the coast from an ascent of one of the principal summits, to advise me to shoot this unfortunate being if ever I saw him ; and he added that if this madman should see me, unobserved, he would either run away or take his opportunity of killing me. However, I made several excursions into the interior afterwards ; but I never fell in with him.

CHAPTER X.

THIS vocabulary was formed in great part by Lieutenant A.
Leeper, to whom I may take this opportunity of expressing my
thanks for his kindness, in thus placing it at my disposal. I have
supplemented this list from smaller vocabularies made by Lieutenant
C. F. de M. Malan and by myself. It is to be regretted that, owing to
Lieutenant Malan taking up a Colonial appointment in Fiji during the
last year of the commission, we were unable to avail ourselves in a
further degree of his knowledge of the Fijian tongue, and of his
general acquaintance with the construction of the Polynesian
languages. We are, however, especially indebted to him for the
recognition of the pronominal suffixes.

The spelling follows to a great extent the mode adopted in the
missionary alphabet of Professor Max Müller, as given on page 116
of the Anthropological Notes and Queries drawn up at the request
of the British Association. The vowels and dipthongs are pronounced as in the following examples ;— *a* as *a* in father, *e* as *a* in
fate, *i* as *i* in marine, *o* as *o* in note, *u* as *oo* in moon, *ai* as *ai* in aisle,
au as *ou* in proud. Where there has been an evident want of agree-
ment in the three vocabularies, I have given the different words or
the different spellings, as the case may have occurred. We have
thus been, in some degree, "checks" to each other : and I hope we
have avoided, in this manner, many of those errors into which the
unassisted framer of a vocabulary is so liable to fall. The accented
syllable is thus indicated (') in most instances where it is needed,
the accent being usually placed on the penultimate.

Miscellaneous Words

Afraid............Fulau.
Angry............Fangolu.   Gafolu.
Armlet............Pago.
Arrow............Iliu.
Ashes............Oafu.
Awl............Nila.
Axe ....Libba-libba.   Levo-
                        levo.

Back............Aro.
Bad ....Paiténa.
Bag............Ko-isa.
Basket ....Koko.   Besa.
Beat (to)............Lapu.
Before............Gaga.
Behind ....Arogu.
Big............Yolulla.   Kana-kana.
Blood............Masíni.
Blow............Ifu.
Bow............Lili.
Boy ....Taui.
Break (to)............Taposha.
Bring............Galómi.
Brother............Manai-ina.
Bury (to)............Nafu.
Buy............Fúna-aili.

Calico............Bauro.
Canoe............Obuna.
Cap............So-so.
Capsize (to)............Igomo.
Charcoal............Sibi.
Chew ....Tatau.
Chief ....Lálafa.   Yolóna.
Chief's eldest sonNatuna.
Clean ....Lapu.   Sapolu.
Club ....Peko.
Club (dancing)..Toko.   Toku.
Cold ....Lulu-gulu.
Comb ....Supi.
Cut............Ausi.

Dance............Gatu.
Dark ....Lali.
Day ....Bol.
Dead ....Mate.   Imati.
Deaf............Kipau.
Devil (*i.e.*, bad
        spirit)....Nito paitéua.
Dig (to)............Eli.
Dirty ....Mati.
Drift (to)............Ali.
Drink (to)............Atali aoa.

Drinking-vessel (a cocoanut).
    with neck of
        bamboo..Dogo.
    without neck....Droo.
Dry ....Dúgga-dúgga.

Earthquake............Nono.
Eat (to)............A-am.
Egg ....I-au.
Empty............Golu.
Enough............Sumána.

Fall............Kappa.
Fan ....Etif.
Far............De-apína.
Fat............Hatutu.
Father............Apa.
Few............Alua-tapoína.
Fight............Tala.
Finish (end)......Egáfulu.
Finished ....Sumána
Fire............Feli.
Fish-hook............A-ili
Flint............Kilifela
Fly (to)............Lofu
Food............Dorómi.   Darámi.
    „   (cooked)...Selo-selo.
Full............Forna.

Gift ....Teletafala.
God (*i.e.*, good
        spirit)....Nito drékona.
Good............Drékona ; Dékona.
Great............Yolulla; Kana-kana.

Half............Koputi.
Heaven ....Lavin.
Heavy............Mamma.
Hot ....Posella.
House ....Numa ; Fale-fale.
    „   (tambu)...Olatu.
Hungry............Belu.

Inside............Uni ; Fakoria.

Jew's harp............Mako-mako.
Jump (to) ....Subolosa.

Kick (to)............Savulu.
Kill (to) ....So-orti.
Kneel (to)............Fasiliki.
Knife............Papalana.
Know (to) ....Atai.

Lick (to) ....Damíti.
Lift (to) ....Ikoti.
Light (in weight) Dùgga-dugga.
Live (to).........Pcoka.
Long.............Deapa.

Mad.............Kipau.
Man.............Kániga ; Tium ; Ká-
        niga-tium.
Many ....Tapóina.
Mat ....Sararang ; Pota.
    (The names of the two pan-
    danus trees, from the leaves
    of which the mats are made.)
Match ....Sararang (vide pre-
                ceding).
Moon.............Ilala; Ilolla.
Mother.............Unka.

Naked ....Ampea-paiia.
Net (fishing) .....Sorau (large).
        Sai-aili (small).
        Awi-sulu.
    (The plant supplying the fibre
    is named awi-sulu, probably
    a species of "Lyonsia.")
New ....Faolu.
Night ....Lali.
No ....Api ; Apea.
Noise ....So-orli.
None ....Ausaka.
Now ....Ivai.

Old ....Purafalu.
Open ....Kapeta.
Outside ....Ampapaluna.

Paddle (noun
    and verb)...Fosi ; Fose.
Pay ....Aili.
Path ....Poa.
Pearl ....Bor-otulu.
Pestle and mor-
    tar (wooden),
    used for pound-
    ing food........ Tagero.
Plane (a).........Ketuma.
Plenty ....Tapóina.
Pot (cooking)....Kore.
Present (a) ......Teletafala.

Quarter ....Totoli.
Queen ....Mamaifi.

Quick ....Fakare.

Rain ....Laiti.
Resin .... { Anóga, for torches.
    „ .... { Tita, for canoe seams
Rope ....Fili.
Ruu ....Gágona.

Same ....Umbilua.
Sea ....Keno ; Kelo.
Short.............Papa.
Shut ....Dakopi.
Sick.............Mate ; Sali.
Sing (to) ....Gatu.
Sister ....Fafini.
Sit ....Ahotu.
Sky ....Abu ; Avu.
Sleep ....Suéli.
Small ....Kaidakina.
Smoke ....Tula.
Speak ....Arei ; Selli-selli.
Spear ....Portulu.
Spirit ....Nito ; Nitu.
Star ....Bito-bito.
Stone ....Patu.
Stop ....Aru.
Sun ....Feo ; Isang.
Swim (to) ....Usu.

Tail.............Aukuna.
Tambu (forbid-
        den)...Olatu.
Tear ....Igati.
Thin.............Morsu.
Thirsty.........Fana-oa.
To-day.........Ibai.
To-morrow ....Boiwa
Town.............Famaca.
Tray ....Kisu ; Kishu.
    (The name of the palm supply-
    ing the material for making
    the trays is also "kisu.")
Tree ....Au ; Ava.

Waist-cloth ......Malioto.
Wait ....Au.
Walk (to) ....Dagona.
Wash (to) ....Sisi.
Water ....Ateli (fresh).
    „ ....Kelo ; Keno (salt).
Wet.............Pu-un.
What ?.............Afana ?
When ? ....Lefila ?

¹ These are also the native names of the trees supplying the resins, the anoga being probably a species of "Canarium," the tita, "Parinarium laurinum."

Whistle (to) ..... Faso.
Wife .... Ewa.
Wind .... Oa.
Woman .... Batafa ;   Bataha ;
            Talai-ina.
Wood .... Au.

Work .... Karre.
Worn .... Tualina.

Yes .... O-o.
Yesterday .... Lafi.

Numerals.

One .... Ilia ; Kala.
Two .... Elua.
Three .... Épisa ; Ébisha.
Four .... Efáte ; Efatsi.
Five.............. Lima.
Six .... Onomo ; Onoma.
Seven .... Fito ; Fit.
Eight .... Alu.
Nino .... Ulia.
Ten.............. Láfulu.
Eleven........... Láfulu kala.
Twelve .... Láfulu élua.
Thirteen .... Láfulu épisa
Fourteen .... Láfulu efáte

Fifteen .... Láfulu lima.
Sixteen .... Láfulu ónomo.
Seventeen ...... Láfulu fito.
Eighteen .... Láfulu alu.
Nineteen........ Láfulu úlia.
Twenty .... Tanugo ; Tana oge.
Thirty .... Pisa-vulu.
Forty .... Fatia-vulu.
Fifty .... Lima-hulu.
Sixty .... Nomo-fulu.
Seventy .... Fitua-fulu.
Eighty........... Alua-fulu.
Ninety........... Tia-fulu ; Sia-fulu
Hundred .... Latu ; Latu-u.

Parts of Body.

Ankle .... Sapolu.
Arm .... Pagolo.
Beard .... Polu.
Cheek .... Papala.
Chest............ Ate.
Chin .... Ali.
Ear .... Tana.
Elbow........... Tau.
Eye .... Mata ; Shol.
Eyebrow......... Metapolissi.
Face .... Laia.
Finger.......... Kim.
Fist .... Gogumu.
Foot .... Toto.
Hair .... Tawo ; Untu.

Hand .... Imai ; Ime.
Head .... Alapatu ; To-o.
Leg .... Tatabua ; Nanabu ;
Lip .... Ulu.   [Tato.
Mouth .... Uruguru.
Neck .... Lua.
Nose .... Leo ; Lo-u.
Shoulder .... Fali.
Stomach......... Muru.
Thumb .... Gagata.
Toe............. Kuri-kurisi.
Tongue .... Miata.
Tooth .... Nifo ; Nifa.
Trunk .... Tia.
Waist........... Buli.

Geographical and Nautical.

Cape .... Manavo.
Drift............. Ali.
Hill.............. Soma.
Island .... Nua-nua ; Pete.
Land............. Mesola.
Mountain......... Olo.
Passage.......... Ai.
Rain....... .... Laiti.
Reef............. Aru-oshe ; Butulu.
River............ Ateli;Atele;Sallile.
Rock............ Pushai.

Sand............. Mesola-lanun
Sea............... Keno ; Kelo.
Shallow.......... Seala.
Sky.............. Abu.
Steep (to)........ Suele.
Stream........... Ateli;Atele;Sallile.
Tide............. Tofala.
Wind............. Oa.

Rowing { Pull ..... Fosi.
       { Back ... Palma.
      { Stop..... Atti-horsi.

Animal Kingdom.

Ant...	Doau.	Hornbill	Po-po.
Bat (Pteropidæ)	Dramo.	Lizard	Kurru-rupu.
Bird	Maraka; Maruka.	Opossum (Cuscus).	Mali.
Butterfly	Bebe.	Osprey	Manuella.
Cockatoo	Anau.	Parrot	Karro.
Crocodile	Umau.	Pig	Boa.
Dog	Au-au.	Pigeon	Baólo.
Eel	Tolo.	Rat	Kuáki.
Fire-fly	Bito-bito.	Shark	Bao.
Fish	Ianna; Ienna.	Snake	Nifii.
Fly	Lau-au.	Turtle	Palúsi.
Fowl	Kokole.	Turtle-shell	Purai.
Frog	Appa-appa.		

Pronouns.

My	Gu, as a suffix, *e.g.*	You	Maito.
	Toto-gu, my foot.	Him.	Ealai.
Your	Ng, as a suffix, *e.g.*	These	Ea.
	Toto-ng, your foot.	Those	Oa.

Names of Natives.

Men.—Gorai ; Mule ; Kópana ; Krepas; Kurra-kurra; Erosini; Tutu; Lawi ; Sege; Fauli; Kiliusi; Gégora; Nito ; Émara ; Olega ; Malakolo; Butiu ; Igeti ; Ki'kila ; Totono ; Gélesi ; Dúkutau ; Alisa ; Iri-isa ; Sahi ; Oisi ; Karubo ; Devi ; Dansi ; Kamo ; Fulagi ; Pilaisi ; Maluka ; Tokura; Misiki; Levo; Tunu; Biro. Women.—Kaika ; Bito ; Siali ; Évenu ; Bose ; Omakau ; Domari ; Duia.

Vegetables, Fruits,[1] &c.

Banana	Toitoi.	Sago	Nami; Bia.
Wild Plantain	Kalula.	Taro (small)	Koko.
Breadfruit	Balia.	Taro (large)	Karafai.
Betel-nut	Olega.	Tobacco	Brubush.
Cocoa-nut	Niu.		

Short Sentences and Phrases.

Where have you come from?...	Tiga fina ?	What do you want? A hana pe-una ? Ahampeo ?.	
I come from Alu..	Tiga Alu.	What do you do ?.	Ahana wussa ?
I want it	Ai peko.	What is this?	Mai-ito ahampeo ?
I do not want it...	Abu ai peko.	I go	Falalau.
I give you	Fantellao.	Go away	Fato.
Give me	Tellao.	He goes	Onalau.
Will you give me ?	Tellao fa ?	Let me see	Fanaroro.
I do not give you.	Abu hanatellao.	Take it	Na.
Do I go this way ?	Fina fanato ?	I take it	Nto.[2]

[1] The native names of most of the common plants will be found in the list given on pages 291-304. *Vide* also remarks on page 280.

[2] This is an expression of acknowledgment rather than of thanks.

In a recent work on the Melanesian languages, the Rev. Dr. Codrington[1] deals with the languages of the islands of the Solomon Group which lie east of New Georgia. Some of them, as he observes, fall naturally into two divisions: those which belong to Ulaua, Malaita, Ugi, San Cristoval, and the part of Guadalcanar adjacent; and those of Florida, the parts of Guadalcanar opposite, and the nearest extremity of Ysabel. In the first region, the language of Fagani on the north coast of San Cristoval, is somewhat distinct; and in the second, that of Savo is strangely different in some respects.[2]

The languages of the large islands of Choiseul, Bougainville, and Bouka and of the numerous smaller islands in their vicinity, or, in other words, the languages of the western portion of the Solomon Group have hitherto scarcely come within the cognizance of the philologist, and are therefore not referred to by Dr. Codrington in his comprehensive work. It is probable that that of the islands of Bougainville Straits may form the centre of another group of the Solomon Island languages, as it is spoken by a dominant tribe of natives who have extended their raids to the island of Bouka. Yet, it is a singular circumstance that the natives of Takura, a village on the adjoining coast of Bougainville, cannot understand the language spoken by the inhabitants of the islands of Bougainville Straits. I met twelve of the Takura men visiting the island of Faro, who were only able to make themselves understood by the Faro people through the medium of an interpreter.

Little communication appears to take place between the natives of the Straits and those of the islands of Vella-la-vella, Ronongo, and Simbo (Narovo) to the eastward; and judging from a vocabulary obtained by Captain Cheyne[3] in 1844 from the inhabitants of Simbo, or Eddystone Island as it is also called, a native of this island would be scarcely able to make himself understood by the people of Treasury Island nearly eighty miles away. As shown in the footnote[4] where the numerals up to ten are compared, all the Simbo

[1] "The Melanesian Languages," by R. H. Codrington, D,D. Clarendon Press, 1885.

[2] For instance, the Savo notation forms an exception to the decimal system of counting which prevails in the Solomon Islands.

[3] "A Description of Islands in the Western Pacific Ocean." London 1852.

[4]	One	Two	Three	Four	Fire	Six	Seven	Eight	Nine	Ten.
Simbo......Kamee Karu		Kuay	Mantee	Leema	Wouama	Weetu	Kalu	Seang	Manosa.
Treasury {Ilia / Kala	Elua	Episa	Efate	Lima	Onomo	Fito	Alu	Ulia	Lafulu.
	Sun	Moon	Fire	Sleep	Spear	Bad	Star.
Simbo........Gawaso	Popu	Eku	Puta	Opuree	Ekarenah	Keenda.
Treasury {Feo / Isang	Ilella	Feli	Sueli	Portulu	Paitena	Bito-bito.

numbers with the exception of those signifying *five*, *seven*, and *eight* are apparently distinct. Many of the common terms are equally different; so that it would appear that the inhabitants of this island speak a language referable to a distinct group of the Solomon Island languages, probably to be classed with those spoken by the natives of Ronongo, Vella-la-vella, Kulambangra, and perhaps New Georgia.

I forbear from making many remarks on the general affinities of the language of the islands of Bougainville Straits, and prefer to leave such a comparison to those qualified to pronounce on the subject. There are, however, certain points to which I will briefly refer.

Professor Keane, to whom I sent a portion of this vocabulary, informs me that whilst the structure of the language and most of the words are distinctly Papuan, the numerals and several terms are Polynesian. However, whilst I was engaged in collecting plants and making general botanical notes in this locality, it occurred to me that by comparing the names of the common littoral trees with those of the same trees in other Pacific groups and in the Indian or Malay Archipelago, I might obtain some important additional clues as to the sources of the language. In so doing I have obtained some interesting results, to which I have briefly alluded on a previous page, and which go to show that the peoples who originally migrated from the Indian Archipelago to the various Pacific groups carried with them the names of several of their common littoral trees, some of which may still be found in the intermediate groups of islands, such as the Solomon Islands, which have served as stepping-stones or halting places along the line of migration. On page 101 I have taken "Barringtonia speciosa" as an illustration. I will now refer to some other instances.

After examining the pages of Crawfurd's Malay Dictionary, together with the extensive list of the native names of plants obtained by G. J. Filet, I have ascertained that the following names of pandanus-trees belonging to languages of the Indian Archipelago may be traced across the South Pacific to the Austral Islands, viz., *Harassas*, *Haragh-hagh*, *Pudak*, *Putih*.[1][2]   In the

---

[1] *Pudak* (Pandanus inermis), *Pandan-pudak* (P. moschatus), *Pandan-putih* (P. leucacanthus). *Vide* Crawfurd's Malay Dictionary.

[2] *Hara-hagh* (Pandanus moschatus) Sundaneesch, *Harassas leutiek* (P. humilis) Sundaneesch, *Harrassas gedeh* (P. caricosus) Sundaneesch. *Vide* "De Inlandsche Plantennamen," by G. J. Filet, published in "Natuurkundig Tijdschrift voor Nederlandsch Indie." Deo xix. vierde serie, deel v. Batavia, 1859. Another list by J. C. M. Radermacher occurs in "Bataviasch Genootschap," deel i. p. 87.

islands of Bougainville Straits the four common pandanus-trees are known as *Darashi, Sararang, Pota,* and *Samala.* In the Sikyana or Stewart Islands off the eastern end of the Solomon Group, the pandanus is named *Dawa.*[1] The Fijians name the "Pandanus odoratissimus" *Balawa.*[2] In the Hervey Group and in the surrounding islands, as we learn from Mr. Wyatt Gill,[3] the " Pandanus odoratissimus " is the *Ara* of the natives, whilst the "Pandanus utilis " is the *Rauara;* the first being the Thatch-tree, and the last the Mat-tree. In the Austral Islands further to the eastward, the names of the pandanus-trees were ascertained by Dr. G. Bennett to be *Hoshoa, Sahang,* and *Pauhuf* (" Pandanus odoratissimus.")[4]

Indian Archipelago..............Haragh-hagh...Harrassas...Pudak, Putih.
Bougainville Straits............Sararang.........Darashi......Pota.
Sikyana Islands....................................Dawa.
Fiji Group.......................Balawa.
Hervey Group, and vicinity...Rauara, Ara.
Austral Islands.................Sahang...........Hoshoa......Pauhuf.

By arranging these names as in the above list, the important bearings of such a comparison are at once seen ; and I may here remark that I have attached no weight to the non-retention of the same native name for the same species of " Pandanus " in different localities, since as in the instance of " P. odoratissimus," there is no evidence that would lead us to expect such a close agreement. Most of the common pandanus-trees have a very similar appearance, and there is often a general name given to them in addition to their distinctive names. Thus the natives of the Bougainville Straits often designate all the species by the term *Sararang.* In the Indian Archipelago, the general names are *Pandan, Haragh-hagh, Harassas, Pudak, Rampai,* &c. These are the names which would be applied to any new kind of pandanus-tree during the migration eastward of the races of this archipelago ; and it is manifest that as the separate Pacific groups of islands came to be occupied by different offshoots of the main migration, the same tree might have received a different general name. Therefore, in investigating the nomenclature of the pandanus-trees throughout the Pacific, we should concern ourselves not with a comparison of the names of identical

[1] Scherzer's "Voyage of the Novara," vol. ii. p. 617.   London, 1861-63.
[2] Seemann's "Mission to Viti." London, 1862.
[3] " Jottings from the Pacific," pp. 183, 188. London, 1885.
[4] "Gatherings of a Naturalist in Australasia," p. 389. London, 1859.

species in different groups, but with the general names for the whole genus of "Pandanus." We desire, in fact, to find the equivalent of such terms as the *Ara* of the Hervey Group, and the *Sararang* of Bougainville Straits.

That the names of trees possessing such conspicuous characters as those of the genus "Pandanus," can be traced from the Indian Archipelago eastward through the Solomon Islands, and across the Central Pacific to the Austral Islands, is a circumstance of considerable interest to the philologist and anthropologist. We have already seen (page 101) that in the instance of "Barringtonia speciosa," the name may be similarly traced from the Indian Archipelago across the Pacific to the Society Islands. Another example is to be found in the case of "Morinda citrifolia," the Indian mulberry, a common littoral tree in the Indian and Pacific regions; it supplies a yellow dye extensively used by the inhabitants. It is the *Bangkudu* or *Mangkudu* of the Indian Archipelago and the *Wongkudu* or *Kudu* of Java in particular.[1] In Bougainville Straits it is known as the *Urati*; in Fiji as the *Kura*;[2] and in Tahiti as the *Aari*;[3] names which are evidently different forms of the same word, probably the *Kudu* of the Indian Archipelago. Another tree, "Fagræa Berteriana," the sacred tree of the South Central Pacific groups, is the *Bubulata* of Bougainville Straits, the *Bua* of Fiji,[4] and the *Pua* or *Bua* of the Hervey and Society Groups.[5] I have not yet found the original of this name in the Indian Archipelago, the only suggestive word being *Büa* or *Buwah*, the Malay word for fruit.

Before proceeding further I should observe that an inquiry into the names of the common littoral trees, such as "Barringtonia speciosa," "Morinda citrifolia," and the species of "Pandanus," which are yet preserved in the languages of the islands of the Indian Ocean, might be productive of important results. Being unable to follow up this branch of the subject, I would recommend it to some of my readers. As an encouragement, I would point out that there appears to be a resemblance between the names for the pandanus-tree in northern Madagascar, and in the Pacific

---

[1] Crawfurd's Malay Dictionary.   Raffles' "History of Java."

[2] Seemann's "Mission to Viti."

[3] Bennett's "Gatherings of a Naturalist," p. 399.

[4] Seemann. (Ibid.)

[5] Wyatt Gill's "Life in the Southern Isles" (p. 275), and "Jottings from the Pacific,"

Islands. Thus the *Hoshoa* of the Austral Islands, the *Darashi* of Bougainville Straits, the *Harrassas* of the Indian Archipelago, and the *Vua-tchirié*[1] of North Madagascar, may be the same compound word in different forms. *Vua*, it should be remarked, is a prefix attached to many trees and plants in this part of Madagascar. With this digression, I will now proceed.

Amongst the native names of trees in the Indian or Malay Archipelago which are to be found in an altered form in the islands of Bougainville Straits, I may refer to *Kanari*, which is the common appellation of "Canarium commune," in the former region.[2] The kernels of the fruits of this tree furnish a frequent source of food to the Malay races and also to the inhabitants of the Maclay coast of New Guinea, where the tree is known by the similar name of *Kengar*.[3] In the islands of Bougainville Straits, where the same or an allied species of "Canarium" is found, the fruits of which form a staple article of food, the Malay name of *Kanari* and the New Guinea name of *Kengar* have been contracted to *Ka-i.* . . . The sago-palm ("Sagus," sp.) affords another instance. It is, according to Crawfurd, the *Rámbiya* of the Indian Archipelago.[4] Earl informs us that in Kisa, one of the islands of the Sarawati group in the Banda Sea, it is known as the *Pihir.*[5] On the Maclay coast of New Guinea it is the *Buam.*[6] In Bougainville Straits it receives two names, *Bia* and *Nami*, the former (I think) being applied to the tree and the latter to the sago. . . . Then again, the two similar names, the *Katari* of Bougainville Straits and the *Gutur* of the Maclay coast,[7] are applied in both regions to resin-yielding trees which belong, however, to different genera, the *Katari* being a species of "Calophyllum," and the *Gutur* a species of "Canarium." In both localities the name is also given to the resin itself, which is employed by the natives for various purposes. But the important point is that these two words are merely slightly altered forms of *Gátah*, which is the general name for gums and resins in the Indian Archipelago,[8] and I need scarcely add that gutta-percha is but the *gátah* of the *Párcha* tree,

[1] Rochon's "Voyage a Madagascar et aux Indes Orientales." Paris, 1791, p. 319.

[2] In the numerous works referring to the Indian Archipelago, this word is sometimes written *kanary* or *kanarie*.

[3] Miklouho-Maclay in Proc. Lin. Soc., N.S.W. Vol. X., p. 349.

[4] Crawfurd's "Grammar and Dictionary of the Malay Language."

[5] "Journal of the Indian Archipelago." Vol. II., p. 695 (1848).

[6] Miklouho-Maclay Proc. Lin. Soc., N.S.W. Vol. X., p. 349.

[7] Miklouho-Maclay (Ibid., p. 353, 357).

[8] Crawfurd's "Malay Dictionary."

the familiar "Isonandra gutta" of this region.[1] . . . . Some of the names of trees in Bougainville Straits I have been unable to trace further westward than New Guinea. Thus, the breadfruit-tree ("Artocarpus incisa") is the *Balia* of Bougainville Straits and the *Boli* of the Maclay coast of New Guinea.[2]

The term *Uri*, which is applied in a slightly altered form to different fruits in the Melanesian Islands, would seem to be derived from the Indian Archipelago. Proceeding westward from the Banks Group where *Ur* is the name of the fruit of "Spondias dulcis," we find that in New Georgia in the Solomon Islands *Ure* is a designation for fruit. In the neighbouring islands of Bougainville Straits, several species of "Ficus" and their fruits receive the name of *Uri*. To the westward of the Solomon Islands we come upon the same term in the Mafoor of New Guinea, where the breadfruit is known as *Ur*. Lastly, in the island of Ceram in the Indian Archipelago, the fruit of the banana is called *Uri*.[3]

On this unequivocal evidence of one of the sources of the languages of the islands of Bougainville Straits it is unnecessary to dilate. It should, however, be remembered that other words are distinctly Polynesian in their origin, and must be sought for in the languages of the Pacific groups. Thus, whilst *numa*, the word for "house," finds its counterpart in the Malay *rumah* and the Javanese *uma*, *fale-fale*, which also signifies a house, is the *vale* of the New Hebrides (Lepers Island and Aurora Island), the *vale* of Fiji, the *fale* of Samoa and Tonga, and the *whare* of the Maori. According to Dr. Codrington, these two words signifying a house, *fale* and *ruma*, with their various forms, have an interesting distribution. The first belongs to the eastern Pacific, and the second to the western Pacific; but they overlap in the intermediate districts as in the New Hebrides and the Solomon Islands. It is, however, significant that both these words should be included in the language of Bougainville Straits.

I will conclude my remarks on this vocabulary with a reference to the imitative character of the names of some of the animals. In Bougainville Straits, the frog is known as *appa-appa* in imitation of

---

[1] By an easy transition from *gdtah* through *katari* to *kauri* we have the probable origin of the native name of the resin-yielding "Dammara australis" (Kauri Pine) of New Zealand.

[2] Miklouho-Maclay in Proc. Lin. Soc., N.S.W. Vol. X., p. 348.

[3] I am mainly indebted to Dr. Codrington's "Melanesian Languages" for the distribution of this term.

its cry.   For a similar reason it is known in New Britain as *rok-rok*,[1] in Australia as *twonk*,[2] and in the Malay Archipelago as *codac*.[3]   The lizard is named *kurru-rupu* by the natives of these straits, an appellation which is suggested by its cry; in the Malay Archipelago it is known as *kikia*.[4]   The hornbill is called *po-po* by the natives of Bougainville Straits in imitation of the rushing sound that it makes during its flight, which has been aptly compared by travellers to the noise of a locomotive.   For this reason the natives of New Britain term it *banga-banga*;[5] whilst at Redscar Bay, New Guinea, it is called *pawporo*.[6]   In a like manner the native dog of these straits is named *au-au*, and the bush-hen (Megapod) *kokole*; there is, however, no necessity to supplement these more familiar imitative names from the numerous examples in the languages of neighbouring regions.   The native names, which the frog and the hornbill have received in the localities alluded to, will serve to show how varied may be the form of the name which has been suggested by the noise or cry of the animal.   There would, thus, appear at first sight to be but little connection between the names *po-po* and *banga-banga*; yet those persons who have been familiar with the noise made by the hornbill during its flight will recognise these terms as distinctly imitative of such a sound.   Again, few would guess that such different sounding names, as *appa-appa*, *rok-rok*, *twonk*, and *codac*, have been very naturally suggested by the cry of the frog.

[1] Wilfred Powell's "Wanderings in a Wild Country," &c.
[2] Tylor's "Primitive Culture."
[3] Labillardière's "Voyage in search of La Pérouse." (Vocabularies in Vol. II.)
[4] Labillardière. Ibid.
[5] Wilfred Powell. Ibid.
[6] Macgillivray's "Voyage of H.M.S. 'Rattlesnake.'"

CHAPTER XI

A CONSIDERABLE interest was aroused in the minds of geographers, rather more than a century ago, by the recent discoveries of French and English navigators in that portion of the
Western Pacific in which the Solomon Islands are now known to
lie. M. M. Buache and Fleurieu (pages 263-265.) endeavoured to
show that the islands there discovered were none other than the
mysterious Islands of Solomon discovered two centuries before by
the Spaniards, the existence of which had been long treated as a
myth, and in fact, had almost been forgotten. This view was
opposed by Mr. Dalrymple, one of the foremost of the English
geographers ; and it laboured under the serious disadvantage that
the only existing narrative of this Spanish voyage, on which such a
conclusion could be based, was a very brief and imperfect account
incorporated by Dr. Figueroa[1] in a work that was published at
Madrid nearly half a century after the return of the voyagers to
Peru. There were some reasons for believing that Hernando
Gallego, the chief pilot of the expedition, had kept a journal of the
voyage ;[2] but the geographical writers of the close of last century
failed to have access to such an account, and its existence was
doubted by some of them. The only other account, worthy of the
name, that was known to these writers was one included by Herrera
in his " Descripcion de las Indias Occidentales," a work which was
published at Madrid about the year 1601, or more than thirty years
after the Spanish voyagers had returned to Peru. But this account
was a somewhat vague, general description of the Solomon Islands,

[1] Hechos de Don Garcia Hurtado de Mendoza, Quarto Marques de Canete ; por el Doctor
Christoval Suarez de Figueroa. Madrid, 1613. *Vide* Note I. of the Geographical Appendix.
[2] A MS. journal of Gallego was referred to by Penelo as occurring in the Barcia Library.
(Dalrymple's Hist. Coll. Voy. and Disc : p. 96.)

which, although it contained a few additional particulars, was of little service to the cartographer.

It appears to have been only in the second quarter of the present century that the existence of a journal written by Gallego became known to geographers. It may seem at first sight difficult to explain the reason of this narrative being so long unknown; but its author tells us in his prologue that it was through fear he did not publish it; and from other circumstances, referred to in the succeeding pages, it may be inferred that pressure was brought to bear on him, and that the journal was intentionally withheld in order to keep Drake, who had recently appeared in the South Sea, in ignorance of the position of these islands. The journal has for this reason always remained in manuscript. The original manuscript was a few years since in the possession of Mr. Amhurst. There is a copy in the library of the British Museum, which was purchased of M. Fr. Michelena y Roiss in 1848;[1] and it is a translation of this copy that is given in great part in the following pages. In undertaking this translation, I have been greatly assisted by my acquaintance with these islands; and I have thus been able to avoid the pitfalls into which the somewhat careless copyist might have led me.

If M. M. Buacho and Fleurieu could have had access to this journal of Gallego, they would have been saved much laborious criticism, both on their own part and on the part of others. That they were able to employ the scanty data, furnished by Figueroa, for the identification of the lost Isles of Solomon with the recent discoveries of their own day, is an accomplishment concerning which any adulation on my part would be both unnecessary and unbecoming. Even with the comparative wealth of materials which the journal of Gallego affords, as contrasted with the account of Figueroa, all that remained to be done was to fill in the rude outline originally sketched by the French geographers.

The story of the gradual identification of the Isles of Solomon forms an interesting and instructive episode in the history of geographical discovery. In the sketch which I have given, I have, so to speak, raked up the ashes of a controversy which burnt itself out some generations ago; but the labour expended in its prepara-

[1] The British Museum Reference number is 17,623; and the title is as follows: "Descubrimiento de las Islas Salomon en el Mar del Sur: 1566," by Hernando Gallego, native of Corunna.

N

tion will not have been unprofitable, if I have been successful in placing before my readers a clear and connected account of how the Isles of Solomon were discovered, lost, and found.

We find in the prologue, with which Gallego commences his account of this voyage, an explanation not only of the principal object of the expedition, but also of the motive which led the Spanish navigator to draw up his narrative. It was for the propagation of the Christian faith amongst the peoples of the unknown islands of the West that this expedition was dispatched from the shores of Peru ; and it was to guide the missionary to the field of his labour that the chief pilot drew up his relation of the voyage.

"I understand it to be incumbent"—thus Gallego writes—"on the men who follow the nautical profession, and have had the good fortune, in some degree, to take precedence of their fellows, to give an account of their success. And there are many reasons why it is necessary that from the ignorant these things should not be concealed. But for me, Christian piety affords the principal inducement; and especially since it moved the mind of that most Christian and most Catholic monarch, Don Philip, to write to his Governor, the most illustrious Lope Garcia de Castro, that he should convert every infidel to Christ. Imbued with this feeling, I have made it my first object, by means of this relation and of the additions made by me to the sea-chart, to enable the missionaries, who are to guide the infidels into the vineyard of the Lord, to know where these places will be found and to learn how to navigate these seas exposed to the fury of the winds, and how all dangers and enemies may be avoided. This is my design, unless I am otherwise convinced. Let the curious accept this brief discourse. It is from fear that its author has not wished to print it. This is my object: such is my desire. Receive, reader, this token of esteem, and be steadfast in God. Farewell!"

Before proceeding with the journal of Gallego, it is necessary for me to remark that I have relegated to an appendix much of that which is of interest to the geographical student. The reason is an obvious one and needs no further reference, since the narrative often takes the character of a sea-log, and the geographical and critical points involved are necessarily only of special interest.

The Governor, Lope Garcia de Castro, gave orders for the equipment of two ships of the fleet for the discovery of certain islands
and a continent (tierra firme) concerning which His Catholic Majesty
D. Philip II. had summoned a number of persons versed in mathe-
matics in order to deliberate on the plan to be followed. After
selecting the vessels, he nominated as Generalin command of the
expedition his nephew, Alvaro de Mendana; as Commander of
the troops (maestre de campo), Pedro de Ortega Valencia; as the
Royal Ensign, D. Fernando Enriquez; and lastly, as Chief-Pilot—
to quote the words of the journal—"myself, the said Hernando
Gallego."

The number of all that embarked on this voyage, including,
besides the soldiers and sailors, four Franciscan friars and the
servants, was a hundred. The preparations were made with such
alacrity and willingness that the ships were fitted out with a dis-
patch that seemed scarcely credible; and on the 19th day of Nov.,
1566,[1] being Wednesday, the day of St. Isabel, the two ships sailed
from Callao, the port of the City of Kings, which is situated, as
Gallego remarks, in 12¼° S. lat. Shaping their course to the south-
west, they had not to allow for the variation of the compass, since
the needle pointed direct to the pole; and reference is here made in
the journal to the circumstance that in Spain, more particularly in
the city of Seville, the needle varied one point to the north-west.
Steering in the same southerly and westerly direction until the 27th
of the same month, they reached the latitude of 15¼°, being by their
reckoning 57 leagues[2] due west from the "morro de Uacaxique,"
which was in the same latitude.[3] They now shaped their course
west, following along the parallel of 15¾°, because "the Lord President had said that in the latitude of 15°, at a distance of 600 leagues
from Peru, there were many rich islands." With the wind "a long
time in the south-east," they accomplished a usual daily run of from
20 to 30 leagues. By the third of December, they were by their
reckoning in the meridian of the bay of Fego,[4] which is stated by
Gallego to be situated in 16° north of the equinoctial and 546
leagues due north of their position. On the 7th of the same
month, the Chief-Pilot recorded his observation that the needle

---

[1] *Vide* Note II. of Geographical Appendix.
[2] Spanish leagues, 17½ to a degree, all through the narrative.
[3] I have not been able to fin l this name in any maps or charts.
[4] In the maps I have examined there is no bay of this name given.

showed no variation from the pole and that it neither dipped nor tilted up.

"At this time," he writes, "I inquired of the pilots as to our position ; but I only provoked their obstinacy : and we went on our voyage sailing across the ocean to discover land. We noticed the flight of the birds that passed us in the morning and evening, and whence they came, and whither they went towards the setting sun. All this was no certain guide, as some flew north and others south ; and there was nothing to justify our pursuing the flying-fish which abounded in those seas." It is right that I should here allude to the importance attached by the voyagers of this period to the flight of birds which had often guided them to the discovery of new lands. It was for this reason, it will be remembered, that Columbus swerved from his westerly course when approaching the American Continent.

Gallego soon began to lose confidence in the opinion of the Lord President, because pursuing their course along the same parallel of $15\frac{3}{4}°$ they failed to observe any signs of land. On the 12th of December, being in the meridian of the harbour of La Navidad (a port on the Pacific coast of Mexico, in lat. 19° 12′ N., long. 104° 46′ W.), there was a consultation between Gallego and the other pilots, when their latitudes were found to agree, but the dead reckoning of the pilots was greater. At length, on the 16th of the month, it was resolved by the Chief-Pilot to leave this parallel and head more to the northward, as they were now 620 leagues rather more than less from Peru and there were no signs of their approaching land.

Accordingly the course was altered ; and for four days they ran west-by-north reaching the latitude of $13\frac{3}{4}°$, and accomplishing 166 leagues. During the 20th and 21st of December they steered north-west for 65 leagues, keeping a good look-out for land, but to no purpose. On the 22nd, after steering to the north-west-by-west for 30 leagues, they reached the parallel of 11°. They then coursed north-west until the 26th, which was St. Stephen's Day, having gone by their reckoning 95 leagues and attaining, as their observations showed, a latitude rather under nine degrees (nueve grados escasos). It is . worthy of note that in the daily record, which was at this time kept by Gallego of the course and distance and of the latitude obtained by observation, it usually happens that the computed latitude is considerably less than that observed.[1] In this journal, however, the latitudes are all those of observation except where it is

---

[1] This circumstance was, probably, due to a strong southerly drift.

otherwise mentioned. During the 27th and 28th of December they stood to the west-north-west for 60 leagues; and on the two following days they steered west-by-north for 62 leagues, reaching the latitude of 6¼°. It is here recorded that the needle was deflected a third of a point to the north-west. On the last day of the year they sailed 30 leagues to the west, experiencing strong currents.

Hitherto no signs of land had been observed, and, in consequence, symptoms of uneasiness showed themselves amongst the crews. As they sailed along, they were led in their imaginations to believe that they were always on the point of making the land; but no land appeared. "The pilots told me," writes Gallego in his journal, "that I was the only person who was not disheartened after having sailed so many leagues without seeing land: and when I told them that they would suffer no ill and that, with the favour of God, they would see the land at the end of January, they all kept silent and made no reply."

The 1st of January, 1567, found the Spanish voyagers steering west along the parallel of 6¼°; and in accordance with the opinions of his fellow pilots, Gallego kept this course until the 7th, traversing in the time about 125 leagues.[1] They now experienced unsettled weather, the wind shifting to the north and subsequently to the north-east. Although steering west-by-south, they did not change their latitude as much as they expected; and, on the 10th, after accomplishing 30 leagues on this course during the past three days, they found their latitude in 6¼°. During the 11th and 12th with a very favourable wind they sailed 55 leagues to the west on the same parallel. Heavy rain-squalls here overtook them; and they ran along under easy sail.

"On this day," writes Gallego, "they signalled from the "Almiranta" (the general's ship) to ask where the land should be. I replied that it lay, in my opinion, 300 leagues away; and that at all events we should not sight it until the end of the month. At this time some of the people began to doubt whether we should ever see the land. But I always told them that, if God was with them, it would be His pleasure that they should not suffer ill." During the 13th they steered west 25 leagues and found themselves in the parallel of 6°. On the following day they ran in the same

---

[1] For one day, Saturday the 3rd, there is no record in the Journal of the distance run. To allow for this omission, I have taken 18 leagues as being the average daily run during this week.

direction for 30 leagues, experiencing much rain and varying winds. Their water supply was failing, and the minds of many were the more depressed; for these reasons they ran on with eased sheets and did not shorten sail.

But the long-expected land was near, and I will permit Gallego for the time to tell his own story. " On the Thursday the 15th of January, we had heavy showers of rain and such thunder and lightning as we had not seen in all the voyage. We were distant from the land of Peru, on the course which we had steered, 1450 leagues. In the following[1] morning we ran with a light wind 15 leagues south-west-by-west, and were in the latitude of $6\frac{1}{4}°$. A seaman went to the top and discovered land in the shape of a small island, which appeared on the port hand to the south-west-by-west. We were about six leagues from it, because being a low island it could not be seen at a greater distance. Keeping away, we reached it at sunset. This island is low and level. It has many reefs around it, and has quite a bay of the sea in the middle of it. After we had arrived, I found the latitude to be $6\frac{3}{4}°$. We were eager to send a boat in; but, however, it was thought best to await the arrival of the 'Almiranta' which was much behind us.

" In the meantime seven canoes full of people started from the island. Some turned back to the shore and the remainder came off to the ship. But when they saw so many persons, they returned to the beach and made great bonfires. That night they put up flags, seemingly for the protection of the island. We were not able to determine whether they were mats of palm-leaves or of cotton, they were bleached so white.[2] The people in the canoes were naked and of a tawny hue. When the 'Almiranta' arrived, we agreed that no boats should land until the next day, as it was then evening. And when it dawned, it blew so strong from the north-west that we drifted a quarter of a league to leeward of the island. I wished to reach it, but could not, as the wind was so strong that we could carry no sails. I advised that, if we beat up to reach the island with the wind so strong and contrary, the ships might be broken in pieces (on the reefs); that it would not be wise to run the risk of losing all our lives for an island so small; and that seeing that the island was inhabited, the rest could not be far away.

---

[1] The word "following" has been added by me, since from the subsequent remarks of Gallego, it is evident that this land was sighted on the 16th.

[2] Mats of very fine quality are manufactured in many of the Pacific islands.

Although being so near to this island, we could not get bottom with 200 fathoms."

The decision of Gallego naturally caused much discontent amongst the crews. "The soldiers murmured"—thus the Journal continues—"because they were unwilling to leave this island, notwithstanding that they would run the chance of losing their lives. Being weary of the voyage, they took no pains to conceal their displeasure. But I cheered them and consoled them with the assurance that they would meet with no misfortune, and that with the grace of God, I would give them more land than they would be able to people; for this island (as I pointed out to them) was not more than five or six leagues in size. I gave it the name of the Isle of Jesus, because we arrived at it on the day after that which we accounted the 15th of January."[1]

As the Spanish voyagers were now approaching the scene of their future discoveries, their course becomes of peculiar interest to the historical geographer.[2] Continuing their voyage on the 17th of January, they had before them a long and tedious passage, having to contend with contrary winds and being swept north and south in turns by the currents. On the 23rd, they were in the latitude of 6°, and on the 28th in 5¼°. At length on Sunday the 1st of February, when they were according to their reckoning 165 leagues from the Isle of Jesus, they discovered two leagues away[3] some banks of reefs with some islets in the middle of them. "These shoals"—as described by Gallego—"ran obliquely from north-east to south-west. We were not able"—so he writes—"to get their extremity within our range of sight; but as far as we could see them they extended more than fifteen leagues. We gave them the name of 'Los Bajos de la Candelaria,' because we saw them on Candlemas Eve: and I took the latitude near them, when we lay east and west with their centre, and found it to be 6¼°." On referring to the present Admiralty charts, it will be noticed that the name "Candelaria Reef," is applied to an atoll lying about eighty miles to the north of the large island of Isabel in the Solomon Group and named "El Roncador" by Maurelle the Spanish navi-

---

[1] It is scarcely possible to identify this island with any of the islands marked in the latest Admiralty charts. *Vide* Note III. of the Geographical Appendix.

[2] I would direct the nautical reader to Note V. of the Geographical Appendix which refers to Gallego's observations of latitude in this group. He will thus be saved some confusion in comparing the Spanish latitudes with those of the present charts.

[3] Thus the distance of these shoals from the Isle of Jesus would be probably about 167 leagues in all. Figueroa gives the distance as 160 leagues.

gator in 1781.   Now, seeing that this atoll is not more than six
miles across, it cannot possibly be identical with the extensive reefs
which are above described by Gallego under the name of the
Candelaria Shoals.   As shown in the appendix,[1] it is highly probable that these shoals are the same with those which lie about
35 miles to the north of the Roncador Reef, where they constitute
an atoll fifty miles in width which was discovered by the Dutch
navigators Le Maire and Schouten in 1616, and was named "Ontong
Java " by Tasman in 1643.

Leaving these shoals, they steered south-west, expecting to
sight land, which could not have been, in the opinion of Gallego,
more than fifty leagues distant.   During the night, however, they
had to heave-to on account of the heavy weather; and on the
following day, which was the day of our Lady of Candlemas, they
experienced the same weather and were obliged to take in all sail.
During the next day, which was the 4th of February, the weather
improved; and steering at first west-by-north they subsequently
stood to the south-west; and as night approached they shortened
sail, in the event of there being other reefs and shoals such as those
they had already passed.   The prevailing winds had been north-
west; but on the following day the wind went round to the west
and fell very light.   For four days they had been unable to take
observations on account of the thick weather.   On the 5th,[2] their
latitude was found in 7° 8', from which Gallego inferred that in
those four days they had drifted fifteen leagues to the south-by-west.
They now made sail and headed north.[3] (?)

" This day," writes Gallego, " was Saturday, the 7th of February,
and the 80th day since we set out from Callao, the port of the City
of the Kings.   In the morning I ordered a seaman to go aloft to the
top and scan the south for land, because there seemed to me to be
in that quarter an elevated mass; and the seaman reported land.
The land soon became visible to us; and a signal of our discovery
was made to the ' Almiranta ' which was half a league from the
' Capitana ' (Gallego's vessel).   Every one received the news with
feelings of great joy and gratitude for the favour which God had
granted them through the intercession of the Blessed Virgin, the

---

[1] *Vide* Note IV. of the Geographical Appendix.

[2] There is apparently an error in the journal with reference to this date, since the 6th is
omitted altogether.

[3] The subsequent remarks relative to the course show that there is here an error in the
M.S., or in the original journal.

Glorious Mother of God, whom we all believed to be our mediator; and the 'Te Deum laudamus' was sung."

They were distant from the land, when they first saw it, about 15 leagues. It is described in the journal as "very high." Turning the ships' heads in that direction, after they had gone 3 or 4 leagues, they discovered much more land belonging to the same island which appeared to be a continent. They did not get up to it until the evening of the next day, which was Sunday the 8th of February.

"Shortly after we arrived," continues Gallego in his narrative, "many large and small canoes came off to see us, displaying signs of amity. But they did not dare to come alongside the vessels; and as we approached the land, they kept away. However the General threw them some coloured caps, and being thus assured they came alongside the ship. The boat was launched, and in it went Juan Enriquez with eight musketeers and target-men (rodoleros) to see if they could find a port to anchor in, and also to search for the place whence the canoes had come. The rest of the natives became more confident, and some of them came on board the ship. As they behaved well, we gave them things to eat and drink; and they remained on board until it began to grow dark, when they got into their canoes and went ashore. And those who had gone away in the boat, seeing that it was getting dusk, returned without having found any port. As soon as it was dark we stood out to sea, and the natives in the canoes returned to their homes. They told us that for the sake of friendship we should have gone with them, and that they would have entertained us and given us plenty to eat.

" We stood to windward that night with a light wind; and the currents carried us more than three leagues to the west-north-west, bringing us over some reefs on which we might have been lost as the sea was breaking around them. Finding ourselves in seven fathoms of water, we at once made course to stand clear of them. We remained under easy canvas until it dawned, when we saw that the currents had carried us right upon the shoals; and as the sea broke around us, we made more sail. I hailed the 'Almiranta' to make the best of her way out of her position among the shoals; and we accordingly stood away until we found a sufficient depth."

Juan Enriquez was now dispatched in the boat to find a harbour for the ships; but he was deterred by the sight of all the reefs and returned to the ship. He was ordered by the General to go back

again and carry out his search, and "I told him "—adds Gallego—
"that it was necessary for the safety of the ships that he should
find a port without delay." The position of the Spanish vessels was
a truly critical one ; and only those who have been similarly situated
in a sailing ship in unsurveyed waters, studded with unknown coral
reefs, can realise how anxious the moment was.

"Committing ourselves to God "—thus Gallego writes—" I sent a
man aloft to the fore-top, and placed another on the bowsprit, and I
told them to notice where the shoals were white. The sounding-
lead was kept in hand ; and in the event of our having to go about
or to anchor, we stood by the sheets and bowlines and had the
anchor cleared. I steered for the place where we found seven
fathoms of water, as it seemed to me that we should not find a less
depth. The boat had not yet reached the shore, so I determined to
sound and I got twelve fathoms with a clear bottom ; and farther
on it was deeper and also clear of rocks. Although it was mid-day,
a star appeared to us over the entrance of the reef. Taking it as a
guide and as a good omen, we were cheered in spirit and became
more hopeful. As we proceeded, the water deepened little by little :
and I informed the General that we were already clear of the reefs . . .
I signalled to the 'Almiranta' to follow us. As we neared the
harbour where the boat had gone, they signalled to us that they had
found a good anchorage. Presently we entered the harbour with
the star over the bow, and we anchored, the 'Almiranta' entering
shortly afterwards. At the entrance of the port is a rock (or islet),
in size larger than the ship.

"It was the day of Santa Polonia, the 9th of February. The
harbour, which is in the latitude of 7° 50", we named the port of
Santa Isabel del Estrella ; and we named the island, Santa Isabel.
The Indians called the island Camba ; and their cacique is named
Billebanarra. This harbour lies nearly in the middle of the north
coast of the island, and is 26 leagues north-east and south-west from
the reefs.[1] Having disembarked with the other captains, I took
possession of the island in the name of His Majesty. A cross was
erected : and I chose a convenient place for building a brigantine."

On the following day, Gallego landed with the carpenters ; and
they began with all diligence to fell the trees and to saw the planks

[1] The reefs, here referred to, are evidently the Candelaria Shoals. This bearing of the
harbour with these shoals does not warrant the position which has been assigned to Estrella
Bay in the present Admiralty Chart, its position there being due south of these reefs.

for the construction of the brigantine. Meanwhile the General had sent Pedro Sarmiento with thirty men into the interior. They penetrated about five leagues, and met with some Indians, one of whom they took as a hostage. This native was treated kindly by the General; and he was set at liberty in order that he might carry a favourable account to the other natives of the island. During this incursion, a soldier had been struck by an arrow, but received no hurt. Shortly afterwards, a larger force was dispatched under Pedro de Ortega to explore the interior. The expedition included 52 persons, and comprised 35 soldiers, with some seamen and negroes. They were absent seven days from the ship; and from the account of Gallego, we may infer that but little discretion was employed in their dealings with the natives. They burned "many temples dedicated to the worship of snakes, toads, and other insects;" and, as the result of such proceedings, two soldiers were wounded, one of whom subsequently died of tetanus. His name was Alonzo Martin, and he bore the character of a good soldier.

"These people," writes the Chief Pilot, "are tawny and have crisp hair. They go naked, wearing only short aprons of palm leaves. They have as food some maizes or roots which they call *benaus* and plenty of fish. They are, in my opinion, a clean race, and I am certain that they eat human flesh." On the 15th of March, whilst the Spaniards were at mass on shore, a fleet of fourteen canoes arrived at the place where the brigantine was being built. The cacique, who was in command, sent the General a present of a quarter of a boy, including the arm and hand, together with some roots (benaus), which he requested him to accept. In order that the natives should understand that the Spaniards did not eat human flesh, the General ordered it to be buried in their presence, at which they were abashed and hung their heads, and returned to an islet which was situated at the entrance of the harbour. This cacique, who is termed in the Journal the Taurique Meta, lived at a place fifteen leagues from the harbour to the west-by-north. Pedro de Ortega, with the two pilots, Pedro Roanges and Juan Enriquez, were sent with thirty soldiers and four Indians to visit the place where this taurique lived. They were absent four days, and effected nothing except the capture of four Indians, two of whom they retained as hostages in order to compel the natives to bring them provisions.

On the 4th of April, the brigantine was launched, and the

rigging was set up. It having been resolved that she should proceed on a voyage to discover the other islands and harbours, Gallego,
Ortega, with 18 soldiers[1] and 12 sailors, embarked on board; and
on the 7th of April they left the port. Following the coast along
to the south-east, they came to two islets, lying six leagues away
from the port of Santa Isabel de la Estrella, and situated, according
to an observation of Gallego, exactly in the latitude of 8°. On
these islets were many palms which were deemed to be palmettos
and cocoa-nut trees. "This land," as the Chief Pilot remarks,
"trends south-east and north-west. The needle stood a point to
the north-east and there remained. Proceeding on our cruise, we
saw many islets in the same direction . . . . [2] 5 leagues from
where we had started; and we anchored at an islet in which we
found a canoe and three houses. We landed 7 soldiers; and they
went up towards the houses in search of the Indians, who, however,
carried off their canoe. On reaching the houses, the soldiers found
a quantity of provisions, which they brought on board the brigantine. Continuing our voyage along the coast, 17 canoes came out
to us. In them came an exceedingly daring Indian, who, calling
himself the cacique Babalay, held his bow towards us, and signified
to us that we should go with him, and that, if we should not wish
to go, he would carry us by force and would kill us. On account of
his audacity, the "maestre de campo" ordered them to fire and
knocked him down with a shot; and when those in the canoes saw
him fall, they all fled to the shore. Shortly afterwards, I tacked
towards the shore in order to make a port, as the wind was strong.
In a little time we came to an anchor, and I found by observation
that the latitude was 8¼° . . . . [3]" Leaving this anchorage,
they stood out to sea, with the wind in the north-north-west; and
in a short time they kept away and followed the coast along to the
south-east-by-east.

"And as we sailed on," continues Gallego, "the mast sprung and
nearly fell on us. Seeing what had happened, I ordered the sails to
be secured and the tackle to be brought to the weather side, and in

[1] According to the MS. in this passage, only 10 soldiers embarked; but on one occasion
during the cruise it is stated that 18 soldiers were landed (vide p. 207), a number which agrees
with that given by Figueroa.

[2] The words omitted here are in the Spanish: "hasta la provincia de Vallas."

[3] Reference is here made to the fact that the coast ran north-west-by-west with the
island of Meta, which was seven (?) leagues distant. This island of Meta was probably a
small coast island on which the chief of that name lived.

this manner the mast was "stayed." When the night overtook us we were without knowledge of any port, having much thick weather with wind and rain. Guided by the phosphorescence of the sea we skirted the reefs; and when I saw that the reefs did not make the sea phosphorescent, I weathered the point and entered a good harbour at the fourth hour of the night, where, much to our ease, we passed (the remainder of) the night.[1] This port is 6 leagues from where we set out, and is in a great bay. It is capacious and has 7 or 8 inhabited islands. The next day I disembarked the people to get water and wood; and we saw coming to the beach more than a hundred Indians, carrying their bows and arrows and clubs with which they are accustomed to fight. The 'maestre de campo' ordered those on shore to embark, fearing some ambuscade. Soon the Indians arrived but they did nothing, and a canoe came. Seeing that they made no attack, the 'maestre de campo' ordered four soldiers to go ashore and fire three or four shots to frighten them; and when this was done and the Indians saw it, they shot their arrows and took to flight. Thus passed the 12th of April.

" Whilst in this bay we saw to seaward a very large island which lies east and west with this bay. This island is called in the language of those Indians, Malaita. The west extreme of this island lies east and west with the point of Meta.[2] This island lies with the shoals of Candelaria north-west-by-west and south-east-by-east 52 leagues;[3] and the extremity of this island of Malaita is in 8°; it is distant from the island of Santa Isabel 14 leagues; it has 5 or 6 islets at the extremity, which are, each of them, 2 leagues in circuit. There are two islets in the middle, between the two large islands. The name of the Isle of Ramos suggested itself for this Island of

---

[1] To find in a dark night and in thick weather an opening in a line of coral-reef on an unknown coast, is an undertaking fraught with the greatest hazard, even for a ship possessing steam power. The only available guide is that which was followed by this clear-headed navigator; but it is one which, as it depends on the luminosity of the sea, can only be of occasional service. When the sea has been unusually phosphorescent, each roller, as it breaks on the weather-edge of the reef, is marked by a disconnected line of light, reminding one of the straggling fire of a line of musketry. I once saw this phenomenon splendidly exhibited on the coast of Japan, the sea-surface being crowded with myriads of "Noctilucæ."

[2] The point of Meta is probably near the place where the chief of that name lived. *Vide* page 203.

[3] "Norueste sueste quarta de leste hueste" is the bearing given in the MS. The distance of 52 leagues very closely corresponds with the distance indicated on the present chart between the west end of Malaita and Ontong Java. (*Vide* appendix: note iv.)

Malaita, because it was discovered on Palm Sunday (Domingo de Ramos).[1]

"Coasting further along from this bay, we saw a fleet of more than seven large canoes making for the shore where there were fisheries. The canoes came on with us; and many Indians shot their arrows at us with great shouting. The 'maestro de campo,' on seeing their daring, ordered some muskets to be fired; and one Indian was killed and the rest took to flight. On the following day, which we made the 14th of April, running further along the coast to the east-south-east (?) we sailed nearly 6 leagues. Here the Indians came out to us in a friendly manner, bringing cocoa-nut and other things which we needed. Here we saw a hog, which was the first we had seen. The next day we went further out in quest of the point and extremity of this island, running to the south-east. From the bay to the point of the island, the coast ran north-west and south-east. There are some islets near this point; and from this point to the bay is 14 leagues. I took the latitude and found it to be barely 9°. At this point, two canoes came out to us with fighting-men, in order to question an Indian whom we had on board, one of the two we took from Meta. They shot their arrows at us; and when we fired a musket to frighten them, they fled.

"On the following day, which we reckoned the 16th of the month, being at the extremity of this island, we named it Cape Pueto;[2] and from here we discovered some islands to the south-east,[3] which are 9 leagues from this cape. Some lie north-by-west and south-by-east;[4] and others north-west and south-east. And we approached them this day with a fair wind, sailing to the south-east. We arrived at ten o'clock in the night at an island which was a league and a half in circuit; and there we anchored. It is

---

[1] Through an unconscious error in the translations by Mr. Dalrymple and Capt. Burney of the account given by Figueroa, the name "Isle of Ramos" has been applied in modern charts to an islet nearly in the middle of the passage between Isabel and Malaita. For further particulars consult Note VI. of appendix.

[2] The name of this cape is spelt in three different ways in this MS., viz., Puerto, Pueto, and Prieto. The latter is that adopted in Figueroa's account. Puerto seems to be the correct name as no reason is given in the journal for using the epithet of "black" (prieto); but the last is employed in the present chart.

[3] In the account of Figueroa this bearing is given as south-west, which, as pointed out by Pingré, Fleurieu, and Burney, is in contradiction to the other bearings, and was by all three authors replaced by that of "south-east."

[4] Norte sur quarta del noroeste sueste."

low and beset with reefs. We sailed around it. It has many palms, is inhabited ; and it was there we passed the night. When it dawned, we were desirous to land but could not on account of the numerous shoals and reefs. It was named 'La Galera.' Here a canoe came off to us carrying 50 men whom we perceived to be ready for battle. . . .[1] It preceded us to another large island which was a league distant. It was soon joined by many canoes both small and large ; and in (one of) them came a leading taurique. He came and approached us in a friendly manner, and gave us beads (chaquiza), of the kind they wear, which resemble those that are found in Puerto-viejo.[2] The ' maestre de campo ' gave him a good reception ; and in token of peace presented him with some things which we had on board. Soon the taurique commanded the men in the canoes to take the brigantine in tow and bring us into the harbour, which they did. After we were inside, the ' maestre de campo ' landed with 18 soldiers ; and I remained with 12 on board the brigantine. The Indians soon took up their weapons, and hurled stones at us, and jeered at us because we asked for provisions. Seeing their insolence, some shots were fired at them, and two Indians were killed. Thereupon they fled, leaving their houses defenceless. This island is called in the language of the Indians, Pela.[3] And there is a chain of five islands, which lie east and west one with another. The first of these, which we came to, was at the east end, for we were pursuing our discoveries from East to West ; it lies with the Cape Prieto north-west and south-east, 9 leagues from the said cape. It will be in circuit 12 leagues. It is well peopled by natives and has many huts and towns and. . . .[4] To this island we gave the name of Buena Vista from its appearance ; it seemed to be very fertile, and was well-peopled ; and the rest are as above mentioned. They go naked, without any covering *whatever*, and have their faces patterned (tattooed).[5] There are many inhabited islands around. I took the latitude

---

[1] As the meaning is obscure, I have here omitted the following : "and coming close to us " which is followed in the Spanish by "no nos dijo cosa nise movieron contra nosotros," which I have left untranslated.

[2] A town in the province of Quito, in the kingdom of Peru.

[3] Gela is the present native name of the Florida Islands. (Codrington's "Melanesian Languages," p. 522, *cited*). Consult Note VII. of the geographical appendix.

[4] "Lugares formados y juntos." These words, which I have not translated, are to be found unaltered in Figueroa's account, and have been rendered thus by Dalrymple " places cultivated and enclosed."

[5] " Las caras labradas."

here, and found it to be 9½° south of the equinoctial. It runs east and west.

"On Good Friday of this same year we went from this island to another a league distant. We found in it abundance of cocoa-nuts; and we placed a quantity on board the brigantine for our sustenance. Whilst we were at this island, a canoe came off to us with three Indians; they left us to go from there to the large island; and they offered us hogs, but we did not want them.

"On arriving at the large island, the 'maestre de campo' landed and came to a town which was on high-ground. Here they gave him two hogs, which he brought off with him to the ship, having met with no bad treatment; and we returned to pass the night at the islet (?). This day was Holy Saturday. On the following day, which was the Feast of the Resurrection, we skirted the south coast of the island; and from here we went to another island, which is a league from it. On our arrival, there came off to us more than 20 canoes of fighting-men, who planned taking us to their town and capturing us, and displayed much delight amongst themselves. I ordered the anchor to be weighed that we might get to a better place, because we were almost touching the shoals. When the Indians saw that we were about to shift our position, they got into their canoes in a great hurry with their bows and arrows, and clubs, and many stones; and in a very fierce manner they began to shoot their arrows and stones at us. Seeing their daring, we replied with the muskets; and many Indians were killed, and the whole were repulsed; and they rallied and came on to the attack with greater fury; but this time they suffered even more, and for the second time they were repulsed and routed. There were more than 700 Indians. We took three canoes; but afterwards we abandoned two and kept the other. Deserting their towns, they went off with many howls and cries to the higher land in the interior. Soon the 'maestre de campo' landed with 20 men: and he endeavoured to bring off some provisions to the brigantine, and to restore friend-ship with the natives; but from their dread of the muskets they would never approach; and they kept much in advance of them calling to each other by conch-shells and with drums. Seeing that there was no help for it, we set fire to a house, after having taken possession of the island in the name of His Majesty, as in the case of the other islands; and we gave it the name of 'La Florida.' This island is in latitude 9½° and lies east and west with the island of

Buenavista. It is 25 leagues in circuit, and is a fine island in appearance, with many inhabitants, who are also naked as in the other islands; and they redden their hair, eat human flesh, and have their towns built over the water as in Mexico.[1]

"This day we went on to other islands which are further to the east in the same latitude. The first has a circuit of 25 leagues. We had not resistance from them (the Indians); because they had already come to know that they could not overcome us, if we were prepared for them. To this island, we gave the name of San Dimas. We did not go to the remaining islands that we might not hinder ourselves. We named the one San German, and the other the Island of Guadalupe." (*Vide* Note VII. of the Geographical Appendix.)

" The next morning we went to another very large island which is on the south side of the five islands. In the middle of the way, or half-way between them, is an island which we named Sesarga. It is 8 leagues in circuit. This island is high and round and well-peopled; with plenty of food, *mames* and *panales*[2] and roots and hogs [which have no grain to eat ?]. In the middle of this island there is a volcano, which is continually emitting great smoke. It has a white streak which resembles a road descending from the higher parts down to the sea. This island is in latitude 9¾°. With the island of Buenavista it lies north-west and south-east (?).[3] Five leagues from this island, there came out 5 canoes; and they gave us a fish, telling us by signs that we should go with them to their island, and that they would give us hogs. The Indians went away; and we slept this night at sea.

"On the next day, which was the 19th of April, we arrived at the great island, which we had seen, and came upon a town of the Indians. There is a large river here; and there came out canoes to

---

[1] In the present day the natives of Florida built their houses on piles. See p. 60, of this work.

[2] Figueroa gives for *mames*, *ynaninus*; and for *panales*, *panays*. In the first instance, "yams" are probably meant ; whilst, in the second case, Burney suggests that by *panays* the "breadfruit" may be referred to. Fleurieu hints that it may be the application of the name of the "parsnip" to some other vegetable. The "taro" is evidently here alluded to.

[3] In Note VII. of the Geographical Appendix, I have treated of the question relating to the identification of the islands which lie between Cape Prieto and the north coast of Guadalcanar, with the Spanish discoveries. In so doing, I have re-opened a discussion that excited considerable interest a century ago, but which has since, notwithstanding the efforts of Burney and Krusenstern, been almost forgotten. Those acquainted with these islands will recognise in Sesarga the present Savo.

o

the brigantine, and some Indians who were swimming, and some
women and boys. They gave us a rope, and towing us, carried us to
the shore. When we were close to the beach, they began to throw
stones at us, saying, 'Mate,' 'Mate,' meaning that they were going to
kill us.[1] Some shots were fired, which killed two of them, and
immediately they left us and fled. The 'maestre de campo' landed
with 20 men, and took possession as in the case of the other islands.
In the town was found, in small baskets, a large quantity of provisions, of roots, and ginger which is plentiful in this island. We
put on board the brigantine what we could, including a hog. The
same evening, we embarked; and we gave this island the name of
Guadalcanal and to the river that of Ortega. I took the latitude,
and found it to be in $10\frac{1}{2}°$. With the higher part of Buenavista, it
lies north and south 9 leagues, and with that of Sesarga north-west
and south-east. From here we determined to return to where we
had left the ships. We, therefore, started on the return voyage.
Running back to the island of Santa Isabel, we passed by the island
of Sesarga, which is called in the language of the Indians 'Guali.'
Pursuing our way, we came close to Cape Prieto. We sailed along
the south coast and arrived at an island, 7 leagues from Cape Prieto,
which lies with the island of Sesarga north-by-west[2] 15 leagues.
The taurique of this island, Beneboneja by name, called it the island
of Veru. It is a league from that of Santa Isabel. The passage
(entrada), which is on the south-east side of the island of Beru
(Veru), has a fine harbour that is able to hold a thousand ships: it
is 6 leagues in length, has a depth of 12 to 8 fathoms, is very clear
(of shoals), and has an outlet to the north-west a league in length.[3]
This channel[4] runs west-north-west to the cape of this island, where
there is a large town which has more than 300 houses. The Indians
received us in a friendly manner, giving us a hog: and because they
would not give us more than a hog, we seized three canoes; and
when they saw that we had taken these canoes, they ransomed
them, giving for two canoes two hogs. We saw in this island some
pearls that the Indians brought, which they did not hold in

[1] There is here a strange coincidence. The natives in using the word " mate "—a widely
spread Polynesian word for " dead "—were unconsciously making a correct use of the
Spanish verb " matar," to kill.

[2] Norueste quarta del norueste (?).

[3] This fine harbour is at present known as Thousand Ships Bay. It was visited by
D'Urville, in 1838, who named his anchorage Astrolabe Harbour.

[4] The outlet to the northwest has been named Ortega Channel. It was explored by the
officers of D'Urville's expedition.

much esteem. They also brought us some tusks[1] that seemed to belong to some large animal, of which they have many: and they told us that we should take them and give them back their canoe. I considered that we should restore canoe their and accept these tusks: but the 'maestre de campo' was not willing to do so. This island is in · latitude 9¼°. We named it the island of Jorge.[2]

"We continued our return journey, sailing to the west-by-north around the said island of Santa Isabel. When we were a third part from the south-south-east portion of this island, we saw two large islands. We did not go to them, because *we had not reached the extremity of the island which we should have to round*,[3] and also because the coast is beset with many reefs and shoals which we could scarcely pass through in the brigantine, it being impossible to sail through them in ships. These islands would be 6 leagues from Santa Isabel; they are in latitude 9¼° S., as they lie east and west with the island of Veru 10 leagues. These islands, which we passed, bear east and west one with the other. The land runs much further to the west-by-north. The needle declined to the N.W.[4] I observed the sun near the river and found myself in 9° full (9 *grados largos*). In this island we saw many bats (*murcielagos*) of such a size that the wings from tip to tip measured 5 feet in expanse. This island has a breadth of 20 leagues; for I took the sun on the north side, where the ships lay, and now on the south side; and in this last I found the latitude to be 9° full (*largos*), whilst on the north side the latitude is 8° minus 8 minutes, lying north-north-east and south-south-west 20 leagues. To the two large islands, which we saw, we gave the following names, to the one San Nicolas, and to the other, which lies more to the west, the Isle of Arracises (Reefs), because there are so many reefs to pass through that it is impracticable to sail round the island.[5]

"After running for four days, but not through the nights, we

---

[1] Probably boar's tusks.

[2] The St. George's Island of the present chart.

[3] The general sense of this passage italicized is here given.

[4] For N.W. read N.E. There is evidently a mistake in the MS., as Gallego previously found the needle to vary one point to the north-east, when a few leagues from Estrella Harbour (see p. 204).

[5] These two islands were probably, from their bearing with the island of Veru or St. George, the two mountainous islands in the south-east part of New Georgia, which, as observed by Gallego, runs much further to the westward. Their distance, however, from Veru, is more than double that which Gallego gives.

could scarcely sail along,[1] on account of the many reefs; and we entered a passage a quarter of a league further on, but seeing that there was no outlet we had to return by the aid of the oars.[2] At this time many Indians came out against us, from among the reefs, with their bows and arrows. We made sail, and as we were proceeding in the same direction, 18 canoes full of fishermen, in each canoe 30 Indians, with their bows and arrows, came to shoot at us. We fired some shots, and so they went away and left us.

"On the 26th of April, we reached some reefs and grounded on them . . .[3] Some Indians came out at this time with bows and arrows; and we fired some shots, but because the Indians did not leave us, we did not repeat this. There are many islets near, both inhabited and uninhabited. The island became narrower as we arrived at a point of this island which is from the extremity 6 leagues north-west to south-east. We entered a passage separating the island from the other islets around, which are many and inhabited. This is the west part of the island; and I took the sun at its extremity and found myself in $7\frac{1}{2}°$. This island is 95 leagues in length, and in circuit more than 200.[4] As we sailed on, some canoes came out to us; and on our firing some shots, they left us, because . . . *(porque nos afliriun)*.

"Issuing from the passage, we saw, towards the east-by-south,[5] 6 leagues away, a large island. We did not go to it, so as not to delay ourselves. We gave it the name of San Marcos.[6] It is in latitude $7\frac{3}{4}°$. This island lies with that of Santa Isabel west-by-north and east-by-south. All this people, which we have hitherto seen, are naked, and are as the Moors of Barbary, and do not confess the Lord.

"Sailing on to the 28th of the month, there came out to us 34 canoes in line of battle, in order to stop us. Three large canoes, which passed astern, followed us for more than 2 leagues. When we saw their determination to overhaul us *(que trahian)*, we fired

---

[1] *Lit* " we were unable to sail along."

[2] This blind passage may be the one indicated in the present chart in the vicinity of Nairn Island, an off-lying islet.

[3] The following sentence, being unintelligible to me, has not been translated, "porque en esta isla hay muchos sueños que llaman fuenos forzado volver atras para salir."

[4] These dimensions are very greatly in excess.

[5] This bearing is evidently an error; the correct bearing is given a few lines below.

[6] The island of San Marcos is evidently the Choiseul Island of the present chart, as named by Bougainville in 1768; and the passage through which the brigantine had just passed, is that known as Manning Strait between Choiseul and Isabel.

at them with a small cannon and some muskets. At this, they took to flight . . . (*mas que de paieia*). Although we had been away from the ships a long time and were endeavouring to return, we were delayed in arriving at them, as we were opposed by the east winds.

"Being anchored on Sunday at a small uninhabited island, we determined to send before us a canoe with nine soldiers, a sailor, and an Indian who had always accompanied us. Whilst they were coasting along, not daring to stand out to sea, they got on some reefs. Through their negligence, the canoe was broken in pieces; and by God's mercy, the people escaped with the loss of what they carried, their muskets and ammunition being wetted. When they were all collected together, they resolved to return to the brigantine; and the Indian ran away from them, although he did not belong to that land. Having walked all that night over the stones and rocks along the coast, for fear of meeting the Indians, they came to a point where they found a cross which they had put up when they passed by there; and they worshipped it, and determined to await there the arrival of the brigantine. They put up a flag *which was seen by us as we came along* . . .[1] We went to receive them and found them in a sorry plight (*maltratados*). Continuing our voyage, we came to where they had been wrecked amongst some reefs close to an islet, in which they had left two hogs that they carried with them. A canoe was sent for them (the hogs) and they were taken. Near here we anchored, because there was much wind. As the weather was fine and the wind was off the land, we went inside the reefs, looking out for our ships all that day and part of the night. We made sail the next day at dawn, and arrived at the port of Santa Isabel de la Estrella, where we found the ships, to the no small satisfaction of both those on board and of ourselves.[2]

"The same day on which we arrived at Santa Isabel de la Estrella, I told the General that it was necessary to refit the ships, and that soon afterwards we should proceed further on to follow up what we had begun. Accordingly, on the 8th of the said month,

---

[1] "Visto por losque en el veniamos soyechamos lo que podia ser."

[2] From the context it may be inferred that the brigantine completed the circuit of the island of Isabel. Figueroa, in his narrative, expressly states that the brigantine turned the west end of the island, and encountered head easterly winds in her return to the ships. Figueroa also tells us that during the absence of the brigantine some of the men in the ships had died of sickness; but Gallego does not refer to this circumstance.

we left the port of Santa Isabel de la Estrella, on our way out, passing by some reefs which are at the entrance of the harbour. We
sailed on until the end of two days. The brigantine, being unable
to keep up with the ships, drifted towards the land, so much so that
at dawn she was nearly out of sight, although there came in her
the pilot Gregorio Gonzalez with some of the soldiers and sailors
who had (previously) gone in her. Being afraid of losing her, I
made signals to her to go about and make a reach to seaward. I
deemed that unless one of the ships turned back to take her in tow,
we should lose her. Seeing that, on account of the many reefs, she
was so essential to us for the exploration of those islands, and had
been built by us after so much labour and through my diligence, I
left the ' Almiranta ' to go on, and turned back in the ' Capitana '
to get her. We kept the sounding-lead in hand for fear of the
reefs ; and about 6 leagues out to sea (seis leguas de la mar) I found
myself in 6 fathoms. I went about immediately, and it pleased
God that we found deeper water. We found the brigantine in the
hours of the night ; and we took her in tow with no little labour,
going after the ' Almiranta ' which had followed the course I had
advised in order to avoid the many reefs existing here, and leaving
behind in her course the islands of Veru and Flores,[1] and many
others which were discovered in the brigantine, without touching at
them. At the end of four days, we saw the ' Almiranta ' right
ahead of us, not having yet found a port.

"On Tuesday, the 12th of May, we arrived at a port in the
island of Guadalcanal, to which we had gone from Santa Isabel ;
but we were not able to arrive at the river of Ortega which lay two
leagues to windward of where we were. This day, the wind blew
so hard from the east that our cable parted and we lost an anchor.
On the following morning I went in a boat to find a good anchorage, for we were anchored on an (open) coast ; and I went a league
from here to the rear of an islet which was close to this island of
Guadalcanal ; and having sounded everywhere I found that it was
clear (of shoals) and afforded a good anchorage for the ships, since
it had a large river which was named by us Rio Gallego. It is in
latitude 10° 8'. From here I returned to the ships, and brought
them to this port which we named Puerto de la Cruz.[2]

---

[1] The island of Florida is probably thus referred to.

[2] The position of this harbour is shown on the present chart ; but it is placed too much to
the eastward ; since, from the narrative, it is apparent that it lies near Sesarga, which is
the present Savo.

. "This same day, the General landed with all the soldiers and self; and he took possession of this island in the name of His Majesty as in the case of the other islands. A cross was erected on a little eminence that was there; and we all paid our adoration. Some Indians, who stood near to look on, commenced to discharge their arrows; and some shots were fired at them, by which two Indians were killed; and so they left us and fled, and we embarked for that night.

" On the following morning, when we intended to land to say mass, we noticed that the Indians had pulled up the cross and had carried it off. On account of their audacity, the General ordered the soldiers to get themselves ready to go in search of the cross and to put it in its place: and whilst they were going ashore in the boat, we saw the Indians return and endeavour to set it up. When it was in its place, they went away; but it appeared that they had not thrust it in sufficiently, and it fell. Presently, the same men attempted to erect it; but, from fear of us, they did not stop to set it up quite straight and fled; and herewith our people reached the shore and disembarked. The General sent Pedro Sarmiento with some soldiers to look at the cross; whilst he himself remained on the beach with the rest of the people. On reaching there, they found that the cross was not upright; and they placed it as it was at first. Pedro Sarmiento then returned, and they all embarked and came back to the ships.

" In order not to lose time, I gave the order to repair the brigantine, as she was very leaky. She was repaired accordingly; and then it was determined that Don Fernando Henriquez, the chief-ensign (alferez general), and I, the said Hernan Gallego, should go in the brigantine with 30 soldiers and sailors to discover the remaining lands of the same island of Guadalcanal. On the 19th of May, we sailed in the brigantine along the coast of the said island which is named, in the language of the natives, Sabo.[1] And on the same day, the General sent Andres Nuñez with 30 soldiers to see what the land possessed, and to endeavour to make a search in cracks or broken ground, because the miners, who understood it, said that it was a land for gold. And so they carried out this

---

[1] The name of Savo is at the present day given to the volcanic island, named by the Spaniards, Sesarga, which lies off the north-west coast of Guadalcanar: Savuli is the name of a village at the west end of Guadalcanar (*ride* map in Dr. Codrington's "Melanesian Languages").

object in an excursion of 7 days. Whilst they were endeavouring
to make a trial of the ground in a large river, so many natives
crowded around them that they had to give it up, because they
would not suffer them to do it. By a sign which they gave, they
said that there was gold. They have . . . .[1]; and here were found
the first hens of Castile. They brought back two young hens and a
cock, which they all received with much satisfaction, understanding
that they would discover better land." (These birds were evidently
the "bush-hens," *Megapodidæ*, of these islands.)

"Those in the brigantine, as they sailed along the coast of this
island from the south-east to the north-west,[2] saw many villages
near a river that was nigh to the ships. We passed a league further
on, and after another league came to the river of Ortega. All this
coast is full of villages; yet we did not stop to have seen more of it.
Going further along the coast, we came to a river and anchored in
it; and we resolved to land to see the people who were there. More
than 200 Indians came out to meet us in a friendly manner, with
their bows in their hands and the clubs with which they fight.
They gave us some plantains *(platanos)* which abound here. After
we had seen this, the people embarked; however, they threw some
stones at us as we were embarking. We were from the ships 12
leagues. Proceeding on our course to the south-east, we saw in
another river a large population of natives, and we named it Rio de
San Bernardino because it was that same day. It is in the latitude
of $10\frac{1}{3}°$, and bears . . . .[3] There is a very high round hill here.
This river is 4 leagues from where we started from, as I have
said.[4]

"We continued coasting along this same island; and two leagues
from this river, we came to a great village on the bank of a small
river. Don Fernando landed, and took a canoe which he found in
the river, and also some roots, that they call "mames" (yams) and
others, "names," which they found in cases. We told the natives to
give us some hogs, and they should have their canoe back. They
said that they would give them to us with the intention of detaining
us whilst they collected their numbers. Thereupon they began to
play their instruments for the battle. By the time we were em-

---

[1] "muchas guacanaras en este entrada."
[2] A perplexing error. Read instead, N.W. to S.E. Figueroa gives the course as E.S.E.
[3] "Nor norueste subueste" (an impossible bearing).
[4] The sense of this sentence is not intelligible to me.

barked, more than 600 ruffians (*gandules*) had assembled. Coming to the beach with their bows and arrows, and clubs, and stones, they began to shoot; but no musket was fired at them, although they did not cease from shooting at us. Some took to the water and swam off to the brigantine endeavouring to cajole us with fair words, asking us for the canoe and promising us a hog. They tried to take it from astern: and when we observed this, we threatened them and they went ashore.

" The Indians then brought on a pole a bundle of dry grass in imitation of a hog; and they placed it on the beach. Some came off to the brigantine and said that there was the hog, that we should go for it, and should give back the canoe. We saw the deceit that they intended; and when they perceived that we understood what it was and did not go for it, they threw stones at us and rushed into the sea, swimming with their weapons in their hands. Withal, we did not wish to harm them until we saw their boldness, and that they were coming to the brigantine to shoot at us with their arrows. To frighten them, some shots were fired high in the air, which did not wound any one: and so we went further along the coast, whilst they returned to the shore and followed us until we arrived off another large river, with many people as numerous as themselves, whom they joined.

" On the 22nd of May, we named this river Santa Elena. There is much level ground here which is covered with palms and cocoanut trees. This island has a very lofty *cordillera* in its interior and many ravines from which these rivers issue; whilst between the mountains and the sea there are eight leagues of level country. In the mouth of the river there are many sandbanks; but we did not anchor there, and sailed a long way from the coast to double a point of reefs, where we anchored. The wind blew so strong from the south-east that we ran much risk when seeking shelter to leeward of the shoals that run out from the river. Here I anchored, and although there was much wind, it was fine weather at sea.

" The Indians, who were more than a thousand in number, swam out to us with their bows and arrows; and they dived and plunged beneath the water to lay hold of our anchor and carry the brigantine ashore. Seeing their determined perseverance, we fired some shots, and having killed some, we ceased firing; and they made for the shore, where they raised some mounds of sand for their protection. As we were short of water, we were compelled to get more; and when we headed towards the shore, a great number of the natives assembled together to menace us lest we should take up a position in the rear of their works, from which they defended themselves. We loaded a small cannon with small shot, and discharged it against their mound-works, by which some were wounded and one killed. Seeing that they could not hold the works, they left the beach and withdrew to the mountain slope.

"And we found a place to get water in the canoe that we had; but it was brackish; and I told them that unless they brought sweeter water they should not come on board the brigantine. The Indians said that they would fetch it in the earthen jars which were given them for it; and taking them, the Indians went and brought it sweet and put it on board the brigantine. Soon they all came on board, and they did not follow us any more. Continuing our voyage along the same coast for another 6 leagues, we anchored off a great town, which was more than three leagues in extent (*mas de tres leguas de poblacion*), whence there came out to us more than 3,000 (!) Indians, who gave us a hog and many cocoa-nuts; and they filled the earthen jars with water and brought it off in their canoes, and they came on board the brigantine to visit us without arms. Close to the shore there are two inhabited islets lying about half a league to sea; and further on to the north-west of these two islets, there is another islet of sand. Soon we steered our course to the south-east, following the trend of the coast for two leagues. There are two other islets, and another of sand, near them, which were not inhabited.

"On the 24th of May we sailed further along; and there came off to us 18 canoes, which accompanied us until sunset. When they were about to go, they menaced us with their bows; and on some shots being fired to disperse them, they quickly left us. Accordingly, we kept our course until the extremity of this island, which runs from north-west to south-east. We went to look for a port for the ships in case it should be needed; and we found at the point of this promontory many islets with shoals between them. Among them is a large island with a good port. We were in want of water, and two canoes that accompanied us showed us where to get it, with the intention of luring us there and killing us; for they came with their weapons. They were joined by 30 other canoes, one of them carrying 30 Indian warriors. Arriving whilst we were watering, they landed, and having got plenty of stones and arrows and spears, some went to attack the brigantine, whilst the others went to attack those who were getting water on shore. When we saw their determined daring, shots were fired by which some were killed and many wounded; and so they fled, leaving behind two canoes empty, and carrying off the rest. The large canoe was much injured, and in their precipitation they threw themselves into the sea; but we took the canoe with four Indians, two wounded and two unharmed. We landed them, and treating them well, gave them their liberty and restored their canoe. And so they went away; and I kept a boy that I took here. I found the latitude to be in $10\frac{1}{2}°$. On the south-south-east side of the point, the coast trends from north-east to south-west, but from this point we could not see the end of it. The port is 40 leagues from where we left the ships.[1]

" We left this port with some difficulty as it lies among the reefs. We saw to the south-east-by-east an island 7 leagues away;[2] but we did not go to it, as we were going to the island of Malaita, as the Indians name it, which lies with the island of Guadalcanal, and with the point where we had been, north-east-by-east. We sailed to the north-east-by-east for 16 leagues, and arrived at a good harbour which has many reefs at the entrance. There came out 25 canoes with warriors who discharged their arrows. Some shots were fired at them, which killed some and wounded others. This port, which is on the south-south-west coast, is in the latitude of $10\frac{1}{2}°$; and the name, Escondido, was given to it, because it is almost enclosed by reefs.[3] In this island we found apples of some size, oranges, a metal that seemed to be a base kind of gold, and, besides, pearl-shell, with which they inlay the club they use in battle, being the one they usually carry. These natives, like the rest, go *completely* naked. In the name of His Majesty we took possession of this island, to which we gave the name of the Isle of Ramos." (*Vide* Note VI., Geographical Appendix.)

" Leaving this port, we sailed to the south-east for four leagues, and discovered an entrance to a harbour resembling a river dividing

---

[1] The description of this part, its situation, and relative position to the adjoining coasts of Malaita and St. Christoval, as stated below, all point to its identity with Marau Sound. In the Geographical Appendix reference is made to the discrepancies in the distances and latitudes of Gallego.

[2] This island is evidently St. Christoval.

[3] Future visitors to the southern portion of Malaita will doubtless be able to identify this port with some anchorage on the west coast to the northward of the Maramasiki Passage. In so doing they should not forget the usual error of Gallego's latitudes (Note V. of the Geographical Appendix).

the lands from each other.[1] We could not see the end of it; and
on account of the strong current we were unable to enter. We
accordingly passed on another four leagues, where we found a good
port: and in it I took the latitude, and found it to be $10\frac{1}{3}°$ south of
the equinoctial. It has an islet at the entrance which should be left
close on the starboard hand in entering the port. Two hundred
Indians came out and attacked us. To this port we gave the name
of La Asuncion, because we entered it on that day.[2] This day we
sailed out and proceeded further along the coast to the south-east.
Close to the extremity of the island, we put into a *small bay*,[3]
where they discharged some arrows at us, and on our firing some
shots they left us. Quitting the small bay, we sailed as far as the end
of the island which is in $10\frac{1}{4}°$.[4] It lies north-east and south-east with
the isle of Jesus, which is the first island we saw, and lies in 7°.
[With the other end of Malaita, which is to the north-east, and lies
east and west with Meta in 8°, it is 85 leagues. There. is another
point in 7°, with which the Isle of Jesus lies north-east-by-north
135 leagues.[5]]

"This island of Malaita has a length of 114 leagues. We did
not go to the north side, and for that reason we cannot say what is
its breadth. The island of Guadalcanal is very large. I do not
estimate its size, because it is a great land and half a year is needed
to sail along its shores.[6] That we sailed along its length on the
north side for 130 leagues and did not reach the end, shows its
great size. Moreover, on the east[7] side of the extremity, the coast
trended to the west, where I saw a great number of fine towns.[8]

"From the extremity of this island of Malaita we saw another
island, which lies east and west from this cape 8 leagues, to which
we went, arriving in the night. We anchored in front of a town on

---

[1] This is without a doubt the Maramasiki Passage which cuts through the south-eastern
portion of Malaita.

[2] Port Asuncion may, perhaps, be the large bay of Su Paina.

[3] *Caleta* in the Spanish. This anchorage may, perhaps, be identified with Su Oroha or
with one of the inlets or coves nearer to Cape Zélée, such as Te Oroha or Te Waina.
("Pacific Islands:" vol. I.; "Western Groups:" p. 61, 62; "Admiralty publication," 1885.)

[4] This latitude is not consistent with that given above for the port of Escondido, which,
according to the journal, lies more than half a degree to the north-west.

[5] I have endeavoured unsuccessfully to get at the meaning of the two sentences enclosed
in brackets.

[6] "*Para anda*'*læ es menester medio anno.*"

[7] This should be "west."

[8] See Note VIII. in Geographical Appendix for remarks on the eexaggerated ideas as to the
size of this island.

the coast, which has a small river; and whilst we were anchoring, two canoes came off to see us, but they soon returned. At dawn we sent the people on shore to get water : and the natives came out peacefully with their women and their sons. They are all naked like the others. The women carry in their hands some things like fans, which they sometimes place before them. When the water was procured, we asked for a hog, and they brought it; and placing it so that we should see it, they returned and carried it off. But we did not injure them in any way; and accordingly embarked and proceeded out to sail round the island. When the natives saw that we were going, most of them came out in their canoes with their bows and arrows in pursuit of us. The first man who was about to aim, we knocked over with a shot. At this, they turned and fled ; and we pursued them as far as the port, capturing some canoes that had intended to take us. A friendly Indian, whom we carried with us, climbed a palm tree and saw how the Indians came in regular bodies' bearing their shields. We went to arms, and sent three soldiers to see in what force the people were. They came in their canoes in two or three divisions to attack the brigantine: and we began to bring our musketry into action, killing two Indians and an Indian woman. They soon retired ; and our men who were on the shore having embarked in the brigantine, we went on in pursuit of our quest. The island is named Uraba[1] in the language of the Indians. We gave it the name of La Treguada because they led us into a treacherous truce.[2] This island is in latitude 10¼°. It is well peopled, and has plenty of provisions of their kind. Although small, it has an area of 25 leagues. There is communication with the neighbouring islands, and with a cape that lies to the north-west. It trends north-west and south-east until the middle of the island, where we found these 10°, and the other . . . . . (milad) trends north-north-west until the end of the island.

" To the south-by-west of the point of the island there are low islands, with many shoals around them, which are three leagues dis-

[1] The reader will have already inferred that the island of Uraba is the Ulaua of the present chart, and will have noticed that the name of the island has remained the same during the last three centuries. It is the Ulawa of the present natives, and the Contrarieté of Surville.

[2] One must judge Gallego in the spirit of his times. Humane as he really was, we cannot free him from his share in this unfortunate conflict with the natives of Ulaua : and the name of La Treguada had been better never bestowed. The next navigator who visited this island was Surville in 1769 ; who, following up his previous proceedings at Port Praslin in Isabel, repelled its inhabitants with grape shot.

tant from this island of La Treguada, to which we went and obtained water. They are inhabited; and we gave them the name of Las Tres Marias. They trend west-by-north and east-by-south.[1]

"There is another island which lies three leagues from Las Tres Marias. It is low, and the inhabitants are like those around. We named it the island of San Juan, and found in it a good harbour. We took possession of it in the name of His Majesty, as in the case of the other islands. It is 6 leagues in circuit; and is in latitude $10\frac{2}{3}°$.[2]

"We went thence to another great island,[3] which lies north and south with it, 2 leagues away. Before we arrived, 93 canoes with warriors came out to us and . . . . . [4] We took an Indian chief and placed him below the deck. He seized a sword, and defending himself attemped to escape, until at last the sword was taken from him and he was bound. We sent the people on shore, intending to take possession; but so many natives attacked them that we were not able to do so, and we returned to the island of San Juan. I offered to Don Fernando to take possession of it before dawn; and it was done. In the island of San Juan, they ransomed the Indian, and gave us for him three hogs, to which he added some beads. As a sign of friendliness, Don Fernando Henriquez embraced him.

"On the following day, which was the 2nd of June, we arrived at dawn off the island of Santiago.[5] More than 50 canoes came out

---

[1] These three islands are without doubt identical with the three small islands which are named the Three Sisters in the present chart. Surville, the French navigator, who saw them in 1769, gave them the name of Les Trois Sœurs, which they still retain. At the present day they are uninhabited, and any water that could be obtained would be of a very doubtful quality. Flourieu hints at the identity of Les Trois Sœurs and Las Tres Marias.

[2] The San Juan of Gallego is evidently the island now known as Ugi. There is no apparent reference in this journal to the small adjacent island of Biu.

[3] Apparently this is the island named Santiago below. It is without doubt St. Christoval.

[4] "y tuvimos gran guasavara."

[5] The reader will now require to use some caution in following this part of the narrative, since Gallego seems to have fallen into much confusion respecting the island of St. Christoval. The name of Santiago was evidently applied by him to the north side of the island west of the prominent headlong of Cape Kelbeck, which he might easily have taken for the extremity of the island. The name of San Urban was in all probability given to the peninsula of Cape Surville, which, as I have myself remarked while off the St. Christoval coast, has the appearance of a detached island when first seen, in approaching it from the northward and westward. This deceptive appearance, when viewed from a distance, is due to the circumstance that the neck of the peninsula of Cape Surville is raised but a few feet above the level of the sea, and is in consequence below the horizon when this cape is first sighted.

to us; and they planned to carry us off to their towns. It was necessary to fire some shots in order that they should quit us; and they left us and returned. Possession was taken of this island in the name of His Majesty; and we did no injury to the people. This island is 40 leagues in length on its north side: and it is narrow, and in part mountainous, and is well peopled. The Indians of this island go naked and eat human flesh. Its eastern extremity is in latitude $10\frac{3}{4}°$; and lies north-west and south-east with the island of Treguada 12 leagues. The south-east extremity lies north-west and south-east 18 leagues with the island of Malaita.

"When we were all embarked to proceed further on, a violent north-east wind overtook us, and drove us to the extremity of Santiago, whence we saw a large island to the south-east that trended westward. It was 18 leagues distant. It is in latitude $10\frac{1}{2}°$ south of the equinoctial; and is 4 leagues distant from the island of Guadalcanal. We gave it the name of the island of San Urban.

"On account of the sickness of myself and of some of the soldiers, we did not proceed further: and, keeping away to leeward, we arrived at the island of Guadalcanal. We landed at a town where the Indians gave us. . . . . . .[1] when we intended to get water, and where we set free the three Indians in the canoe; and they gave us a hog and *panales*. But they were in great fear of us, and leaving us they returned to the town. Beads were given to them as a sign of friendship. Leaving there, we continued our cruise to return to the ships, and touched at some places where we had been before, the natives receiving us in a friendly manner, and giving us what they had, because they were much afraid of the muskets we carried. We sailed further on to a port, where, during our previous stay, we had been received peacefully. We got water there; and they gave us a hog and almost filled the brigantine with *panoes*, which is the food they eat. It is a very good harbour for the ships, and lies under the shelter of an island. There are many inhabitants.

"We continued our return cruise, intending to explore a river where we had been before. Sailing into the port to obtain provisions,

The distance of San Urban from Guadalcanal, as given above, is inconsistent with the rest of the journal; and for 4 leagues, 40 leagues was evidently intended, the omission of the cipher being probably a clerical error. The name of St. Christoval was subsequently given, as shown further on in the narrative, when the Spanish ships visited the south coast of this island.

[1] " La Guacanara."

we arrived close off a town which the Indians abandoned when they saw us. We found there, many *panoes* and *ñámes* (yams) with which we loaded the brigantine. I tried to catch a tame white parrot, which the Indians had together with many others of various hues. When the Indians saw that we did no harm, they all assembled, and came and gave us a hog to induce us to go. Presently we sailed on to another river, on the bank of which there is a large town ; we anchored in it. The Indians began to make fires, and to cast the fire in the air ;[1] it was a thing we had, not seen in any other part.

"On the next day, which was the 6th of June, the Feast of the Holy Ghost, we reached the ships, and found them all very sad. It appeared that on the Day of the Ascension, the steward with four soldiers and five negroes were sent on shore for water. As on previous occasions, they were sent because the cacique of that tribe was a friend and used to come off to the ships to give us cocoa-nuts, whilst his men used to fetch the water in the earthen jars, and because we trusted them for the friendly manner in which they behaved in their dealings with us. This day, however, when they were gone for the water, it seemed that the boat got aground because they had not taken care to keep her afloat as she was being filled. At this moment, the Indians rushed out from ambush with their weapons and were upon them ; and they did not leave a single soul alive except a negro of mine who escaped. All the rest they hewed to pieces, cutting off their heads, and arms, and legs, tearing out their tongues, and supping up their brains[2] with great ferocity. The negro who escaped took to the water to swim off to an islet that was near. However, they swam in pursuit, and with a cutlass, which he carried in his hand, he defended himself from them in such a manner that they left him, and he reached the islet. From there he began to make signs, and to shout out to those in the ships, which they perceived ; and as quickly as possible the General went ashore to see what had happened. When he reached there, the ill tidings were told. The Indians retired to the hills. In a short time, the dead Christians were recovered ; and they buried them in the place where they used to say mass, the soldiers

---

[1] "hechar por lo alto."

[2] The New Ireland cannibals of the present day are fond of a composition of sago, cocoa-nut, and human brains. ("The Western Pacific and New Guinea." London 1886: p. 58 : by H. H. Romilly.)

in one grave, and the negroes in another. Of the negroes, one belonged to the King, two to ourselves, and one to the boatswain. It was a thing to hear their shouting, and the noise that the Indians made with their drums. It appeared to be a general assembling day with them, because more than 40,000 Indians[1] had gathered together for this purpose. When our people had buried the dead, they embarked in the ships, being in great grief with what had occurred.

" As I understand, the cause of the Indians coming to attack us was this. The cacique came off to the 'Capitana' to entreat that our people would give him back a boy belonging to his tribe, whom they had taken. He offered a hog for him; but they would not give him up. On the following day, the cacique brought a hog off to the ship, and said that, if they gave him the boy who was a kinsman of his, he would give them the hog. But they would not give him up, and took the hog by force. When the cacique saw how he had been treated, he went away and did not return to the ships again. In a few days, the disaster happened.

" On the day after this unfortunate event, the General ordered Pedro Sarmiento to land with as many men as he could muster to inflict punishment. He burned many towns, and killed more than 20 Indians. Then he returned to give account of what he had done. Each day that they landed they endeavoured to punish them the more. On a subsequent occasion, because no more Indians were seen whom they could punish, the General ordered Pedro Sarmiento to proceed to a point that lay to the south-east a league and a half from the ships. For he considered that all the Indians had been concerned in the treachery and in the death of the Christians. Having embarked 50 soldiers in two boats, Pedro Sarmiento went there, but he found no Indians as they had fled to the hills. After he had burned all the buildings and habitations that he could find, he turned back on his way to the ships. Some Indians, who came out from a point, followed him slowly ; and our people lay in ambush and killed three or four Indians, the rest escaping in flight. They then returned to the boats, and embarking came back to the ships. An Indian, whom we took, informed us of those who were concerned in the death of our men. He said that the leader was a taurique, named Nobolo, who lived on the bank of the river that lay a league to the east of the Rio Gallego ; and that with him there

[1] This is either an exaggerated statement, or it is an error in transcribing.

P

were many others who had collected together for that object and
with the said result.

"On Wednesday, the 9th of June, the men of the 'Almiranta'
were engaged in making a top-mast on the islet close to where the
ships were anchored. Some musketeers and targeteers (*rodeleros*),
who were eight in number, were in guard of the carpenter's party.
As it happened, the Indians were then preparing for another attack;
and more than 300 of them lay in ambush, ready for the assault.
About 10 Indians crossed over to the islet with bows and arrows
concealed; and they brought a hog, intending to beguile our men
by occupying their attention in talking, whilst the other Indian
warriors should be arriving. When I saw the Indians crossing over
and this canoe heading for the islet where our people were making
the top-mast, I ordered some musketeers into the boat; and
accompanied by Pedro Sarmiento, we steered so that the islet concealed us from those in the canoe. Approaching the islet, we
passed between it and the main island and came close up with the
canoe which had only one Indian on board, the others having thrown
themselves into the sea. The canoe was captured together with the
hog which they had brought to deceive us. When we had joined
the party who were making the top-mast, we returned to the ships
after having killed those who came in the canoe. This was the
most effective attack that was made, for the Indians went away
much discouraged.

"On the 12th of the same month of June, the General took the
brigantine and a boat with nearly all the people, in order to inflict
further punishment at a river which lay a league to the east of the
place where the ships were anchored; and I accompanied him. An
hour before the dawn we arrived close to the river; and we were
about to conceal ourselves and fall upon the Indians, when we
were seen by their sentinels and they went to arms. I remained
with four musketeers in charge of the brigantine and the boat in
the mouth of the river, so as not to allow any canoe to escape. The
General on arriving at the town, which had more than 200 houses,
found it deserted. He set fire to it; and then we returned to the
ships.

"The next day, which was Sunday the 13th of June, we made
sail during the night and proceeded in the ships to follow up the
discoveries of the brigantine. When we had sailed about 8 leagues
to the south-east, we anchored because the wind was contrary. The

General landed here to get some provisions for the sick, of whom there were many. In a short time he returned to the ships, when we made sail with the land-breeze. Now died the pilot, Paladin, an experienced seaman. We lost sight of the brigantine, as she went ahead of us: and we did not see her until we found her anchored in a port off an islet that lay half a league to windward of where we had anchored in the brigantine during our voyage of discovery. There were many inhabitants here; and they came off to us as friends. On account of it being Corpus Christi Day, we remained here all the day. Mass was said at the islet which is close to the anchorage. We watered the ships there. The Indians gave us of their own free will two hogs and many cocoa-nuts and *ñames* (yams). The cacique of this tribe was named Meso, and the town was called Urare. This people is at war with the people of Feday, which is the name of the place where we were anchored. . . . . .[1]

"On the 18th of June, we left this port, and proceeded on our voyage, seeking the island of Santiago or San Juan,[2] which was the island that we had discovered and named. • We beat to windward against a strong head wind in our endeavour to arrive at the island of Santiago; but on account of this contrary wind and the bois-terous weather, we did not fetch it; and I determined to steer to the south of the island of Santiago, the wind and the contrary currents not allowing us to find a harbour. We coasted along an island, not seen in the brigantine[3], and we held on our course for fourteen days, endeavouring to reach the end of the island; but in the middle of the island, on account of the contrary wind and currents, what we gained one day we lost the next. Accordingly I went to find a port. We named this island San Christoval.[4] It was our Lord's pleasure that after so much difficulty I should find a very good port for the ships; and on the following day I returned to the ships. We sailed to windward that night on account of the boisterous weather, which obliged us to shorten sail and lie-to[5] for the night. When it dawned, we found ourselves three leagues to

[1] " que nos maron gente."

[2] Gallego here seems to have forgotten that he had previously applied these two names to different islands, that of San Juan to Ugi and that of Santiago to the large island south of it, viz., the present St. Christoval (see p. 222).

[3] This remark is inconsistent with the previous reference to their steering south of Santiago.

[4] I should here call attention to the circumstance that the Spaniards were navigating the south coast of this island. Further proof of this is given in succeeding pages.

[5] " Sin velas de mar a el traves.'

leeward of the port, which we tried in vain to reach ; and since we
kept falling to leeward, I was compelled to take the brigantine and
go in search of another anchorage, with the understanding that
when I had found one, I should signal to the ships to follow the
brigantine. The signal being made, I guided the ships to the
brigantine, which lay outside a point of reefs that formed the
harbour ; and so we entered it.

"It is a good and secure anchorage ; and there is a town there
which has eighty houses. The General landed with the captains
and the soldiers to obtain provisions and to take possession of
the island, in the name of His Majesty, which we did without
opposition, for the Indians received us peacefully. The same
evening we landed, and went in marching order to see the
town, but without doing them any injury ; and we returned to
the ships with the agreement that on the following morning
we should revisit the town to get provisions, of which we were
in need.

"On the morning of the 1st of July, we all landed with the
determination to obtain provisions for our present necessities ; and
the General entered one part of the town with the greater number
of our people, whilst Pedro Sarmiento with twelve soldiers entered
another part. When the Indians saw our determination, and that
we entered the town in two places, they began to arouse themselves and to take up their weapons, making signs that we should
embark. They held a consultation in a small hollow, where Pedro
Sarmiento and his party entered. One of the headmen was seen
to make incantations and invocations to the devil, which caused
real terror, because it seemed as though his body was possessed of
a devil. There were two other Indians, who, whilst making great
contortions with their faces and violently shaking themselves,
scraped up the sand with their feet and hands and threw it into the
air. They then made towards the boats with loud shouting and
yells of rage, and tossed the water in the air. At this, our
people sounded the trumpets to assemble where the General was ;
for there were all the Indians with their bows and arrows and darts
and clubs, which are the weapons with which they fight. They
came very close to us, bending their bows and bidding us to depart.
It became necessary for us to fire ; and accordingly some were
killed and others were wounded. Thereupon they fled and
abandoned the town, in which there was a great quantity of *panaes*

and *ñames* and many cocoa-nuts and almonds,[1] which were sufficient
to load a ship. Presently we set about carrying to the boats all
that we found, and nothing more was done that day. The Indians
did not dare to return to the town again, and that night we
embarked. This port is in 11° south latitude. It is in close
proximity to the island of Santiago, to the south-east; it is narrow
and mountainous, and the inhabitants are like the rest.[2]

"After three days had passed, the General ordered that the
brigantine should proceed on a voyage of discovery; and Francisco
Muñoz Rico, with ten soldiers, and I, with thirteen seamen, embarked. We left this port on the 4th of July, and coasted along
this island of Paubro, as it is called in the language of the natives,
being that which we named San Christobal.[3] Until the middle of
the island, the coast trends north-west and south-east for 20 leagues
and a point nearer east and west; and the other half trends west-
by-north and south-by-east. We entered a harbour, which was the
first we discovered in this cruise ; and there we remained for the
day.

" On the following morning we left there, and proceeded further
along the coast to the east-by-south. We entered a small bay,
enclosed by reefs, near which were three towns. We seized two
boys here. The officer in command of the soldiers went with all our
people to reconnoitre the town that was a league away ; and I
remained behind in charge of the brigantine with no small risk, for
there were only three soldiers left with me to defend it. In a few
hours the people returned with two canoes that they had taken,
and five sucking-pigs, and some *panaes*, and plantains, with which
they embarked. We then made sail to proceed further along the
coast.

" On the next day a canoe with two Indians came off to us. They
were friendly, and one of them came on board the brigantine. We
sailed on in order to reach a harbour, and proceeded further along
the same coast, on which there were many towns, and the people of
them were, as we expected, very turbulent; for a canoe preceded

---

[1] These almonds were without doubt the almond-like kernels of the fruit of a species of
Canarium, a common article of food at the present day.

[2] This sentence refers to the island, and not to the port, judging from the context.

[3] This reference to the native name of *Paubro* is interesting, since at the present day St.
Christoval is largely known by the native name of *Bauro*, which is evidently the same.
This is also without a doubt the "large country named *Pouro* " of which the natives of
Taumaco (Duff Group) informed Quiros about forty years afterwards (*vide* Geographical
Appendix, Note XV.).

us, giving warning in such a manner that in all this island we were not able to capture anything. As we approached a promontory (*morro*), many Indians came out and threw stones at us with much shouting ; and at the extremity of this island we discovered two small islands. The end of this island is in 11½° south of the Equinoctial. This island is a hundred leagues in circuit and seven leagues in width, and is well peopled.

" From the extremity, we went to one of the small islands which was the smallest and lay to the south side.[1] On arriving there we anchored ; and there came off to us twelve Indians who came on board the brigantine and spent some time with us. On their being asked by signs what further land there was in that part, they said that there was none ; but towards the west, where we pointed, they said that there was much land. We saw it, and because there was no time or opportunity we did not go to it.[2] Through the day and night we had much wind. As we were about to disembark, the natives began to throw stones at us ; and when some shots were fired for our own defence, they fled. Accordingly, we landed and went to the town, where we found some hogs and a quantity of almonds and plantains. I ordered a sailor to climb a high palm to see if he could descry land to the south, or south-east, or north-west (?)[3] but no further land appeared. There came from that quarter a great swell which was a sign of their being no more land there. This island, we named, Santa Catalina ; in the language of the natives it is called Aguare.[4] It is 40[5] leagues round, and it is low and level. It has many palms and is well peopled. It has

[1] This small island was subsequently named Santa Catalina ; and the circumstance of the Spaniards going to it before they visited the adjacent small island of Santa Anna, is a proof of their having coasted along the south side of St. Christoval. Then, the description of the trend of the coast (*see* page 229) applies rather to the south than to the north coast ; and this is further confirmed by the circumstance that when the Spanish ships were soon afterwards leaving the group on their return voyage to Peru, they weathered or doubled the two islands of Santa Anna and Santa Catalina. Again, no reference is made to the islands visible off the north coast, which would have been certainly referred to, even although they had previously visited them in the brigantine. I lay stress on this point as it clears up the confusion of the different names applied to St. Christoval.

[2] There is some obscurity in this passage, and in rendering it I have been guided by the account of Figueroa.

[3] " North-west " is an error, which the context indicates, even excluding other circumstances ; it should be " south-west."

[4] The present native name is Orika, or Yoriki of the Admiralty chart.

[5] An evident mistake, and one inconsistent with the context. The island is scarcely two leagues in circuit.

many reefs. It is in latitude 11⅔°, and it lies two leagues south-east from the extremity of San Christobal.

" On the 11th of this month, we went from this island to the other island which lies with it north-north-west and south-south-east,[1] a short league distant from it.[2] It is distant 3 leagues, east-by-south, from the end of San Christobal; and is in latitude 11° 36'. We named it Santa Anna; it is called Hapa[3] in the language of the natives. It is 7 leagues in circuit; and is a low round island with an eminence in the centre, like a castle; it is well peopled, having abundant provisions, with pigs and hens of Castile; and there is a very good port on the east side.[4]

" On arriving there, we landed the people, and the Indians commenced to attack us.[5] On an Indian being killed, they began to fly, and deserted the town. Our men entered the houses in search of provisions, but they found only three hogs, as all the rest had been placed in safety. At nightfall we embarked in the brigantine and stood off the land ; and all the night we heard no sound except the crowing of many cocks. The next morning, which was the 13th of July, we landed the people to obtain more provisions to carry back for the sick in the ships ; and when the Indians saw our people landing, they got into ambush. I was left with four soldiers in charge of the brigantine. The Indians, with loud cries, began to attack our men, discharging many darts and arrows. Their bodies were painted with red stripes, and they had branches on their heads.[6] They wounded three Spaniards and a negro of mine ; and also the officer in command, Francisco Muñoz, a dart piercing the shield and arm and projecting a hand's breadth on the other side of the shield. Rallying our men, we attacked them valiantly, killing some Indians and wounding many others, so that they abandoned the place and fled. We burned the town, and took water. From the higher ground near by we tried to discover any appearance of

[1] This bearing is only approximate, the magnetic bearing being nearly north and south.

[2] This distance agrees nearly with that on the chart which is about two miles. Figueroa, in his account, gives the distance as three leagues.

[3] The village, situated on the shores of Port Mary on the west coast of the island, is at present called Sapuna by its inhabitants. Allowing for the variation in the spelling of native names, we can here recognise the Hapa of the Spaniards. Oo-ah or Oa, is the name of the island.

[4] This is a good description of the appearance of this island. The port is, however, on the west side ; and the circumference of the island is not half this amount.

[5] " A dar nos guacanara." What " guacanara " means, I can only guess at.

[6] I cannot gather the meaning of this latter part of the sentence and have rendered it literally. The same expression occurs in the account of Figueroa.

land ; but as we saw none, we embarked on our return voyage to
the ships.

"Sailing all this day with a fair wind, we arrived at the island of
San Christobal; and that night we entered a port because there was
a threatening appearance in the weather. We landed in a town that
was there, and the Indians fled, discharging some arrows. A soldier
was wounded in the throat, but not seriously, and he was able to
swallow some food. As we wished to leave the port with the rising moon, we embarked ; and we named the port La Palma.

"We continued our voyage back to the ships; and when we had
sailed about 4 leagues from the port, a canoe came off to look at us
and to learn what people we were. As we had need of Indians for
their language, we endeavoured to take the canoe; and so we coaxed
them on, and of four which came in the canoe we took three alive,
and one died whilst defending himself. In the evening, we arrived
at the Puerto de la Visitacion de Nuestra Senora, where the ships
lay.[1] I found that, on account of bad treatment, all the Indians
whom we had taken in the islands had gone.

"I gave a report to the General of what we had seen and accomplished in the expedition, telling him that there was no appearance
of land further (in that direction), but that all the mass of the land,
which was endless, lay to the west ; and that, from this, he would
perceive what ought to be done. A council of the captains and
pilots was held to determine what steps should be followed in the
prosecution of the voyage ; and it was decided to refit the ships for
this purpose ; this, therefore, was the result of the general consultation. The ships were accordingly refitted ;[2] but on Saturday, the
7th of August, in the same year of 1568, all mustered together and
made a protestation to the General and the captains with reference
to the plan to be pursued. I told them briefly that because the
ships were getting worm-eaten and rotten, and the rigging and
cordage were not of much good, we should be determined to complete, without delay, the object for which we had come. The
General, in reply, said that it would be well that the brigantine
should go in search of more provisions, of which we were in want ;
but I pointed out that this should not be done, because all the

---

[1] From the short description of this harbour given on page 228, it is probably not Makira
Harbour on the south coast of St. Christoval ; although from the time occupied by the
brigantine in her return voyage along this south coast from Santa Anna to the ships, it must
be in its vicinity.

[2] Figueroa refers to the ships being heaved down in this harbour.

islands that we had visited were aroused, and the provisions hidden. They asked for my opinion as to returning to Peru, whence we had come; and I told them that we should not sail to the south of the Equinoctial, as we should be lost, on account of there being many people, scanty provisions, and but little water. I also said that if we were to direct our course to positions in latitudes which we should have time to reach, we should not have time to find land to the south-south-west and south, which would be a work of difficulty; and that such a new navigation, with 1,700 leagues of sea to cross on our return voyage, did not seem prudent. I therefore gave it as my opinion that we should steer north to reach the latitude of the first land we found, because it would be necessary, in order to shape a course from Peru, to go beyond the south tropic for thirty degrees and more; and I also said that when they should venture to make the return voyage, they should carry an abundance of water and provisions, because, otherwise, they would run the risk of all perishing. And so the pilots came to my view, which satisfied the protest that had been made; and I gave my opinion in the presence of a clerk who was Antonio de Cieza. Concerning the idea of my asking to found a settlement in these islands, I said that in that matter I did not know what the General intended to do, since the instructions concerning it were in his keeping. To this opinion they all came, and were of one mind without one that did not assent.[1]

" At midnight on the following Monday, when all were asleep, the General ordered Gabriel Muñoz and myself to go with some soldiers and make an entrance into a town in order to seize some Indians for interpreters (*para lenguas*). We went with 30 men, and took an Indian with his wife and young son; and all the rest of the Indians fled. We then returned to the ships; and straightway we made preparations for prosecuting our voyage.

" On the 11th of August of the same year, we left the Puerto de Nuestra Senora, which is in 11° south of the Equinoctial, in order to follow our voyage to Peru. Sailing to windward, at the end of 7 days after we had left the port, we weathered the island of San Christobal with the two islands of Santa Catalina and Santa

---

[1] The impression, which this interesting passage leaves on my mind, is that the Chief-Pilot prefers in his narrative to gloss over an incident which must have been full of disappointment to himself. Further on in the narrative, he writes more freely on the subject (page :37). In Note IX. of the Geographical Appendix, I have given some further remarks on this passage.

Anna. On the Tuesday evening, having shortened sail, we had reached the islands of Santa Catalina and Santa Anna, which lay three leagues to the north-north-west. Looking around we did not see any more land, and here a strong south-east wind overtook us; and we shaped our course to the north-east-by-east."

In this manner the Spaniards left behind them the Isles of Salomon after a sojourn of six months in these islands; and, perhaps, a few reflections on their discoveries in this group, and on their dealings with the inhabitants, may be here apposite. They seem to have landed on, and to have taken formal possession of, almost every island of any size from Isabel eastward; they named all the large islands in the group with the exception of Bougainville; and the majority of the smaller islands also received their names. In the Geographical Appendix, I have given a list of the islands named by the Spaniards, which do not at present bear the names given them by their original discoverers.[1] It would be a graceful compliment to the memory of the gallant Gallego, who was the central figure of this expedition, if, after the lapse of more than three centuries, the Spanish names should be associated with these islands in the Admiralty charts. The reason why such islands as Choiseul, Contrariété, Les Trois Sœurs, and the Ile du·Golfe (Ugi), at present bear the names given to them by the French navigators, Bougainville and Surville, rather more than a century ago, is to be found, not in any intended act of injustice to the Spanish discoverers, but in the circumstance that the imperfect account of Figueroa,[2] which omits many of the discoveries made in the brigantine, has been the only source of information available in the construction of the Admiralty charts. Those who have written most on the history of geographical discovery in these regions, Pingré, Dalrymple, Buache, and Fleurieu a century ago, and Burney in the early part of the present century, had only the account of Figueroa at their disposal.[3] The Journal of Hernan Gallego, the existence of which was doubted, would have been invaluable to them; and although a non-professional writer, I may be pardoned when I express my admiration at the manner in

[1] *Vide* Note X.

[2] Translated in great part from the original in the works of Pingré, Dalrymple, Fleurieu, and Burney. (Hechos de Don G. H. de Mendoza: par Dr. C. S. de Figueroa.)

[3] Pingré's "Memoire sur le choix et l'état des lieux ôu le passage de Venus du 3 Juin, 1769;" Dalrymple's "Historical Collection of Voyages;" Fleurieu's "Découvertes des François ou 1768 and 1769 dans le sud-est de la Nouvelle Guinée" (also Eng. edit.); Burney's "Chronological History of Voyages and Discoveries," &c.

which M. M. Buache and Fleurieu arrived at such correct inferences, based as they were on such scanty premises. One or two mistakes have arisen in the nomenclature of the present chart, which are due to misconceptions in the English translations of the account given by Figueroa, to wit, I may cite the instance of the Isle of Ramos. . . . . . . The additional names which the Journal of Gallego enables us to identify with existing islands are, in truth, to be found in the general description of the Salomon Islands, which Herrera incorporated in his " Descripcion de les Indias Occidentales," which was published about 1601. But this description was, as just remarked, of a general character, and beyond confirming the suspicion that there were other accounts of Mendana's discoveries besides the relation of Figueroa, it was but of little service to the nautical geographer.

I come now to a less pleasant task, that of reviewing the character of the intercourse that prevailed between the Spaniards and the natives. It has been remarked by Commander Markham in his spirited sketch of the discoveries of Mendana, that the conduct of the Spaniards, in their intercourse with the islanders, was not otherwise than humane;[1] but I feel assured that a different opinion would have been expressed, if the writer had extended his inquiries further into the narrative of Gallego. During their six months' sojourn in this group, the loss of the Spaniards was but trifling in comparison with the losses they inflicted on the natives. In these numerous conflicts the natives must have lost not less than a hundred killed, whilst the Spaniards lost ten of their number; but a large proportion of these unfortunate islanders fell victims to the lamentable succession of reprisals for the massacre of the watering-party at the Puerto de la Cruz, an act of retribution which the Spaniards had entirely brought upon themselves. In the great majority of instances the natives assumed the aggressive, but not in all; and although the Spaniards were often justifiably compelled to employ force in obtaining provisions, yet there was often nothing to excuse them in seizing the canoes, in cajoling natives alongside in order to capture them, or in carrying off with them from the group an unfortunate native with his wife and child. The natives kept on board the ships escaped on account of ill-treatment; and, as Gallego also writes, all the islands were aroused to such a degree by the visit of the Spaniards, that they concealed their provisions, and

[1] " The Cruise of the ' Rosario,' " 2nd edit., 1873 (p. 6).

the ships began their return-voyage to Peru with scanty supplies of food and water. . . . . . We must, however, judge of the conduct of the first discoverers of the Solomon Islands in the spirit of the age to which they belonged. The zeal, which led them to burn the temples dedicated to the worship of snakes and toads in the interior of Isabel, was appropriate to the spirit of an age in which expeditions were fitted out for the double purpose of discovering new territories and of reclaiming the infidel. Yet, if we lay aside the religious element, I doubt very much whether the lapse of three centuries has materially raised the standard by which our dealings with savage races should be guided. The white man kidnaps; the savage revenges the outrage on the next comer ; the ship-of-war in its reprisal is of necessity equally indiscriminate ; and thus feuds are re-opened with no single effort at conciliation.

We left the Spanish vessels when on the eve of their departure from the Isles of Salomon. Little could Mendana or Gallego have then believed that two centuries would pass away before the white man should again visit the scene of their discovery. The Chief-Pilot kept in his journal an almost daily record of the course and usually of the distance during the first portion of this return voyage; but as he was not so regular or so precise in noting the distance of each day's run, the latitudes, which he frequently records, enable me to follow this portion of the track with some degree of confidence.[1] It was on the 18th of August that they bore away to the north-eastward (N.E. by E.) with a strong south-east wind. Experiencing rain-squalls and calms, they kept a little to the north of this course, and on the 23rd they were in latitude 7° (full *largos*), being, as they computed, 36 leagues W. by N. from the Isle of Jesus.[2] It is apparent from the Journal that Gallego expected to find more land in this vicinity, and that he would willingly have gone in search of it. But the expedition had lost heart in the enterprise, and all that they desired was to return to Peru. A look-out was kept for several days, but not a sign of land was seen ; and thereupon Gallego, stifling his own desire, thus records his lament in his journal : "As in the case of the archipelago of the islands, they did not allow me to explore further where I wished. And I hold for certain that if

[1] I have only indicated the general course in the return voyage, as a full translation would be tedious to the reader and would occupy too much of my space.

[2] The bearing was to the southward of west, as the Isle of Jesus, according to Gallego's own observation, was in latitude 6¾°. Three days after, when they were in latitude 5¼° S., Gallego gives their distance and bearing from the Isle of Jesus as 45 leagues W. by N.

they had allowed me to go further, I should have brought them to
a very prosperous and rich land, which will be discovered at God's
pleasure by whomsoever He wills. We were not far from it now,
and of its goodness I did not wish to speak, because they were all
disheartened and desired to return to Peru."

Heading north-eastward with uncertain winds, they were obliged
to steer S.E. by E. for six days as the wind shifted to the north-east.
Finally, they headed to the northward again, and in the last day of
August they passed the 3rd parallel of south latitude. "Between 2°
and 4° of south latitude," as Gallego writes, "we met abundant signs
of land, such as palm-leaf matting, burnt wood, sticks, and *rosuras*,[1]
which the sea derived from the land. From these signs we knew
that we were near the land, although we did not discover it. We
thought that it was New Guinea,[2] because it is not in a greater
latitude than 4° south of the Equinoctial."

New Guinea, however, lay some 1200 miles away; and the
Spanish vessels were in the vicinity of the Gilbert Group, which lay
probably about 300 miles to the eastward. On September 5th, with
shifty and contrary winds, they crossed the Equator at about the
168th meridian of longitude east of Greenwich. The course pursued, in which it would appear the Chief-Pilot had not been consulted, was the subject of a protest made to the General. Thus
writes Gallego : " I said to the pilot, Juan Henriquez, that we ought
to petition the General to direct our course to one place or another
or to steer for one pole or the other, as we were expending our provisions and water in beating to windward. Since the General
followed his own opinion and showed no desire to consult me, I
made this request in the presence of Antonio de Cieza, Clerk, all of
which appears more fully in the said .petition, which is in the possession of the said Clerk."

Steering to the north and subsequently to the N.E. by E., they
reached the 4th parallel of north latitude on September 8th. "This
day," writes the Chief-Pilot, "·I signified to the 'Almiranta' that
they should keep a good look-out from 6° up to 11°, as we were
heading for the land." Altering their course to N.N.W., they

---

[1] Not translated.

[2] Gallego here adds : "Inigo Ortez de Retes discovered it (*i.e.*, New Guinea) and no
other : but Bernardo de la Torre did not see it : nor is there such a Cabo de Cruz (Cape of
the Cross) as he says." I have placed this interesting reference to the discovery of New
Guinea in a foot-note, as it is suddenly interposed in the narrative. In Note XI. of the
Geographical Appendix, the reader may learn more, if so desirous.

reached the parallel of 6° on the 14th, the needle showing no declination to the north-east. On the 15th and 16th, they headed north-east, and on the 17th, steering north, they found themselves in 8°. The surmise of Gallego proved correct. In this parallel, they discovered land.

"Two hours before dawn," as the Chief-Pilot writes, "we came upon the shoals and islands of San Bartolomeo, which trend north-west and south-east and are 15 leagues in length. The south-east extremity is in 8°, and the north-west extremity lies in 8⅔°. There are two lines of reefs with apparently channels between them. There seems to be another line about half-a-league distant. At the north-west, there are two islets, which lie one with the other east and west one league. The coast is steep-to; and we did not find any depth to anchor on the west side. There were many houses and much people and *villos* in these islands. Between the islands, which number more than 20, a canoe was under sail, but it made for the shore. We launched the boat to go for water. They could only obtain a cock of Castile, which they brought back with them. The people fled, abandoning their houses. They came upon a chisel made from a nail, which appears to have belonged to some ships that had been there, and some pieces of rope. They did not find water, but the cocoa-nut palms were cut which showed how the inhabitants got their water.[1] These Indians drink "chicha,"[2] which is made from some fruits like pine-apples; and on this account there is an infinite number of flies. We beat to windward for three hours trying to find depth to anchor; but the water was a thousand fathoms (*estados*) deep. When the boat returned, we continued our voyage."

Figueroa, in his scanty account, neither gives the name nor the latitude of this discovery, so that previous writers, who derived their information entirely from this source, were unable to identify these islands with those in the charts. However, with the materials afforded to me by the journal of Gallego, I have been able, after carefully following the track of the Spanish ships, to identify this discovery with the Musquillo Islands in the Ralick Chain of the Marshall Group. Having followed their course northward from the vicinity of the Gilbert Group, to which I referred above (page 237),

---

[1] This probably refers to cocoa-nut palms that had been cut for making "toddy," a practice to be found amongst the natives of the Line Islands at the present day.

[2] An Indian name for a drink prepared from maize.

it was evident that they were about to pass through the Marshall Islands, and that if they should sight land, I had only to compare the description of Gallego with the present chart of this group, in order to identify this discovery with one of the atolls that there exist. (*Vide* Note XII. of the Geographical Appendix.)

Continuing their course to the northward, they began to get short of water, and the people sickened and . . . . . [1] On the 22nd of September, they attained the latitude of 11½°, and running due north along the meridian, they reached the latitude of 19¼° on October 2nd, when they discovered " a low islet enclosing the sea after the manner of a fishing-net, and surrounded by reefs." " We were hove-to all that night," . . . writes Gallego, . . . " believing that it was inhabited, and that we should be able to obtain water. But there were only sea-birds living on it; and its surface was sandy with some patches of bushes. It is probably two leagues in circuit: and is in latitude 19¼° north of the Equinoctial. As it was the Day of San Francisco, we named it the Isle of San Francisco."

This island of San Francisco has not been identified by previous writers with any island in the present chart, as Figueroa supplied them with the latitude alone, but gave no reliable account from which they might be able to follow the previous track; nor, in fact, in the times of Burney and Krusenstern, who were the last to devote any considerable attention to the discoveries of Mendana, was this part of the Pacific sufficiently well known to enable even a confident surmise to be made. Commodore Wilkes, amongst others, has swept more than one phantom-island from this region. The track of the Spanish ships northward from the Marshall Group brought them, in fact, to a little coral-atoll, named Wake's Island in the present chart, and lying in 19° 10' 54" N. lat. This is the Isle of San Francisco, which is but little altered in appearance in our own day.[2]

Keeping the same northerly course, they passed the limit of the tropic of Cancer on October 7th; and in another week they had reached the latitude of 30°. They now shaped their course north-east; and Gallego consulted the other pilots as to the position of the land, and as to the bearing of the Cabo de Fortunas [3] (Cape Fortune). " They told me in reply," . . . . as the Chief Pilot informs us, ... " that we were already in the vicinity of land, that this cape lay, in

---

[1] "Murieron hartos." To avoid falling into a serious mistake, I have not translated this, more especially as Figueroa refers to no deaths on board during the voyage to Peru.

[2] *Vide* Note XIII. of the Geographical Appendix for further information on this subject.

[3] This cape is evidently referred to as on the Californian coast ; I cannot identify it.

their opinion, 70 or 80 leagues to the north-by-west, that we were much to leeward of the land, that it was not practicable to reach the cape with this wind as the coast trended north-west and south-east, and that we could not live unless we fell in with the land."

Could the Spaniards have known at this time what lay before them, the bravest heart amongst them would have quailed. Instead of being in the neighbourhood of the Californian coast whither they were steering, they had more than 3,000 miles of ocean to traverse and two long dreary months to struggle through, before they were fated to sight the land. They were destined to pass through storms, the like of which Gallego had never witnessed during his 45 years' experience of the sea. The two ships were to be parted; and each was to pursue its solitary way in the fear that the missing ship had foundered. Such was the lot before them with sickness already amongst them, and with a failing store of water and provisions.

The Chief-Pilot thus continues his narrative—"On the 14th of this month (October), I continued to steer both ships in close company to the north-east. In the middle of the night there came a squall with a little rain. We shortened sail; and at that time the 'Almiranta' was to windward; but she allowed herself to fall to leeward for an hour, and when it dawned we could only see her from the top. Hoping to fall in with her, we carried only the fore-sail, and made no more sail all that day and night. We headed to the north-east until the second hour of the day; and because we did not see her, we took in all the sails. This was the 16th day of the month of October.

"Two hours after noon on Sunday the 17th, whilst we were yet hoping, we shortened sail because there was much wind from the south-east. We were driven before the gale; and as we were lying in the trough of the sea without any sails, the wind came upon us with all its fury from the north-east, such as I never beheld during the 45 years that I have been at sea, 30 of which I have served as pilot. Such boisterous weather, I have never witnessed, although I have seen storms enough. For a squall to take us when we were without sail, this was what frightened me. A sea struck us on the port side from the water-line to the middle hatch, which was battened down and caulked as I had ordered. We were deluged with water. Everything went its own way; and the soldiers and sailors were swimming about inside the ship, as they were trying to launch the boat, which was smashed and full of cables and water. The sailors were not able of themselves to do it; but God and His Blessed Mother willed that it should be done.[1] Then I ordered the sailors to unfurl a little of the sail; but before two gaskets were loosed, the fore-sail went into two thousand pieces, and only the bolt-ropes remained. For more than half-an-hour the ship was in great peril until the main-mast was cut away.[2] And soon I ordered them to make a sail of a *frecada*,[3] and of a piece of a bonnet (*boneta*); with this the ship was able to answer her helm . . . . . .[4] The weather began to clear. We were driven from our course more than 50 leagues, because the storm overtook us in latitude $32\frac{1}{2}°$, and when it began to clear we found ourselves in 30°. When this weather came upon us we were 70 leagues south-east-by-south [5] from the Cabo de Fortunas; and when it began to clear we were 120 leagues, rather more than less.

" We headed on our course with only the fore-sails, as we had no other sails, since the sailors had lost the bonnets overboard. On the 21st of October, the wind went round to the opposite quarter, and lasted until the 29th. Coursing north-east with much wind and sea, we sailed close-hauled on one tack or the other, because it was no longer possible to sail free as the sea would engulph us. The ship did not behave well in a beam sea, for soon she shipped seas on either side, and she lost as much way as she made. On the evening of the 29th of October, the wind went round to the south-east, and there was a heavy sea. The wind was so strong that we were unable to make any sails, as they were carried away. All that night we lay in the trough of the sea with much wind and thunder and lightning, so that it seemed like the overwhelming of the world.[6] On the following morning I ordered them to clear away the sprit-sail and use it as a fore-sail, so that we might steer the ship. Before we had run for a watch to the north-east, the wind went round to the south, and with such force that it carried away the sails and we

---

[1] This reference to the launching of the boat, in order, I infer, to lighten the vessel, is ambiguously expressed. Figueroa, in his account, would appear to imply that the boat was merely relieved from its weight of ropes and water ; but further on in his account, Gallego expressly refers to their being without a boat.

[2] Figueroa adds to this account. He says that the General gave the order to cut away the mainmast, and that it carried away a portion of the bulwarks.

[3] *Frazada* in the account of Figueroa.

[4] " Para atras hechamos el camaroto de popa a la mar."

[5] I cannot understand this bearing.

[6] Figueroa in his account states that there was always a foot and a half of water in the hold.

Q

were left without any sail. We employed *las frescadas* (blankets?)
for sails, and thus we went this day. Soon the wind lessened, and
we hoisted the fore-sail and coursed north-east until the next day,
which was the last day of October."

The "Capitana," to which ship the narrative for a time alone
refers, was now in 29° N. lat. A very strong north-east wind, lasting until November 4th, drove them to the south-east in latitude 26°.
These north-easterly winds continued to prevail; and being unable
to sail close to the wind, the Spaniards could not keep their latitude
and were being driven from their course, to the south-east.[1] "We
were," . . . . as Gallego writes, ... "much wearied and suffered
from hunger and thirst, as they did not allow us more than half a
pint of stinking water and eight ounces of biscuit, a few very black
beans, and oil; besides which there was nothing else in the ship.
Many of our people were unable from weakness to eat any more
food. A soldier, who had gambled with his allowance of water and
had lost it, became desperate with thirst and cried out all the day.
Being without a boat, we could do nothing on approaching a harbour.
We resolved to trust that God would send us the means of help.
He provided for us in His great mercy, and on the day of St. Isabel
(November 19th) he gave us a (fair) wind, and we sailed in the lati-
tude of 28° and up to 30°. This weather lasted until the 26th of
November, and we were 125 leagues further on our voyage."

During the first week of December they experienced foul winds
and thick weather: but on the 9th the wind went round to the
south-south-east; and they reached the latitude of 31° on the 12th.
Signs of the vicinity of land were now observed, such as sea-birds
and a goose. A sailor leapt into the sea after a floating piece of a
pine, and brought it on board, in order to bring fair weather. Rain
fell, and enough water was collected for three days. At length the
land was sighted by the watchful eye of Gallego. "It was the eve of
our Lady the Virgin " . . . . . he writes . . . . . "and whilst standing
at the side of the ship, I saw the land. Some of us, who despaired
to see it, said that it could not be the land. Sailing through the
night, two hours before the dawn we found ourselves close to two
islets that lay a league from the mainland in latitude 30° north of
the Equinoctial.[2] "

[1] Figueroa in his account tells us that they rigged a jury-mast, making use of a top-mast
for this purpose.

[2] Gallego here observes that the day before the land was sighted, the needle remained
pointing north.

At length the Spaniards had reached the coast of Old California. "The mercy of God"—as Gallego writes—"had brought us safely through so many storms and privations that the soldiers had despaired of seeing it. Following along the coast, as it trended to the south-east, we entered a bay which resembles in form a pen for shoeing cattle (*corral de herrar ganado*). We could not see the outside point on account of its great distance. We found ourselves embayed; and it was necessary to steer west to weather this point. . . . . . We were detained three days with calms and north-west winds, as we had to beat to windward to weather this point. We named this bay *la bahia de San. tome*: it is in latitude 27⅘°. At the point of this bay there are two large islets, named the Isles of Cacones.[1] We doubled the point on the 23rd of December. We beached the ship for 12 days between these islets. Having lost our boat at sea, we went ashore on a raft of casks to get water. There we made another raft of rushes and some casks, on which we carried on board 12 casks of water and many fish that we caught."

Having obtained timber for making another boat, they continued their voyage, as the Indians were hostile. A foul wind caused them to pass by the port of Xalosco, and they "tacked to seaward to double the Cabo de Corrientes, which is in 21°, in order to reach the port of Santiago, which is 50 leagues beyond Xalosco."

On the 24th[2] of January, 1569, they entered the port of Santiago. The Chief-Pilot tells us in his journal that he was well acquainted with this coast and with its people: this port,[3] he says, lies six leagues from Port Natividad, and is in latitude 19½. Before they left Santiago a joyful surprise awaited them. "On the day of St.

---

[1] This large bay, which deeply indents the Californian peninsula, is named in the present maps the bay of Sebastian Vizcaino, after the Spaniard who surveyed this coast in 1602. Gallego's name of San. tome, which may be a contraction for San. Bartolomeo, has, therefore, the priority of some 30 years and more. The prominent headland, which they had to double, is at present called Point Eugenio. The two *large islets* off this point are now called Cerros and Natividad Islands.

[2] This should be the 22nd of January, as Gallego observes subsequently that the "Almiranta" arriving on the 25th came three days after them.

[3] During his passage from the Californian to the Mexican coast, Gallego seems from some observations in his journal to have been puzzled by getting a latitude of 23° 26' before he arrived at the extremity of the Californian Peninsula. He speaks of San Lucas as being "at the end of California in the tropics;" but this observation apparently did not clear up his doubt on the matter; and in fact on first touching the Mexican coast, the number of small bays made him think that it was still the coast of California. The latitude of Cape San Lucas, the extremity of the Californian Peninsula, is 22° 52': it is, therefore, well within the tropics.

Paul's Conversion, three days after our arrival, the 'Almiranta'
. . . . . hove in sight. She was much in want of water and provisions ; and she carried no boat which, like ourselves, she had cast
over in the great storms ; and her main-mast was cut away. They
did not recognize the coast. It was our Lord's good will to bring
us together in this port. God knows how glad we were to see each
other. In preserving us through such great tempests, our Lord
had worked a miracle . . . . . They told us what had happened
during the great storms : and that when they arrived, they had only
one vessel (*botija*) of water remaining . . . . . Sama, the alguacil-
mayor of the city of Mexico, came with some people of the town of
Colima to see who we were, and he talked with the General."

The two ships left the port of Santiago on the 10th of March.[1]
Nine days afterwards, they sailed into the port of Atapulco
(Acapulco) to obtain news from Peru : but learning nothing, they
left in an hour. Gallego adds that this port is the nearest to the
city of Mexico, and that it lies in 17°. Proceeding along the
Mexican coast, they anchored outside the port of Guatulco (lying
according to Gallego in 15¼°); and they sent a boat on shore to
learn news of Peru and to get wine and biscuits . . . . . "All the
people of the town," . . . . . the Chief-Pilot writes . . . . . " were
scared and fled into the interior, because they had heard in Mexico
that we were a strange Scotch people " (*gente estrangera escoceses*).

Through a jealousy exhibited by the pilots of the "Almiranta"
towards Gallego, the " Capitana " was left behind at this port for a
day and a night, for which, says the object of their jealousy, the
General was very angry with them. However, the " Capitana "
arrived in the port of Caputla nine days before the other ship. The
people there were at first much disturbed ; but on recognising
Gallego, who had been there on previous occasions, they were re-
assured ; and they carried the news ashore that the voyagers had
come from " the discovery of the islands." On the 4th of April the
" Capitana " arrived in the port of Realejo on the Nicaraguan coast,
and was followed five days after by the " Almiranta " . . . . . " In
this port," . . . . . continues the Chief-Pilot . . . . . " we beached
the ships and caulked the seams, and set up lower-masts and top-
masts, of which we had need, in order to be able to lie up for Peru.
With all our necessity in this port, neither the officials of the govern-

---

[1] Gallego refers to an eclipse of the moon at nine in the night of the 10th of March. "At
the end of an hour the moon was clear."

ment nor any other persons would give or lend money to us for the repair of the ships. Perceiving that otherwise the ships would be lost, and that it was indispensable for the service of His Majesty, I lent the General all the money which I had of my own, and I received an acknowledgment for 1400 *pesos* (dollars), with which the ships were refitted; and they were victualled for another piece of gold of 400 *pesos*: all this I lent for the service of His Majesty.

" We left this port, which is in latitude 12½,° on the 28th of May. Sailing to the Cabo de Guion (Cape Guion), we lay up thence for the coast of Peru. On the 4th of June we lost sight of the coast of Nicaragua; and on the 5th we passed to leeward of Mal Pelo Island.[1] On the morning of the 11th we were off Facames,[2] which lies four leagues below the Cabo del San Francisco (Cape San Francisco) on the coast of Peru. On the 14th we anchored in Puerto-viejo; and on the 19th we reached Point Santa Elena. On Sunday, the 26th of June,[3] Don Fernando Henriquez left with the news for Lima or the City of the Kings."

LAUS DEO.

[1] The Malpelo Island of the present charts.
[2] This is evidently Atacames, which has the position described.
[3] The two last dates are referred to as July. This is apparently a mistake, and I have, therefore, corrected it in the translation.

CHAPTER XII

THE most interesting feature in the history of the discovery of the Solomon Group is the circumstance that during a period of two hundred years after it was first discovered by the Spaniards it was lost to the world and its very existence doubted. In the belief that I shall be treading on ground new to the general reader, I will at once pass on to relate how this large archipelago was lost and found again.

Fancied discoveries of the precious metals in the island of Guadalcanar inflamed the imaginations of the Spaniards: and the reports, which they gave on their return to Peru, in 1568, of the wealth and fertility of the newly-found lands, cast a glamour of romance over the scene of their discoveries which the lapse of three hundred years has not been able altogether to remove.

To colonize his new discovery and add one more to the vast possessions of Spain, became the life-long ambition of Mendana. In order to further his great aim, he gave to these islands the name of the "Isles of Salomon," to the end that the Spaniards, supposing them to be the islands whence Solomon obtained his gold for the temple at Jerusalem, might be induced to go and inhabit them. Thus, the name of the new discovery was itself a "pious fraud," if we may believe the story of Lopez Vaz,[1] a Portuguese, who was captured by the English, nearly twenty years afterwards, at the River Plate. This seems to me to be the explanation of the name, which we ought, in fairness, to receive; since, after reading the narrative of Gallego, it is scarcely crediting the Spaniards with ordinary reasoning faculties to imagine that Mendana and his officers really thought that they had found the Ophir of Solomon.

However, many years rolled by; and Mendana had arrived at

---

[1] "Purchas, his Pilgrimes," Part IV., Lib. VII.

an elderly age before any further undertaking was attempted. The appearance of Drake in the South Sea, some years after the return of the expedition to Peru, caused the scheme of colonization to be abandoned. The Spaniards now found a rival in the navigation of that ocean which, under the sanction of a Papal decree, they had hitherto regarded as exclusively their own. The dread that they would be unable to hold the "Isles of Salomon" against the attacks of the powerful nation now intruding in their domain, caused them to relinquish the coveted islands; and "commandement was given, that they should not be inhabited, to the end that such Englishmen, and of other Nations as passed the Straits of Magellan to goe to the Malucos (Moluccas), might have no succour there, but such as they got of the Indian people." [1] To prevent the English obtaining any knowledge of these islands, the publication of the official narrative of Mendana's voyage was purposely delayed. So strong a pressure was brought to bear upon Gallego, the Chief-Pilot of the expedition,[2] that he was afraid to publish his journal, which has not only remained in manuscript up to the present day, but was not brought to light until the second quarter of the present century. Thus, it happened that for nearly half-a-century after the return of Mendana, there was no account of the expedition:[3] no chart preserved its discoveries, it being considered better, as things were then, to let these islands remain unknown.[4]

The popular ignorance of these islands naturally increased the mystery that surrounded them; and their wealth and resources were soon increased ten-fold under the influence of the imaginative faculties of the Spaniards. Lopez Vaz, the Portuguese already referred to, writing about the year 1586 of the recent American discoveries, remarked that "the greatest and most notable discovery that hath beene from those parts now of late, was that of the Isles of Salomon." But romance and fact are strangely mingled in his story. We learn from him, for the first time, that the Spaniards, although "not seeking nor being desirous of gold," brought back with them, from the island of Guadalcanar, 40,000 *pezos*[5] of the precious metal. No reference is made to such a find of gold on the part of the Spaniards in the accounts of Gallego and Figueroa: and

[1] "History of Lopez Vaz: Purchas, his Pilgrimes," Part IV., Lib. VII.
[2] *Vide* prologue to "Gallego's Journal," page 104.
[3] *Vide* page 102.
[4] Letter from Quiros to Don Antonio de Morga, Governor of the Philippines.
[5] Dollars.

it is probable that the reports to this effect may have originally
arisen out of the circumstance that, when the ships were being refitted and provisioned at the port of Realejo, on the Nicaraguan
coast, for the completion of their voyage to Peru, the necessary
expenses, which amounted to 1800 *pezos*, were defrayed by the
Chief-Pilot, Gallego.[1]

If the English captain, Withrington by name, who elicited this
information from his Portuguese prisoner, Lopez Vaz, had hoped to
have obtained any satisfactory account of the position of these
vaunted islands, he must have been grievously disappointed. He
learned from him that the Spaniards, having coasted along the island
of Guadalcanar until the parallel of 18° S. latitude without reaching
its extremity, were of the opinion that it formed " part of that continent which stretches to the strait of Magalhanes " (Magellan).
From this misconception, the idea arose that the Spaniards had discovered the southern continent and that Gallego was the discoverer,[2]
and so vague was the information of the extent of the newly-dis-
covered islands that, when in 1599, an English ship was carried by
tempest to 64° S. lat., the captain, on sighting some mountainous
land covered with snow, considered that it extended towards the
islands of Salomon.[3]

But to return to the long-deferred project of Mendana. Years
of delay seemed only to increase the desire of the first discoverer of
this group to complete his work. A change occurred in the vice-
royalty of Peru ; and under the auspices of the new Viceroy an
expedition of four ships was fitted out, on which were embarked
sailors, soldiers, and emigrants to the total number of four hundred.
In 1595, more than a quarter of a century after the return of his
first expedition, Mendana, now an elderly man, sailed from Peru
accompanied by his wife, Donna Isabella Baretto. Fernandez de
Quiros, who had braved with his leader the perils of the first voyage
and had shared with him in the disheartenings arising from a hope
so long deferred, now served under him as chief pilot. Their destination was St. Christoval, the easternmost of the Solomon Group.
The imperfect knowledge of the navigator of those days was curiously
exhibited during this voyage. With the means at his command, it
was a comparatively easy matter to follow along one parallel of

---

[1] *Vide* page 245.
[2] Dalrymple's "Historical Collection of Voyages," &c., Vol. I., p. 90.
[3] "Purchas, his P.lgrimes," Vol. IV., p. 1391.

latitude or " to run down his latitude " as the sailor terms it; but to
ascertain with any approach to accuracy his meridian of longitude
was scarcely within the power of the Spanish navigator. When
only about half-way across the Pacific and about the same distance
on their voyage to the Solomon Group, they discovered a group of
islands, which, from their latitude, they believed to be the object of
their quest. Further exploration, however, convinced Mendana of
his mistake; and he named his new discovery Las Marquesas de
Mendoza, a name which this group at present in part retains. On
continuing the voyage, the crews were assured that in three or four
days they would arrive at the "Isles of Salomon," which were in
point of fact more than three thousand miles away. The three or
four days wearily spun themselves out into thirty-three. General
discontent became rife; and murmurs of dissatisfaction arose which
might have shortly ended in open revolt. At length, late one night
they were overtaken by one of the rain-storms so common in those
regions; and when the clouds lifted, they saw within a league of them
the shores of a large island. The discovery was signalled from the
flag-ship, the "Capitana," to the other three ships: but only two
replied. The missing vessel, the "Almiranta," had been last seen
between two and three hours before. No trace was ever found of
her. Whither she went, or what fate befell her, are questions which
have remained amongst the many unsolved mysteries of the sea.
There is something tragical in this disappearance of a large ship
having probably over a hundred souls on board, men, women, and
children, when apparently the goal of the expedition had been
attained.

The appearance of the natives of this large island at first induced Mendana to believe that he had at last arrived at the lands
he had been so long seeking. But his belief was short-lived. The
new island was named Santa Cruz; and having abandoned the
original object of the expedition to establish a colony on the island
of St. Christoval, the Spaniards commenced to plant their colony on
the shores of a harbour which they named Graciosa Bay. Disaster
upon disaster fell on the little colony. Disease struck down numbers
of the settlers, and the poisoned weapons of the natives ended the
lives of many others. Mutiny broke out; and the extreme punishment of death was inflicted on the conspirators. The foul murder
of the chief who had steadfastly befriended them was punished, it
is true, by the execution of the murderers; but the enmity of the

natives could not thus be pacified. Broken-hearted and overcome by disease, Mendana sickened and died; and the heavens themselves must have seemed to the superstitious Spaniards to have frowned on their design, for a total eclipse of the moon preceded by a few hours the death of their commander. The brother of Donna Isabel had been selected by Mendana as his successor; but a fortnight afterwards he died from a wound received in an affray with the natives. It was at length resolved to abandon the enterprise; and rather over two months after they had first sighted the island, the survivors of the expedition re-embarked for Manilla. Hoping to learn something of the missing ship before finally steering north-ward, they directed their course westward until they should reach the parallel of 11° of south latitude, when they expected to arrive at St. Christoval whither the "Almiranta" might have gone. The course[1] which they steered under the guidance of Quiros, the pilot, must have soon brought them on this parallel; and they appear to have followed it with a favourable wind until the second day,[2] when seeing no signs of land, they were urged by the increasing sickness and by the scarcity of water and provisions to give up the search, and to this change of plans Quiros gave his consent. In a few hours, if they had continued their course, the mountain-tops of St Christ-oval would have appeared above the horizon and the "Isles of Salomon" would have been found. But such was not to be; and when probably not more than fifty miles from the original destination of the expedition, the ships were headed N.N.W. for Manilla. Such a course must have brought the Spanish vessels yet closer to the eastern extremity of the group; but the night fell, and on the following morning the Solomon Islands were well below the western horizon. Of the three ships, two only reached the Philippines. The "Fragata" lost the company of the other ships and "never more appeared." It was subsequently reported that she had been found driven ashore with all her sails set and all her people dead and rotten.[3]

Thus terminated the attempt of the Spaniards to found a colony in the Solomon Islands; and the ill fate which it experienced was scarcely calculated to encourage others to undertake a similar

[1] The course is differently given, by Quiros as W. by S. and by Figueroa as W.S.W. (Dalrymple's Historical Collection: vol. I., 92.)

[2] Figueroa implies the second day; whilst Quiros speaks of "two days."

[3] Dalrymple's Historical Collection of Voyages: vol. I., 58.

enterprise. Barely half of the four hundred souls who had left
Peru under such bright auspices could have reached the Philippines.
Among them, however, was Quiros the pilot of Mendana, who,
nothing daunted by disaster and ill-success, returned to Peru and
endeavoured to re-awaken the spirit of discovery which was losing
much of its enthusiasm with the departing glory of the Spanish
nation. The Viceroy of Peru referred him to the Court of Spain ;
and, after experiencing for several years the effects of those intrigues
which seem to have been the accustomed fate of the early navigators,
Quiros set sail from Callao at the close of 1605, to search the Southern
Ocean once again for the Isles of Salomon and the other unknown
lands in that region. He had been supplied with two ships, and
was accompanied by Luis Vaez do Torres as second in command.
It is unnecessary to enter here into the particulars of the voyage
across the Pacific. It will be sufficient for my purpose to state that
Quiros finally sought the parallel of 10° south, and sailed westward
in the direction of Santa Cruz, which he had discovered with
Mendana ten years before. Being rather to the northward of the latitude of Santa Cruz, he struck a small group of islands, the principal
of which was called Taumaco by the natives. These islands have
been identified with the Duff Group, which lies about 65 miles
north-east of Santa Cruz. Nearly two centuries had passed away
before these islands were again seen by Europeans, when they were
sighted by Captain Wilson of the missionary ship " Duff," in 1797.
During the ten days spent by the Spaniards at Taumaco, Quiros
obtained information of a number of islands and large tracts of
land in the neighbourhood, which seemed to confirm him in his
belief in a vast unknown extent of land in the Southern Ocean.
The list of these islands are included in a memorial[1] subsequently
presented by Quiros to Philip II. of Spain, which contains many
particulars of the discoveries of the expedition in this region. Some
of them I have been able to identify with names on existing charts,
but referring my reader to Note XIV. of the Geographical Appendix,
I will only allude here to the most interesting reference in this
memorial, which is to a *large country named Pouro*, that is without
doubt the large island of St. Christoval in the Solomon Group,
which lay rather under 300 miles to the westward. The central

---

[1] Dalrymple's Hist. Coll. of Voyages: vol. I, p. 145. This memorial is given in the
original in Purchas, (His Pilgrimes, Part VI, Lib. VII, Chap. 10.) *Vide* also De Brosses
" Histoire des Navigations aux Terres Australes : " tom. I, p. 341 : Paris 1756.

portion of St. Christoval is at present called *Bauro*, and by this name the whole island is often known to the natives of the islands around. Thus, without suspecting it, Quiros had described to him an island of the lost Solomon Group, and the very island which had been more completely explored than any other by the expedition of Mendana nearly forty years before. Had he been in possession of Gallego's journal, in which the native name of *Paubro* is given to St Christoval, he would have at once recognised in this *Pouro* of the Taumaco natives the *Paubro* of Mendana's expedition. His informant spoke to him of silver arrows which had been brought from *Pouro*, but this circumstance did not set him on the right track ; and thus for the second time this enterprising navigator unwittingly let the chance pass by of finding the Isles of Salomon.[1]

The opportunity had gone ; and, for this reason, the remainder of this voyage of Quiros has no interest in connection with the Solomon Group. The information which he had obtained of the numerous islands and tracts of land in the vicinity of Taumaco seems to have banished from his mind all thoughts of the missing group. Steering southward, and passing without seeing the island of Santa Cruz of which he had been in search, he reached the island of Tucopia, of which he had previously obtained information from the natives of Taumaco. Continuing his course, he finally anchored in a large bay which indented the coast of what he believed was the Great Southern Continent. The name Australia del Espiritu Santo was given by him to this new land, when flushed with the success of his discovery. In the hour of his supposed triumph, fortune again frowned on the efforts of the Spanish navigator. A mutiny broke out on board his ship, and Quiros was compelled by his crew to abandon the enterprise. Without being able to acquaint Torres of what had happened, he left the anchorage unperceived in the middle hours of the night, and after making an ineffectual attempt to find Santa Cruz, he sailed for Mexico. Torres, after ascertaining that the supposed southern continent was an island,[2] continued his voyage westward, and, passing through the straits which bear his name, ultimately arrived at Manilla.

The results of the expeditions in which Quiros had been engaged

---

[1] The question of this name of Pouro is further treated in Note XV. of the Geographical Appendix, since an attempt has been made by Mr. Hale, the American philologist, to identify it with the Bouro of the Indian Archipelago.

[2] This island is one of the New Hebrides, and still retains its Spanish name of Espiritu Santo.

could hardly have been looked upon with feelings of great satisfaction at the Spanish Court, where the veteran navigator in the
true spirit of Columbus now repaired to advocate the colonization
of the Australia del Espiritu Santo he had just discovered. The
Isles of Salomon had been also discovered, it is true; but two
succeeding expeditions had failed to find them. Santa Cruz had
similarly eluded the efforts of Quiros; and his last discovery of the
supposed southern continent had been proved by his companion,
Torres, to be an island. Several years had passed away, and Quiros
was an old man before his wishes for a new expedition were
granted. In furtherance of the exploration of the Isles of Salomon
and the Australia del Espiritu Santo, he is said to have presented
no less than fifty memorials to the king; in one of which, after
painting in the brightest colours the beauty and fertility of his last
discovery, he thus addresses his Sovereign : " Acquire, sire, since you
can, acquire heaven, eternal fame, and that new world with all its
promises." Such appeals coming from one who might fitly be called
the Columbus of his age could scarcely be rejected by the monarch.
In 1614, Quiros, bearing a commission from the king, departed from
Spain on his way to Callao, where he intended to fit out another
expedition. Death, however, overtook him at Panama on his way
to Peru ; and with Quiros died all the grand hopes, which he had
fostered, of adding the unknown southern continent to the dominion
of Spain. Had he lived to carry out his project, Australia
might have become a second Peru. The spirit of enterprise
on the part of the Spanish nation never again extended itself
into this region of the Western Pacific. During the next century
and a half the large island-groups, which the Spaniards had discovered in these seas, were not visited by any European navigators;[1]
and it is surprising how few benefits have accrued to geography
from these three Spanish expeditions to these regions. Their discoveries have had to be rediscovered ; and it has been only by a
laborious process on the part of the geographer that the navigator
has been able to make any use of the imperfect information, which
the Spanish navigators have bequeathed to us of their discoveries
in these seas.

The death of Quiros deepened more than ever the mystery that

[1] In 1616, the Dutch navigator, Le Maire, when he discovered and named the Horne
Islands in lat. 14° 56' S. and Hope Island in 16° S. thought that he had found the Solomon
Islands ; but these islands lie more than a thousand miles to the eastward of this group.
Dalrymple's Hist. Coll., vol. II., p. 59.

was thrown over the Isles of Salomon. Although Herrera[1] had published in 1601 a short description of these islands, which he must have derived from official sources, no account of the first voyage of Mendana was published until nearly half a century after the return of the expedition to Peru, when in 1613 a short narrative appeared in a work written by Dr. Figueroa.[2] However, the exaggerated description, such as Lopez Vaz had given, obtained by virtue of prepossession a stronger hold on the memories of the seafaring world. The same spirit of jealousy against other nations, which had compelled Gallego to suppress his journals, and had so long withheld any account of Mendana's discoveries, now doomed to destruction the several memorials and documents of Quiros; but fortunately the work of destruction was not completed. The consequence of such proceedings was to greatly heighten the exaggerated misconceptions relating to the Isles of Salomon. We learn from Purchas[3] that Richard Hakluyt was informed in London in 1604, by a Lisbon merchant, of an expedition which had left Lima in 1600 and had fallen in "with divers rich countries and islands not far from the islands of Salomon. One chief place they called Monte de Plata, for the great abundance of silver there is like to be there. For they found two crowns' worth of silver in two handfuls of dust, and the people gave them for iron as much and more in quantity of silver."[4] Amongst the misconceptions which prevailed is one which we find in a memorial addressed by Dr. Juan Luis Arias to Philip III. of Spain,[5] where he refers to the discovery of "New Guadalcanal" and "San Christoval" as quite distinct from Mendana's subsequent discovery, as he alleges, of the Isles of Salomon ; and he alludes to the opinion of some that New Guadalcanal was a part of New Guinea. In Peru the actual existence of these islands came to be doubted ; and successive viceroys held it a political maxim to treat the question of the existence of the Solomon Islands as a romance.[6]

The jealous attitude, assumed by Spain towards other nations with reference to these discoveries, succeeded only too well in be-

[1] *Vide* page 192.

[2] *Vide* page 192.

[3] "His Pilgrimes," vol. IV., p. 1432.

[4] Geographical writers are not agreed as to whether this allusion refers to one of the voyages of Quiros or not. From the date it would appear probable that it refers to Mendana's second voyage, when Quiros was chief pilot.

[5] A translation is given by Mr. Major in his "Early Voyages to Terra Australis."

[6] Pinkerton's Voyages, vol. XIV., p. 12.

wildering the geographers who endeavoured to ascertain the true position of the Solomon Islands; and so varied were the opinions on the subject, that the latitude assigned to them varied from 7° to 19° south, and the longitude from 2400 miles to 7500 miles west of Peru. Acosta, in 1590, ignorant of the materials several years after placed at the disposal of Figueroa, located these islands about 800 leagues[1] west of Peru, and Herrera gives them the same position,[2] a longitude which Lopez Vaz had previously given them in the account obtained from him in 1586 by Captain Withrington. The discoverers themselves, if we may trust the estimates given in the accounts of Gallego and Figueroa, and in the memorials of Quiros, considered that the Solomon Islands were removed about double this distance from the coast of Peru. Their estimates vary between 1500 and 1700 Spanish leagues, whereas the true distance is about 2100 leagues or from 1500 to 2000 miles west of the position assigned by the discoverers. In his second voyage, Mendana was misled by this small estimate when he at first mistook the Marquesas for his previous discovery, the Isles of Salomon. I am inclined to consider that the Spanish navigators purposely under-estimated the distance of these islands from the coast of Peru, and that in so doing they were actuated by two motives. In the first place, they would be desirous to bring their discoveries within the line of demarcation fixed by the Papal Bull after the discovery of America by Columbus, by which the hemisphere west of a meridian 370 leagues west of the Azores was assigned to Spain, and that to the east of this meridian to Portugal. Thus it was that Spain had had to deliver the Brazils to Portugal; and in possessing herself of the Moluccas she had appropriated by a geographical fraud lands which should have belonged to that nation.[3] Their other motive is probably to be found in that jealousy of spirit which, in order to prevent Drake and the English from finding their discoveries, caused the suppression of Gallego's journal and the burning of many of the memorials of Quiros.

Similar confusion prevailed amongst the early cartographers as to the position which they should assign to the Solomon Islands. As M. Buache[4] points out, the first charts representing the Isles of

[1] Spanish leagues, 17½ to a degree.
[2] Herrera at the same time places them 1500 leagues from Lima !
[3] I am indebted to Mr. Dalrymple (Hist. Collect. of Voyages, vol. I., p. 51) for this explanation of the small estimates of the Spanish navigators.
[4] "Memoir concerning the existence and situation of Solomon's Islands," presented to the Royal Academy of Sciences in 1781. (Fleurieu's "Discoveries of the French in 1768 and 1769.")

Salomon, which were published at the end of the 16th century, made a near approximation to their true position by placing them to the east and at no great distance from New Guinea. Subsequent cartographers, however, were less happy in their guesses at the truth. In the "Arcano del Mare," published by Dudley, in 1646, the Solomon Islands were transported to the position of the Marquesas, with which they were thought identical. This position was generally received until early in last century, when Delisle adopted a position much nearer to that given in the early maps. M. Danville, however, later on in the century, being unable to reconcile the Spanish discoveries with the more recent discoveries in the South Seas, suppressed altogether the Isles of Salomon in his map of the world; and his example was followed by several other geographers, who were equally anxious to expunge the lost archipelago from their maps and to relegate it to the class of fabulous lands.

After the death of Quiros, the Spanish nation ceased to favour any further enterprise in search of the missing archipelagos, which do not appear to have engaged the special attention of any nation. Generations thus passed away, and the Solomon Islands were almost forgotten. But there lingered amongst the sea-faring population in Peru, memories of the missing islands of Mendana and Quiros, which were revived from time to time by some strange story told by men, who had returned to Callao from their voyage across the Pacific to Manilla. Even in the first quarter of last century, the mention of the Isles of Salomon suggested visions of beautiful and fertile lands, abounding in mineral wealth, and populated by a happy race of people who enjoyed a climate of perfect salubrity. This we learn from the narrative of Captain Betagh,[1] an Englishman, who, having been captured by the Spaniards in 1720, was detained a prisoner in Peru. He speaks of the arrival, not long before, of two ships at Callao, which, though cruising independently in the Pacific, had both been driven out of their course and had made the Solomon Islands. A small ship was despatched to follow up their discovery: but as she was only victualled for two months, I need scarcely add that she did not find them. It is very probable that the islands made by the two ships were the Marquesas.

Not very long after this attempt to find the missing group, Admiral Roggewein,[2] the Dutch navigator, in his voyage round the

---

[1] Pinkerton's "Voyages and Travels," vol. XIV., p. 12.
[2] Dalrymple's "Hist. Coll. of Voyages," vol. II.

world, sighted, in 1722, two large islands or tracts of land in the
Western Pacific, which he named Tienhoven and Groningen (the
Groninguc of some writers). Behrens, the narrator of the expedition,
considered them to be portions of the Terra Australis. Geographers,
however, have differed widely in their attempts to identify these
islands. Dalrymple and Burney held the opinion that these islands
were none other than the Solomon Islands; but the question is of
little importance to us, as no communication took place with the
natives.

In his "Histoire des Navigations aux Terres Australes," which
was published in Paris, in 1756, De Brosses, after referring to the
circumstance that geographers differed a thousand leagues in locating
this group, inserts, as giving quite another idea of their position, the
story of Gemelli Careri, when on his voyage from Manilla to Mexico,
in command of the great galleon. It appears that when they were
in 34° north lat., a canary flew on board and perched in the rigging.
Careri at once inferred that the bird must have flown from the
Solomon Islands, which lay, as he learned from the seamen of his
vessel, two degrees further south. The source of the Spanish commander's information might have suggested some rather odd reflections: however, De Brosses, as if to justify this belief of the
sailors of the galleon, refers to two islands, Kinsima (Isle of Gold)
and Ginsima (Isle of Silver), lying about 300 leagues east of Japan,
which, having been kept secret by the Japanese, had been in-
effectually sought for by the Dutch in 1639 and 1643.[1] De Brosses,
it should be remembered, was writing when the Isles of Salomon
were in the minds of many a myth. That this notion of the seamen
of the galleon should suggest to him two legendary islands placed
east of Japan, islands believed by the Dutch not to belie their names
in mineral wealth, sufficiently shows how wild speculation had become with reference to the position of this mysterious group.

In a few years, however, there was a revival of the spirit of
geographical enterprise in England, under the enlightened auspices
of George III.; and the time was approaching when, in anticipation
of the transit of Venus in 1769, the attention of the English and
French astronomers and geographers was more specially directed to
the South Pacific, with the purpose of selecting suitable positions
for the observation of this phenomenon. M. Pingré, in his memoir
on the selection of a position for observing the transit of Venus,

which was read before the French Academy of Sciences in December, 1766, and January, 1767, gave a translation of the account given by Figueroa of Mendana's discovery of the Solomon Islands; but he did not throw much new light on their supposed position.

Whilst the attention of geographers was thus once more directed towards this part of the Pacific, the two English voyages of circumnavigation under Commodore Byron and Captain Carteret[1] supplied them with information, which pointed to the correctness of the view of the old cartographers that the Solomon Islands lay to the east, and not far removed from New Guinea. That Commodore Byron, when sailing in the supposed latitude of these islands in 1765, expected to fall in with them more towards the centre of the Pacific, is shown by the circumstance that he at first believed one of the islands of the group, subsequently named the Union Group, to be the Malaita of the Spaniards, an island which actually lay more than 1500 miles to the westward. However, he continued his course in the track of the missing group, until he reached the longitude of 176° 20′ E. in latitude 8° 13′ S., a position more than 800 miles to the eastward of that assigned to the Solomon Islands in his chart. Giving up the search, Commodore Byron steered northward to cross the equator, and ultimately shaped his course for the Ladrones. His remark in reference to his want of success augured ill for the future discovery of the Solomon Group, since he doubted whether the Spaniards had left behind any account by which it might be found by future navigators.

In August, 1766, another expedition consisting of two ships, the "Dolphin," and the "Swallow," under the command of Captain Wallis, and Captain Carteret, sailed from Plymouth with the object of making further discoveries in the southern hemisphere. After a stormy passage through the Straits of Magellan, the two ships were separated just as they were entering the South Sea. This accidental circumstance proved fortunate in its results for geographical science, as each vessel steered an independent course. Whilst Captain Wallis in the "Dolphin" was exploring the coasts of Tahiti, Captain Carteret in the "Swallow" followed a track more to the southward, and ultimately brought back to Europe tidings of the long lost lands of Mendana and Quiros. In July, 1767, Captain Carteret being in 167° W. long. and 10° S. lat., kept his course westward in the same parallel "in hopes"—as he remarks—"to have fallen in

[1] Hawkesworth's Voyages (vol. I.) contains the accounts of these expeditions.

with some of the islands called Solomon's Islands." After reaching the meridian of 177° 30' E. long. in 10° 18' S. lat., a position five degrees to the westward of that assigned to the Solomon Islands in his chart, Captain Carteret came to the conclusion "that if there were any such islands their situation was erroneously laid down." He was afterwards destined to discover, unknown to himself, nearly a thousand miles to the westward, the very group whose existence he doubted. Continuing his westerly course, he arrived at a group of islands, the largest of which he recognised as the Santa Cruz of Mendana, which had not been visited by Europeans since the disastrous attempt to found a Spanish Colony there more than 170 years before. With a crazy ship, and a sickly crew, Captain Carteret desisted from the further prosecution of his discoveries in those regions; and shaping his course W.N.W., he sighted in the evening of the second day a low flat island, one of the outlying islands of the Solomon Group, which, without suspecting the nature of his discovery, he called Gower Island, a name still preserved in the present chart.[1] During the night, the current carried him to the south, and brought him within sight of what he thought were two other large islands lying east and west with each other, which he named Simpson's Island, and Carteret's Island. Captain Carteret communicated with the natives, but did not anchor. These two islands have proved to be the forked northern extremity of the large island of Malaita. Keeping to the north-west, he subsequently discovered, off the north-west end of the group, a large atoll with nine small islands, which are known as the Nine Islands of Carteret. On the following morning he was fated, without being aware of it, to get another glimpse of the Solomon Islands. A high island, descried by him to the southward, which is named Winchelsea Island in his text, and Anson Island in his chart of the voyage, was in all probability the island of Bouka visited nearly a year afterwards by Bougainville, the French navigator. Thus the missing group was at length found, but without the knowledge of the English navigator who discovered it. He had, in truth, expected to find it 20° further to the east. It was reserved, however, for the geographer in his study to identify the discoveries of Carteret with the Isles of Salomon of Mendana.

At the end of June, 1768, Bougainville the French navigator,[2]

---

[1] Captain Carteret communicated with the natives, but did not anchor.

[2] "Voyage autour du Monde en 1766-1769:" second edit. augmentee : Paris 1772.

coming northward from his discovery of the Louisiade Archipelago and of the Australia del Espiritu Santo of Quiros, made the west coast of a large island, now known as Choiseul Island, one of the Solomon Islands. When the ships were about twenty miles south of the present Choiseul Bay, boats were sent to look for an anchorage, but they found the coast almost inaccessible. A second attempt was made to find an anchorage in Choiseul Bay, but, night coming on, the number of the shoals and the irregularity of the currents prevented the ships from coming up to the anchorage. In this bay the boats were attacked by about 150 natives in ten canoes who were dispersed and routed by the second discharge of fire-arms. Two canoes were captured, in one of which was found the jaw of a man half broiled. The island was named Choiseul by its discoverer, and a river from which the natives had issued into the bay was called "la riviere des Guerriers." Passing through the strait which bears his name, the French navigator coasted along the east side of Bougainville Island, and passed off the island of Bouka. The natives who came off to the ship in their canoes displayed the cocoa-nuts they had brought with them, and constantly repeated the cry, "bouca, bouca, onellé." For this reason, Bougainville named the island, Bouca, which is the name it still retains on the chart. It is, however, evident from the narrative that the French navigator never regarded this name as that by which the island was known to its inhabitants. When Dentrecasteaux, during his voyage in search of La Pérouse, lay off this island in his ships in 1792, the natives who came off from the shore, as Labillardière informs us,[1] made use of the same expression of "bouka." This eminent naturalist considered that the word in question was a term in the language of these islanders; and he refers to it as a Malay expression of negation, except when a pause is made on the first syllable when it signifies "to open." On leaving behind him the island of Bouka, Bougainville quitted the Solomon Group; but from his account it is apparent that he had no idea of having found the missing archipelago. Referring to these islands in the introduction to his narrative, he writes :—"supposing that the details related of the wealth of these islands are not fabulous, we are in ignorance of their situation, and subsequent attempts to find them have been in vain. It merely appears that they do not lie between the eighth and twelfth parallels of south latitude." In Bougain-

---

[1] Labillardière's "Voyage a la recherche de la Pérouse : " Paris 1800 : tome I., p. 227.

ville's plans and charts, these discoveries are referred to as forming
part of the Louisiade Archipelago which he had found to the southward. In the general chart showing the track of his voyage, the
Solomon Islands are placed about 350 miles north-west of the
Navigator Islands ; and they are there referred to as "Isles Salomon
dont l'existence et la position sont douteuse."

In June of the following year, 1769, there sailed from Pondicherry
an expedition commanded by M. de Surville,[1] who was bound on
some enterprise with the object of which we are still to a great extent unacquainted. It is, however, probable as we learn from Abbé
Rochon,[2] that some rumour of an island abounding in wealth and
inhabited by Jews, which was reported to have been lately seen by
the English seven hundred leagues west of Peru, had led to the
fitting out of this expedition. Not unlikely, stories of the wealth of
the missing islands of Mendana had been revived by the arrival in
India of some ship that had come upon them in her track across the
Pacific ; and the reference to their being populated by Jews may be
readily understood when I allude to the fact that the form of the
nose in one out of every five Solomon Islanders, and in truth in
many Papuans, gives the face quite a Jewish cast. In October, 1769,
Surville discovered and named Port Praslin on the north-east coast
of Isabel, which was the same island of the Solomon Group that
Mendana had first discovered two hundred years before. Here he
stayed eight days, during which time his watering-parties came into
lamentabl econflict with the natives. Sailing eastward from Port
Praslin, he sighted the Gower Island of Carteret, which he named
Inattendue Island. Subsequently he reached Ulaua, which he
called, on account of the unfavourable weather which he experienced
in its vicinity, Ile de Contrarieté. The attempt to send a boat ashore
was the occasion of another unfortunate affray with the natives, who
were ultimately dispersed with grape-shot. It will be remembered
that just two centuries before, the Spaniards in the brigantine came
into conflict with these same islanders, and that they named their
island La Treguada in consequence of their supposed treachery (vide
anteâ). In the neighbourhood of Contrarieté, Surville sighted three
small islands, which he named Les Trois Sœurs (Las Tres Marias of
the Spaniards), and near them another island, which he called Ile du

---

[1] An account of this expedition is given in Fleurieu's "Discoveries of the French in 1768
and 1769 to the south-east of New Guinea :" London, 1791.
[2] " Voyages à Madagascar et aux Indes Orientales :" Paris, 1791.

Golfe, the Ugi or Gulf Island of the present chart. Sailing east-ward, he apprehended from the trend of the neighbouring St. Christoval coast that he would become embayed; but his apprehensions were removed when he arrived at the extremity of this land, which he named Cape Oriental, and the two off-lying small islands of Santa Anna and Santa Catalina were called Iles de la Déliverance in token of the danger from which he had apparently been delivered. In total ignorance of the fact that he had been cruising amongst the islands of the lost archipelago of Mendana, Surville now directed his course for New Zealand; and on account of sangu-inary conflicts with the natives of Port Praslin and Contrarieté, he named his discoveries Terre des Arsacides or Land of the Assassins.

In 1781, Maurelle, the Spanish navigator, in command of the frigate "Princesa," during his voyage from Manilla to San Blas on the west coast of Mexico,[1] came upon the Candelaria Shoals of Mendana, which lie off the north coast of Isabel Island. I have shown on page 200 that these Candelaria Shoals are no other than the Ontong Java of Tasman, which was identified by M. Fleurieu[2] with the discovery of Maurelle. To the south-east of these shoals the "Princesa" approached another, which on account of the roaring of the sea was named El Roncador: this has been erroneously identified with the Candelaria Shoals by M. Fleurieu, and it is so named on the present Admiralty charts. Thus it nearly fell to the lot of the Spanish nation to be amongst the first to find the group they had originally discovered; but Maurelle was not acquainted with his vicinity to the missing Isles of Salomon, and turning the head of his ship eastward, he proceeded on his voyage.

In July, 1788, Lieutenant Shortland, when returning to England from Port Jackson in convoy of a fleet of transports, made the Solomon Group near Cape Sydney on the south coast of St. Chris-toval. He skirted the south side of the group until he arrived at Bougainville Straits, and received the impression that he was coast-ing along an apparently continuous tract of land, to which he gave the name of New Georgia. Passing through Bougainville Straits, which, in ignorance of the discoveries of the French navigator, he named after himself, Lieutenant Shortland continued on his voyage.

[1] An account of this voyage is given in " Voyage de la Pérouse autour du Monde," par Milet-Mureau: London, 1799: vol. I., p. 201.

[2] " Discoveries of the French in 1768 and 1769," etc.: pp. 179, 18 .

The names of the numerous headlands[1] on the south side of the Solomon Group, bear witness in the present chart to the accurate observations of the English navigator: and from him Mount Lammas, the highest peak of Guadalcanar, received its name. Like Bougainville and Surville, Shortland was not acquainted with the nature of his discoveries.[2]

It now remained for the geographers to avail themselves of the materials placed at their disposal by the voyages of the French and English navigators. M. Buache in a "Memoir on the Existence and Situation of Solomon's Islands,"[3] which was presented to the French Academy of Sciences in 1781, deals with the discoveries of Carteret, Bougainville, and Surville. The steps by which he arrived at the conclusion that the groups of islands discovered by these navigators were not only one and the same group, but that they were the long-lost Isles of Salomon of Mendana, afford an instructive instance of how a patient and laborious investigator, endowed with that gift of discrimination which M. Buache employed with such laudable impartiality, may ultimately attain the truth he seeks, invested though it be in clouds of mystery and contradiction. Groping along through a maze of conflicting statements, to which both navigators and geographers had in equal share contributed, M. Buache finally emerged into the light of day, when he asserted in his memoir that between the extreme point of New Guinea as fixed by Bougainville and the position of Santa Cruz as determined by Carteret, there was a space of 12½ degrees of longitude, in which the Islands of Solomon ought to be found. In this space, as he proceeded to show, lay the large group discovered by Bougainville and Surville which, he with confidence asserted, would prove to be none other than the long-lost islands of the Solomon Group.

But such a view of the character of the recent French discoveries in these seas was received by English geographers with that spirit of partiality from which the cause of geographical science has so frequently suffered. Mr. Dalrymple in his "Historical Collection of Voyages," published in 1770, before he had become acquainted with the discoveries of Carteret, Bougainville, and Surville, stated his conviction that there was no room to doubt that what Mendana

[1] Capes Philip, Henslow, Hunter, Satisfaction, etc.
[2] Shortland communicated with the natives of Simbo. An account of this voyage is given in the "Voyage of Governor Phillip to Botany Bay:" London, 1789.
[3] This memoir is given by Fleurieu in the appendix of his work.

called Salomon Islands in 1567, Dampier afterwards named New Britain in 1700. In the introduction to the narrative of his second voyage round the world, when he followed up Bougainville's exploration of the Australia del Espiritu Santo of Quiros,[1] Captain Cook supported this view. The arguments, however, of M. Buache had no weight with Mr. Dalrymple, who in 1790 re-stated his opinion that the Solomon Islands of the Spaniards and the New Britain of Dampier were one and the same, and he referred to the discoveries of Bougainville and Surville as showing no similitude in form to the Solomon Islands of the old maps.[2]

But in the minds of French geographers there was little doubt as to the correctness of the views of M. Buache. Amongst the detailed geographical instructions given by Louis XVI. in 1785 to La Pérouse, when he was setting out on his ill-fated expedition, was one which directed the attention of this illustrious navigator to the examination of the numerous islands of the Solomon Group, and especially to those which lay between Guadalcanar and Malaita.[3] It was considered almost indubitable, as M. Fleurieu informs us, that the intended exploration by La Pérouse of this archipelago would convert probability into certainty. But when in the vicinity of the islands he was never destined to behold, La Pérouse experienced that mysterious fate which has excited sympathy throughout the civilised world. On the reef-girt shores of Vanicoro his ships were wrecked, and the French commander and his men were never seen again by any Europeans. As Carlyle wrote, . . . " The brave navigator goes, and returns not; the seekers search far seas for him in vain, ... and only some mournful mysterious shadow of him hovers long in all heads and hearts."[4]

The ominous silence that had fallen over the doings of the absent expedition, on account of the non-arrival of the long expected dispatches, must have been, in a double sense, a cause of disappointment to M. Fleurieu, who had hoped to demonstrate the correctness of the views of the French geographers by the results of the explorations of La Pérouse. It was with the object of showing that the New Georgia of Shortland was one and the same with the Terre des

---

[1] This group, which had been previously named by Bougainville, L'Archipel des grandes Cyclades, was designated The New Hebrides by Cook, a name which it retains on the present charts.

[2] "Nautical Memoirs of Alexander Dalrymple."

[3] "Voyage de la Pérouse," redigé par M. L. A. Milet-Mureau; London, 1799.

[4] Carlyle's "French Revolution," ch. V., p. 37.

Arsacides of Surville and the Choiscul of Bougainville, and that the
French and English navigators had independently of each other
discovered the lost Solomon Group, that M. Fleurieu published in
Paris in 1790 his " Decouvertes des François en 1768 et 1769 dans
le sud-est de la Nouvelle Guinée."[1]   " The desire of restoring to the
French nation its own discoveries, which an emulous and jealous
neighbour has endeavoured to appropriate to herself, induced us,"
thus the author wrote in his preface to his work, " to connect in one
view, all those that we have made towards the south-east of New
Guinea ; and particularly to prove, that the great land, which Shortland imagined he discovered in 1788, and to which he gave the
name of New Georgia, is not a new land, but the southern coast of
the Archipelago of the Arsacides, the famous Islands of Solomon,
one part of which was discovered after two centuries by M. de Bougainville in 1768, and another more considerable by M. de Surville
in 1769." I need not refer to the detailed arguments of this learned
geographical writer. Under his arguments, Surville's appellation of
Terre des Arsacides and Shortland's of New Georgia,[2] finally gave
place to the original title given by the Spanish navigator. " It was
the work of M. de Fleurieu," thus writes Krusenstern,[3] the Russian
voyager and hydrographer, " that removed once and for all any
doubt that might have been held about the identity of the discoveries of Bougainville, Surville, and Shortland, with the Solomon
Islands." Another illustrious navigator, Dumont D'Urville,[4] thus
alludes to the successful labours of his countrymen, . . . " Le labo-
rieux Buache et l'habile Fleurieu travaillèrent tour à tour à établir
cette identité qui, depuis, est devenue un fait acquis à la science
géographique ; les îles relevées par Surville et par Bougainville sont
réellement l'archipel Salomon de Mindana." Thus the lost archipelago was found, not so much by the fortuitous course of the
navigator as by the patient investigations of the geographer in his
study. The result is intrinsically of little importance to the world
at large ; but, as an example of the success of a laborious yet dis-
criminate research, it may afford encouragement to all who endeavour
to add something to the sum of knowledge.

     I will now refer briefly to the voyagers who subsequently visited

[1] English translation published in London in 1791.
[2] The designation of New Georgia has been retained in the modern charts for that portion
of the group which is known as Rubiana.
[3] " Recueil de Mémoires Hydrographiques," St. Petersburgh, 1824. Part I., p. 157.
[4] " Histoire Générale des Voyages," Paris, 1859 ; p. 229.

this group, after its identity had become established. In May 1790, Lieutenant Ball,[1] in the "Supply," when on his voyage to England from Port Jackson *via* Batavia, made the eastern extremity of the Solomon Islands. He sailed along the north side of the group until opposite the middle of Malaita, when he headed more to the eastward and clear of the land. He correctly surmised that he was sailing along the New Georgia of Shortland, but on the opposite side of it: though he looked upon the islands of Santa Anna, Santa Catalina, and Ulaua as his own discoveries, and he named them respectively Sirius's Island, Massey's Island, and Smith's Island. In December 1791, Captain Bowen of the ship "Albemarle," during his voyage from Port Jackson to Bombay, sailed along the coast of New Georgia, and reported that he had seen the floating wreck of one of the vessels of La Pérouse; but this report was discredited by Captain Dillon in the narrative of his search after the missing expedition.[2] In 1792, Captain Manning,[3] of the Honourable East India Company's Service, during his voyage from Port Jackson to Batavia in the ship "Pitt," made the south coast of the Solomon Group off Cape Sidney, which was the headland first sighted by Lieutenant Shortland. Sailing westward, he imagined St. Christoval and Guadalcanar were continuous, and he thus delineates their coasts in his track-chart much as Shortland did. The Russell Islands he named Macaulay's Archipelago, a name which ought to be retained as a compliment to their discoverer. He then passed between Rubiana and Isabel, naming the high land of the latter island Keate's Mountains. Passing through the strait between Choiseul and Isabel, which bears his name, Captain Manning proceeded northward on his voyage.

At this time, a French expedition, under Admiral Dentrecasteaux, was cruising in the same part of the Pacific with the object of ascertaining the fate of La Pérouse. Amongst the instructions embodied in a "Mémoire du Roi," which were given to the French admiral, was the following one referring to the Solomon Islands: . . "Qu'il s'occupe à détailler cet archipel, dont il est d'autant plus intéressant d'acquérir une connoissance parfaite, qu'on peut avec raison le regarder comme une découverte des François, puisqu'il étoit resté ignoré et inconnu pendant les deux siècles qui s'étoient écoulés

---

[1] *Vide* "An Historical Journal," &c., by Capt. John Hunter. London, 1793; pp. 417-419.

[2] "Voyage in search of La Pérouse's Expedition." London, 1829.

[3] "Chart of the track and discoveries of the ship 'Pitt,' Capt. Edward Manning, on the western coast of the Solomon Islands in 1792."

depuis que les Espagnols en avoient fait la première decouverte."[1] In July 1792, when on his way from New Caledonia to Carteret Harbour in New Ireland, in prosecution of his search for the missing expedition, Dentrecasteaux made the Eddystone Rock which had been thus named by Shortland, and passing by Treasury Island, he skirted the west coast of Bougainville and Bouka. In May of the following year, when on the passage from Santa Cruz to the Louisiade Archipelago, the expedition sailed along the south coast of the Solomon Islands as far as Rubiana. Passing between St. Christoval and Guadalcanar, Dentrecasteaux sailed close to the island of Contrarieté and communicated with the natives. Whilst one of his ships lay off the north-west part of St. Christoval, the natives of Gulf Island (Ugi) discharged a flight of arrows from their canoes and wounded one of the crew. It is satisfactory to learn that her commander contented himself with firing a musket and discharging a rocket at them without effect, and that no other retaliatory measures were taken to intercept them in their flight. Turning back on his course, the French admiral was almost tempted to explore the group of islands between Guadalcanar and Malaita, to which the work of Fleurieu had directed his attention, and had he done so, he would have cleared up the confusion with which the vague description of Figueroa has surrounded these islands; but his instructions and the object of his voyage led him along the south coast of Guadalcanar on his way to the Louisiade Archipelago.

To the voyagers who visited this group during the first half of the present century, I can only briefly allude. The Solomon Islands were seldom visited during the early portion of it, except, perhaps, by occasional trading-ships whose experiences have rarely been made known, a loss which may not be a subject for our regret. However, in March, 1834, there sailed from New York the clipper " Margaret Oakley," bound on a trading and exploring voyage in the South Pacific.[2] She was commanded by Captain Morrell, who was accompanied by a young American, named Jacobs, to whom we are indebted for a very singular narrative of the cruise, which, for private reasons, was not published till 1844. Into the extremely questionable proceedings of Captain Morrell,[3] in his dealings with

[1] "Voyage de Dentrecasteaux," redigé par M. de Rossel. Paris, 1808; tom. i., p. xxxiii.
[2] "Scenes, Incidents, and Adventures in the Pacific Ocean." By T. J. Jacobs. New York, 1844.
[3] When Dumont D'Urville was in London, shortly before he started on his last voyage, he was asked his opinion of Morrell with reference to his cruises in the high southern lati-

the natives during his sojournings in the Western Pacific, I need not here enter. It will be sufficient for me to remark that they had better have been buried in the oblivion which is most fitting for such deeds of heartless cruelty. Mr. Jacobs, in his attempt to describe the discoveries of the voyage with which we are more particularly concerned, exercises an amusing freedom in dealing with the explorations of the famous early navigators in this region. Instead of adding to our knowledge of these seas, by his presumption, he has thrown discredit on the whole of his narrative; and it is only by the insertion in his account of a rude sketch-map of New Guinea and the islands south-east of it that he has rescued his narrative from utter confusion. There we see, that by Bidera he means New Britain; by Emeno, New Ireland; Bougainville is honoured by the retention of his name for the large island which he discovered; whilst the other large land-masses of the Solomon Group would have had their identities hopelessly lost in the narrative under the appellations of Baropee, Soterimba, and Cambendo, had it not been for the rude map attached. References to dates are systematically avoided by Mr. Jacobs; however, it would appear that probably, in 1835 or 1836, they extended their cruise to the islands of the Solomon Group. Coasting along the west side of Bougainville Island, they sailed through the straits of that name, and skirting the north coasts of Choiseul (Baropee) and Isabel (Soterimba), they turned Cape Prieto and steered S. by E. Sailing by a singular rock like a ship under sail (the Two Tree Islet of the chart), their course lay through beautiful verdant islands; and then passing a volcanic island with steam issuing from the crater on its summit (the Sesarga of the Spaniards and the Savo of the present day), the lofty lands of Cambendo (Guadalcanar) appeared in view. Coasting westward, along the north side of Guadalcanar, they were visited by Tarlaro, the King(?) of Cambendo, who was accompanied by a great number of natives. On the following day, they visited a large village, where they were friendly received; and shortly afterwards they left the group, steering southward and passing Rennell Island.

In November, 1838, Dumont D'Urville,[1] the French navigator, sighted the Solomon Group, in his passage westward from Santa

tudes. His reply was that he was already acquainted with him as " un fabricateur du contes." (" Voyage au Pole Sud." 1837-1840. Introduction, p. lxvii.)
[1] " Voyage au Pole Sud et dans l'Oceanie." 1837-40. Paris, 1841.

Cruz. Coasting along the north side of St. Christoval and the south side of Malaita, he recognised in Surville's Terre des Arsacides the Malaita of the Spaniards. He then set himself to work to clear up the difficulty with reference to the position of the islands named by the Spaniards, Galera, Florida, Buena Vista, Sesarga, &c., islands which had never been since explored, but he ultimately contented himself with viewing these islands from off the north coast of Buena Vista. After endeavouring imperfectly to identify them with the description of their first discoverers, he anchored in Thousand Ships Bay, which was originally discovered by Gallego and Ortega; and he named his anchorage Astrolabe Harbour, after one of his ships. From the circumstance that the natives, who came off to the ships, made use of such expressions as "veri gout," "captain," "manoa" (man of war), D'Urville concluded that they had recently been visited by other voyagers.[1] Leaving Thousand Ships Bay, he sailed along the south coast of Isabel, and passing through Manning Strait, he skirted the north side of Choiseul and Bougainville Islands and then left the group.

Dumont D'Urville was the last of the French navigators to whom the re-discovery and exploration of the Solomon Islands are in the main due. A singular fatality seems to have attended the careers of nearly all the French commanders who visited these seas. With the exception of Bougainville, who lived to superintend, in 1804, the fitting out of the flotilla, at Boulogne, for the invasion of England, all died during the voyage or shortly after their return. Surville was drowned on his arrival at Peru. La Pérouse met with his untimely fate at Vanikoro, and neither of the two commanders of the expedition that was sent in search of him survived the voyage; Dentrecasteaux died from scurvy off New Britain, and Huon Kermadec died before the ships left New Caledonia. Lastly, D'Urville was killed in a railway accident at Paris, whilst engaged in the completion of the narrative of his expedition.

In July, 1840, Captain Sir Edward Belcher,[2] whilst on his voyage to New Ireland, in H.M.S. "Sulphur," made the south coast of Guadalcanar; but after looking in vain for an anchorage, he continued his course. In 1844, Capt. Andrew Cheyne, in the trading-schooner "Naiad," visited Simbo Island and the neighbouring islands.

---

[1] According to his narrative, Jacobs, in the "Margaret Oakley," anchored in the vicinity of Thousand Ships Bay, two or three years (?) before the visit of D'Urville.

[2] "Narrative of a Voyage round the World in H.M.S. 'Sulphur:'" vol. II., p. 70.

We are indebted to him for much information concerning this part
of the group.[1] About 1847, Monsignor Epalle, a French Roman
Catholic Bishop, was landed, with eighteen priests, on the island of
Isabel, for the purpose of founding a mission. On first landing, the
bishop strayed from the rest of the party and received his death-blow
at the hands of the natives, who are supposed to have been tempted
by his dress and ornaments. In April of 1847, three French missionaries, living at Makira, were murdered by the hill-tribes of St. Christoval; and in March of the following year, M. Dutaillis,[2] in command
of the French corvette "L'Ariane," anchored at Makira, and sent an
expedition into the interior by which the villages of the murderers
were destroyed and many of the natives killed and wounded.

In September, 1851, the ill-fated yacht "Wanderer,"[3] with her
owner, Mr. Benjamin Boyd, on board, visited the Solomon Group.
Cruising along the south coast of St. Christoval, the yacht put into
Makira, where she lay at anchor nearly three weeks. Friendly
intercourse was established with the inhabitants and frequent shooting excursions were made into the interior. Mr. Boyd thought so
highly of the advantages of Makira and its harbour, that he intended
to return there with the intention of entering into a treaty with the
principal natives of the locality for the purpose of acquiring it for
future commercial purposes. However, the careers, both of the
yacht and of its owner, were drawing to a close. From Makira,
they proceeded to Guadalcanar. Leaving his vessel anchored in
Wanderer Bay, as it has since been named, Mr. Boyd landed with
his gun, accompanied by a native of Panapa. Neither of them were
ever seen again; and they appear to have met with their deaths at
the hands of the natives soon after landing. A great number of the
natives attacked the yacht, but they were repulsed by the crew of
the "Wanderer" with grape-shot and musketry. An ineffectual
search was made for Mr. Boyd and his companion: and before the
yacht left the locality, round and grape-shot were poured into the
villages, canoes and houses were burned, and probably a large
number of natives were killed and injured. The "Wanderer" now
left the group; and in the following month she was totally lost on
the bar of Port Macquarie on the Australian coast.

[1] "A Description of Islands in the Western Pacific Ocean." London, 1852.
[2] "Annales Hydrographiques;" tome I. 1848-49. "Last Cruise of the 'Wanderer,'"
by John Webster, p. 73.
[3] "Last Cruise of the 'Wanderer.'" By John Webster.

In 1854, there were rumours in Sydney, that Mr. Boyd was still alive and that his initials had been seen carved on trees in Guadalcanar. A skull, which had been bought from a chief by the captain of a trading-ship as that of Mr. Boyd, proved, on examination, to belong to a Papuan. However, in December of this year, Captain Denham, in H.M.S. "Herald," visited the scene of the tragedy; and after making inquiry into the matter, he came to the opinion that the unfortunate owner of the "Wanderer" had been killed directly after he landed, and that the various stories current respecting his being alive were inventions of the natives.

I now bring to a close this short sketch of the history of the Solomon Group since its identity was established by the French geographers towards the end of the last century. During the last thirty years there has been greatly increased intercourse with the natives of these islands; the Melanesian Mission has firmly established itself; numerous traders have resided in the more friendly districts; and the visits of men-of-war and trading-ships have been very frequent. But this increased intercourse with the outer world of savage peoples, who can with difficulty distinguish between a stranger and a foe, has been accompanied, as we might naturally have expected, by many tragic episodes, some of which we can deplore, most of which we can only reflect upon with mingled feelings of shame and regret. The reprisals on the part of men-of-war have not been always satisfactory in their results; and the effect of the labour-traffic has been to undermine the confidence which the missionary and well-intentioned trader have been long endeavouring to create. The quiet heroism of the members of the Melanesian Mission, under circumstances often the most dispiriting and insecure, it would ill become me to praise. It will be sufficient, however, to remark that it has been the only redeeming feature in the intercourse of the white man with these islanders during the last twenty-five years.

GEOGRAPHICAL APPENDIX.

NOTE I.

THE ACCOUNTS OF GALLEGO AND FIGUEROA COMPARED.—On carefully comparing these two accounts, I have no doubt that Figueroa derived almost all his information from the journal of Gallego. He, to a great extent, employs his own phraseology; but in the description of the islands and of the natives, the words and expressions employed are often identical, and the mode and order of description are evidently supplied by the journal of Gallego. An indirect proof of the source, whence Figueroa drew his materials, is to be found in the circumstance that, after the two vessels were separated during the voyage back to Peru, he confines his account to the experiences of the "Capitana," which was Gallego's vessel; and here his account is substantially a condensed form of Gallego's journal which is occasionally quoted literally. Figueroa, however, does not inform us of the source of his information; and he has evidently, in some measure, endeavoured to infuse his own method of expression into the account. There are not wanting proofs, however, that he was assisted from other sources, but only in a small degree. For instance, he occasionally intercalates a circumstance to which Gallego does not allude; and he varies in the accounts of the conflicts with the natives: thus he refers to some of the Spaniards having died at Estrella Harbour, to there being a foot and a half of water in the hold of one of the ships during the return voyage, to the ships being heaved-down at St. Christoval, and to a few other similar occurrences unrecorded by Gallego. The account of Figueroa differs in the date of the year of the voyage. It contains only a bare reference to the cruise of the brigantine to St. Christoval and its adjacent islands, whilst the vessels lay at the Puerto de la Cruz on the coast of Guadalcanar. It is from this cause that the names of all the islands visited and named during this cruise of the brigantine are not given in Figueroa's account. Herrera, however, in his short description of these islands, gives a full list of the names of the islands, and, in this respect, his description is superior to that of Figueroa.

NOTE II.

DISCREPANCIES IN THE DATES OF THE YEARS.—There is a strange discrepancy in the dates of the years during which this expedition was away from Peru. The year 1566, is given on the title-page of the British Museum copy of Gallego's Journal; and the author expressly states that the expedition left Callao on November 19th, 1566; he carries this year on, naming the following year, 1567; but in August he gives the year as 1568, and makes the return to Peru to be in 1569. It is evident from the narrative that the ships were absent from Peru about nineteen months, from November of one year to June of the second ensuing year; and it is highly probable that the year of their departure was 1566, and that of their return 1568. . . . Figueroa differs strangely in the dates he gives.[1] In the first line of his account he says that the ships were dispatched in 1567; and in the succeeding paragraph he gives January 10, 1568, as the date of their departure from Callao, thus being quite at variance with Gallego, both as regards the day, the month, and the year. The ships reached the coast of Mexico on their return voyage in January 1568, according to Figueroa. From this inconsistency it may be inferred, that 1567 was intended as the date of the departure from Peru. . . . Herrera,[2] in his description of these islands, states that they were discovered in 1567, which accords with the narrative of Gallego. . . . Arias[3] in a

[1] "Hechos de Don Garcia H. de Mendoza," por el Doctor Christoval S. de Figueroa. Madrid, 1613.
[2] "Descripcion de las Indias Occidentales." (Madrid, about 1601.)
[3] "Early Voyages to Terra Australis," by R. H. Major (p. 1). Hakluyt Society, 1859.

memorial addressed to Philip III. of Spain, says that Mendana discovered San Christoval in 1565; but his account is both short and confused, and was evidently not derived from original sources. . . . Notwithstanding the conflicting character of the dates, the probable dates would appear to be as follows.—The ships left Peru on November 19th, 1566, discovered the Isles of Salomon on February 7th, 1567, and arrived at Peru on June 19th, 1568.

NOTE III. (Page 199.)

THE ISLE OF JESUS.—Burney [1] estimated the longitude of this island to be 172° 30′ East of Greenwich; Krusenstern, [2] on surer grounds, fixed it at 171° 30′; but both estimates were based on an erroneous longitude of the Candelaria Shoals. . . . I have shown in note iv. that these shoals are probably identical, not with the Roncador Reef as is implied in the present charts, but with the islands of Ontong Java, to the northward; however, this correction affects but little the question of longitude. Taking the longitude of the centre of Ontong Java at about 150° 30′ E. (in lat. 5° 25′ S.), the longitude of the Isle of Jesus, 167 Spanish leagues to the eastward (in lat. 6° 45′ S.), would be about 169° E. The only island shown on the present charts in the vicinity of this position is Kennedy Island, also called Motuiti, the existence of which is stated to be doubtful. Its position, as determined by the "Nautilus" in 1801, was 8° 36′ S. 167° 50′ E. [3] However, in 1883, the German war-vessel "Carola" failed to find it in this position in the chart, and the initals E. D. are there attached to the name. The difficulty may, I think, be explained by the existence in this region of some atoll of no great size, the position of which has been never correctly determined. It would appear that a similar view is held by Captain Wharton, the present Hydrographer, since in the Sailing Directions for these seas issued in 1885, the island is still given prominent mention. [4] Not improbably the missing island will be found between the 6th and 7th parallels, and near the position assigned to the Isle of Jesus.

Herrera gives the name of another island, "El Nombre de Dios," which is said by him to lie in 7° S. lat., and to be 50 leagues distant from Santa Anna; Gallego does not refer to any island with this name; and since Herrera makes no reference to the Isle of Jesus, it is possible that this isle may be here alluded to, as its latitude corresponds somewhat with that of "El Nombre de Dios." M. Fleurieu [5] identifies this island, however, not with the Isle of Jesus, but with an island off the north end of Malaita which was named Gower I. by Captain Carteret in 1767, and Inattendue I. by M. Surville, in 1769.

NOTE IV. (Page 199.)

THE CANDELARIA SHOALS.—The shoals were identified by Fleurieu with the Roncador Reef discovered by Maurelle in 1781; and Krusenstern subsequently confirmed this opinion. Gallego, however, describes shoals trending N.E. and S.W. for more than fifteen leagues, which cannot possibly be the Roncador Reef of the present chart, which is not more than six miles across. These Candelaria Shoals, on the other hand, correspond in their size with the large atoll of Ontong Java lying about 35 miles to the north of the Roncador Reef, and being about 50 miles in width. The apparent difference in latitude between Ontong Java, which lies in about 5° 25′ S., and the Candelaria Shoals of Gallego, which were placed by him in 6° 15′ S., may be explained by the circumstance that the majority of Gallego's observations of latitude in the Solomon Group were about two-thirds of a degree in excess of the true latitude. [6] By making this correction, the latitude of Ontong Java and of the Candelaria Shoals will be found to closely approximate. The bearing and distance of the Candelaria Shoals from the west end of Malaita (as given by Gallego on p. 202) and from Estrella Harbour (as given on p. 205) go to support my view that the Candelaria Shoals of Gallego and the Ontong Java of Tasman are one and the same.

1 " Chronological History of Voyages and Discoveries in the South Sea." Vol. I. p. 289. London, 1803.
2 " Recueil de Memoires Hydrographiques." St. Petersburg, 1824.
3 Findlay's " Directory of the Pacific Ocean." Part II 900. (London, 1851.)
4 " Pacific Islands." Vol. I. p. 50. (Western Groups.) 1885.
5 " Discoveries of the French, 1768-1769, to the S. E. of New Guinea," p. 181. (London, 1791).
6 Vide Note V. of Geographical Appendix.

274 GEOGRAPHICAL APPENDIX.

NOTE

THE LATITUDES OF GALLEGO IN THE SOLOMON GROUP.—On making fourteen comparisons of the latitudes obtained by Gallego with the latitudes of the same places in the most recent Admiralty charts, places about which there can be no doubt as to their identity, I find that all but two are in excess of the true latitude. The excess varies between 11′ and 1° 7′ (about); and since seven of the twelve latitudes vary between 38′ and 46′ in excess, we may take 40′ *plus* as about the probable and average prevailing error of Gallego's observations of latitude in this group. A constant error points to some constant defect of observation; whether it may be instrumental or otherwise, I must leave to the judgment of my nautical readers. . . . . It may be inferred from his journal that Gallego did not endeavour to make his latitudes by observation accord with his bearings, as they are so often at variance. This circumstance should be borne in mind in order to explain the discrepancies that occur.

NOTE VI. (Page 206.)

THE ISLE OF RAMOS AND THE ISLAND OF MALAITA.—On referring to the account of Figueroa in the original Spanish, I find that, like Gallego, he applies the name of Ramos to Malaita. Pingré, who published a translation of Figueroa's account in 1767 at Paris,[1] associates the two names together. Dalrymple[2] in his translation, published in 1770, laid the ground for future misconception, by so pointing the sentence that the name of Ramos might be taken as intended for one of the "two islets" in the middle of the passage between Malaita and Isabel. Fleurieu,[3] in his translation of Figueroa published in Paris in 1790, applies the name of Ramos to Malaita. Burney,[4] in his version (1803), apparently applies this name to one of the islets above referred to. The authority of Dalrymple and Burney would appear to supply an explanation of the circumstance that in the present Admiralty charts this name of Ramos is applied to an islet between Malaita and Isabel; but Dalrymple's version is susceptible of two meanings, and may be urged with equal justice on either side. Gallego and Figueroa both apply the two names to the same island; so that circumstance alone is sufficient to justify the restoration to Malaita of the Spanish name of "The Isle of Ramos." The original cause of the mistake is to be attributed to the first discoverers, who gave their own name and were not content with the native name. Herrera[5] has fallen into the opposite error, since, in distinguishing between Malaita and Ramos, he gives the latter a circuit of 200 leagues.

NOTE VII. (Pages 207-209.)

THE ISLANDS BETWEEN CAPE PRIETO AND GUADALCANAR.—These islands which occupied the attention of Fleurieu and Burney, and excited the curiosity of Dentrecasteaux, and which D'Urville had intended to have completely explored, have long baffled the efforts of geographical writers, who have endeavoured to identify them with the islands mentioned by Figueroa in his brief account of Mendana's discoveries in this region. His description is evidently derived from that of Gallego, of which it is but an imperfect and erroneous extract: and I will therefore disregard it. The island of Galera is apparently a small island, not named in the present chart, which lies close to the north-west coast of Buena Vista. The neighbouring large island, a league distant, to which Gallego only applies the native name of Pela,[6] is, as I apprehend, the Buena Vista of the present chart: the Buena Vista of the Spaniards is apparently an island, not named in the chart, which lies west of the present Sandfly Passage. The remaining four of the five islands may be in the future identified with the incompletely surveyed intersected mass of land to which the general name of Florida is applied in the present chart. The island of Sesarga is without doubt the volcanic island of Savo: but I must refer the reader elsewhere for further information on this subject of Sesarga.[7]

1 "Mémoire sur le choix et l'état des lieux où le passage de Venus du, 3 Juin, 1769." (Paris, 1767.)
2 "Hist. Coll. of Voy. and Discov.," London, 1770.
3 "Discoveries of the French in 1768 and 1769."
4 "Chronol. Hist. Voy and Discov.," vol. i.
5 "Descripcion de las Indias Occidentales."
6 At the present day the whole of the Florida sub-group is known to the natives as Gela. (Codrington's "Melanesian Languages," p. 522.)
7 The evidence is given in my volume of Geological Observations.

NOTE VIII. (Page 220.)

THE EXCESSIVE DIMENSIONS OF GUADALCANAR.—How could such misconceptions have arisen? They are totally inconsistent with the rest of the journal; and to such statements must be attributed the exaggerated reports which long prevailed with reference to the size of this island. The lengths of the islands of Isabel, Malaita, and St. Christoval, as given by Gallego, are greatly overstated; in the case of the two former islands they are at least double the true dimensions, and they completely disagree with the latitudes and bearing, which are noted in the journal.

NOTE IX. (Page 233.)

THE CONSULTATION AS TO THE FUTURE COURSE OF THE EXPEDITION.—The ignorance in which Mendana seems to have kept his officers with regard to the character of his instructions considerably hampered the captains and pilots in their consultation. We learn subsequently (page 237) that it was originally intended to prosecute the voyage westward in order to explore the extensive lands that lay in that direction. However, the protest made by the crews seems to have caused a change of plans. They were to steer northward for the Isle of Jesus, where Gallego apparently expected to find more land, as they provided themselves with natives as interpreters (page 233) before quitting the group. This northerly course found favour, when Gallego pointed out that it was on the track of their return voyage.

NOTE X. (Page 234.)

ISLANDS IN THE SOLOMON GROUP WHICH DO NOT AT PRESENT BEAR THE NAMES GIVEN TO THEM BY THE SPANIARDS:—

Present name.	Spanish name.
Ugi	San Juan
Three Sisters	Las Tres Marias
Ulaua (Contraried.)	La Treguada
Malaita	Ramos (Isle of)
Savo	Sesarga
Ontong Java	Candelaria Shoals
Choiseul	San Marcos
New Georgia (?)	San Nicolas / Arraciaes (Reefs).

NOTE XI. (Page 237.)

INIGO ORTEZ DE RETES AND BERNARDO DE LA TORRE.—We learn from Galvano's "Discoveries of the World,"[1] that in 1545 Captain Inigo Ortez de Retha was dispatched from Tidore to New Spain. He sailed to the coast of Papua, and not knowing that Saavedra had discovered it in 1528, he assumed the honour of the discovery. Mr. Coutts Trotter in a recent article[2] refers to him as Ortiz de Retez or Roda, and he informs us elsewhere[3] that Antonio de Abreu was probably the first discoverer of New Guinea in 1511. According to Galvano (page 234), a Spanish officer named Bernaldo de la Torre started from the Philippines in 1543, on a voyage to New Spain.

NOTE XII. (Page 238.)

THE ISLANDS OF SAN BARTOLOMEO.—The Musquillo Islands of the Marshall Group, with which I have identified this discovery of the Spaniards, were thus named by Captain Bond in 1792.[4] They form a double atoll about 38 miles in length and trending N.W. and

1 Hakluyt Society's Publication, 1862, p. 238.
2 Encyclopædia Britannica (Article on "New Guinea.")
3 Proceedings, Royal Geographical Society, 1884, p. 190
4 Purdy's "Oriental Navigator" p. 689

S.E. The N.W. end is in latitude 8° 10' N., and the S.E. end is in latitude 7° 46' N. Captain Bond ranged along the coasts of above 20 small islands. At the N.W. end and solated from the rest are two small islands about three miles apart. On comparing this description with that given by Gallego, the reader will have little doubt as to the identity of the Musquillo Islands with the Spanish discovery. It is probable that Gallego considered this discovery to be near the position of an island discovered in 1536 in 14 ° N lat. by Toribio Alonzo de Salazar,[1] 328 Spanish leagues from the Mariana Islands, and named by him San Bartolomeo. This discovery of Salazar is marked in Krusenstern's General Atlas of the Pacific.

NOTE XIII. (Page 239.)

THE ISLE OF SAN FRANCISCO.—Wake's Island, with which I have identified the Isle of San Francisco, was discovered in 1796 by the "Prince William Henry.". Commodore Wilkes, who fixed its position in 1840 (lat. 19° 10' 54" N. ; long 166° 31' 30" E. of G), thus describes it. "Wake's Island is a low coral one, of triangular form and eight feet above the surface. It has a large lagoon in the centre, which was well filled with fish of a variety of species ; amongst these were some fine mullet. There is no fresh water on the island, and neither pandanus nor cocoa-nut tree. It has upon it the shrubs, which are usually found on the low Islands of the Pacific, the most abundant of which was Tournefortia. The short-tailed albatross is found here ; birds quite tame though not as numerous as in other uninhabited islands. The appearance of the coral blocks and vegetation leads to this conclusion that the island is at times submerged or that at times the sea makes a complete breach over it."[2] Wake's Island is about the size of the island described by Gallego. Its latitude, its isolated position, and the close agreement of Wilkes' description with that of Gallego, leave no room to doubt that Wake's Island and the Isle of San Francisco are one and the same . . . Burney refers to a small island named San Francisco which is placed in the chart of the Galleon in Anson's voyage in lat. 19½ north and 84° east of the Strait of San Bernardino ; but he adds that it is too far to the east to be identified with the island discovered by Mendana.[3]

NOTE XIV. (Page 251.)

THE LIST OF ISLANDS IN THE VICINITY OF TAUMACO WHICH WAS OBTAINED BY QUIROS IN 1606 FROM ONE OF THE NATIVES.—They are as follows, Chicayana, Guantopo, or Guaytopo, Taucalo, Pilen, Nupan, Pupam, Fonfono or Fonofono, Mècaraylay, Manicolo, Tucopia, Pouro. More than half of these islands can be identified with certainty, even after an interval of nearly three centuries.

Chicayana may be without a doubt identified with Sikyana or Sikai-ana, the present native name of the Stewart Isles which lie about 250 miles to the north-west of Taumaco, or as the Taumaco people reckoned, four days' sail in their large canoes. In fact, the native from whom Quiros obtained his information was originally from Chicayana, having been carried by contrary winds to Taumaco whilst endeavouring with a number of his fellow-islanders to reach the island of Mecaraylay. The Chicayana natives were described to Quiros as being very fair with long loose red hair, some, however, being darker like mulattoes, but with hair neither curled nor quite straight. They possess much the same characters at the present day.[4]

Guaytopo or Guantopo was a larger island than those of Taumaco and Chicayana. Since it is placed three days' sail (native reckoning) from Taumaco and two days from Chicayana, it may have been one of the eastern islands of the Solomon Group. The in-

1 Krusenstern's "Memoires Hydrographiques," St Petersburgh, 1827 : Part II, p. 49.
2 "Narrative of the United States Exploring Expedition," vol V. p. 267.
3 "Chronol. History of Voy. and Disc. " vol I, p. 291.
4 These islands, as far as is known, were not visited by Europeans until nearly two centuries after the visit of Quiros, when Captain Hunter came upon them in 179:.

habitants were said to have skins as fair as Europeans and red or black hair. They punctured their bellies in a pattern of a circle around the navel; and painted their bodies red down to the waist. The women were very handsome and were clothed with some light material from head to foot. The natives of Guaytopo, Taumaco, and Chicayana, were on very friendly terms and spoke the same language.

The islands of Pilen and Nupan are evidently the Pileni and Nupani of the adjacent Matema or Swallow Islands, which lie to the northward of the large island of Santa Cruz. Fonofono or Fonfono, which is stated to lie near Pilen and Nupan, may perhaps be the Lomlom of the same small group. It was described to Quiros as being "many islands, small and flat," with a good port. The inhabitants were said to be dun-coloured, and very tall. Tucopia was subsequently visited by the Spanish navigator. In later times it has obtained a melancholy interest in connection with the fate of La Pérouse. Mécaraylay is apparently in the vicinity of Guaytopo, but possessing a different language, its inhabitants being noted for the use of tortoise-shell ornaments. Its name suggests that of Makira, on the south coast of St. Christoval, in the neighbouring Solomon Group. Taucalo may perhaps be the volcanic island of Tinakula lying off the north coast of Santa Cruz Island. It is stated to be near Taumaco.

The "large country" called Manicolo is to be identified with the adjacent large island, named Vanikoro in the present Admiralty charts, which lies about 100 miles to the southward of Taumaco. It is referred by Captain Cook[1] to the Mallicolo of the New Hebrides, lying 4° further south, which he visited in 1774; but this view cannot be sustained. In the first place, it is stated to lie two days' sail from Tucopia. The following evidence, however, is sufficient of itself to settle the point. When Captain Dillon[2] was on his way to Vanikoro in 1827, to ascertain the fate of La Pérouse, he learned from the natives of the neighbouring island of Tucopia that the island he was going to was called *Malicolo :* but he subsequently ascertained on visiting the island in question, that it should be more correctly called *Manni-colo* or *Vannicolo.* In his chart of the island, Captain Dillon calls it Mannicolo. The resemblance in name between these two islands in the New Hebrides, and Santa Cruz Groups has been a frequent cause of misconception in references to the narratives of the early navigators.

NOTE XV. (Pages 100, 251.)

THE POURO OF QUIROS.—A native of Chicayana, whom Quiros had captured at Taumaco, told the Spanish navigator that there dwelt in Taumaco "an Indian, a great pilot," who had brought from "a large country, named Pouro," certain arrows, with points, in the form of a knife, which, from the native's description, Quiros concluded were of silver. Pouro, he learned, was very populous, and its inhabitants were dun-complexioned.

When I first came upon this reference to Pouro, I at once recognised it as an allusion to the Bauro (St. Christoval) of the Solomon Group, lying rather less than 300 miles to the westward of Taumaco. Mr. Hale,[3] the philologist of the United States Exploring Expedition, under Commodore Wilkes, endeavours to identify the Pouro of the Taumaco natives with the Bouro in the Malay Archipelago, an island lying more than 2,000 miles further westward : and he refers to the circumstance of the silver arrows that were brought to Taumaco as supporting his view. Regarding Bouro as the island referred to in the traditions of the Fijians, Tongans, and Samoans, relating to the origin of their race, Mr. Hale finds in the Pouro of the Taumaco natives an allusion to this sacred island, and in the circumstance of the silver arrows he finds evidence of communication between these two regions. There can, however, be little doubt that by this Pouro the Bauro of the Solomon Group was meant. The presence of the silver arrows may be easily explained, when we remember that about forty years before, the Spaniards were exploring this island of Bauro, or Paubro as Gallego gives it (page 229).

[1] "Voyage towards the South Pole and round the World," vol. II., p. 146.
[2] "Discovery of the fate of La Pérouse,' London, 1829; vol. I., p. 85.
[3] "Ethnography and Philology of the U. S. Exploring Expedition," p. 105.

NOTE XVI.

THE EDDYSTONE ROCK AND THE SIMBOO OF LIEUTENANT SHORTLAND.—For a considerable time after the re-discovery of the Solomon Islands by the French and English navigators, few islands were better known in the group than Eddystone or Simbo Island. In thus naming this island, however, there has been a singular misconception; and since the name of Simbo has been omitted in the latest Admiralty chart (August, 1884) of the group, some explanatory remarks may be of interest.

In August, 1788, Lieutenant Shortland,[1] whilst sailing along the south coasts of the Solomon Group on his voyage from Port Jackson to England via Batavia, approached " a rock which had exactly the appearance of a ship under sail, with her top-gallant sails flying; " and so striking was the resemblance that a signal was made to the supposed vessel. The ships did not approach within three or four miles of this rock. It was named the Eddystone and was placed in lat. 8° 12' S., bearing S.S.W. a league from two remarkable hills which were named the Two Brothers. A point running south from these two hills was named Cape Satisfaction. Whilst the English ships were off the Eddystone, some natives came to them in their canoes, from whom Shortland learned that they had come from " Simboo," a place which lay, as they indicated by their gestures, near Cape Satisfaction. In the chart of his discoveries, this officer assigns this name to some land lying east of the Two Brothers near the position of the island at present called Gizo, but it is evident both from his chart and from his narrative that he considered Simboo as the general name for the land to the east of Cape Satisfaction ; and Fleurieu, when remarking on his discoveries, made the suggestion that the Simboo of Shortland might prove to be the Choiseul of Bougainville.[2]

In what manner, we may now inquire, have the discoveries of Shortland been identified with the islands that are laid down in the latest charts of this group? For half a century and more the name of Eddystone has been attached, not to a rock such as that to which it was originally given, but to the adjacent volcanic island about four miles in length and about 1100 feet in height ; and the name of Cape Satisfaction has been given to the south end of Ronongo which lies ten miles N.N.E. of Eddystone Island. This cape is stated by Shortland to run south from the two remarkable hills which he named the Two Brothers. The island of Ronongo, however, has a long and level summit destitute of peaks ; and it is evident that we must look elsewhere for the Cape Satisfaction of Shortland. In Eddystone Island, there are two singular conical hills which might very fitly have been named the Two Brothers, and it will be seen from the sequel that it must have been to the south extremity of this island that the name of Cape Satisfaction was in the first place given. I shall also point out that the original Eddystone rock is represented at the present day by a bare rock which rises out of the sea at a distance of about a third of a mile from the south-west coast of Eddystone Island, and that the Simboo, from which the natives came to visit Shortland, was a diminutive island on the opposite or south-east side of this same island.

When, in July 1792, the French expedition under Dentrecasteaux arrived in this locality, the Eddystone rock was at once recognised by the description of Shortland. . . . . " nous aperçûmes "—thus wrote Labillardière [3] the naturalist of the expedition—" le rocher nommé Eddystone. De loin nous le prîmes, comme Shortland, pour un vaisseau à la voile. L'illusion étoit d'autant plus grande, qu'il a à peu près la couleur des voiles d'un vaisseau ; quelques arbustes en couronnoient la sommité. " In the Atlas of this voyage (carte 24), this rock is placed off the south-west end of the island at present named Eddystone Island, and exactly in the position of the bare rock above alluded to, which will be found marked in the plan of this island made by the surveying officers of H.M.S. " Lark " in 1882. Lieutenant Malan tells me that this rock at the time of the survey was quite bare of vegetation. It rises in two conical masses from the water between which a boat can pass in calm weather. Although it has a height of 30 feet, it is frequently washed over by the heavier seas. The

1 The narrative of Lieut. Shortland's voyage is given in " The Voyage of Governor Phillip to Botany Bay in 1787 " : London, 1789.
2 " Discoveries of the French, 1768-1780, to the S.E. of New Guinea :" London, 1791, p. 196.
3 " Voyage à la recherche De la Pérouse," par Labillardière : Paris, 1800 : tom i, p. 215.

change in the appearance of this rock, since the visit of Dentrecasteaux in 1792 when it summit was crowned with shrubs, has been probably due to a movement of subsidence which has affected the adjacent coast of Eddystone Island in recent years (*vide below*). To such a change must be attributed the confusion which has arisen with reference to the Eddystone rock; and cartographers, failing to identify it, have applied its name to the adjacent volcanic island on which they have also bestowed the name of Simbo. During his survey of this island in 1882, Lieutenant Oldham ascertained that this name of Simbo actually belonged to a small island bordering its south-east coast with which it was connected by coral reefs. The true native name of Eddystone Island, he found to be Narovo, and in the latest Admiralty charts it is thus designated; the name of Simbo is there attached to the small adjacent island which is, I have no doubt, the Simboo from which the natives came, who visited Shortland's ships in 1788 as they lay off the Eddystone rock. At the present day the larger island of Narovo is but thinly populated, and its inhabitants are under the sway of a powerful chief who resides on the small island of Simbo. There be rules over a warlike and adventurous people who by their head-hunting raids have established the fame of their diminutive island throughout a large portion of the Solomon Group.

[In my volume of Geological Observations I have described the movement of subsidence, to which is due the confusion concerning the original Eddystone rock].

CHAPTER XIII

M Y botanical collections were made during 1884 in the islands of Bougainville Straits; and in order to add to the completeness of this section of my work, I will briefly refer to the physical character of this locality. The principal islands of this sub-group are Treasury Island, the Shortland Islands, and Faro, or Fauro, Island; whilst around these lie numerous smaller islands and islets. The largest is not more than twelve miles in length, and none of them attain an elevation exceeding 2000 feet, Faro being about 1900 feet, Treasury about 1100, and Alu, the principal of the Shortland Islands, about 500 feet. In geological character they differ widely, Treasury being, for the most part, of recent calcareous formations, Faro of volcanic formations, whilst Alu is formed of rocks of both these classes. Of the numerous smaller islands and islets which dot these straits, some are of volcanic, and others of coral rocks.

In my botanical excursions in these islands, I received the greatest assistance from the natives; and I was particularly struck with the familiar knowledge of their trees and plants which these islanders possessed. They have names for not only nearly all the trees, but for several of the grasses; and, in the case of the former, when I was uncertain as to whether I had come upon any specimen before, they would obtain its flower, or fruit, or foliage, and point out to me its comparative characters. The superior knowledge, which these natives possess of each plant and its uses, has often led me to reflect on the meagre acquaintance with the commonest trees, shrubs, and herbs, which the ordinary white man can claim. Had my native companions asked me to instruct them in a similar manner on the vegetation of an English woodland—if such a rapid change of scene were possible—they would probably have regarded me as a very ignorant and unobservant fellow. They have names for and display a familiarity with many plants that can be of no service to them, a somewhat puzzling circumstance, which may be perhaps explained by their employing instinctively a method of exclusion in the selection of those plants that are of service to them. For the building of his house, the cultivation of his ground, the construction of his canoe, the manufacture of his spears, clubs, and other weapons, and for his many other wants, the native has to resort to the vegetable kingdom for the requisite materials. An extensive acquaintance with the vegetation of his island-home is unconsciously acquired by a native who has himself to provide for all his necessities: but his knowledge extends far beyond that limit which mere utility would appear to demand. In a paper published recently in an American serial,[1] Mr. Matthews combated the notion that savages are versed only in the knowledge of plants and animals that contribute to their wants. He found that the Indians are incomparably superior to the average white man, or to the white man who has not made zoology or botany a subject of study. In this respect, his experience accords with my own. The native of the Solomon Islands will point out by name, in some remote inland dell, an insignificant plant, which, he says, is of no service to him: he names all the weeds of his cultivated patches; and he is similarly acquainted with all the wild fruits, usually distinguishing them by their edible or injurious qualities. Yet, in arriving at such a conclusion, it behoves one to be wary, as I have sometimes found that the native applies the name of a useful plant to all other useless plants (usually of the same genus or family) that resemble it in their more conspicuous characters. Then, again, I have often been surprised at the singular holes and corners in the vegetable world which the native ransacks to supply his wants. A fern that clothes the higher slopes of Faro Island, and which is known to the natives as " sinimi," and to the botanist as a species of *Gleichenia*, furnishes the material for their plaited armlets. For this purpose they employ narrow strips of the vascular tissue that forms the firm central portion of the stem. I had previously looked upon this fern as of little use to these islanders, and on learning of the ingenious purpose for which it was employed, I became very careful in the future when pronouncing on the utility or inutility of any familiar plant.

[1] " Bulletin of the Philosophical Society of Washington," Vol. VII.

With these preliminary remarks, I will proceed to describe the
general characters of the vegetation of these islands; and, in order to
connect my observations together, I will treat of them in the form of
a series of excursions made in different districts.

An ascent of one of the larger streams in the Shortland Islands.—
In the lower part of its course, the stream follows a circuitous course
amidst the gloom and dismal surroundings of a mangrove swamp.
It is difficult to convey in words a true idea of such a scene. The
features most imprinted on my memory are those of "a slow and
silent stream" of dark turbid water, traversing a swamp of black,
repulsive-looking mud, in which the crocodile finds a congenial home.
The light of day is subdued into a depressing gloom by the foliage
of the mangrove forest: the air, charged with the miasma of decaying vegetable life, is impregnated with a sour, unpleasant odour;
and the silence that prevails is interrupted only by the fall of a
branch, or by the startled cry of some wading-bird disturbed in its
haunt. Nipa palms line the banks in places, and occasionally
occupy the swamp for some distance on either side of the stream.
Overhead, perched high upon the branches of the tall mangroves,
occur the two singular epiphytes, *Hydnophytum* and *Myrmecodia*,
both of which have been found to be species new to science (*H.
Guppyanum*, Becc. : *M. salomonensis*, Becc.). From the following
remarks, my readers will be able to observe the peculiar features
of these interesting rubiaceous plants. The large swollen base of the
stem, sometimes eighteen inches in length, is occupied by cavities
which are usually infested by ants that actively resent any attempts
to carry off their home. It has been considered that this swollen
mass and its chambers are due to the irritation produced by the ants
gnawing at the base of the young growing stem, and that the plant
cannot thrive without the ants; but from observations made by Mr.
H. O. Forbes,[1] in Java, on the origin of "this curious-galleried structure" in a species of *Myrmecodia*, it would seem that this swollen
mass and its chambers are produced without the presence of ants,
and that in their absence the plant may thrive vigorously. Not
unfrequently, I found the ants in scanty numbers, and sometimes
they were absent altogether. In the case of *Myrmecodia salomonensis*, and *Hydnophytum inerme*,[2] they are found in considerable
numbers. The chambers of *H. Guppyanum* are usually nearly full

[1] "A Naturalist's Wanderings in the Eastern Archipelago," p. 81. (1885.)
[2] This species was obtained at Ugi.

of dirty rain-water, and contain scarcely any ants, a few cockroaches being generally found in the cavities. Those specimens which I examined of another species of this genus (*II. longistylum*, Becc.), that occurs on the coast trees, contained a few cockroaches, but no ants; and, on the outer surface of one of the swollen masses, I found a small crab. From my own cursory notes, it would therefore seem probable that these epiphytes may thrive without the presence of ants. . . . . With this digression, I return to my description of the ascent of the stream.

Leaving behind the slime and gloom of the swamp, the rising ground is reached, at the base of which the vegetation is of the most luxuriant character, and often have I lingered here in my Rob Roy canoe to admire the luxuriance of plant-growth that surrounded me. For on account of the lowness of the district, it shares the dampness though not the infertility of the swamps below. The soft clayey rock, which is exposed in the banks of the stream, affords a rich and even too productive soil. Nature runs riot and becomes prodigal in her profusion ; and thus growth is too often associated with decay to present on all occasions a pleasing picture to the eye. Here the tree-fern, the croton, the wild plantain, and numerous areca palms flourish ; but the alpinias, heliconias, and other scitamineous plants form the chief feature of the vegetation on this gently rising ground.

Higher up the stream, tall forest trees rise on each side often enveloped partially by a drapery of runners and climbing plants, their leafy branches spreading over the water. Stout lianas hang in festoons across the stream. Partly hidden amongst the greater vegetation may be seen the fan-palm of the district (*Licuala*, the " firo " of the natives), and another pretty little palm known as the " sensisi," *Cyrtostachys*, together with the handsome foliage of a *Plerandra* (" fo ") and numerous areca palms. An occasional *Dolichololbium* (" lowasi ") with white flowers distributes its fragrance around. Ferns abound along the banks, varying in size from the small *Trichomanes* to the tree-fern, twenty feet in height, and the *Angiopteris* with its magnificent spreading fronds fifteen feet and more in length. If one leaves the stream for a few minutes at the foot of the hills, a moist, low-lying district is traversed, the home of the scitamineæ and the areca-palms, which latter are distinguished amongst the natives as the " momo," " niga-solu," " niga-torulo," and " au-au."

Ascending the hill slopes towards the source of the stream, numerous palms rise up on either side. The *Caryota* ("eala") with its branches resembling the fronds of a huge adiantum, the handsome "kisu" (probably a species of *Drymophloeus*) and a tall areca known as the "poamau," are those which frequently meet the eye. Interspersed among them we notice the lesser areca-palms and the fan-palm before alluded to. On the crest of the hill, at a height of some 200 or 300 feet above the sea, are found tall forest trees, some of them of gigantic size and attaining a height of 150 feet and upwards. Amongst them occur the banyan ("chim"), other ficoid trees with the flange-like buttresses, and the "katari," a species of *Calophyllum* which supplies the natives with a resin for their torches. In the following description of the interior of the forest in this region I have referred at some length to the larger trees.

The interior of the forest . . . To obtain a true idea of the forest-growth in these islands, it is necessary to traverse one of the more level districts in the interior, which is removed from the vicinity of the cultivated patches of the natives. Entering the confines of the forest direct from the full glare of the tropical sun, one experiences a peculiar and often oppressive sensation, which may be attributed to the combined influences of the warmth, the humidity, and the effluvia arising from the decaying vegetation, to the impressive silence that reigns, and to the subdued light or dusky atmosphere that there prevails. Meeting overhead at a height of some 150 feet from the ground, the foliage and the smaller branches of the lofty trees form a dense leafy screen roofing over, as it were, a series of lofty corridors in which the palms and the lesser trees flourish. The gloom that there prevails is rarely lightened by the direct rays of the sun, except here and there through the gap left by the downfall of one of the huge trunks that now lies rotting on the ground. Nor is the silence that reigns often broken, except by the cooing of the fruit-pigeons overhead or by the rushing flight of the hornbill startled from its repose. Here the steady blast of the trade is no longer felt and is only perceptible in the movements of the foliage of the tallest trees. Yet there is little in such a scene that would strike the mind of the merely æsthetic lover of nature. Flowers he rarely sees: they are only to be found where the sunlight can reach them in the partially cleared spaces in the midst of the forest, or on the sides of ravines, or along the coasts. On the other hand, however, he cannot fail to be impressed by the luxuriance and magnifi-cence of the vegetation in this conservatory of Nature.

Under such conditions the palms flourish. The *Caryota*, the "kisu" palm, numerous areca-palms, with the tree-fern, give the character to the lesser vegetation. Huge climbing stems, such as the "droau," the "aligesi" (*Aleurites ?*), the "nakia" (*Uvaria*), the "awi-sulu" (*Lyonsia*) lie in coils on the ground and rising vertically reach the lower branches of the trees some fifty to a hundred feet overhead. The large purple papilionaceous flowers of the "droau" sometimes strew the ground at the bases of the tallest trees. If the forest be situated on a hill-side, the slope is clothed by *Selaginellæ* which often display in the midst of their dark-green foliage pretty bleached fronds that form a striking contrast to the prevailing hue. Mosses, small ferns, and fungi, such as the massive expansions of *Polyporus* and the more delicate plates of *Hexagona apiaria* and others, conceal in some degree the unsightliness of the decaying log. A drapery of lycopods and of trailing and climbing ferns, such as *Trichomanes* and *Lygonia* more or less completely invests the lower portions of the trunks of the larger trees. Seventy or eighty feet overhead the wide-spreading fronds of the birds-nest fern (*Asplenium nidus*) appear half-suspended in mid-air, as they project from their point of attachment to the tree. Lower down the trunk, the handsome aroid *Epipremnum* may be observed. Epiphytic orchids form no marked feature in this forest-scene, preferring, as they do, those situations where the direct sunlight can reach them, as at the coast and on the sides of ravines. Terrestrial orchids, however, with inconspicuous and sombre-coloured flowers thrive in the gloom and moisture of the forest.

The larger trees, to which I have not yet referred, often attain a height of 150 feet and over. Here the banyan and more than one species of *Canarium* including the "ka-i" or Solomon Island Almond tree, together with a *Ratonia* ("nekale"), a *Vitex* "(fasala"), the "katari" (*Calophyllum*) before mentioned, and numerous ficoid trees known to the natives as the "uri,' the "ilimo," and the "nie," figure amongst the more conspicuous of the forest trees. Many of them possess at the base of the trunk large buttresses or flanges, which, as in the "tobu," "ilimo," "nie," and "maranato" (*Sapotacea ?*), may rise twelve to fifteen feet up the trunk and extend some twenty feet away along the ground. Some of the ficoid trees throw off at a height of from twenty to thirty feet, large flange-like buttresses,

which, on reaching the ground, form natural arches. These lofty
trees, as I have already remarked, meet together overhead to form
a leafy screen, which, whilst it excludes the direct rays of the sun,
admits and confines both the moisture and the heat. This conservatory of nature contains within its own precincts the conditions
for its preservation. Here the young tree grows up, its safety
ensured, until at length it becomes a pillar in the edifice in which it
was itself reared. The open character of the wood and the absence
of scrub and undergrowth, more especially on level ground, have
often been a cause of surprise to me. I have often walked without
impediment through the gloomy corridors of such a forest, brushing
past the huge trunks of the tallest trees, and winding in and out
amongst the palms that number as many years in age as their
giant compeers count decades.

On first treading in such a forest, the visitor is much impressed
by the imposing appearance and size of the banyans and the
buttress-trees. With mingled feelings of awe and pity he will perceive that between these monarchs of the forest there is waged an
unequal struggle, in which the huge buttress-tree always succumbs
to the rough embraces of its foe. He will observe all the stages in
the struggle. Here the buttress-tree may be seen in its prime, but
in part embraced at its lower part by the tightly clasping offshoots
of the young banyan. Further on, in the midst of the interlacing
columns of the banyan, the buttress-tree may be seen partially
strangled. Dry rot has attacked its trunk reaching almost to the core,
so that a sheath-knife sinks readily up to the handle in its substance;
yet, far overhead the wide-spreading branches of this forest potentate
are covered with green foliage, and still wave defiantly in the trade.
In the prolonged contest the buttress-tree is dying hard, and in fact
it is the stout investing trunks of the banyan that alone hold its
victim erect. Near by may be another banyan of larger size and
presenting the appearance of a maze of columns which may cover
an area thirty to forty feet across. Its victim has long since disappeared, and a hollow in the centre of the maze of stems alone
marks the former situation of the huge buttress-tree.

What finer or more impressive simile could be employed to illustrate the gradual degeneration and final downfall of a nation under
the choking influences of vice, corruption, luxury, and misgovernment?
A mighty forest tree is slowly strangled by the caresses of an insidi-
ous creeper. With advancing decay its tottering stem is alone sup-

ported by the tightening grasp of its foe. Yet its higher branches
retain their vitality to the last; and when the end comes, its ashes
add fertility to the soil and vigour to the growth of its destroyer.

It is not to be surprised that this battle of the trees should be
included in the mythical lore of some of the inhabitants of the Pacific
islands. Dr. George Turner, in his recent work entitled "Samoa, a
hundred years ago and long before," gives the following legend of
the banyan. . . . . . "A report reached Samoa that the trees of
Fiji had fought with the Banian tree, and that it had beaten
them all. On this the Tatangia (*Acacia laurifolia*) and another tree
went off from Samoa in two canoes to fight the Fijian champion.
They reached Fiji, went on shore, and there stood the Banian tree.
'Where is the tree,' they inquired, 'which has conquered all the
trees?' 'I am the tree,' said the Banian. Then said the Tatangia,
'I have come to fight with you.' 'Very Good, let us fight,' replied
the Banian. They fought. A branch of the Banian tree fell, but
the Tatangia sprung aside and escaped. Another fell—ditto, ditto—
the Tatangia. Then the trunk fell. The Tatangia again darted
aside and escaped unhurt. On this the Banian tree 'buried its eyes
in the earth' and owned itself conquered."

An ascent to the summit of the Faro Island. . . . . . In making
an ascent to the higher districts of this island, which attains an
elevation of about 1900 feet above the sea, a little may be learned
perhaps of the vertical distribution of the coast flora in this portion
of the Solomon Group. The cycad (*Cycas circinalis*) grows most
frequently just within the trees that immediately line the beach and
may be often observed at all heights up to 400 feet above the sea,
but it is not usually found at greater elevations.[1] The following
large trees commonly occur on the hill-slopes up to an elevation of
a thousand feet, the "fasala" (*Vitex*), the "toa" (*Elæocarpus*), the
"opi-opi," the "ka-i" (*Canarium*), the "katari" (*Calophyllum*), and
others; whilst the palms such as the fan-palm (*Licuala*), the *Caryota*
("cala"), the "kisu" (*Pinanga*) and the arecas, fill up the intermediate
ground, the fan-palm growing in great numbers and often mono-
polising the slope.[2] The smaller trees, of a height usually of sixty

[1] At Treasury Island I found a solitary cycad at a height of a thousand feet above the
sea. As it was in the vicinity of a plantation of sago palms, it is probable that it had been
planted by the natives who employ the fruits for medicinal purposes.

[2] This fan-palm, the "firo" of the natives, was in 1884 only represented in Treasury by a
single individual which had been brought a few years before from Bougainville, where the
leaves are employed in making a conical hat that is commonly worn.

or seventy feet, which are more frequently observed during the lower half of the ascent, are, a species of *Cerbera* ("anumi"), the "kunuka" (*Gnetum*), the "palinoromus" (*Couthovia*), the "poporoko," and others; whilst on the hill-slopes below the elevation of 500 feet the small conifer *Gnetum Gnemon* ("mcriwa") may be commonly seen. In three different localities, at elevations of between 1,000 and 1,100 feet above the sea, I came upon brakes of fine bamboos (*Schizosta-chyum ?*) 35 to 40 feet in length which are employed as fishing-poles by the natives. This bamboo, both in Treasury and Faro Islands, does not appear to occur below this height ; whilst in the Shortland Islands, although found at a lower elevation, it selects the higher regions of the island.

Above a thousand feet, many of the trees and palms so frequent below become less common or disappear. The fan-palm (*Licuala*) which grows in such numbers in the lower levels did not come under my notice above this elevation. On account of the absence of large trees near the summit, the lesser vegetation receives more of the sun's rays ; and thus at 1,600 feet above the sea the alpinias, such as the "vitoko" and the "kokuru" re-appear, plants which usually abound in the lower levels in all open situations, as on the banks of streams. For the same reason, we find near the summit of the island at elevations of 1,600 to 1,700 feet the tall composite shrub, *Wedelia biflora*, which is one of the commonest of the plants that grow at the margin of the beach. On account of this absence of large trees, and the consequent increased exposure to the sun's rays, the smaller trees with conspicuous flowers find a congenial situation at this elevation : here are found the species of *Dolicholobium* ("lowasi"), which is common on the banks of the streams in the lower levels, the *Fagræa Berteriana* ("bubulata") which grows also at the coast, a wild nut-meg tree (*Myristica*), a species of *Harpullia* ("wawaupoko), the "pakuri" (*Eugenia*), the "baimoloi" and others. In these higher regions tree-ferns grow to a height of thirty feet; and here the areca-palms, "momo" and "niga-torulo," are also found. Here flourishes the *Gleichenia*, a fern which does not usually grow at elevations under 700 feet above the sea, and which is represented by two common species : it is the "sinimi" of the natives who, as I have already remarked, work the fine strips of its vascular tissue into armlets which they commonly wear. Near the summit and all down the slopes is found a species of *Begonia*, a genus, as I am informed by Baron von Mueller, not before recorded from islands east of New Guinea.[1] A dense growth of the trailing stems of a *Freycinetia* and of ferns clothes the rocky sides of the highest peak, which is almost bare of trees. Here however I found a new genus of the *Pandanaceæ*, which, like some other pandanus trees, is known to the natives as "sararang." It grows to a height of fifty feet, and was only observed by me on the highest peak of the island and for two or three hundred feet below. It has a very conspicuous white "branching female spadix," three to four feet in length; and I learn from Professor Oliver that the same or a near ally of it, though not in a condition to describe, was collected by Signor Beccari in Jobi Island off the north-west coast of New Guinea.

The coast vegetation of the larger islands. . . . It is in the coasts of such an island as Treasury or Faro Island, where the strictly littoral and more inland plants become intermingled, that the Solomon Island vegetation in some degree redeems its character. Here the prevailing sombreness and inconspicuous inflorescences give place to bright hues and to a variety of flowers. Here are seen the handsome white flowers of a rubiaceous tree, a species of *Bikkia*; the yellowish flowers and bright red fruits of *Harpullia cupanioides* (" kolon "); the crimson flowers of an *Erythrina* (perhaps *indica*); the yellow flowers of *Cæsalpinia Nuga*; the large pods of *Pongamia glabra*; and the fruits of a wild nutmeg (*Myristica*, sp.). *Hernandia peltata* and *Clerodendron inerme* may also be here found. The conspicuous flowers of *Hibiscus tiliaceus*, *Thespesia populnea*, and of other littoral trees such as *Cerbera Odollam* and *Guettarda speciosa*, add their brightness to the scene. Amongst the foliage of the trees twine a species of *Ipomæa* with handsome white flowers, and here are seen the wax-like flowers of more than one species of asclepiad (*Hoya*, sp.). Orchids, some of striking beauty, hung from the trunks of the trees and form a conspicuous feature in the scene. Among them occur species of *Dendrobium*, *Coelogyne*, *Cleisostoma*, etc.

The littoral vegetation, as exhibited in a coral islet. . . . I will take the case of one of the many wooded islets that have been formed on the coral reefs by the action of the waves. On the weather side of such an islet, which may be termed its growing edge, the vegeta-

[1] A species of *Ophiorrhiza* is in Treasury Island usually associated with this *Beyoni* and is found at all elevations.

T

tion is scanty, and there are but few trees. A binding weed and
more than one species of *Ipomœa* loosely cover a surface composed
almost entirely of calca·eous sand, broken shells, coral debris, and
pumice pebbles; and it is on such an unproductive soil that two or
more species of *Pandanus* and *Casuarina angustifolia* flourish.
Here at the margin of the beach may be seen in profusion the tall
composite shrub, *Wedelia biflora*, and another common shrub, *Scœvola
Kœnigii*. Two climbing peas prefer the sandy soil in this situation,.
one with yellow flowers, *Vigna lutea*, and the other with pink
flowers, *Canavalia turgida*; whilst a dense growth of *Flagellaria
indica* often conceals from view any rocky slope overlooking the
beach. Just within the line of vegetation immediately bordering the
beach, the following trees commonly occur, *Ochrosia parviflora*
("pokosola"), *Heritiera littoralis* ("pipilusu"), *Terminalia catappa*
("saori"), *Cycas circinalis*, and one or more species of *Pandanus*.
Here also a species of *Crinum* (the "papau" of the natives) and the
Tacca pinnatifida ("mamago") may be usually found. (I hoped to
have referred to the ferns of such a coral islet; but my endeavours
to obtain any information of my collection have been unavailing).

On the lee side of such an islet, which is the oldest portion of its
surface, the vegetation is much denser and of a different character.
Here, the trees form a thick belt, their branches overhanging the
rising tide. Those of most frequent occurrence are, *Barringtonia
speciosa*, *Calophyllum inophyllum*, *Hibiscus tiliaceus*, *Thespesia
populnea*, *Guettarda speciosa*, *Morinda citrifolia*, *Cerbera Odollam*,
Pongamia glabra, *Tournefortia argentea*, and other The trunks of
the larger trees often lean over the beach or lie partly procumbent on
the sand. Amongst the foliage of these coast trees, many of which
have large conspicuous flowers, climbing asclepiads of the genus
Hoya with their equally conspicuous flowers may be frequently
observed. Orchids, often of considerable beauty, hang from the
reclining trunks of the trees. Here, as in the case of the coasts
of the large islands, we perceive how pleasant is the contrast which
the littoral vegetation presents when compared with the gloomy and
apparently flowerless forests, where the tallest trees possess but an
inconspicuous greenish inflorescence.

In the interior of such a coral islet, huge banyans and other trees
having wide-spreading buttresses are to be found. Many of them
attain a height of 150 feet and upwards, and afford a home to numbers of fruit-eating pigeons which largely subsist on their fruits, and

through whose agency the interiors of coral islets are stocked with these large trees. Conspicuous amongst the trees is a species of *Canarium* (the "ka-i" of the natives), the disgorged nuts of which frequently strew the ground beneath ; a banyan (*Ficus*) with large oblong fruits and another species with small spherical fruits ; other ficoid trees with large buttresses, such as the "uri"; a species of *Eugenia*, probably a variety of *Eugenia jambos* ; together with several other trees.

This description of the vegetation of a coral islet brings me to refer to the manner in which such an islet, which is usually of very recent origin, has become stocked with its plants : and in so doing I shall be treating of a very important matter, *the oceanic dispersal of plants*. Fortunately for me, my notes and collections relating to this subject had an increased value at the time of my arrival in England, and in this respect I have been able to accomplish one of the principal aims of a young traveller, that of supplying trustworthy materials to those engaged in the particular line of research to which his notes and collections relate.[1]

The picturesquely wooded islets of these seas have been stocked through two principal agencies. Winds and currents drift to their shores the fruits and seeds of the littoral trees which ultimately form the margin of the vegetation ; whilst the fruit pigeons disgorge the seeds or fruits of those often colossal trees which occupy the interior.

I will first refer to the former of these agencies. Lines of vegetable drift, intermingled with floating pumice, are frequently observable whilst cruising among the islands of the Solomon Group. The floating fruits commonly found belong to the most familiar littoral trees of this region, those of *Barringtonia speciosa* and *Calophyllum inophyllum* being especially frequent ; and on more than one occasion the solitary fruits of the former were noticed at sea by Lieutenant Oldham and myself at distances of from 130 to 150 miles to the southward of the group, being probably derived from one of the islands of the New Hebrides to the eastward. Other fruits or seeds occurring frequently in the drift are those of *Nipa fruticans* and of two or more species of *Pandanus*; numerous

[1] Mr. Botting Hemsley was on the point of completing his report on the oceanic dispersal of plants in connection with the Botany of the "Challenger" Expedition. Such of my collections, as referred to his work, were placed at his disposal by Sir Joseph Hooker; and my notes were incorporated in volume I. of the Botany of the "Challenger" (Part III. p. 309), to which I must refer my readers who are more specially interested in this subject

beans (species of *Mucuna, Canavalia, Dioclea*), the long germinated seeds of the mangrove (*Rhizophora*), an occasional cocoa-nut, the cones of *Casuarina equisetifolia, Terminalia catappa, Lumnitzera coccinea, Guettarda speciosa, Ochrosia parviflora, Heritiera littoralis* and others.[1]

The foregoing seeds and seed-vessels with many others may be observed washed up by the waves on the surface of the bare sandy islets or sand-keys, which exhibit the first stage in the growth of those picturesquely wooded coral islets that are ultimately formed on the reefs. On such a sand-key, not more than some 25 or 30 yards across, I have counted as many as 30 different kinds of seeds and fruits, all collected together in the centre, which was only washed over at spring-tides. One of the first trees to establish itself is the mangrove (*Rhizophora*), which by its reclaiming agency adds to the area of the islet and enables other trees, such as *Lumnitzera coccinea*, to take up their abode. *Pari passu* with the seaward extension of the reef, the islet increases in size; and in time the winds and currents bring other fruits and seeds which germinate and form ultimately the belt of littoral trees bordering the beach. In this manner *Barringtonia speciosa, Calophyllum inophyllum, Thespesia populnea, Hibiscus tiliaceus, Cerbera odollam, Ochrosia parviflora, Heritiera littoralis, Terminalia catappa*, different species of *Pandanus, Casuarina equisetifolia*, and *Cycas circinalis* with many others referred to on a previous page, become established. It is worthy of note that the fruits of the great majority of trees which form the margin of the vegetation, whether on the lee or weather side of such an islet, float in salt water.[2] The small cones of the *Casuarina* however, require a certain amount of drying before they can be transported by the waves. The green fruits of the *Cycas* usually sink in salt water; but I found that one out of ten specimens floated, an exceptional circumstance which sufficiently accounts for the occurrence of *Cycas circinalis* on these coral islets.

Whilst through the agency of the winds and currents the waves have stocked the islet with its marginal vegetation, the fruit pigeons have been unconsciously stocking its interior with huge trees, that have sprung from the fruits and seeds they have transported in their crops from the neighbouring coasts and islets. Perched up in

---

[1] Other fruits found floating were a second species of *Calophyllum*, a species of *Gomphrandra, Harpullia* sp., and some *Scitamineæ*.

[2] The results of some experiments I made are given on page 305.

the branches of the trees, these birds disgorge the seeds they have brought from other localities ; and the rejected seeds and seed-vessels lie strewn on the ground beneath. The soft and often fleshy fruits, on which the fruit pigeons subsist, belong to numerous species of trees. Some of them are as large even as a hen's egg, as in the case of those of the species of *Canarium* ("ka-i ") which have a pulpy exterior that is alone digested and retained by the pigeon. The fruits of the banyans and other ficoid trees, which with the *Canarium* are amongst the most conspicuous trees in the interior of the coral islets, are apparently preferred by the fruit pigeons, since they occur commonly in their crops. A species of *Eugenia* common in the interior of these islets possesses fruits found in the crops of these birds. Amongst other fruits and seeds on which these pigeons subsist, and which they must transport from one locality to another, are those of a species of *Elæocarpus* (" ton "), a species of laurel (*Litsea*), a nutmeg (*Myristica*), an *Achras*,[1] one or more species of *Areca*, and probably a species of *Kentia*. There is, however, another bird common on these coral islets, the ground pigeon *Geophilus nicolaricus*, known commonly as the Nicobar pigeon, which transports seeds in its gizzard cavity that on account of their hardness are not fed upon by the ordinary fruit pigeon (*Carpophaga*). The peculiar structure of the gizzard, which is described on page 323, enables the Nicobar pigeon to crack seeds that can only be broken by a sharp blow with a stone. I have found inside this organ, the hard red seeds of a leguminous plant, very probably *Adenanthera pavonina*, of which one seed is occasionally found to be cracked. We may therefore consider that many small hard seeds and seed-vessels, which would be refused by the common fruit pigeon of these islands, are transported from one locality to another in the gizzard cavity of the Nicobar pigeon.

From the foregoing remarks it may be inferred that the pigeons in these islands play a very important part in the dispersal of plants, to which, as Mr. Botting Hemsley remarks in his report (page 313), they have perhaps contributed more than any other animal. In the Solomon Islands the fruit pigeons, as dusk approaches, frequent the islets on the coral reefs in great numbers, and from their unwillingness to leave their roosts in the trees they fall an easy prey to the sportsman. In one afternoon, on one of the islets of Choiseul Bay,

---

[1] I am indebted to Mr. Charles Moore of Sydney N.S.W., for the identification of this fruit. (*Vide* also " Journal and Proceedings of the Royal Society,, N.S.W.," XVII., p. 226.)

57 birds fell to the guns of Lieutenant Heming and Lieutenant
Leeper; and it is to these two officers that I am indebted for my
opportunities of collecting the fruits taken from the crops of these
pigeons.

In drawing my botanical remarks to a close, it may be fitting to
recall the more lasting impressions which I have received of the
vegetation of these islands; and I may do so in a very few words.
The characteristic features of the vegetation are to be found in the
number and variety of the areca palms; in the abundance of the
alpinias, heliconias, and other scitamineous plants; in the imposing
size and form of the banyans and the buttress trees; and in the profusion of the ferns. I have not previously dwelt upon the important
part which the ferns take in the vegetation of these islands, because
I had hoped to have heard something of my collection which I presented to the British Museum eighteen months ago; but, to my
great chagrin, I have been unable, after repeated application, to
learn anything concerning it. I may here state that ferns abound
everywhere; in moist and dry situations; in sheltered and exposed
districts; now decking the tree-trunks with their draperies, or con-
cealing the unsightliness of the decaying log; here covering the bare
slopes of some lofty hill-top, or clothing the surface of some treeless
tract. The tree-fern and the wide-spreading *Angiopteris* are to be
found on the banks of streams or in some inland dell. The former
avoids the coast, and occurs at all elevations up to 2000 feet and
over: it flourishes at the heads of valleys.

LIST OF PLANTS COLLECTED IN THE ISLANDS OF BOUGAINVILLE STRAITS, SOLOMON GROUP, DURING 1884.[1]

ANONACEÆ.

Uvaria, sp. . . vulgo "Nakia." A stout climber.

GUTTIFERÆ.

Ochrocarpus ovalifolius, T. And v. O (Calysaccion) tinctorium, Seem. ?
    vulgo "Kokoilo." A littoral tree about thirty feet high.
Calophyllum Inophyllum, L., vulgo "Bogoau."

---

[1] I am mainly indebted to the kindness of Professor Oliver for the list of the plants collected by me in the Solomon Islands, most of which were sent to Kew. The ferns are in the
British Museum, but I can learn nothing of them. Fortunately, the fungi were not included;
and for a list of them I am indebted to Mr. Baker. Most of the orchids, and some of the
asclepiads, were given by me to Baron von Mueller, who intends to examine them in connec

Calophyllum sp. . . vulgo "Katari." Two tall trees apparently distinguished by the size of the fruits. (Flowers not obtained.) A dark resin oozes from the bark, which the natives burn in torches.

MALVACEÆ.

Hibiscus tiliaceus, L. : vulgo "Dakatako."
Thespesia populnea, Corr. : vulgo "Kai-kaia."

STERCULIACEÆ.

Kleinhovia Hospita, L. : vulgo "Lafai."
Heritiera an H. littoralis, var. angustifolia ? vulgo "Pipilusu."

TILIACEÆ.

Triumfetta procumbens, Forst.
Elæocarpus sp. . . vulgo "Toa" A tree about seventy feet high, with conspicuous blue fruits, eaten by fruit-pigeons.

OXALIDACEÆ

Oxalis corniculata, L.

SIMARUBEÆ

Soulamea amara, Lam.

RUTACEÆ.

Evodia hortensis, Forst. : vulgo "Luk-a-luk."
Rutacea (§ Toddaliæ ?). Detached leaves and flowers picked up from the ground at the foot of a tall forest tree. Flowers "4-meri ; petala imbricata libera ; stamina 4 libera, pet. alterna, ovarium liberum integrum, 4-loc ?"

BURSERACEÆ.

Canarium sp. . . No flowers obtained. A tall forest tree. a hundred feet and upwards in height. Vulgo "Käi" Known as the Solomon Island almond tree. The kernels afford a common article of food in August and September.
Canarium ? vulgo "Nie." A tree with buttresses, a hundred feet high.
Canarium ? vulgo "Nie." A tall forest tree, with buttresses, 100 to 150 feet high.

OLACINEÆ.

Gomphandra sp. . . vulgo "Ninilo," or "Ningilo." A tree thirty to forty feet high. Fruit eaten by wild pigs.
Lasianthera sp. . . nov ? vulgo "Porutolo." A tree sixty to seventy feet high.
Olacinea (dub) : vulgo "Poporoko." A tree sixty feet high, having a light reddish wood, and a dark red sap.

tion with subsequent collections. I take this opportunity of expressing my sense of the great kindness he showed me with reference to my plant collections. To Signor Beccari I am also indebted. Owing to my inexperience in botanical collecting, the specimens were often inadequate for descriptive and specific determination ; but my deficiencies will appear more excusable when I state that I devoted my attention more particularly to the trees. Professor Oliver, however, informs me that, in spite of its defects, my collection gives an excellent conception of the flora of the islands visited.

CELASTRINEÆ.

Salacia sp. . . nov ,

RHAMNACEÆ.

Colubrina asiatica, Bngn.

AMPELIDEÆ.

Leea sambucina, L. (A Gr. U.S. Expl. Expn.)

SAPINDACEÆ.

Schmidelia aff. S. obovatæ, A Gr. A littoral tree, thirty feet high.
Harpullia cupanioides, Roxb. : vulgo " Koloa." Littoral.
Sapindacea an aff. Harpulliæ ? vulgo "Wawau-poko." Growing 1400 feet
    above the sea.
Ratonia sp. . . vulgo " Nekale." A forest tree, a hundred feet high and
    over, with inconspicuous buttresses.
Ratonia sp. . . vulgo " Nekale." A forest tree, a hundred feet high and
    over, with buttresses.

ANACARDIACEÆ.

Mangifera indica, L. ? vulgo " Faise." Mango tree, growing in plantations.
    Fruit ripens in August. Height, thirty feet.

LEGUMINOSÆ.

Crotalaria quinquefolia, L. : vulgo " Kokila."
Desmodium umbellatum, D.C., vulgo " Meki," forma stenocarpa.
Desmodium ormocarpoides, D.C. ?
Desmodium polycarpum D.C.
Erythrina : flowers only. E. monosperma perhaps, or E. indica.
Mucuna gigantea, D.C.? vulgo "Faso-gasuga."
Mucuna sp. . . vulgo " Wassa-wassawa."
Mucuna sp. . .
Papilionacea (dub) ; vulgo " Droau." A stout climber on forest trees, with
    large purple flowers.
Canavalia turgida, Grah.
Vigna lutea, A. Gray.
Pongamia glabra, Vent. ? vulgo " Ausapo."
Sophora tomentosa, L.
Cæsalpinia Nuga, Ait.
Adenanthera Pavonina, L. (probably). Seeds only obtained.
Leucæna sp. . . ?? vulgo "Gehala." A tree thirty to forty feet high.

CHRYSOBALANEÆ.

Parinarium laurinum, A. Gr. : vulgo " Tita." A tree about sixty feet high.
    From the fruit is obtained a resin used by the natives for caulking
    the seams of their canoes.

ROSACEÆ.

Rubus tilaceus, Sm.

COMBRETACEÆ.

Terminalia Catappa, L. : vulgo " Saori." Seeds eaten by the natives.
Lumnitzera coccinea, W. and Arn.

MYRTACEÆ.

Eugenia sp. . . vulgo "Pakuri." A tree thirty feet high, growing 1600 feet above the sea.

Eugenia clusiæfolia, A. Gray (allied to E. Jambolana).

Eugenia sp. . . vulgo "Tsugi." A littoral tree.

Eugenia, aff. E. Richii, A. Gr. : vulgo "Malapo." A tree eighty feet high, with buttresses, growing on coral islets.

Barringtonia speciosa, F.

Barringtonia cf B. edulis, Seem. and B. excelsa, Huds. (New Hebrides) : vulgo "Borolong." A tree thirty to thirty-five feet in height, growing in plantations. Flowers gathered into very conspicuous pendent yellow spikes, two and a half feet long. Kernel of fruit edible.

Barringtonia aff. B. racemosæ, BL : vulgo "Misioko." A tree forty feet high, growing near coast.

Barringtonia ? ? vulgo "Sioko." A tree fifteen to twenty feet high, growing in plantations. Fruit edible.

MELASTOMACEÆ.

Medinilla sp. . . A climbling plant around the trunks of trees.

LYTHRACEÆ.

Pemphis acidula, Forst.

CUCURBITACEÆ.

Cucumis Melo, L., forma ?

ARALIACEÆ.

Panax fruticosum, L.

Plerandra, near Pickeringii, A. Gray : vulgo "Fo."

Araliacea (dub ?) : vulgo "Bubolio." A littoral tree, fifteen feet high.

RUBIACEÆ.

Hedyotis Auricularia, L.

Ophiorrhiza aff. O. cantonensis, Hance.

Ophiorrhiza sp. . .

Dolicholobium aff. D. longissimo an D. longissimum, Seem. forma macranthus : vulgo "Lowasi." A tree fifty feet high and under, common along the sides of streams.

Geophila reniformis, C. and S.

Morinda citrifolia, L. : vulgo "Urati."

Guettarda speciosa, L. : vulgo "Orgoi."

Myrmecodia salomonensis, Becc. A new species separated from M. samoensis, Becc. Noticed commonly on tall mangrove trees bordering the sides of streams in the lower part of their courses. The swollen tuberous stem measures as much as one and a half feet in length, and is usually occupied by many ants.

Hydnophytum longistylum, Becc. Found on coast trees. Those I examined contained no ants, but, instead, a few cockroaches. On the outside of one of them I found a crab.

Hydnophytum Guppyanum, Becc. A new species. Noticed commonly on the tall mangrove trees bordering the sides of streams in the lower part of their courses. The swollen tuberous portion of the stem has a characteristic scaphoid form ; those I examined being nearly

full of dirty rain-water, and almost free from ants ; a few cockroaches occurred in all ; some of them are one and a half feet in length.
(Hydnophytum inerme, a specimen I obtained from Ugi Island at the east end of the group in 1882, and identified by Mr. C. Moore of Sydney.)
Psychotria sp. . . vulgo "Popotu."
Psychotria, aff. P. Forsterinæ, A. Gr.
Bikkia sp. . . A littoral tree, twenty feet high, with large handsome white flowers.

COMPOSITÆ.

Vernonia cinerea, Less.
Adenostemma viscosum, Forst.
Blumea aff. B. glandulosæ, D.C.
Eclipta alba, Hassk.
Bidens pilosa, L.
Wedelia biflora, D.C. A very common littoral plant, but in one instance I found it 1600 feet above the sea.

GOODENIACEÆ.

Scœvola Kœnigii, Vahl. vulgo "Nano." A very common littoral shrub.

SAPOTACEÆ.

Sapotacea ? Seeds only obtained.
Sapotacea (dub) : vulgo "Maranato." A forest tree, a hundred feet high with large plank-like buttresses.

APOCYNEÆ.

Ochrosia parviflora, Hensl : vulgo "Pokosola."
Ochrosia aff. O. (Lactaria) calycarpæ (Miq.). Tree 30 feet high.
Ochrosia sp. . . vulgo "Bararai." A tree 30 to 40 feet high.
Cerbera Odollam, Gœrtn : vulgo "Lukapau."
Cerbera sp. . . vulgo "Anoumi." A tree about 50 feet high, growing away from the coast.
Lyonsia ? ? : vulgo "Awi-sulu." A stout climber : its bark supplies the fibres used for making fishing-lines.

ASCLEPIADEÆ.

Hoya australis, Br. ? (H. bicarinata, A. Gr.) forma : vulgo "Alulu."
Hoya sp. . . (narrow-leaved species).
Hoya Guppyi, Oliv. sp. nov. Ramulis ultimis parce hirtellis dense glabratis, foliis petiolatis coriaceis late ellipticis breviter acuminatis cuspidatisve base late rotundatis subcordatisve supra glabris, subtus præcipue versus basin plus minus hirtellis, umbellis pedunculatis, pedunculis pedicellisque glabris, calyce parvo tubo corollæ 2-4-plo breviore 5-partito lobis ovatis obtusis ciliolatis, corolla rotata lobis patentibus ovatis v. late ovato-lanceolatis acutatis medio depressis intus hirtellis extus glabris sinubus reflexis, coronæ foliolis cartilagineo-incrassatis disco ovato lanceolatis concavis obtusis basi angustatis dorso profunde excavatis marginibus lateralibus utrinque carinatis, folliculis subteretibus parce hirtellis.
    Folia 3½-4½ poll. longis, 2¼-2½ poll. latis ; petiolo hirtello ¼-¾ poll. longo ; umbella 10-14 flora ; pedunculo 2 poll. longo,

pedicellis 1-1½ poll. longis. Corolla 1-1¼ poll. diam. rubro-pur-
purea. Follicula 8-9 poll. longa.
Faro Island : Bougainville Straits : "A climber on coast
trees."

LOGANIACEÆ.

Couthovia, nearly allied to C. Scemanni A.Gr., if not a variety with inflor-
escence throughout tawny-puberulous. Vulgo "Palinoromus." A
forest tree 70 feet high.
Fagræa Berteriana A.Gr. ? vulgo "Bubulata."
Fagræa morindæfolia, Bl. forma. Vulgo "Kirofe."
Fagræa sp. . . vulgo "Mamuli." A tree twenty-five feet high.

BORAGINEÆ.

Tournefortia argentea, L. f. vulgo "Diave."
Cordia subcordata, Lam.
Cordia ? (Corollas picked off ground.)

CONVOLVULACEÆ.

Ipomœa denticulata, Chy.
Ipomœa (Calonyction) grandiflora, Lam ?
Ipomœa pes-capræ, Roth.
Ipomœa sp. . .

SOLANACEÆ.

Solanum repandum, F ? vulgo "Kirkami." }
Solanum repandum, F ? vulgo "Kobureki." }
Natives distinguish these two plants, which grow in their planta-
tions, as shrubs 4 to 6 feet high. Fruits edible when cooked.
Solanum vitiense, Seem. vulgo "Koriele."
Physalis angulata, L.

SCROPHULARINEÆ.

Vandellia crustacea, Bth.

CYRTANDREÆ.

Cyrtandra v. gen. nov. aff.

ACANTHACEÆ.

Adenosma cœrulea, R.Br. ?
Bœa Commersoni, R.Br. fide F. von. Mueller.
Hemigraphis reptans, T. And.
Hemigraphis reptans, forma.
Ruellia sp. R. arvensis. S. Moore var ? v. sp. nov. aff. Growing beside a
stream, 1½ feet high, with light-yellow flowers.
Acanthus ebracteatus, V.
Eranthemum variabile, Br. var. ? Very common in the waste ground of
plantations and by the sides of paths : 1½ to 2 feet in height.

VERBENACEÆ.

Premna obtusifolia, R.Br. an P. taitensis Schr? vulgo "Demoko." A
littoral tree 12 to 15 feet in height. '

Vitex an V. acuminata, Br.? vulgo "Fasala." A large forest tree, a
hundred feet and over in height, with small buttresses, supplying
wood for paddles and canoes.
Clerodendron inerme, Br.
Verbenacea dubia? vulgo "Au-au." A tree fifty to sixty feet high.

LABIATÆ.

Moschosma polystachyum : Bth : vulgo "Pipituan."
Ocymum sanctum, L: vulgo "Kiramma."
Plectranthus v. Coleus? vulgo "Momauri." Leaves, when crushed, give a
reddish-brown stain, and used for staining the skin. Height 1½ feet.
Plectranthus parviflorus, W.

AMARANTACEÆ.

Amarantus melancholicus, L.
Cyathula prostrata, Bl.

PIPERACEÆ.

Piper Betel var. (Chavica Siriboa, Miq.) vulgo "Kolu."

MYRISTICACEÆ.

Myristica sp. . . vulgo "Ito-ito." Coast tree fifteen feet in height.
Myristica sp. . . vulgo "Baimoloi." A tree fifty feet high, growing 1600
feet above the sea.

LAURACEÆ.

Litsæa sp. . . vulgo "Pitoponkano." A tall forest tree.

HERNANDIACEÆ.

Hernandia peltata, Meiss : vulgo "Koli."

EUPHORBIACEÆ.

Euphorbia pilulifera, L.
Euphorbia Atota, Forst.
Phyllanthus (§ Emblica) sp., allied to P. bæobotryoides, Wall? vulgo
"Mefuan." A tree 15 to 20 feet high.
Mallotus tiliæfolius, M. Arg. M. acuminatus, Juss? Tree twenty feet high,
growing at the coast on the border of swampy ground.
Macaranga sp. . . vulgo "Balako." A tree forty to fifty feet high, with
ringed trunk.
Aleurites? vulgo "Aligesi." A stout climber on forest trees. Kernels of
fruit edible.
Sapium indicum, Willd? vulgo "Aligesi." A tree seventy feet high, grow-
ing on the verge of a mangrove swamp.
Excœcaria Agallocha, L.
Codiæum sp. . . (♂)
Codiæum variegatum. A. Juss : vulgo "Tiatakush."

URTICEÆ.

Trema (Sponia) sp. . . : vulgo "Kio." A tree seventy to eighty feet high.

Ficus nr F. theophrastoides. Seem ? vulgo "Tutubolo." Growing in plantations. Probably 10 to 12 feet high.

Ficus sp. . . vulgo "Uri." A tree eighty to ninety feet high, with buttress roots. Growing on coral islets.

Ficus sp. . . vulgo "Sii." A banyan growing at or near the coast and on coral islets. Multiple trunks, some cylindrical and erect, others plank-like and arching. Height eighty or ninety feet and over.

Ficus sp. . . vulgo "Chim." A banyan often growing on the crest of inland ridges. The multiple trunks are all cylindrical and erect, and individually smaller than in the case of the Sii : they are also more closely arranged. Height a hundred and fifty feet and over.

Ficus ? vulgo "Ilimo." A tall forest tree over a hundred feet in height, with magnificent buttresses.

Artocarpus incisa, L. There appears to be but one variety of the Breadfruit tree in the islands of Bougainville Straits. The fruit ? stalked, seedless, and rough externally, the leaves pinnatisect, wit smooth surfaces. Fruit ripens in August. Vulgo "Balia."

Artocarpus sp. . . vulgo "Tafati." Perhaps a variety of the Jack-fruit Tree (A. integrifolia). Sixty feet high. Fruit larger than the common breadfruit, but more irregular in shape : seeded : edible.

Fleurya interrupta, Gaud. (F. spicata, var.)

Elatostemma integrifolium, Wedd. ?

Elatostemma ? vulgo "Obu-obu."

Procris integrifolia, Don ? ?

Pellionia sp. . .

Leucosyke an L. corymbulosa ? Coast tree fifteen feet high.

Pipturus velutinus, Wedd ? v. P. argenteus ? vulgo "Dilipoa." A tree thirty to fifty feet high ; trunk partially ringed ; aerial roots.

CONIFERÆ.

Gnetum Gnemon, L. vulgo "Mariwa."

Gnetum sp. . . : vulgo "Kunuka." A tree sixty feet high, prominently ringed. Kernels of fruits eaten by the natives.

CASUARINEÆ.

Casuarina angustifolia F.

ORCHIDEÆ.

Dendrobium hispidum, Rich. (fide F. v. Mueller).

Dendrobium sp. . . near D. dactylodes, R. fil ?

Cœlogyne sp. . .

Cleisostoma sp. . .

SCITAMINEÆ.

Alpinia sp. . . vulgo "Karu."

Alpinia sp. . . vulgo "Vitoko."

Alpinia sp. . . vulgo "Konkoku."

Costus or Alpinia sp . . vulgo "Makisa."

Alpinia Boia, Seem ? v. sp. aff. vulgo "Pai-yang-pipiula."

Riedelia curviflora, Oliv ? vulgo "Kokuru."

Canna indica, L. ? vulgo "Sati."

Marantacea aff. Phrynio ? vulgo "Sinoili." Flowers in two collateral pairs in each spathe with linear bracts between the pairs. Ovary shortly

stipitate, ovule erect.   Fruit 3-locular, cells 1-seeded, seeds with
crustaceous muricate testa.
Heliconia ? vulgo " Kiari."
Clinogyne grandis Bth and Hook ? (near C. dichotoma and affs) vulgo
" Nini."
Scitaminea (dub) : vulgo " Temuli."   A plant 1 to 1½ feet high growing
in the waste ground of plantations.   The roots have medicinal pro-
perties, according to the accounts of the natives, and they have a
yellow juice which is used for staining. ,
Scitaminea (dubia) : vulgo " Nakia : " a wild ginger.

AMARYLLIDEÆ.

Crinum sp. . . vulgo " Papau."   Grows near the beach.   Height four feet.
Curculigo sp. . vulgo " Bulami."   Growing 2 to 2½ feet high on the banks
of streams.

LILIACEÆ.

Cordyline sp. . . vulgo " Dendiki."   Tree twenty feet high ; growing near
the coast.

COMMELYNACEÆ.

Commelyna nud.flora, L.

DIOSCOREÆ.

Dioscorea sativa, L. ? vulgo " Alapa."

JUNCACEÆ.

Flagellaria indica, L. var.

TACCACEÆ.

Tacca pinnatifida, Forst. : vulgo " Mamago."   The natives do not appear to
make use of the arrowroot-like starch obtainable from the tubers.

PANDANACEÆ.

Pandanacea : genus novum,[1](♀ flowers only and leaf collected).   The only
locality where I found it was the summit of Faro Island, where it grows
to a height of fifty feet, and has a long white female branching spadix,
three to four feet in length.   The same, or a near ally, was obtained
by Signor Beccari in Jobi Island, off New Guinea.   (*Vide* page 289.)

The natives distinguish several species of Pandanus trees, of which I
was only able to obtain the fruit.   The " darashi " " sararang," and " pota,"
grow at the coast, and have a height of from thirty to forty feet.   The
" darashi " has narrow leaves, and, if the ground is not rocky, aerial roots
are often absent : the fruit is smaller than that of the two other littoral
pandanus trees.   The " sararang " has broad leaves, and always aerial roots :
the fruit is often more than a foot in diameter.   The " pota " has broad
leaves, with contracted acuminate apices, two inches long : the fruit is about
a foot in diameter : aerial roots are always present, and rise often fifteen

---

[1] I learn from Professor Oliver that Count Solins confirms the generic distinctne s.

feet from the ground. The segments of these pandanus trees all contain edible kernels. The broad leaves of the "pota" are employed in making mats. . . . There is another pandanus tree, the "samala" of the natives, which often grows away from the coast, as on the banks of streams: it has an erect, stout trunk, thirty-five to forty feet high, without aerial roots, and does not branch.

Freycinetia sp. . .
Freycinetia sp. . .
Nipa fruticans.

PALMACEÆ.

Cyrtostachys sp. . . vulgo "Sensisi." Growing up to fifty feet high on the banks of streams.

Palmacea dub. (cf. Drymophlorus): vulgo "Kisu." Growing seventy to eighty feet high. The tough sheathing at the bases of the branches is employed for making the native dishes.

Pinanga sp. . . vulgo "Kisu": conf. the "Kisu" above. Growing up to seventy or eighty feet high.

Caryota sp. . . vulgo "Eala." Growing up to fifty feet high.

Licuala sp. . . vulgo "Firo." Grows up to thirty-five or forty feet in height. More common on volcanic soils. Absent from Treasury Island, with the exception of one imported tree. Said to be very numerous in the large adjacent island of Bougainville, the leaves being there used in making conical hats.

Palmacea dub.: vulgo "Poamau." Grows up to seventy or eighty feet high. Its fruit, which is eaten by the women, is said to have a stimulant effect like the betel-nut. Its wood supplies the material for spears.

Areca sp. . . vulgo "Momo." Grows up to thirty-five or forty feet high. Small fruits (¼ inch) sessile on a branching stalk.

Areca sp. . . vulgo "Niga-torulo," or "Torulo." Grows up to thirty-five or forty feet high. Fruits larger (1—1½ inch) sessile, and gathered thickly together on an undivided stalk.

Areca sp. . . vulgo "Niga-solu." Grows up to fifty feet high. Fruits (1—1½ inch) sessile, gathered thickly together on an undivided stalk.

[*Note.*—The three kinds of areca palms just mentioned are very common on the low ground at the foot of hills. They all have a general resemblance, and their fruits are often chewed in lieu of "betel-nuts." They are distinguished from each other readily by the size and mode of attachment of the fruits, and by the number of ribs on the lateral pinnæ.]

Areca sp. . . vulgo "Poamau." Growing up to eighty feet high.

Areca sp. . . vulgo "Au-Au." Grows up to twelve feet high. Aerial roots rising from stem 1½ feet above the ground.

Areca sp. . . vulgo "Olega." The betel-nut palm of the Solomon Islands. Planted by the natives in the vicinity of their villages. Height up to thirty feet.

Sagus sp. . . vulgo "Bia," "Nami." Height up to sixty feet. Dry situations.

AROIDEÆ.

Schizmatoglottis sp. . . vulgo "Kuraka." Growing wild along the banks of streams. The natives make a savoury vegetable broth of the leaves and unopened spathes.

Epipremnum cf. E. mirabile, Sch.   Found on trees.
Scindapsus sp. . . vulgo " Kurricolo."   Grows on sandy soil near the coast.
Pothos ?

CYPERACEÆ.

Cyperus (Mariscus phleoides, Nees).   Height two to two and a half feet.
Cyperus canescens, Vahl.   Height two feet.
Cyperus (Mariscus umbellatus, V.).   Height one foot.
Kyllinga monocephala, Rottb.   Six to eight inches high.
Mapania sp. . . Three feet high.

GRAMINEÆ.

Eleusine indica, Gœrtn.
Panicum (Digitaria) sanguinale, L.
     „   radicans, Retz. ?
     „   carinatum, Presl.
     „   neurodes, Sch.
Pennisetum (Gymnothrix Thouarsii Beauv. ?).   Also
Pennisetum macrostachys, Trin. (fide F. v. Mueller): vulgo "Orsopa."
     Growing in waste ground of plantations to a height of eight or nine
     feet.
Coix Lachryma, L.: vulgo Ken-ken."   The natives do not appear to make
     use of the seeds as beads. Growing in the waste ground of
     plantations.
Pollinia obtusa, Munro ?
Schizostachyum ? ?   A bamboo usually found at elevations of 1000 or 1100
     feet above the sea. The canes grow to a length of thirty-five to
     forty feet, and are used as fishing-rods.

MUSCI.

Octoblepharum (Leucophanes) squarrosum, Brid.

HEPATICÆ.

Marchantia linearis, L. and L. ?

FUNGI.

Agaricus (perhaps mollis, Schff.).
     „   (Inocybe) maritimus, Fr.
Hygrophorus metapodius, Fr. prox.
Lentinus submembranaceus, B.
     „   dactyliophorus, Lev.
     „   velutinus, Fr.
Polyporus (Mes.) xanthopus, Fr.
     „   (Pleur.) affinis, Nees.
     „   (Pleur.) luteus, Nees.
     „   (Pleur.) lucidus, Fr.
     „   (Placo.) australis Fr.
Hexagona apiaria, Fr.
     „   similis, B.
Cladoderris dendritica, Fr
Thelephora lamellata, B.
Hirneola auricula-judœ, Fr.
Lycoperdon gemmatum, Fr.
Bovista sp. . . (uncertain).
Wynnea macrotis, Berk.

The Flotation of Fruits in Sea-Water.—I made a few experiments on the fruits of this region, the results of which I here append. The fruits were all ripe and not dried.

(1.) Fruits that *float* in sea-water.[1]

Cocos nucifera.
Areca catechu (Betel-nut).
Cycas circinnlis.[2]
Pandanus (three littoral species).
Nipa fruticans.
Barringtonia speciosa.
Calophyllum inophyllum.
Calophyllum sp. (katari).

Ochrosia parviflora.
Heritiera littoralis.
Cerbera odollam.
Harpullia cupanioides.
Myristica sp. (ito-ito).
Riedelia curviflora.?
Thespesia populnea.
Gomphandra sp. (ningilo).

(2.) Fruits that *sink* in sea-water.

Parinarium laurinum.[2]
Licuala sp. (firo).
Areca sp. (torulo).

Areca sp. (momo).
Caryota sp. (cala).

The weeds, rubbish-plants, and shrubs, commonly found in old clearings and in the waste-ground of the cultivated patches in Bougainville Straits.

One of the commonest plants in the islands of Bougainville Straits is the *Erianthemum variabile,* which is frequently found growing at the sides of the paths. The spurges, *Euphorbia pilulifera* and *E. Atoto,* are usually found in the waste-ground around villages. In the cultivated patches clumps of the handsome flowering reed, *Pennisetum macrostachys* ("orsopa"), which grows to a height of nine or ten feet, are often conspicuous. In one place may be seen the tall shrub, *Kleinhovia Hospita* ("lafui"), the inflated fruits of which are eaten by the cockatoos. In another place the botanist may recognise the *Canna indica* (Indian Shot: "sati"), and near by perhaps *Coix Lachryma* (Job's tears : "ken-ken"), both of which plants have been probably introduced originally from the Malay Archipelago. Solomon Islanders occasionally wear the seeds of *Coix Lachryma* as a personal ornament. They are also used for this purpose by the Admiralty Islanders, and by the natives of some parts of New Guinea. Scented labiate plants are very frequent in the waste-ground of the plantations, and the natives are fond of wearing them in their armlets. Amongst them I may mention *Moschosma polystachyum* ("pipituau") and *Ocymum sanctum* ("kirimma"). The "luk-a-luk" (*Evodia hortensis*), which is a favourite scented plant, is commonly found in the same situations. The tiny plant, *Oxalis corniculata,* may clothe a bare patch of ground ; whilst in another part of the plantation, *Commelyne nudiflora* may similarly be observed. Numerous composite plants, such as *Vernonia cinerea, Adenostemma viscosum,* etc., form a conspicuous feature among the rubbish-plants in these cultivated patches. The *Codiæum variegatum* ("tiatakush"), with its very singularly-

[1] The following fruits and seeds, taken from my dried collection of plants, float in sea-water. I did not experiment on them in the green condition. . . . Pongamia glabra : Coix Lachryma : Scævola Koenigii : Tournefortia argentea.·

[2] Out of ten fruits experimented on, only one floated.

[3] This tree is widely distributed throughout the group, which may be due to the circumstance of its resin being generally employed in caulking canoes.

U

shaped leaves, is also to be seen : and, amongst other plants, I should refer to *Solanum vitiense* and *Crotalaria quinquefolia.* Tall sedges, such as *Cyperus canescens* and *Mariscus phleoides*, are to be commonly observed. Lastly, I should notice two small scitamineous plants, the "nukia," a wild ginger, and the "temuli," the root of which has medicinal properties, whilst its yellow juice is used for staining purposes.

A species of Pachyma ? ?

Whilst at the island of Santa Anna in October, 1882, my attention was directed by Mr. William Macdonald and Mr. Houghan to a curious vegetable substance, not unlike a yam in appearance, which is found *lying loose on the soil.* The specimens I obtained varied between one and five pounds in weight, but much larger examples have been obtained. The interior of the substance is white in colour, and sometimes has a waxy look. A large slab which had been whittled out by a native resembled a cake of compressed flour. There were many curious speculations as to the nature of these growths. In the estimation of the inhabitants of the island, they are poisonous, and they have received from them the name of " testes diaboli ; " but I could gather but little information from the natives on the subject except to the effect that they are also commonly found on St. Christoval.[1] However, some time later I was informed by Mr. Stephens of Ugi that some mushroom-like growths were borne by a specimen that he kept, which after a few weeks fell away. I subsequently gave some of these singular masses to Mr. Charles Moore, the Director of the Sydney Botanic Gardens.

Three years passed away and I had almost forgotten about the matter, when I accidentally came upon some substances, closely resembling these masses, which are exhibited in the Botanical Department of the British Museum. They are libelled *Pachyma Cocos* (Fries) from China. On my asking Mr. George Murray concerning their nature, I was pleased to learn that he had been taking a special interest in these growths ; and he showed me a specimen obtained by the Rev. Mr. Whitmee in Samoa, from which a funnel-shaped fungus, about six inches high, was growing. This specimen was very similar to those of the Solomon Islands.

Very recently, Mr. G. Murray has embodied the results of his investigations of these growths in a short paper read before the Linnean Society, in which Mr. Whitmee's specimen is figured (Trans. Linn. Soc., 2nd ser. Bot., vol. ii., part 11). From this source I learn that Rumphius was the first to describe these tuberous masses and their associated fungi from Amboina. The former, which he named *Tuber regium*, were stated to afford remedies useful in diarrhœa, fevers, &c. The fungi were said to shoot out from them during showers of warm rain on a fine day, or when there was thunder in the air. From the description and illustration given by Rumphius, Mr. Fries regarded the growth as a fungus belonging to the genus *Lentinus*, springing from a *Pachyma* (of which the Indian Bread of North America, *Pachyma cocos*, is an example). Strange to say, however, these tubers, which are found also in China and other parts of the world, have never been found with a fungus attached since the time of Rumphius. Mr. Whitmee's specimen, therefore, had considerable interest. It is shown by Mr. Murray to correspond strikingly with *Tuber regium* and to have the structure of a true " sclerotium " (not of *Pachyma*), with a fungus of a species of *Lentinus* growing from it. All the facts go to prove that the fungus and the tuberous mass do not form part of the same growth, but

---

[1] In the event of its proving edible, Mr. Houghan cooked a specimen, but only a taste'eæ substance resulted.

are distinct organisms. A spore having germinated on the surface of the mass, its mycelium penetrates the interior, and becoming perennial, produces successive crops of fungi.

Residents in the Indian Archipelago and in the Pacific Islands might throw considerable light on the subject of these growths by careful notes and collections. It is important to discover the origin of the tuberous mass which become, so to speak, a convenient nidus for the fungus. How do such masses perpetuate themselves? A considerable number should be kept under observation, and the mode of appearance of the fungus carefully noticed. Experiments might be made with the spores of the fungus by dusting them over the surface of the masses. Such notes and collections should be forwarded to Mr. Murray, at the British Museum of Natural History.

CHAPTER XIV.

REPTILES AND BATRACHIANS.

IN a memoir on the Reptiles and Batrachians of the Solomon Islands, which was read before the Zoological Society, on May 6th, 1884,[1] Mr. Boulenger remarked that very little was known about the herpetology of these islands until two important collections, which I sent to the British Museum in 1883 and 1884, brought to light several new and interesting forms, such as could hardly have been expected from this region. " The position of this group of islands on the limits of two great zoological districts,"—this author proceeded to observe—"renders the study of its fauna of special interest, as it is the point where many of the Papuasian and Polynesian forms intermingle. Curiously, all the Batrachians belong to species not hitherto found elsewhere, and one of them is even so strongly modified as to be the type of a distinct family."

According to Mr. Boulenger, the Reptiles may be grouped under four headings, viz. :—

1. Species belonging to both the Papuasian and Polynesian districts.

2. Indo-Malayan or Papuasian species, not extending further east or south-east.

3. Polynesian species, not extending further north and west than New Ireland.

4. Species not hitherto found elsewhere than in the Solomons (and New Ireland.)

1

Gymnodactylus pelagicus
Gehyra oceanica
Mabuia cyanura
Platurus fasciatus.

[1] Published in the Transactions of the Society ; vol. xii., part i., 1886. The diagnoses of most of the new species in my collections were given in the Proceedings for 1884 ; p. 210. Vide also " Annals and Magazine of Natural History " (5) xii., 1883.

2

Crocodilus porosus
Gecko vittatus
Varanus indicus
Keneuxia smaragdina
Enygrus carinatus
Dipsas irregularis.

3

Gonyocephalus godeffroyi
Mabuia carteretii
    „   nigra
Enygrus bibronii.

4

Lepidodactylus guppyi, *n sp.*
Lipinia anolis, *n sp.*
Corucia zebrata
Dendrophis solomonis
Hoplocephalus par, *n sp.*

All of these 19 Reptiles were included in my collection, with the exception of *Corucia zebrata*, which, however, came under my observation. I will now proceed to refer more particularly to the Reptile-fauna of this region.

CROCODILES.—The species of Crocodile (*Crocodilus porosus*, Schneid,) which is so common in the Solomon Group, ranges from India and South China through the Malay Archipelago and Papuan Islands to North Australia. In these islands crocodiles appear to frequent in greatest numbers the swamps and sandy shores of uninhabited coral islands, such as those of the Three Sisters, and the coasts of the larger islands in the vicinity of the mouths of the streams and rivers. I frequently surprised them basking on the sand under the shade of a tree. On one occasion I was standing on the spreading roots of a tree that were exposed on the beach, when one of these reptiles darted out from under my feet and dived into the sea. Of the marks that they make on the sand when lying at rest, an oblong shallow impression corresponding to the head, and a curved well-defined grove caused by the tail are alone specially recognisable. When they are not alarmed and move leisurely along, they leave a double row of footprints on the sand, with a narrow median furrow produced by the weight of the tail; but when they have been disturbed and make a rush to escape, they raise their tail and leave only the tracks of their feet on the sand. These crocodiles are equally at home in salt and fresh water. I have frequently passed them in my Rob Roy canoe when they have been floating as though asleep at the surface of the sea; and it was always in the sea that they found a refuge when my little craft intruded itself within their haunts. They came under my notice in the fresh-water lakes of Santa Anna and Stirling Island, and in the lower courses of the streams in several localities. They are apparently in no uncongenial conditions in the salt-water lagoon of Eddystone Island, although its waters receive the hot sulphureous vapours of submerged fumaroles.

These crocodiles do not apparently attain a greater length than 12 or 13 feet. Mr. Sproul shot one at Santa Anna which measured 9¼ feet. A female that I shot in the Shortland Islands, measured 11 feet. One of the seamen of the "Lark," named Prior, obtained from the natives the skull of a rather larger specimen. Out of half-a-dozen individuals seen on the Three Sisters, not one measured more than 7 or 8 feet.[1] Mr. Bateman, a trader resident at Ugi, told me that at Wano on the St. Christoval coast he saw a very large crocodile which, from his description, appears to have been twice as long as any that I saw. It was, however, dusk at the time; and in connection with this circumstance I should add that I have found actual measurement to reduce the apparent length of a crocodile from 14 to 11 feet.

Natives are rarely attacked by these reptiles, and they show little or no fear of them. I have seen a full-grown crocodile dart under a line of swimmers without causing any dismay. Of the numbers I saw, all were but too anxious to get out of my way; and their cowardly nature is well shown in the account of my capture of a specimen which is given below. However, I came upon a man of Santa Anna who had had his leg broken by one of these reptiles. The natives of Rubiana hold the crocodile in veneration and work without fear in the places which it frequents. They believe that only faithless wives are seized and carried off by the monster. Pigs are occasionally the prey of the crocodile;

[1] A skull given to me by Mr. Nisbet, the government-agent of the "Redcoat," at Ugi, was 12 inches long. It was obtained from the natives of Guadalcanar.

but its usual diet appears to be opossums (*Cusci*), large lacertilians, and fish.

The following account of the capture of a crocodile may interest some of my readers. It was effected by no more formidable weapons than by a number of long staves and a small "bull-dog" revolver. Accompanied by six natives I was making the ascent of a large stream on the north-west side of Alu, when some of my companions espied a large crocodile at the bottom of a deep pool about 200 yards from the mouth of the stream. In setting to work to effect its capture my men proceeded very methodically to work, and evidently knew the tactics which the creature would employ. Standing in the water just below the pool, we stood awaiting the descent of the crocodile down the stream, whilst one of the natives was rousing it up with a long pole to make it leave its hiding-place. After a little time it began to get uneasy, and leaving the pool began to descend the stream. Where we were standing, the stream was only knee-deep, and as the reptile passed us in the shallow water some natives hit it on the head with their poles, whilst others hurled their poles sharpened at the ends, striking it in several places, and I planted a bullet behind its neck. The creature showed no fight and immediately hid itself in the pools near the mouth of the stream. During two hours, after we had been driving it from one pool to another by means of our pointed poles and staves, we seemed no nearer to its capture. At length there was a loud out-cry from the natives. The crocodile was making a final rush for life to cross the bar at the mouth of the stream and escape into the sea. We all followed, some in the canoe and some through the water; and for a short time I thought that the creature would escape. But being a little disabled by our previous attacks, its progress across the bar was somewhat checked; and the foremost of my men caught hold of its tail just as it was getting into deep water. Very quickly we all came up, and assisted in drawing it high and dry on the beach; and whilst two of our number kept hold of its tail, the remainder belaboured its neck with rocks and sticks until it died.[1] Its length proved to be 11 feet. Throughout the whole chase the reptile made no outcry, and even when we were belabouring it to death it only gave a kind of growl. In its stomach I found a large quantity of partially digested food

[1] An illustration in Mr. Bates' "Naturalist on the Amazons" represents a very similar scene.

with the remains of an opossum (*Cuscus*) and a large lizard 1½ feet long (probably *Corucia zebrata*). It was a female, and in the oviduct I came upon an egg, which my natives appropriated, saying that it was very good food; but they do not usually eat the flesh. I was unable from want of space to keep more than the head of the animal, which I cut off and carried back in my canoe to the ship. The skull is now in the British Museum.

LIZARDS. The Lacertilians are well represented in these islands. Those at present described are given in the subjoined list.

Geckonidæ

Gymnodactylus pelagicus
Gehyra oceanica
Lepidodactylus guppyi. *n. sp.*
Gecko vittatus
„ var. bivittatus

Agamidæ

Gonyocephalus godeffroyi.

Varanidæ

Varanus indicus

Scincidæ

Mabuia carteretii
„   cyanura
„   nigra
Keneuxia smaragdina
Lipinia anolis *n. sp.*
Corucia zebrata.

The lizards, which most frequently meet the eyes of the visitors in the vicinity of the beaches, are the two skinks, *Mabuia nigra* and *cyanura*. As a rule those species that are common at the coast have a wide range, extending either into Polynesia or Papuasia or into both these regions (*vide* page 307). The species peculiar to these islands came less frequently under my observation. Thus, that of *Lepidodactylus guppyi,* is founded on a single (female) specimen I found in Faro or Fauro Island in Bougainville Straits. *Corucia zebrata* never came under my notice alive; it is said at Ugi to find its home in the foliage of the higher trees. Doubtless if I could have penetrated to the higher regions of the large islands, I should have obtained a large number of new species. My collections refer for the most part to the sea-border and its vicinity. In the elevated interior of such an island as Guadalcanar there is *a region of great promise* for the collector ; but I shall have a further occasion to refer to this topic.

The Monitor, *Varanus indicus*, may be often seen at the coast, basking in the glare of the mid-day sun on the trunks of prostrate trees or on the bare rocks. It is considered edible by the natives of Bougainville Straits. Whilst we were anchored at Oima Atoll, Lieutenant Leeper captured a very large specimen (5 feet 7¾ inches long)[1] on the rocks close to the sea, and towed it off alive to the ship. After we had tried in vain to strangle it by a cord, a lead was fastened to it and it was sunk overboard, but an hour passed before we could say that the reptile was really dead. This Monitor is probably able to swim considerable distances. It very likely owes its wide range (from Celebes to the Solomon Group including Cape York) to the agency of floating trees. On examining the stomach and intestines, I found them empty. An enormous quantity of fat, developed in two large lobes in connection with the *omentum* or some other part of the *peritoneum*, almost filled the abdominal cavity. With this store of sustenance and heat, these reptiles must be able to live without food for a long time.[2]

SNAKES. Hitherto, the following six species of Ophidians have been found in the Solomon Group. All of them were included in my collection and one of them has been described by Mr. Boulenger as a new species.

Boidæ

Enygrus carinatus

    ,,   bibronii

Colubridæ

Dendrophis solomonis

Dipsas irregularis

Elapidæ

Hoplocephalus par *n. sp.*

[1] A specimen shot in the Florida Islands measured 3 feet 8 inches.

[2] As an instance of the tenacity of life that some reptiles possess, I may refer to the case of a young terrapin which I kept inadvertently for nearly five months on the coast of China without any sustenance except the dry rust of a tin can.

Hydrophiidæ (Water-snakes)

Platurus fasciatus [1]

One of the commonest of snakes throughout these islands is
Enygrus carinatus, a harmless species of the Boa family. It often
possesses considerable bulk in proportion to its length. One
specimen which I obtained in Treasury Island measured $3\frac{1}{2}$ feet in
length and 6 inches in girth. I handled a good many living snakes
whilst in these islands, since the natives used to bring them in
numbers to me both on board and on shore. The statements of the
natives and of the white men resident in this region and the
general appearance of the snakes had led me to believe that there
were no poisonous species in the group. I was therefore somewhat
surprised when, on my arrival in England, I learned from Dr.
Günther that I had found a new species as poisonous as the Cobra.
On being shown the specimen by Mr Boulenger, I at once recognised an old friend which had been brought on board in a
bamboo by the natives at Faro Island and had got loose on the deck.
Whilst the men standing round were preparing to kill it with more
regard for their own safety than for my feelings, I caught it quickly
around the neck and held it under water until it was dead. The
natives certainly were not aware of its venomous character, nor was
Mr. Isabell, who was my right-hand man in these matters, and used to
manage the ticklish progress of removing the snakes from their
bamboo-tubes in a manner only suitable in the case of harmless
species. I only obtained one specimen of this snake, which was
about $2\frac{1}{2}$ feet in length. It is named *Hoplocephalus par* and belongs
to the *Elapidæ*, a family of poisonous colubrine snakes which possess
the physiognomy of the harmless snakes of the same sub-order, and
include the Indian and African Cobras with other well known
venomous species. In the footnote I have quoted Mr. Boulenger's
description of its general appearance for the information of those
who visit the group.[2]

[1] I was indebted to Lieutenant Symonds of H.M.S. "Diamond" for this snake.

[2] The upper surface of the head is uniform b ackish brown. The body is crossed above by
broad red-brown bands separated by narrow white interspaces. The lower surface of the
head and body are uniform white, except on the posterior extremity of the body where the
red and black extend as lines along the sutures of the ventral shields. On the tail the red
forms complete rings. Nearly every one of the dorsal scales have a blackish brown border.
The head is depressed, moderately large, and slightly widened posteriorly. The eye has a
vertical pupil.

BATRACHIANS.—The Spanish discoverers in 1567 remarked that the natives of Isabel worshipped the toad (*vide* page 203), and one of the officers of Surville's expedition in 1769, described in his journal a remarkable toad from the same island;[1] yet it is only within recent years that any Batrachians have been collected in this region. Before I arrived in the group only two species were known to science, and to this number my collections, which were made in the islands of Bougainville Straits, have added seven new species, including a type of a new family. The following list represents the Batrachian fauna of the Solomon Islands, as far as it is at present known:

Ranidæ.

Rana buboniformis, *n. sp.*
Rana guppyi, *n. sp.*
Rana opisthodon, *n. sp.*
Rana krefftii.
Cornufer guppyi, *n. sp.*
Cornufer solomonis, *n. sp.*

Ceratobatrachidæ.

(New family characterised by both jaws being toothed, and by the diapophyses of the sacral vertebra not being dilated.) ·
Ceratobatrachus guentheri, *n. sp.*

Hylidæ (Tree-frogs.)
Hyla macrops, *n. sp.*
Hyla thesaurensis.

The natives of the islands of Bougainville Straits, where, as I have just remarked, my batrachian collection was chiefly made, have given frogs the general name of " appa-appa " in imitation of their noise, just as they have named the smaller lizards " Kurru-rupu " for the · same reason. Amongst the particular species of frogs, I may refer to the large toad-like *Rana buboniformis*, which I found in Treasury Island, and on the highest peak of the island of Faro. *Rana guppyi*, according to Mr. Boulenger's report, attains a larger size than any

[1] "Discoveries of the French in 1768 and 1769," &c., by M. Fleurieu: London, 1701; p. 134.

other species of the genus, with the exception of the Bull-Frog of
North America. *Rana opisthodon* affords an instance of a Batrachian[1]
which dispenses with the usual larval or tadpole stage, "the metamorphoses being hurried through within the egg." On this subject
I made the following notes. Whilst descending from one of the
peaks of Faro Island, I stopped at a stream some 400 feet above the
sea, where my native boys collected from the moist crevices of the
rocks close to the water a number of transparent gelatinous balls
rather smaller than a marble.[2] Each of these balls contained a
young frog about 4 lines in length, apparently fully developed, with
very long hind legs and short fore legs, no tail, and bearing on the
sides of the body small tufts of what seemed to be branchiæ. On
my rupturing the ball or egg in which the little animal was doubled
up, the tiny frog took a marvellous leap into its existence and disappeared before I could catch it. When I reached the ship an hour
after, I found that some of the eggs which had been carried in a tin
had been ruptured on the way by the jolting, and the liberated frogs
were leaping about with great activity. On placing some of them
in an open bottle 8 inches high, I had to put the cover on as they
kept leaping out. Mr. Boulenger remarking on this observation
says, that there are no gills, but that on each side of the abdomen
there are regular transverse folds (with an arrangement like that of
the gill-openings of Plagiostomous Fishes), the function of which
probably is that of breathing-organs. The tip of the snout is, he
says, furnished with a small conical protuberance, projecting slightly
through the delicate envelope of the egg, and evidently used to perforate that covering. In the instance also of *Cornufer solomonis*,
another new species included in my collection, Mr. Boulenger remarks that there is every reason to believe that the young undergo
the metamorphoses within the egg.

With regard to the interesting species, *Ceratobatrachus guentheri*,
which forms the type of a new family, *Ceratobatrachidæ*, the same
writer observes that it is remarkable for the numerous appendages
and symmetrical folds which ornate its skin. It is, in fact, "all
points and angles," and may be truly termed a horned frog. There
is great variation both in the coloration and in the integuments.
"Out of the twenty specimens before me," thus Mr. Boulenger
writes, "no two are perfectly alike." The development is presumed

---

[1] Hylodes martinicensis affords another instance. Mon. Berl. Ac., 1876, p. 714.

[2] According to Mr. Boulenger, they measure from 6 to 10 mm. in diameter.

to be of the type in which the metamorphoses are hurried through within the egg. These horned frogs are very numerous in the islands of Bougainville Straits, and so closely do they imitate their surroundings, both in colour and pattern, that on one occasion I captured a specimen by accidentally placing my hand upon it when clasping a tree.

It is particularly important to notice not only that the Batrachians of the Solomon Islands, as far as we at present know, do not occur elsewhere, but also that in this region a distinct family has been produced. These facts support the conclusions deducible from the geological evidence that these islands are of considerable geological age (*vide* page x.). The insular and isolated conditions have been preserved during a period sufficiently extended for the development of a peculiar Batrachian fauna.

The modes of dispersal of frogs and toads, and, in truth, of the whole Batrachian class, are matters of which we are to a great extent ignorant. Frogs are usually stated to be absent from oceanic islands, a peculiarity of distribution which apparently accords with the circumstance that neither they nor their spawn can sustain submersion in sea-water. The occurrence, however, of three species of *Cornufer* in the Caroline and Fiji Islands, and of a species of *Bato* in the Sandwich Islands,[1] affects the general application of this conclusion. It may be suggested that these exceptions are due to human agency; but if so, it is difficult to understand why they have not been found in such a well explored island as New Caledonia.[2]

In concluding this chapter I will refer to the circumstance that my collections of the Reptiles and Batrachians of this large group have only in a manner broken ground in a region which promises the richest results to the collector. It cannot be doubted that in the elevated interiors of the large islands, such as those of Bougainville and Guadalcanar, there will be found a peculiar Reptilian and Batrachian fauna, the study of which will be of the highest importance for the furtherance of our knowledge of these geologically ancient classes of animals. I believe I am correct in stating that it was on account of the highly interesting Batrachian collections I sent to the British Museum, that I received a grant for further exploration from the Royal Society, which, however, I was unfortu-

---

[1] Boulenger's "Catalogue of the Batrachia Gradientia," &c., 2nd edit., 1882.
[2] Perhaps the peculiar geographical distribution of the Batrachia may throw light on this subject. *Ibid.*

nàtely prevented from turning to account. The work has yet to be done, and there can be little doubt that the man who is first able to examine the lofty interior of such an island as Guadalcanar will bring back collections, the importance of which will amply recompense him for any hardship or personal risk he may have endured. My experience was confined to the sea-border and its vicinity. The future explorer will find his field in the mountainous interiors and on the highest peaks.

NOTE (April 19th, 1887).—Since I penned the above, further collections of reptiles and batrachians, made in these islands by Mr. C. M. Woodford, have been described by Mr. Boulenger at a recent meeting of the Zoological Society. I had the pleasure of meeting Mr. Woodford before he left England, and I hope that he has been able to accomplish his purpose of penetrating into the interior of one of the larger islands of the group.

CHAPTER XV.

AMONGST the numerous strange acquaintances which I made in the Solomon Islands, was that of the well known cocoa-nut crab, or *Birgus latro* ; and I take this opportunity of giving my evidence towards the establishment of the fact of its cocoa-nut-eating propensity, for the following reason. When I read my notes on the subject before the Linnean Society of New South Wales on Dec. 27th, 1882,[1] I was surprised at the incredulity shown with reference to this extraordinary habit; and on inquiry, I learned that the evidence on the subject was deficient in one vital point, viz., the production of the writer who had witnessed this habit of the Robber Crab. Accordingly I referred to the various authors who have recorded this habit of the *Birgus*, and in no single account could I find that the writer had witnessed what he described. Neither Mr. Darwin, Dr. Seeman, Messrs. Tyerman and Bennet, Mr. T. H. Hood, the Rev. Wyatt Gill, nor the numerous authors whose accounts I also examined, seem to have actually witnessed the *Birgus* opening and eating a cocoa-nut. Herbst[2] was among the first to refer to this habit ; whilst, long ago, M. M. Quoy and Gaimard[3] asserted, from their own observation, that the crab was fond of cocoa-nuts, and could be supported on them alone for many months, but they made no allusion to its capability of husking and opening them. The evidence on this point appears to have been always tendered by natives, excepting the account given to Mr. Darwin by Mr. Liesk, which is conclusive in itself.[4] Yet, credulous persons had fair grounds to retain their doubts, although in various works on natural history, popular and otherwise, this habit of the *Birgus* was described as an undoubted fact. I therefore submit my evidence ; leaving to my reader to

[1] Proc. Lin. Soc. N.S.W.
[2] Proc. Zool. Soc., 1832, p. 17.
[3] Freycinet's " Voyage autour du Monde," 1817-20 : Zoologie, p. 536. (Paris, 1824.)
[4] " Journal of Researches," p. 462.

reply to the query—Can there be any reasonable doubt on the subject?

The *Birgus* was to be found in most of the islands we visited. It is to be usually observed at or near the coast; but on one occasion, in St. Christoval, I found an individual at a height of 300 feet above the sea. Whilst traversing, in September, 1882, the belt of screw-pines, which borders the beach on the east coast of Malaupaina, the southern island of the Three Sisters, I came upon one of these large crabs, ensconced in the angle between the buttressed roots of a tree, with a full sized cocoa-nut within the reach of its pair of big claws. From the fresh-looking appearance of the shell, it had been evidently, but recently, husked, which operation had been performed more cleanly than if a native had done it. There was an opening at the eye-hole end of the shell of a somewhat regular oblong form, which measured 2 by 1½ inches, and was large enough to admit the powerful claws of the crab.[1] The white kernel, which had the firm consistence of that of the mature nut, had been scooped out to the extent of from 1 to 1½ inches around the aperture; small pieces of the kernel lay on the ground outside the nut, and others were floating about in the milk inside, of which the shell was about a fourth-part full.

I had, without a doubt, disturbed the *Birgus* in the middle of its meal; but, curiously enough, there were no cocoa-nut palms to be seen within fifty paces of the spot where the crab was found in its retreat. Not only had the shell been very recently husked, but it was evident, from the fresh condition of the milk and kernel, that an interval of less than a couple of hours had elapsed since the opening had been made. There was no possible explanation of the crab having got at the edible portion of the cocoa-nut, except through its own agency. The island is uninhabited, being only occasionally visited by fishing-parties of natives from St. Christoval, none of whom were on the island during the ship's stay. There was, therefore, the strongest presumptive evidence that the *Birgus* had not only husked the cocoa-nut, but had also broken the hole at the end, in order to get at the kernel.

I kept the crab alive on board on a diet of cocoa-nuts for three weeks, when, one morning, to my great disappointment, I found it dead. Other foods, such as bananas, were offered to it but were left untouched, and its appetite for cocoa-nuts continued unimpaired to

[1] This shell was presented to the Australian Museum, Sydney.

the last day of its life. Being desirous of observing the manner in which the husk was removed, I had a cocoa-nut with its husk placed in the coop in which the crab was kept. On one occasion the *Birgus* was surprised with the nut between its large claws ; but, notwithstanding that no other food was offered to it for a day and a half, it did not attempt to strip off the husk. So the operation was done for it, and a small hole was knocked in the top of the shell. On the following day I found the shell—a young and somewhat thin one—broken irregularly across the middle, with the soft white kernel already removed and eaten. It was afterwards found necessary to break the nuts for its daily food.

In 1884, when the " Lark " was in Bougainville Straits, three of these crabs were kept on board with the intention of taking them down to Sydney. Mr. W. Isabell, leading-stoker of the ship, looked well after them, as he had also done in the case of the previous crab, but within three or four weeks they had all died. The cocoa-nuts had to be husked and broken for them, as they were in vain tempted to do it for themselves. One crab, however, was frequently observed clasping between its claws a full-grown unhusked nut, the upper end of which showed deep grooves and dents from the blows of its claws ; and Mr. Isabell and I came to the conclusion that the coop, in which these crabs were placed, was too low to allow of the free play of the great claws.

My evidence alone would be sufficient to convict the *Birgus* of this offence : for an offender it would certainly be in the eyes of the owner of a plantation of cocoa-nut palms. I learned from Mr. Isabell that the first crab we had on board consumed, on the average, two cocoa-nuts in three days. A number of these crabs in a cocoa-nut plantation, might therefore prove a considerable pest: for, if this betokens the quantity of food which the *Birgus* consumes in a state of nature, a single crab in the course of twelve months would dispose of about 250 cocoa-nuts, which represent the annual production of three palms and between 20 and 30 quarts of oil.

As these crabs disliked observation, I was unable to gain much knowledge of their habits by watching. During the day-time they were sluggish, did not eat, and kept themselves in the further corner of the coop, as far from the light as possible. At night they moved about very actively and fed vigorously on the cocoa-nuts. The natives of the Shortlands, who were well-acquainted with the cocoa-nut eating habit of the *Birgus*, described to me the mode of

x

husking and breaking the nut, just as Mr. Liesk described it to Mr. Darwin. They esteem as an especial luxury the fat which gives the chief bulk to the abdomen of the crab.

The habit of the *Birgus*, when surprised away from its burrow, is not to turn round and run away, but to retreat in an orderly manner with its front to the foe. Having reached some root or trunk of a tree which protects in the rear its less perfectly armoured abdomen, it makes a regular stand, waves one of the long second pair of claws in the air, and courageously awaits the attack. The attitude of defence is worthy of remark. The two large claws are held up close together to defend the mouth and eyes, but with the pincers pointing downward—the posture reminding me of the guard for the head and face in sword-exercise. One of the long second pair of claws is planted firmly on the ground to give the crab additional support; whilst the other claw is raised in the air and moved up and down in a sparring fashion. The whole attitude of the *Birgus*, when on the defensive, is one of dogged and determined resistance. The big pincers that point downward are ready to seize anything which touches the unprotected under surface of the abdomen; but on account of the position of these claws in front of the eyes, it can only foresee attacks from above, and it therefore cannot ward off a sudden thrust directed against the abdomen, although it may afterwards inflict severe injuries on the aggressor.

There seems to be some doubt whether the *Birgus* ascends the tree to get the cocoa-nuts or whether it contents itself with those that have fallen. Almost every author who refers to this crab alludes to its climbing the tree, and it is also said to climb the pandanus. The testimony in support of its climbing powers is almost conclusive, yet Mr. Darwin was informed by Mr. Liesk that in Keeling Atoll the *Birgus* lives only on the fallen cocoa-nuts, and Mr. H. O. Forbes,[1] who has recently visited this island, confirms this statement.

My readers, after perusing the foregoing remarks, will agree with me that from the lack of actual observation on the part of the authors, who describe the cocoa-nut eating habit of this crab, there has been fair grounds for scepticism. Even now, we are but imperfectly acquainted with the mode of life of the *Birgus*, which is a subject I would commend to the attention of residents in the Indian and Pacific Oceans.

[1] " A Naturalist's Wanderings," etc. : London, 1885, p. 27.

I may add that the *Birgus* is partial to other kinds of fruits beside cocoa-nuts. Different writers mention candle-nuts, nutmegs, figs, and other rich and oily nuts and fruits. In some islands it would seem that the Pandanus fruit is its only diet; and for breaking open these tough fruits, its heavy claws are well adapted, though from personal experience, I should remark that the crab would have its strength and ingenuity taxed almost as much as in the case of the cocoa-nut.

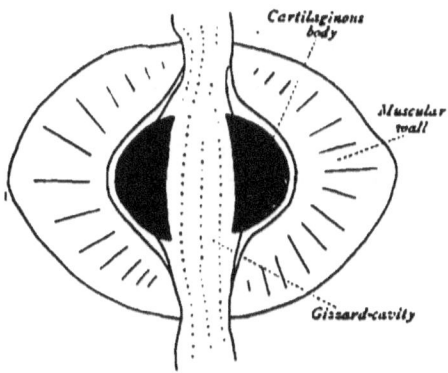

The handsome ground-pigeon, known as the Nicobar pigeon (*Geophilus nicobaricus*), is commonly observed in the wooded islets on the coral reefs of the Solomon Group. As I have remarked on page 293, this bird is probably instrumental in transporting from one locality to another the small hard seeds and fruits which the common fruit-pigeon (*Carpophaga*) refuses. That it is able to crack such hard seeds as those of the leguminous plant *Adenanthera pavonina*,[1] is shown by the fact that I have found these seeds cracked in the cavity of the gizzard, which is in its structure and mechanism a *veritable pair of nutcrackers*. In this bird the muscular stomach or gizzard is of a surprising thickness, and is provided with a very singular mechanical contrivance to assist its crushing power. As shown in the accompanying diagram, it is composed of two muscular halves, each having a maximum thickness of five-eighths of an inch and united with each other in front and behind by a stout distensible membrane, which is the proper wall of the organ. Developed in the horny epithelial lining membrane there are two cartilaginous bodies of hemispherical shape, one in each muscular segment of the gizzard, which measure about one-third of an inch in thickness and

---

[1] The Kuara tree of India, of whose hard seeds necklaces are made.

three-fourths of an inch in diameter. The outer or convex surface of each cartilaginous body fits into a cup-shaped cavity which is lined by a semi-cartilaginous membrane, the whole constituting a "ball-and-socket" joint with well lubricated surfaces. The two surfaces of this pseudo-articulation are capable of easy movement on each other, being retained in close apposition by the attachment to the subjacent tissues of the horny epithelial lining membrane in which the cartilaginous body is developed. The inner or free surface of each hemispherical body, that which looks into the gizzard cavity, is somewhat concave, and projects a little above the surface of the lining membrane ; it is much harder than the opposite convex side of the cartilage and has almost the consistence of bone, the arrangement of the cells into densely packed rows with but little intervening matrix indicating an approach towards ossification.

The firm consistence of these hemispherical cartilages combined with the mechanism of a moveable articulation must greatly assist the already powerful muscular walls of the gizzard ; but there is an additional factor in the crushing power in the constant presence of a small quartz pebble, usually about half-an-inch across. With such a apparatus, I can well conceive that very hard seeds and nuts may be broken, as in the case of the seeds of *Adenanthera pavonina* already alluded to. The Nicobar pigeon is in fact possessed of a nut-cracking mechanism in its gizzard, by which nuts like those of our hazel tree would be cracked with comparative ease.

With reference to the small quartz pebbles found in the gizzards of these birds, I should remark that there is usually only one present, and that it varies in weight between 30 and 60 grains. I was sometimes able to say where the pigeon had obtained its pebble. Thus, in Faro Island the bird often selects one of the bipyramidal quartz crystals, which occur in quantities in the beds of the streams in the northern part of the island, where they have been washed out of the quartz-porphyry of the district. In other instances the pebble seems to have been originally a small fragment of chalcedonic quartz, such as composes some of the flakes and worked flints that are found in the soil which has been disturbed for cultivation. Sometimes the pebble is of greasy quartz ; and now and then in the absence of quartz the bird has chosen a pebble of some hard volcanic rock. It is a singular circumstance that although these pigeons frequent coral islets where they can easily find hard pebbles of coral-rock, they prefer the quartz pebbles which are of comparatively rare occurrence. I never found any calcareous pebble in their gizzards, and was often at a loss to explain how the bird was able to ascertain for itself the different degree of hardness between the two pebbles, when the quartz was of the dull white variety . . . . . I learn from a recent work on New Guinea by the missionaries, Messrs. Chalmers and Gill, that inside the gizzard of each Goura pigeon there is a good-sized pebble much prized by the natives as a charm against spear-thrusts and club blows.[1] The Goura pigeon resembles the Nicobar pigeon in habits ; and I think it probable that its gizzard will be found to present a similar structure and mechanism for cracking nuts and hard seeds. The common fruit pigeons (*Carpophaga*) of the Solomon Islands, living as they do on soft fleshy fruits, and rejecting the hard seeds and kernels, have no peculiar structure of the gizzard, the walls of which are comparatively thin, and are thrown into permanent rugæ somewhat warty on the surface.

One of the most familiar birds in these islands is the "bush-hen," which belongs to the family of the mound-builders (*Megapodiidæ*). They bury their eggs in the sand at a depth of between three and four feet. On one occasion in the island of Faro, Lieutenant Heming and his party found eight eggs, in different stages of hatching, thus buried : they were scattered about in the sand ; and according to the account of the natives only one egg was laid by each bird. The eggs are sometimes found on the surface of the sand. The young birds are able to fly short distances soon after they are hatched. One that was brought on board astonished us all by flying some thirty or forty yards from the ship and then returning to the rigging.

The account recently published by Mr. H. Pryer of his visit to the birds' nest caves of Borneo [2] has opened up the discussion as to the nature of the substance of which the edible bird's nest is composed. Many and varied have been the surmises as to the source of this material ; but nearly all of them have been based on mere speculation, and have been relegated to the limbo of sea-tales. Amongst the earlier explanations, I may allude to those which have been given by early writers. The swiftlets (*Collocalia*), which build their nests in this extraordinary fashion, were considered to gather a gelatinous material from the ocean-foam, or from the bodies of holothurians, or from the skin of the sun-fish. The Chinese fisher-

---

[1] " Work and Adventure in New Guinea " (p. 317): London, 1885.

[2] Proceedings of the Zoological Society for 1884 : p. 532.

men assured Kæmpfer that their nests were composed of the flesh of the great poulpe. A more probable explanation, however, was found by Rumphius in the occurrence on the sea-coasts of a soft almost cartilaginous plant which he with confidence asserted was the material from which these swiftlets constructed their nests; but subsequently this naturalist inclined to the opinion that the substance of which the edible birds' nests are composed is merely a secretionary product. In these two views of Rumphius we have the two sides of the controversy very much as it at present stands. On the one hand, there are those who hold that this substance is a secretionary product: on the other hand, the opinion is held that the nest is constructed of a vegetable matter, usually resulting from the growth of a microscopic alga, which is found in the caves and on the faces of the cliffs where the nests occur. All the weight of experiment and of actual observation tends to negative the view of the vegetable origin of this substance. Sir Everard Home in 1817 declared his opinion that certain peculiar gastric glands, which he found in one of these birds, secreted the mucus of which the nest was formed. In 1859, Dr. Bernstein,[1] after having carefully studied the habits of the birds in question, came to the conclusion that their nests are formed from the secretion of certain salivary glands which are abnormally developed during the nest-building season. M. Trécul, who held the same opinion, showed that the bird constructs its nest by means of a mucus which flows abundantly from its beak at the pairing time.[2] This last view is strongly supported by Mr. Layard, who unhesitatingly pronounces his opinion that these swiftlets build their nests from the secretionary products of their own salivary glands.[3] However, when Mr. Pryer visited in March, 1884, the birds' nest caves in British North Borneo, he considered that he had found the source of the material of which the nests were composed in the occurrence of a "fungoid growth," which incrusted the rock in damp places, and ' which, when fresh, resembled half-melted gum ·tragacanth. Without at present expressing an opinion opinion as to the validity of the inference Mr. Pryer drew from his observations in these caves, I may observe that the "fungoid growth" has been determined by Mr. George Murray,[4] of the Botanical Department of the British Museum, to be the result of the growth

[1] Journ. für Ornithologie, 1859, pp. 112-115; also Proceed. Zoolog. Soc., 1885, p. 610.
[2] "A General System of Botany," by Le Maout and Decaisne : London, 1873, p. 983.
[3] "Nature," Nov. 27th, 1884.
[4] Proc. Zoolog. Soc., 1884 : p. 532.

of a microscopic alga, a species, probably new, of *Glœocapsa*; whilst the edible nests from these caves, according to a chemical and microscopical examination made by Mr. J. R. Green,[1] have been shown to be formed in the great mass of *mucin*, which is the chief constituent of the mucous secretions of animals. After examining various specimens of edible nests from other localities, Mr. Green subsequently confirmed the results of his first experiments. The nest-substance, as he unhesitatingly states, is composed of *mucin*, or of a body closely related to it.[2] So far, therefore, there would appear to be but little evidence to support the view of Mr. Pryer that the species of alga, which he found incrusting the rock in the vicinity of the Borneo caves, supplied the material for the construction of the nests of the swiftlets. However, before proceeding to state my own opinion on the matter, I will refer briefly to my observations in the Solomon Islands relating to this question.

A species of *Collocalia*, which usually frequents inaccessible sea-caves and cliffs, is frequently to be observed on the coasts of the islands of this group. The natives of Treasury Island call this bird " kin-kin ; " but they have no knowledge of the nutrient qualities of the substance of which it builds its nest, and they were much amused when I told them of its being a Chinese luxury. I only came upon the nests of this bird on one occasion, and that was in some caves on Oima Atoll in Bougainville Straits. A description of these caves will be here unnecessary. As in the instance of the birds of the Borneo caverns, these swiftlets shared their retreats with a number of large bats, the accumulation of whose droppings had produced a thick reddish-brown deposit on the floors of the caves. The nests, which were formed for the most part of fibres derived evidently from the vegetable drift [3] at the mouths of the caves, were thickly incrusted with the gelatinous incrustation which projected as winglets from the sides and fastened them to the rock.

A reddish soft gelatinous incrustation occurred on the faces of some of the cliffs in the vicinity of the caves. It was composed of an aggregation of the cells of a microscopic unicellular alga which measure $\frac{1}{2500}$ of an inch in diameter. Unfortunately the specimens of this growth which I collected have been mislaid, but there can be little doubt that it is similar to the "fungoid growth " which Mr.

[1] Proc. Zool. Soc., 1884, p. 532.

[2] ' Nature," Dec. 11th, 1884 and May, 27th, 1886.

[3] The husks of pandanus seeds more particularly.

Pryer describes in connection with the Borneo caves, and which, through the kindness of Mr. George Murray, I had the opportunity of seeing at the British Museum. On the faces of the coral lime-stone cliffs of some islands, such as on the east coast of Santa Anna, a like growth occurs in considerable quantity. In its freshest condition, it may be described as a reddish-yellow, gum-like sub-stance forming a layer ¼ to ⅛ of an inch in thickness. Where it incrusts the overhanging face of a cliff, it is more fluid in consistence and sometimes hangs in little pendulous masses, one to two inches in length, the extremities of which are often distended with water. This alga decomposes the hard coral limestone, making the surface of the rock soft and powdery. All stages in the growth of this substance may be observed. The older portions are very dark in colour and have a tough consistence; and in the final stage it occurs as a black powder covering the rock surface. On examining this alga with the microscope, I found it to be formed almost entirely of granular matter apparently resulting from the death of the cells; whilst the presence of a few cellular bodies alone gave me an indica-tion of its true nature.

From my observations relating to the subject of the edible bird's nest, it may be therefore inferred that in the Solomon Islands, as in Borneo, the occurrence of these nests is associated with the presence of a protophytic alga, which incrusts the rocks of the locality as a gelatinous or gum-like substance. Whether or not the birds em-ploy this material in forming their nests, is a question which would appear to have been already answered in the negative; but it seems to me that those who hold that this material is used for this pur-pose might justly claim that the final judgment should be suspended, until a chemical examination of this vegetable substance has been made with the object of determining whether it might not yield a material closely resembling *mucin*. Amongst the nitrogenous constituents of plants occurs the so-called *vegetable albumen*, which in its chemical composition and in its behaviour with re-agents does not differ materially from the *blood-albumen* of the animal organism, of which in fact it is the source. In suggesting, there-fore, that a *vegetable mucin* may be found in this low plant-growth, I do not pass beyond the bounds of probability.[1]

Small scorpions came under my notice in Faro Island. They are not usually more than 1¼ in length and occur in narrow clefts of

[1] *Vide* a letter by the writer in "Nature," June 3rd, 1886.

rocks and in the crevices of trees. I was stung by one on the thumb, but the pain was trifling and soon passed away.[1]

A species of *Iulus* or Millipede, which attains a length of from 6 to 7 inches, is commonly found in the eastern islands of the Solomon Group on the trunks of fallen trees and amongst decaying vegetable débris. It is often to be seen amongst the rotting leaves that have gathered inside the bases of the fronds of the Bird's-nest Fern (*Asplenium nidus*). These Myriapods seem to be less frequent in the islands of Bougainville Straits towards the opposite end of the group, as I do not remember seeing any large *Iuli* in that locality: their place appears to be taken by another Myriapod, apparently a *Polydesmus*, growing to a length of $2\frac{1}{4}$ inches, which I found amongst decaying vegetation at all elevations up to 1900 feet above the sea, as on the summit of Faro Island. But to return to the *Iuli*, I should remark that this genus of Myriapods evidently possesses some means of transportal across wide tracts of sea, since, amongst other islands similarly situated, it is found in Tristan da Cunha,[2] in the South Atlantic Ocean, and I have found it in the Seychelles, in the Indian Ocean. The habits of these Millipedes would render it highly probable that they have reached the oceanic islands on vegetable drift, such as floating logs. It is, however, a noteworthy circumstance that they do not seem to be able to withstand immersion in sea-water for any length of time. In experimenting on the Solomon Island species, I found that they were able to survive an hour-and-a-half's complete immersion in sea-water, but that an immersion of three hours killed them. One individual, out of several experimented on, survived for twelve hours after it was taken out, but only in a half lifeless condition.[3] It may, therefore, have been that the *Iulus* has been transported to oceanic islands by such agencies as canoes and ships, rather than by means of floating trees.[4]

Like other species of the genus, the Solomon Island *Iulus* exhales a very pungent and disagreeable odour, which is caused by an acrid fluid secreted by small vesicles, of which each segment of the

[1] Specimens of these scorpions were given by me to the Australian Museum, Sydney.
[2] Moseley's "Naturalist on the Challenger," p. 134.
[3] This species of *Iulus* was able to sustain a longer submersion in fresh-water, without apparently any injurious effects. Those experimented on recovered after being kept under water for four hours, but died after a submersion of six hours.
[4] As bearing on this point, it might be interesting to determine whether these large *Iuli* occur on islands far from land which are believed never to have been inhabited.

body contains a pair.[1]   On holding my nose for a moment over the
mouth of a bottle, containing two of these large Millipedes, I experienced a strong sensation in the nasal passages, reminding me
much of the effects of an inhalation of chlorine gas.   I had previously learned from resident traders that these Millipedes have a
habit of ejecting an acrid fluid when disturbed, which, if it entered
the eye, was liable to cause acute inflammation; and the instance
was related' to me of the captain of some ship, trading in these
islands, who lost the sight of one of his eyes from this cause.   Mr.
C. F. Wood learned from the natives of St. Christoval, in 1873, that
these Myriapods "could squirt out a poisonous juice, which was
dangerous if it happened to touch one's eye;" but he adds, "there
seemed no great probability of their doing this."[2]   However, I
usually found that native testimony, in such matters, was very reliable; and in the instance of this reputed habit of the *Iulus*, my
personal experience has convinced me of its reality.   Whilst hand-
ling one of these Millipedes as it lay on the trunk of a fallen tree in
Ugi Island, I felt a sudden smarting sensation in the right eye,
caused apparently by some fluid ejected into it.   Remembering the
injurious effect attributed to this habit of the *Iulus*, I at once
plunged my head under the water of a stream, in which I happened
to be standing up to my waist, and I kept my eye open to wash
away the offending fluid.   During the remainder of the day, there
was an uncomfortable feeling in the eye and somewhat increased
lachrymation; but on the following morning these effects had disappeared.   At the time of this occurrence, my face was removed
about a foot from the Millipede; and, although I was uncertain
from what part of the body the fluid was ejected, I did not care,
under the circumstances, to continue the inquiry.

Amongst the first living creatures to greet the visitor as he lands
on the beach of a coral island in the Pacific, is a small species of
Hermit-Crab, belonging to the genus *Coenobita*, which frequents the
beach in great numbers.   The crab withdraws itself just within the
mouth of the shell, where it forms a perfect operculum, by means
mainly of the large flattened *chelæ* of the left great claw which is
arched over by the left leg of the third pair, whilst the right claw
and the right leg of the second pair serve to complete the shield

---

[1] Hoeven's Zoology. (Eng. edit.) Vol. I., p. 201.

[2] "A Yachting Cruise in the South Seas," p. 131. (London, 1875.)

The most plucky and pugnacious of these little crabs are those which occupy cast-off *Nerita* shells, a character which probably arises from their consciousness of the solid strength of the home they have chosen: and, strange to say, the tiny bosses on the surfaces of the large pincers, which are outermost in the improvised operculum, resemble similar markings on the outer side of the operculum of the *Nerita* (*N. marmorata*, Hombr and Jacq), whose shell they often inhabit. Mr. Darwin[1] observed that the different species of hermit-crabs, which he found on the Keeling Islands in the Indian Ocean, used always certain kind of shells; but I could not satisfy myself that such was the case in the instance of the Solomon Island hermit-crabs. In the case of the common beach species of *Coenobita*, I found, after carefully examining a number of individuals to satisfy myself of their being of the same species, that shells of the genera *Turbo, Nerita, Strombus, Natica, Distorsia. Truncatella, Terebra, Melania*, &c., &c., contained the same species of *Coenobita*, whether the individual was large enough to occupy a *Turbo* shell of the size of a walnut or sufficiently small to select the tiny shell of the *Truncatella* for its home. Another species of the same genus prefers usually the vicinity of the beach; but it may occur at heights up to 200 feet above the sea. It is rather larger than the beach species, and differs amongst other characters in the more globose form of the large claws and in the greater relative size of the left one. It occupies shells of different kinds, such as those of *Nerita, Turbo*, &c. A still larger species, which frequents the vicinity of the beach, usually selects *Turbo* shells, apparently because of their larger size. All the other species of *Coenobita*, which I met with, used, when I touched them, to withdraw themselves within their shells and close them up at once with their claws; but this kind, when I caught hold of the *Turbo* shell that it carried, left the shell behind in my fingers with apparent unconcern and crawled leisurely away, displaying, somewhat indecorously, the rudimentary plates on the back of its abdomen. These are the plates that attain their greatest development in the Cocoa-nut Crab *(Birgus latro)*, which is thus able to dispense with a shell altogether, The greatest heights at which I found hermit-crabs were in the island of Faro on the two highest peaks, which are elevated respectively 1600 and 1900 feet above the sea. In both these localities, the crab had reached the very summit and could not have climbed higher. The

[1] "Journal of the Beagle," p. 457.

species was apparently different from, though closely allied to, the
common beach species, and frequented the shells of a land-snail
(*Helix*). I was indebted to Lieutenant Heming for directing my
attention to the hermit-crab, found 1900 feet above the sea. It
appears to me likely that these hermit-crabs will be found at much
greater heights in this group, since, in this island, their ambition to
rise had carried them up as far as they could go.

Other species of hermit-crabs, that are common in these islands,
belong to the genus *Pagurus*. They are conspicuously distinguished
from the species of *Coenobita*, above described, by their first pair of
claws, which are small and weak and ill-adapted for defensive purposes. For this reason, these species are less able to look after
themselves; and since they cannot form the operculum-like shield
with their claws at the mouth of the shell, they always choose shells
which will permit of their retiring well within it, so as to be out of
the reach of their enemies. Some species are found in the stream-
courses and in the brackish water near their mouths, when they
often frequent cast-off *Melania* shells. Other species (?) prefer the
sea-water on the reef-flats. I noticed one individual that displayed
its eccentricity of disposition, in selecting, as its abode, the hollow
tube of a small water-logged stick, about six inches long, which it
dragged about after it during its peregrinations, and into which it
retreated when alarmed. On one occasion, I observed a large
Dolium shell, moving briskly about in a pool of salt-water, which,
on picking up, I found to be tenanted by a *Pagurus*, so ridiculously
small, in comparison with the size of the shell, that when frightened
it retreated to the very uppermost whorl, and, notwithstanding the
wide mouth of the shell, could not be seen. So light was the weight
of the crab, that, on account of the buoyancy of its shell, it floated
lightly on the surface of the water, on which I had placed it with
the mouth of the shell uppermost, and was blown by a slight breeze
across a pool of water, some twenty yards in width. While it was
afloat, the shrewd little occupant retired to the innermost recess of
its home; but as soon as the shell had grounded, it protruded its
head and pincers and endeavoured to overturn the shell, which it
finally succeeded in accomplishing.

In the case of these two genera of hermit-crabs, *Coenobita* and
Pagurus, it was interesting to notice the relation existing between
the defensive capabilities of the crab, and the relative size of the
shell it selected as its home. The *Pagurus*, with its weak slender

pincers, chooses large shells within which it can retire well out of reach when alarmed. The *Coenobita*, with its stout pincers, prefers shells much smaller, relatively speaking, and ensconces itself snugly in the body whorl, forming an operculum with its claws. As the hermit-crab, *Coenobita*, crawls along the dry sand of a beach, it leaves behind it characteristic pinnate tracks which may be often traced for several feet. The lateral markings are produced by the claws and legs working on each side of the shell; whilst a central groove is formed by the weight of the shell itself. As shown by the arrow in the diagram, the lateral markings point in the direction of the course which the hermit-crab has taken. Sometimes only a single row of lateral tracks accompanies the grooves produced by the shell. Such

markings were produced by a hermit-crab when frightened by my approach. It turned its front towards me, and crawled backwards, by working most of his claws and legs on one side of the shell. In the case of the larger hermit-crabs, which are much less frequent on the beach, each limb produces a distinct print on the sand; but with the small species of *Coenobita* which infests the beach, each lateral marking, as shown in the diagram, is produced by a single movement of the claws situated on the same side of the shell. The hermit-crabs only leave their tracks on the dry loose sand. One individual, that I placed on sand, still wet from the retreating tide, crawled along without leaving any impression. I have described these impressions with some care, as they bear on the origin of the surface-markings of rocks of shallow-water formation, a subject recently discussed in the geological world. It is highly probable that some of the larger and heavier forms of the Anomura (and, in fact, of the Decapoda generally) would produce prints such as I have here described, both on mud-flats left dry by the tide, and on the soft bottom in shallow depths. A cast of the impressions thus produced would have an unmistakeable plant-like form.

Whilst examining the island of Simbo, I noticed some singular Medusæ in a small mangrove-swamp, which is inclosed in the low point that forms the south shore of the anchorage. Numbers of these organisms of a large size (8 or 9 inches across the umbrella), and of a dirty-white colour, were lying on the mud with their

tentacles, uppermost in depths of from one to three feet of water.
I was struck by the handsome mass of arborescent tentacles which
they displayed, and by the peculiarity of their lying upside-down.
The dark mud which formed the bottom of the swamp was composed of decayed vegetable matter, confervoid growths, diatoms,
and a few infusoria: but when I raised up these Medusæ, I found
underneath each a patch of white sand corresponding with the outline of the organism, but completely concealed by the umbrella when
the Medusa lay in its usual position. The sand was derived from
corals, shells, and the volcanic rocks of the island; and the light
patches formed a marked contrast with the dark mud around. I
was unable to find any satisfactory explanation of these curious
patches of sand; and I, therefore, proceeded to interrogate the
Medusæ on the subject by watching them, but to no purpose. So I
had my revenge by turning them all over on their tentacles, when
each one immediately began to contract its umbrella in a most
methodical fashion, and, after swimming a short distance, deliber-
ately resumed its former position of tentacles upward. I had an
extensive experience of mangrove-swamps after we left Simbo;
but these self-willed Medusæ never came under my notice again.[1]

With regard to these Medusæ, I should remark that they belong
to a species of *Polyclonia,* and are classed amongst the Scypho-
Medusæ.[2] Two species of *Polyclonia* seem to be known, *P. frondosa*
(Agassiz) and *P. Mertensii* (Brandt), the first found in the Florida
seas, and the latter in the Carolines. I am inclined to think that
the Solomon Island species is more nearly allied to *P. Mertensii.*
Both species, however, have similar habits, lying on the mud of
mangrove-swamps, with their tentacles uppermost.

The singular habits of these Scypho-Medusæ were noticed by
Brandt in 1838. They have since been remarked by Mosely[3] in
the Philippines, and by Archer[4] in the West Indies. L. Agassiz in
his "Contributions to the Natural History of the United States,"
describes and figures the Florida species (*Polyclonia frondosa*); and

---

[1] I referred to the habits of these Medusæ in "Nature," Nov. 9th, 1882.

[2] I compared my notes with the description and figures given by Agassiz in his "Contrib.
Nat. Hist. U.S.A." (1862: vols. iii. and iv.). In the Solomon Island species, the dendriform
mass resolves itself into 8 principal branches, each ramose, and, all united at their bases by
a common membrane. The umbrella, which was finely lobed or crenulated at its margin,
displayed about 40 radiating canals, each communicating by an anastomosing network with
the canal on either side of it.

[3] Mosely's "Notes by a Naturalist," p. 404.

[4] "Nature" Aug. 4th, 1881.

some additional notes on its habits have been made by A. Agassiz, to whose communication in "Nature" (Sept. 29th, 1881) I have been much indebted.

Whilst we lay at anchor in Treasury Harbour, in April, 1884, a cetacean, unknown to the natives and to ourselves, got partly stranded in the shallow water, and was captured by the villagers. It was nine feet long, and possessed this remarkable character that, although no teeth showed through the gums, each lower jaw possessed a short, conical, hollow tooth an inch long, placed at the anterior extremity. I obtained the head from the natives, and placed it in a safe place, as I thought; but when we returned to Treasury a few weeks after, I found only portions of the skull with the lower jaw-bones, the wild pigs having held a feast over it. The remains, however, together with my notes and a sketch by Lieutenant Leeper were sent to the British Museum. I there learned that it is a species of Ziphius, probably unknown.

The Solomon Islanders believe in the existence of anthropoid apes in the interiors of the large islands, regarding them, however, like the Dyaks of Borneo in the case of the Orang-utan, as "wild men of the woods." In Malaita they are said to be 4½ to 5 feet high, and to come down in troops to make raids on the banana plantations. Captain Macdonald informed me that the natives allege that one of these apes was caught, and, after being kept for some time, escaped. Taki, the St. Christoval chief, told Mr. Stephens that he had seen one of these apes, and pointed out the locality. Tanowaio, the Ugi chief, also made a similar statement. In Guadalcanar, they are believed to live in the trees, and to attack men. Dr. Codrington refers to the prevalence of these beliefs throughout Melanesia (Journ. Anthrop. Inst., vol. x. p. 261). Such beliefs, as experience has shown in the case of the Gorilla and other anthropoids, have undoubtedly some foundation; but whether these mysterious animals are apes is quite another question.

CHAPTER XVI.

LAND AND FRESH-WATER SHELLS.

DURING my numerous excursions in these islands, I had in the majority of instances to follow up the stream-courses in order to examine their geological structure. I had therefore good opportunities in these regions of making a collection of the fresh-water shells, which, together with the land shells I collected, formed a total of between sixty and seventy species, amongst which there were 11 new species and at least 5 new varieties, whilst about 14 would appear to have been never previously recorded from the Solomon Islands, and there were in addition several from new localities in the group. The collection was sent to the British Museum and was examined and described by Mr. E. Smith, to whose paper on the subject[1] I am indebted for my acquaintance with the shells in question, and through whose kindness I have been thus enabled to supplement my other observations in these islands. A list of the shells with the descriptions of the new species is given on page 344. For its size, my collection presented a large amount of novelty, coming as it did from a region the land and fresh-water shells of which were previously considered to be fairly known. There can be no doubt, however, that in the Solomon Islands the conchologist has much work that remains to be done. Not only are the higher regions of the larger islands, entirely unexplored, but it would appear from the collections made up to the present date in this large group, that particular species may be not only confined to a special sub-group of islands but may be restricted to a single island, and that other species more widely distributed through the group may be represented in each island and in different districts of the larger islands by different varieties.

[1] "On a collection of shells from the Solomon Islands" by Edgar A. Smith. (Proceedings of the Zoological Society: June 2nd, 1885.) This paper is illustrated with two coloured plates of the new shells.

Had I been aware of the extent of the influence of locality in this region, I might have made my collection of greater value. It would therefore seem necessary for future collectors in this group to make in every small island and in different districts of the larger islands special independent collections, disregarding the fact that they may have apparently met with the same shell very frequently before, because many of the varieties and some of the species can only be distinguished by the practised eye of the specialist, and a new locality for a previously well-known species may be often unwittingly found.

As an instance of the unexpected results, which may fall to the lot of others in this group, I may here add, that out of eleven land and fresh-water shells that I collected in the small island of Santa Anna, which is only 2½ miles in length, four were new species, and besides there were some new varieties. The stations of these four species may be suggestive. Two of them—*Helix* (*Videna*) *sanctæ annæ* and *Helix* (*nanina*) *solidiuscula*—were generally found on the trunks of the cocoa-nut palms at the coast; whilst the other two occurred in situations far more likely to yield new species, *Melania sanctæ annæ* being obtained from a small stream in the interior of the island, and *Melania guppyi* being found dead in the stomach and intestines of a fish that frequents the fresh-water lake of Wailava. This last shell would appear to live in the deeper parts of the lake, as I only found one living specimen, all the others being obtained from the stomach and intestines of these fish. Mr. Smith describes it as "a very remarkable and distinct species." Its length is about 1¼ inches; and its sharp-pointed spire was to be sometimes seen protruding through the vent of the fish, which evidently digests the animal and ejects the shell. These fish were usually 9 or 10 inches long; but the full-grown shells were found also in fish half this size, when the relation between the length of the shell and the size of the fish was truly alarming. Since the little fish actually swallow sharp pointed shells measuring a fifth of their own length and pass them out through the vent after they have digested the animal, we must credit them with a remarkable capacity for adapting their diet to circumstances.

To exemplify the variation which some species of shells display in this group, I will take the instance of *Helix* (*Geotrochus*) *cleryi*, Récluz. This species is probably distributed through the whole group; but considerable variation prevails in different islands,

Amongst the several forms which I obtained, three were named as
new varieties, var. *meridionalis* from Santa Anna, var. *simboana* from
Simbo or Eddystone Island, and var. *septentrionalis* from the islands
of Bougainville Straits, the localities of the two last varieties being
only 80 miles apart.   Mr. Smith remarks that this species is " subject
to considerable variation in size, colour, and form, apparently resulting from difference of habitat. . . . .   Whether these several
varieties should take specific rank is questionable, for, although there
is a considerable difference between the extreme forms, even in the
series of nearly one hundred specimens under examination, the
gradual transition from one form to another is observable."

Amongst the more singular in appearance of the land shells, I
may refer to the large *Bulimus (B. cleryi)* which I found on the
north coast of St. Christoval.   It attains a length of four inches.   I
was never able to get a living specimen, as they are said by the
natives to live in the foliage of the high trees.   The specimens
which I obtained were empty shells which the natives of the Koofeh
district on the north coast of St. Christoval are in the habit of
throwing into heaps, each man when he picks up a shell throwing it
into the next heap he passes.   I was unable to learn the reason of
this practice and the natives did not seem willing to tell me. . . . .
Two other *Bulimi* I commonly met with.   One was the pretty *Bulimus
miltocheilus* (Reeve), which, when the animal is young and the shell
delicate, has a greenish-yellow hue resembling the colour of the
leaves it feeds upon : as it grows older the shell becomes thicker and
stronger, and in proportion as there is less need for protective resemblance, the greenish-yellow hue fades away, leaving a dull white colour
behind.   This species is found in St. Christoval and the adjacent
islands.   The other *Bulimus (B. founaki,* Homb. Jacq.) which I
found in Faro Island, Bougainville Straits, and which had been only
previously obtained at Isabel Island, attains a length of rather under
three inches.

I come now to refer to the fresh-water shells of these regions.
Stated in their order of frequency, the *Neritinæ, Melaniæ,* and *Navicellæ* are the common fresh-water shells of the e islands.   The *Neritina*
were especially interesting to me.   They abound in the streams :
some of them preferring the moist rocks above the water, others
finding their home in the waters of a quiet pool, whilst others, like
the *Navicellæ,* prefer to buffet the full rush of the torrent.   An
important feature with reference to these fresh-water Nerites or

Neritinœ is their wide dispersal. " Some of these species "—as Mr.
Smith remarks in respect of those in my collection—" range not only
through most of the islands of the Solomon Group, but have a considerably wider distribution." Thus, *Neritina subsulcata* (Sowerby)
and *N. cornea* (Linné), are not only found in the Solomon Islands,
but also occur in the Philippines : *N. macgillivrayi* (Reeve) and *N.
petiti* (Récluz) alike exist in the Fiji and in the Solomon Groups ;
while *N. porcata* (Gould) has been found in Samoa and in Fiji as
well as in the opposite extremities of the group with which I am at
present concerned. Being interested in the question of the mode of
dispersal of these Nerites, I made the following experiment to test
their powers of sustaining submersion in salt-water. · One individual
belonging to the species *Neritina subsulcata*[1]—a species which is
also found as above stated in the Philippines, and at the same time
is the most widely dispersed fresh-water Nerite in the Solomon
Group—survived a submersion of twelve hours ; but not one out of
a dozen individuals was found alive after a submersion of five days,
although the water was changed from time to time. The result was
a surprise to me, as I inferred from the result of Baron Aucapi-
taine's experiments as related by Mr. Darwin,[2] that their close-fitting
stony *opercula* would have enabled them to resist the action of salt-
water. Their death could have been scarcely due to want of food,
since I have kept shells of this species for several months on a very
scanty diet, and since the powers of endurance of other fresh-water
shells are well known. The matter passed out of my mind until
after my arrival in England, when Mr. Smith put the question to me,
as to their mode of dispersal. I then remembered that their calcareous egg-capsules, which are so commonly seen on the rocky sides of
the streams, are in all probability sufficiently thick to resist the
action of salt-water. Here is therefore a probable mode of dispersal,
and I see it is one which Mr. Smith refers to as such in his paper.
These egg-capsules " if attached to floating timber, might be carried
to considerable distances." They are often to be observed on the
outside of the shells of living *Navicellæ*, and I have seen them on the
backs of the valves of a *Unio* which I discovered in the Shortland
Islands.

One common feature of these fresh-water shells, whether

. [1] In his paper Mr. Smith refers to the species experimented on as *N. cornea* : but in my
own list he named a shell belonging to one of the *Neritinæ* in question as *N. subsulcata*.
[2] *Cyclostoma elegans* was the species tested : *vide* " Origin of Species," p. 353; 6th edit. ·

Neritinœ, Navicellœ, or *Melaniœ,* is the extensive erosion of the apices
and surrounding parts of the shells. In some instances I have
noticed that almost the entire exterior of the shell has been extensively eroded, particularly in the case of *Neritina subsulcata,* but I
always found that the erosion was greatest in non-calcareous districts,
where the free carbonic acid in the water is not all consumed in the
solution of the limestone rocks. In volcanic islands the erosion of
the fresh-water shells is greater than in islands of calcareous formation; and in streams, which, like those of the north coast of St.
Christoval, flow in the upper portion of their course through a district
of volcanic rocks and in the lower portion through a district of
calcareous rocks, the same difference in the degree of erosion may be
observed. I learn from a recent work by Professor Semper[1] that it
is the boring of a minute fungus which first exposes the calcareous
substance to the action of the carbonic acid, and that the mechanical
action of the stream in forming tiny whirl-pools in the cavity
probably assists in the erosion.

　There are two common species of *Neritina* in these islands which
I often confounded, viz., *N. subsulcata* and *N. cornea;* and I learn
from Mr. Smith's paper that these two species very closely approach
each other. They, however, are usually to be found in different
stations, *N. cornea* occurring on the trunks of palms and other trees
away from the streams,[2] and *N. subsulcata* preferring the moist rocky
sides of the streams a foot or so above the water.[3] Now and then
they may be found encroaching on each other's domain; for I have
found them together on the trunks and branches of areca palms and
tree-ferns in low lying moist districts, whilst, as at Choiseul Bay, I
found them together in the streams.[4] Now it is a significant circumstance, that the specimen of *N. cornea* in my collection which
was found by Mr. Smith to make the nearest approach to *N. subsulcata* was one which I obtained from a stream in Choiseul Bay. It
had, in this case, not only intruded on the station of *N. subsulcata,*
but had also assumed some of the distinctive characters of that
species. It, therefore, seems to me probable that a graduated series
of the shells of these two species might be formed, which would pre-

[1] "The Natural Conditions of Existence, etc : " London 1881 : p. 212, circâ.

[2] In St. Christoval I found this species on one occasion 150 feet above the nearest stream.

[3] This species often takes to the water. Some individuals that I kept alive on board used
to spend a quarter of an hour at a time in the water eating voraciously all the while.

[4] According to Prof. Semper, these two species in the Philippines live a large portion of
the year high up on the trees in mangrove swamps. (Ibid.)

sent the stages of transition from the one species to the other. If this be possible, then I would suggest that the fresh-water Nerite (*Neritina subsulcata*) may have been transformed into the tree Nerite (*Neritina cornea*) in the following manner.

I have already referred to the circumstance that in the higher portions of the St. Christoval streams, where the rocks are entirely volcanic, the fresh-water shells—and I may here add, especially those of *Neritina subsulcata*—suffer much more erosion than do shells of the same species in the lower parts of the streams where they flow through calcareous districts. Now, the geological structure of this island being mainly ancient volcanic rocks incrusted near the coast by recent calcareous formations, the time will come when these calcareous envelopes will have been entirely stripped off by denudation. How this will influence the Nerites of the streams may be thus explained. At present the normal characters of the species are preserved in the calcareous portions of the streams; but when all the calcareous rocks have been stripped off by denudation, the Nerite through its whole lifetime will be subjected to that extensive process of erosion, which now often denudes almost the entire surface of the shells of those individuals that live in the volcanic portion of the stream's course. Here, Natural Selection may step in to favour the survival of any slight variation that makes the Nerite more suited to lead an entirely arboreal existence. Such a geological agency may in truth lead finally to the expulsion of the Nerite from the stream's course. Varieties will survive only in proportion to their capability of adapting themselves to the new condition; and they alone will perpetuate their kind until a tree Nerite of distinct specific character is produced. . . . . On this reasoning, tree Nerites ought to be more numerous in islands of volcanic formation; but this is a point on which I cannot pronounce from the lack of sufficient evidence.[1]

According to Professor Semper, we have in *Navicella* " a modified form of *Neritina*," which genus it resembles in all essential anatomical characters, but " by long inurement to living in rushing mountain streams, it has had its shell modified in the way most suited to those conditions, while the *operculum*, in consequence of long disuse, has become a peculiar degenerate or rudimentary organ."[2]

[1] Prof. Semper's observations in the Philippines bear on this matter. ("Natural Conditions of Existence," &c., p. 188.)
Ibid, p. 212.

The growth of the fresh-water Nerites would appear to be slow.
I kept a young individual of *Neritina subsulcata* for seven months
in a bottle partly filled with rain-water, and supplied it with decaying leaves for food which it used to eat. Its weight was 37 grains
both at the beginning and the end of the experiment, having only
varied half a grain during the whole time; and its dimensions, as
determined by measurement, were unaltered. This species, when it
is first picked off the rock, ejects a watery fluid with a powerful
musky odour, which effect accompanies the closure of the shell by
the *operculum*. I kept some individuals of this species in rain-water,
containing varying proportions of lime-water, for about three months.
The lime-water was of the medicinal strength of the British Phar-
macopeia. I began with water containing 64 parts of rain-water
to one part of the lime-solution. By the end of the first month the
proportion was increased to 32 to 1; by the end of the second
month it was 16 to 1; towards the end of the third month the
Nerites, having lived for over three weeks in the last solution, began
to die; the survivors were placed in a solution containing the proportion of 8 to 1, but this amount of the lime-solution proved too
much for them. It should be remarked that throughout the experiment, the Nerites used to descend to the water to get their food just
as frequently as in the state of nature: they did not avoid the water;
and after the experiment was over, there was no apparent alteration
in the appearance of the shells. These observations were made in
the north part of New Zealand during the latter part of the summer
and the beginning of the autumn, a circumstance which may partially explain the death of the shells. The temperature there was
about 20° below the temperature they are accustomed to in the
Solomon Islands; this difference is of interest when it is remembered
that *Neritinæ* are mostly found in the streams of tropical regions;
and I may, therefore, infer that this species is capable of adapting
itself to temperatures much lower than that to which it is accustomed, since some individuals survived the voyage to New Zealand
from the Solomon Islands and lived in the climate of the former
region for three months under very unfavourable conditions.

Professor Semper[1] remarks that some *Neritinæ* have the habit
of detaching themselves from rocks on the slightest touch, by this
means, as he considers, escaping the pursuit of their enemies. Some
of them, however, as I observed, detach themselves spontaneously

[1] Ibid, p. 210.

and independently of any alarm. The individuals of *Neritina sub-sulcata* that I kept in a large bottle in my cabin, used frequently in the course of a night to detach themselves from the sides and drop down into the water below. On one occasion when the noise woke me up, I found the culprit voraciously eating a portion of decayed leaf. In the daytime they sometimes dropped, and at other times crawled, down to the water. . . . . . It is probable that the musky water, which this Nerite ejects when it is picked off a rock, may cause a bird to drop it from its beak and thus save its life.

Amongst the new fresh-water shells that I found in this group was a species of *Unio*, to which Mr. Smith did me the honour of attaching my name, it being the first species of this genus of river-mussels that has been found in the Solomon Group. But its occurrence there means something more than a new locality, since, as I believe, I am correct in asserting, we have in it the first record of this widely distributed genus having reached the Pacific islands. I do not think that this species can be generally spread through the Solomon Group. I only found it in one locality, namely the Short-land Islands, near the western end of the group.

A very familiar shell, in low-lying moist and marshy situations throughout the Solomon Islands, is that of the auriculoid, *Pythia scarabæus*, Linné. Being usually accustomed to find it in the low-lying districts, I was surprised on one occasion to find it in the higher parts of Faro Island, which attains an elevation of 1,900 feet above sea. In the mangrove swamps and in the lower parts of the streams at Choiseul Bay, I found a species of *Cyrena* which has not yet been described, together with *Cerithidea cornea* (A. Adams: var.) and *Pyrazus palustris*, the last species occurring also in India. On the moist ground of the taro patches in the islands of Bougainville Straits thrives a species (*S. simplex*, var.) of that ubiquitous genus *Succinea*. The operculated land-snails, of which the *Helicinæ* are the most numerous, are found more frequently in calcareous districts.

LIST OF LAND AND FRESH-WATER SHELLS COLLECTED IN
IN THE SOLOMON ISLANDS[1] DURING 1882 AND 1883.
(EXTRACTED FROM MR. E. SMITH'S PAPER IN THE PRO-
CEEDINGS OF THE ZOOLOGICAL SOCIETY OF LONDON,
JUNE, 2ND, 1885.) THE DESCRIPTIONS OF THE NEW
SPECIES AND VARIETIES FOLLOW:

(1) *Helicarion planospira* (Pfeiffer) *Hab.* Santa Anna, Ugi, St. Christoval,
Guadalcanar.
(2) *Helix (Nanina) nitidissima* (nov. spec.) *Hab.* Treasury Island, a
variety in Guadalcanar.
(3) *Helix (Nanina) solidiuscula* (nov. spec.) *Hab.* Santa Anna, found
generally on the trunks of cocoa-nut palms.
(4) *Helix (Corasia) tricolor* (Pfeiffer) *Hab.* St. Christoval, Ugi, Santa
Anna.
(5) *Helix (Corasia) anadyomene*, A (Adams & Angas) *Hab.* Guadalcanar,
Ugi.
(6) *Helix (Geotrochus) acmella* (Pfeiffer) *Hab.* Faro Island, Bougainville
Straits; Florida Islands, *vide* original paper.
(7) *Helix (Geotrochus) gamelia* (Angas) *Hab.* Isabel, Stephen Island,
Shortland Islands, Treasury Island, Choiseul Bay.
(8) *Helix (Geotrochus) hargreavesi* (Angas) *Hab.* Faro Island in Bougainville Straits.
(9) *Helix (Geotrochus) mendana* (Angas) *Hab.* Shortland Islands, *vide*
original paper.
(10) *Helix (Geotrochus) motacilla* (Pfeiffer) *Hab.* Simbo or Eddystone
Island, also called Narovo.

Note.—In the original paper, Simbo and Eddystone are referred to as
two different islands. This mistake arose from the omission of the name of
Simbo in the latest charts; it is, however, the name usually employed.

(11) *Helix (Geotrochus) guppyi* (nov. spec.) *Hub.* Faro Island in Bougainville Straits.
(12) *Helix (Geotrochus) dampieri* (Angas) var. *Hab.* Choiseul Bay.
(13) *Helix (Geotrochus) eros* (Angas) *Hab.* Isabel, Stephen Island, Shortland Islands.
(14) *Helix (Geotrochus) cleryi* (Récluz) *Hab.* Santa Anna, Ugi, St. Christoval, Guadalcanar, Rua Sura Islets, New Georgia, Simbo or
Eddystone, Treasury, Shortlands, Choiseul Bay. Three new
varieties, var *meridionalis* (Santa Anna), var *simboana* (Simbo or
Eddystone), var *septentrionalis* (Shortlands, Treasury, Choiseul Bay.)

---

[1] The habitats given are confined to the Solomon Group. I have added the new habitats
of species in my collection to those previously ascertained from the collections of Brenchley,
Macgillivray, Hombron and Jacquinot, etc.

(15) *Helix* (*Videna*) *merziana* (Pfeiffer) *Hab.* St. Christoval, New Georgia, Ugi ; *vide* original paper.

(16) *Helix* (*Videna*) *sanctæ annæ* (nov. spec.) *Hab.* Santa Anna, living on the trunks of cocoa-nut palms.

Note.—This species, or a closely similar form, was observed by me in many other islands ; but I neglected to collect it in any other locality than Santa Anna.

(17) *Helix* (*Rhytida*) *villandrei* (Gassies) *Hab.* St. Christoval, Ugi.

(18) *Helix* (*Camœna*) *hombroni* (Pfeiffer) *Hab.* Shortland and Faro Islands in Bougainville Straits, Isabel.

(19) *Helix* (*Chloritis*) *eustoma* (Pfeiffer) *Hab.* New Georgia, Ugi, Faro Island (Bougainville Straits.)

(20) *Bulimus* (*Placostylus*) *cleryi* (Petit) *Hab.* St. Christoval.

(21) *Bulimus* (*Placostylus*) *founaki* (Hombron and Jacquinot) *Hab.* Isabel, Faro Island (Bougainville Straits).

(22) *Bulimus* (*Placostylus*) *miltocheilus* (Reeve) *Hab.* St. Christoval (S.E. part), Ugi, Santa Anna : *vide* original paper.

(23) *Partula*, spec. *Hab.* Guadalcanar, Ugi, Treasury Island, Choiseul Bay : *vide* original paper.

(24) *Succinea simplex* (Pfeiffer) var. *Hab.* Treasury Island, Shortland Islands : living on the moist ground in the taro patches.

(25) *Cyclostoma* (*Adelostoma*) *triste* (Tapparone Canefri), var? *Hab.* Guadalcanar; Santa Anna; Faro and Shortland Islands and Choiseul Bay in Bougainville Straits.

(26) *Leptopoma jacquinoti* (Pfeiffer) *Hab.* Rua Sura Islets off the north coast of Guadalcanar : *vide* original paper.

(27) *Leptopoma vitreum* (Lesson) *Hab.* Santa Anna, Simbo or Eddystone ; Shortland Islands.

(28) *Omphalotropis nebulosa* (Pease) *Hab.* St. Christoval, Guadalcanar, Ugi. I found this shell living on trees clothing a low tract of land skirting the beach.

(29) *Pupina solomonensis* (nov. spec.) *Hab.* Shortland and Treasury Islands in Bougainville Straits : living in the decayed trunks of fallen trees.

(30) *Hargravesia polita*, H. (Adams), var. *Hab.* Faro Island in Bougainville Straits : *vide* original paper.

(31) *Helicina moquiniana* (Récluz) *Hab.* St. Christoval, Guadalcanar, Ugi.

(32) *Helicina egregia* (Pfeiffer) *Hab.* Guadalcanar, Florida Islands.

(33) *Helicina modesta* (Pfeiffer) *Hab.* Guadalcanar, Shortland Islands, Treasury Islands, Choiseul Bay.

(34) *Helicina solomonensis* (nov. spec.) *Hab.* The Islands of Bougainville Straits (Faro, Shortlands, Treasury).

(35) *Pythia scarabæus* (Linné) *Hab.* Santa Anna, St. Christoval, which were the localities of my specimens ; but I observed this species and its varieties in every island I visited. *Stat* : Moist ground usually near the sea.

(36) *Melampus fasciatus* (Deshayes) *Hab.* Isabel, Rua Sura Islets off the north coast of Guadalcanar. I found these shells in the crevices of a log on the beach.

(37) *Melania amarula* (Linné) *Hab.* Ugi, in the streams.

(38) *Melania scabra* (Müller) *Hab.* Ugi, in a stream.

(39) *Melania salomonis* (Brot.) *Hab.* Ugi, in a stream.

(40) *Melania fulgurans* (Hinds) *Hab.* Ugi, in a stream.

(41) *Melania fastigiella* (Reeve) *Hab.* Imbedded in a dark calcareous loam exposed in the banks of a large stream near its mouth at Sulagina, on the north coast of St. Christoval. I could not find any; living specimens.

(42) *Melania* spec. *Hab.* The same as *Mel. fastigiella.*

(43) *Melania verrucosa* (Hinds) *Hab.* The same as *Mel. fastigiella.*

(44) *Melania subgradata* (nov. spec.) *Hab.* The same as *Mel. fastigiella.*

(45) *Melania ugiensis* (nov. spec.) *Hab.* From a stream in Ugi.

(46) *Melania sanctæ annæ* (nov. spec.) *Hab.* A stream in the interior of Santa Anna.

(47) *Melania guppyi* (nov. spec.) *Hab.* From the stomach and intestines of a fish living in the fresh-water lake of Wailava in the island of Santa Anna. This species probably frequents the deeper parts of the lake, as I only found one living individual.

(48) *Cerithidea cornea* A. (Adams) var. *Hab.* Mangrove swamps in Choiseul Bay.

(49) *Pyrazus palustris Hab.* Mangrove swamps in Choiseul Bay.

    Note.—Not referred to in original paper.

(50) *Nerita marmorata* (Hombron and Jacquinot) *Hab.* Living just above high-water level on the surface of the coral-limestone coast, St. Christoval.

(51) *Neritina cornea* (Linné) *Hab.* Star Harbour, St. Christoval, on the trunks of trees 150 feet above the nearest stream ; Choiseul Bay, from a stream ; Shortland Islands, on the stems of tree-ferns and areca palms in a marshy district. I found this species in many other islands ; but did not collect it except in the above three localities.

(52) *Neritina subsulcata* (Sowerby) *Hab.* Streams in St. Christoval and in the islands of Bougainville Straits. In the Shortland Islands I found this species on the stems of tree-ferns and areca palms in a marshy district. I only collected it in these localities ; but I found it in many other islands. When first picked off the rock, it ejects a watery fluid possessing a powerful musky odour.

(53) *Neritina dubia* (Chemnitz) *Hab.* Shortland Islands, in a stream.

(54) *Neritina adumbrata* (Reeve) *Hab.* A stream in Choiseul Bay, and the rocky sides of a stream-course in Ugi.

(55) *Neritina pulligera* (Linné) *Hab.* Guadalcanar, St. Christoval, Ugi, Choiseul Bay, in the streams.

(56) *Neritina petiti* (Récluz) *Hab.* Treasury and Faro Islands, in the streams.

(57) *Neritina olivacea* (Le Guillou) *Hab.* Streams in Treasury Island and at Sulagina, St. Christoval.

(58) *Neritina macgillivrayi* (Reeve) *Hab.* Streams in Guadalcanar and in Faro Island, Bougainville Straits.

(59) *Neritina asperulata* (Récluz) *Hab.* Rocky sides of a stream-course in Ugi.

(60) *Neritina porcata* (Gould) *Hab.* St. Christoval, and Faro Island, Bougainville Straits, in streams.

(61) *Neritina variegata* (Lesson) *Hab.* St. Christoval, Ugi ; Simbo or Eddystone ; Faro Island, Bougainville Straits ; Choiseul Bay ; in streams.

(62) *Neritina turtoni* (Récluz) *Hab.* A stream in the Shortland Islands ; streams in Guadalcanar ; imbedded in a dark calcareous loam exposed in the banks of a large stream near to its mouth at Sulagiua on the north coast of St. Christoval.

(63) *Neritina brevispina* (Lamarck) *Hab.* Streams in Shortland, Treasury, and Ugi Islands. The specimens from Treasury Island were destitute of spines.

(64) *Neritina squarrosa* (Récluz) *Hab.* Streams in Treasury I-land.

(65) *Navicella sanguisuga* (Reeve) *Hab.* Streams in Faro Island, Bougainville Straits.

(66) *Navicella suborbicularis* (Sowerby) *Hab.* Guadalcanar, St. Christoval, Ugi, Treasury and Faro Islands in Bougainville Straits.

(67) *Unio guppyi* (nov. spec.) *Hab.* Streams in the Shortland Islands.

(68) *Cyrena*, spec. *Hab.* In the lower parts of streams and in mangrove swamps, Choiseul Bay. *Note.*—This species is not referred to in the original paper.

Descriptions of the new species and varieties,[1] by Mr. E. Smith.

(2) *Helix* (*Nanina*) *nitidissima*. (Plate XXXVI. figs. 1, 1 *b.*) Shell thin, transparent, very glossy, depressed, narrowly perforate, pale brownish horn-colour above, whitish towards the umbilicus, sculptured with very faint lines of growth. Whorls 4-5, slightly convex, impressed and marginate above at the suture; last whorl large, rounded at the periphery. Aperture obliquely lunate; peristome simple, thin, slightly thickened and reflexed partly over the perforation. Spire low, but very little raised above the last whorl, obtuse at the apex. Greatest diameter 14 millim., smallest 12; height 9.

(3) *Helix* (*Nanina*) *solidiuscula*. (Plate XXXVI., figs. 2, 2 *b.*) Shell very narrowly perforate, depressed, somewhat solid, dark chestnut-brown and a little glossy above, more shining and paler beneath, becoming almost white at the umbilical region; whorls 6½, convex, separated by a deepish suture, and, with the exception of two or three at the apex which are smooth, sculptured with strong, close-set, arcuate, and oblique striæ on the upper surface, crossed with a few more or less distinct spiral lines. Body-whorl rounded at the periphery, or sometimes with the faintest indication of an angle, convex, and only exhibiting fine lines of growth below. Aperture obliquely semilunate; peristome simple, but, owing to the solidity of the shell, seeming slightly thickened, especially on the very oblique columellar margin, which is shortly reflexed above over the perforation. Spire depressed-conoid, having the least convex outlines and an obtuse apex. Greatest diameter 18 millim., smallest 16½, height 12; aperture 8 long, 4½ wide.

This species is well distinguished by its comparative solidity and strong sculpture on the upper surface.

(4) *Helix* (*Corasia*) *tricolor* (Pfeiffer). (Plate XXXVI., figs. 3, 3 *b.*) A specimen obtained on the north coast of the same island of St. Christoval, by Mr. Guppy, is worthy of special mention, and may be termed var. *picta*, on account of the undulating reddish-brown stripes which ornament both the upper and lower surfaces.

A similar example was also collected by Dr. A. Corrie and presented to the Museum. The markings on these two shells are very striking and distinctly visible within the aperture.

(11) *Helix* (*Geotrochus*) *guppyi*. (Plate XXXVI. fig. 4.) Shell elevately conical, thin, pale yellow, ornamented with conspicuous nearly black or black-brown spiral bands, one above and one below the

The numbers refer to the plates in Mr. Smith's paper (Proc. Zool. Soc., June 1885).

sutures of the upper whorls, and three upon the last, one sutural, the second peripheral, and the third basal. Volutions 6, rather slowly enlarging, a little convex, sculptured with fine oblique striæ of growth, not glossy. Three first whorls livid purplish, the last rather sharply angled at the middle, not descending in front, having the basal band broad around the almost concealed perforation, and obsolete within the aperture. The latter is oblique, somewhat narrowed and pouting in front, banded within. with three almost black and two white bands, the central one of the former being squarely truncate at the end, only the lower corner of it touching the margin of the lip, which is pale oblique, receding, a little expanded and reflexed in front and at the columellar margin, the upper end of which is spread over and nearly conceals the small umbilicus. Height 22¼ millim., greatest diameter 19, smallest 16.

This species is remarkable for the striking contrast of its colour-bands and the angular character of the last whorl.

(12) *Helix (Geotrochus) dampieri*, Angas, var. (Plate XXXVI. fig. 5.) Shell imperforate, subglobose, conoid, light brown or fawn-colour, here and there minutely dotted with dark-grey specks, with a broad white band around the middle of the penultimate whorl and two upon the last, one above and the other below the middle, also a narrow white line revolving up the spire beneath the suture, and a dark brown zone surrounding the pale or yellowish umbilical region. Whorls 5, a little convex above, somewhat glossy, obliquely and very finely striated by the lines of growth, the last more or less concentrically striated beneath, shortly descending at the aperture which is white within. Lip a little thickened, edged with reddish brown, only slightly expanded on the right side, more dilated below, produced into a thin transparent callosity over the umbilical region, united above to the upper extremity of the peristome. Columellar margin oblique, white or partly tinged with reddish brown, thickened and terminating below within the edge of the lip. Height 19 millim., greatest diam. 22, smallest 19.

The specimens from the Solomon Islands are smaller than the type with which, through the kindness of Mr G. F. Angas, I have compared them. They also have the peristome brown, and the basal band is darker.

(14) *Helix (Geotrochus) cleryi*, Récluz (Plate XXXVI. figs 6, 6 *b*). The specimens from Santa Anna (var. *meridionalis* fig. 6 *b*) are smaller than the type, pale brown above, with a white thread-like line at the suture, and the acutely keeled periphery, paler beneath, especially towards the centre, and have the aperture particularly acuminate at the termination of the keel.

The specimens from Simbo (var. *simboana*, fig. 6 *a*) are uniformly pale horn-colour, rather sharply carinate at the middle, and have the peristome white, considerably thickened and almost notched at the upper end of the columella, and the body-whorl is more contracted than in the typical form. The examples from Choiseul Bay, Shortland and Treasury Islands (var. *septentrionalis,* fig. 6) are all alike, of smaller dimensions than the normal form, thin pale brownish horn-colour, with rather more convex whorls than usual, the carina at the periphery being acute and thread-like as in the variety *simboana.*

Whether these several varieties should take specific rank is questionable, for, although there is considerable difference between the extreme form seven in the series of nearly one hundred specimens under examination, the gradual transition from one form to another is observable.

(16) *Helix* (*Videna*) *sanctæ annæ*. (Plate XXXVI. figs. 7. 7 *b*.) Shell depressed-conoid, deeply umbilicated, very acutely keeled at the periphery, light brown, sometimes with a few radiating pale streaks on the upper surface, sculptured with oblique lines of growth. Whorls 5, rather slowly increasing, slightly convex, depressed and margined above the suture, last not descending, compressed above and below the keel, a little convex towards the umbilicus, which is moderately large. Aperture transverse, flesh-tinted within. Peristome simple, a little thickened along the basal margin, with the extremities united by a thin callus. Height 7 millim.; greatest diameter 17, smallest 15.

(25) *Cyclostoma* (*Adelostoma*) *triste*, Tapparone Canefri, var. ? Dr. Tapparone Canefri has kindly compared specimens from these islands with his *C triste*, and is of opinion that they may be considered a variety of it; and observes that the New-Guinean form is a little smaller, its spire a little more slender, its surface more glossy, the colour redder, and the apex of the spire darker.

The shells under examination are clothed with a very thin epidermis when in a fresh condition, exhibiting numerous very fine spiral thread-like lines, which entirely disappear in worn shells and can easily be rubbed off with a brush. For several species having a similar epidermis and an incomplete peristome, Dr. Tapparone Canfri has proposed the subgenus *Adelostoma*.

(29) *Pupina solomonensis.* (Plate XXXVI. fig. 9, 9 *a*.) Shell small and very like *P. difficilis*, Semper, and *P. keraudreni*, Vignard. It is of a reddish tint, especially the body-whorl; consists of 5¼ whorls, which are the least convex and exhibit a pellucid line, frequently brown, immediately beneath the suture. Last whorl very obliquely descending behind, narrowed below, and flattened somewhat above the aperture. Columella thickened with callus, white, parted off from the whorl above by an oblique circumscribing red line, truncated rather low down. Outer lip slightly thickened and effuse, and a little paler than the rest of the whorl, produced somewhat at its junction with the body-whorl, which in consequence has the appearance of rising suddenly after an oblique descent. Length 7 millims., diam. 3⅗, aperture 2 long and wide.

(34) *Helicina solomonensis.* (Plate XXXVI. figs. 11, 11 *b*.) Shell small, globose-conical, reddish or yellowish, pale at the apex. Whorls 4— 4½, the least convex above, sculptured with lines of growth and fine spiral striæ both on the upper and lower surfaces, very faintly margined above at the suture; last whorl rounded at the periphery, obsoletely angled near the junction of the outer lip and the least descending in front, so that the faint angulation is visible for a short distance above the sutural line. Aperture somewhat semicircular and oblique, small; peristome slightly expanded; umbilical callosity yellowish or pellucid whitish, defined towards the base of the columellar margin. Greatest width 4⅗ millim., smallest 4; height 3¼.

(44) *Melania subgradata.* (Plate XXXVII. fig. 3, 3 *a*). Shell elongate, turreted, rather solid, covered with an (olive?) epidermis, and marked with fine longitudinal oblique red lines which extend from suture to suture. Whorls probably about 10, flat or even a little

concave at the sides, shouldered above, usually with a spiral shallow groove and a few striæ near the shoulder, and marked with fine incremental striæ. Suture deep, slightly oblique. Last whorl long, finely transversely striated, most distinctly at the base. Aperture elongate-pyriform, acute above, effuse at the base. Outer lip thin, sharp, accurate, and prominent at the middle. Columellar margin rather thickly covered with callus, united above to the outer lip. Length of two specimens, consisting of five whorls 30 and 25 millim.; diameter 11 and 10½; aperture 14 and 12 long, 6 and 5 wide.

(45) *Melania ugiensis.* (Plate XXXVII. fig. 4.) Shell subulate, acuminate, beneath the epidermis (which is wanting in the specimens at hand), of a dirty, pale, livid, or purplish tint. Whorls probably about 14 in number; the eleven remaining are a little convex, rather slowly enlarging, and sculptured with close-set, obliquish, fine riblets, which are crossed by crowded spiral striæ. Last whorl large, with the riblets rather obsolete below the middle, and very close together, much more numerous than those upon the upper whorls. Aperture obliquely pear-shaped. Length 25 millim., diameter 8; aperture 8½ long, 4½ wide.

(46) *Melania sanctæ annæ.* (Plate XXXVII. figs. 5, 5 a.) Shell small, acuminately pyramidal, somewhat eroded towards the apex, covered with a yellowish-olive epidermis, and sometimes marked with a few indistinct, reddish, irregular spots, and lines near the middle of the body-whorl. Whorls 5-6 remaining, flattish at the sides, divided by a slightly, oblique, distinct suture, all with the exception of the last one or two more or less distinctly, longitudinally, finely plicate; the plicæ are more conspicuous in some specimens than in others, being at times entirely eroded. The other sculpture consists of fine lines of growth, and a few rather distant spiral striæ, which cut across the incremental lines and produce a puckered appearance. Aperture elongate, pyriform, pale bluish within. Length of specimen consisting of six whorls 13 millim., diameter 5; aperture 5 long and 2½ wide.

(47) *Melania guppyi.* (Plate XXXVII. figs. 6, 6 a.) Shell slenderly acuminate, covered with an olive-brown epidermis. Whorls about 14, divided by a very oblique, deepish suture, concave above the middle and somewhat convex below it, and then contracted; ornamented with a few spiral series of nodules (about five on the upper whorls) and rather indistinct, very oblique and flexuous, longitudinal ridges, upon which the nodules rests, also exhibiting very sloping and flexuous lines of growth; the most conspicuous rows of granules are near the middle of the whorls. Aperture pyriform. Outer lip thin, remarkably sinuated above towards the suture, and arcuately prominent below. Columellar margin oblique, straightish, covered with a callus, curving into the broad basal sinus. Length 31 millim., diameter 7; aperture 9 long, 4 wide.

This is a very remarkable and distinct species, with a very drawn-out spire, peculiar granuled sculpture, and a deeply sinuated labrum. I have much pleasure in naming it after Mr. Guppy.

(66) *Unio guppyi.* (Plate XXXVII. figs. 8-8 b.) Shell elongate, very inequilateral, usually a little longer than twice the height, compressed, covered with a blackish-brown epidermis, exhibiting strong lines of growth, and very faint radiating substriation, and marked with fine wrinklings at the eroded beaks, which are small and placed quite near the anterior extremity. Dorsal margin behind the um-

bones almost straight or the least excurved for some distance, then at an obtuse angle becoming oblique before rounding into the extremity, which is a little more sharply curved than the anterior end. Ventral outline either faintly excurved, straight, or the least concave. Interior bluish-white, most iridescent at the hinder extremity, generally stained in parts with olive-brown. Cardinal tooth of the right valve moderately large, four or five-lobed at the top, situated just in front of umbo. Between it and the outer margin is a short ridge, the space between the tooth and the ridge receiving the single, smaller, roughened, and striated tooth of the left valve. Lateral tooth of the right valve long, obliquely truncate behind, fitting in between two teeth in the opposite valve. Anterior adductor scar deep, posterior superficial, squarish in front. Pedal scar in both valves under the cardinal tooth very deep. Ligament elongate, prominent.

Length 80 mm. ; height 38 ; diameter 21.
  „   70 mm. ;   „   35 ;   „   18.

This species recalls to mind some of the forms from Australia and New Zealand. Its principal features are the elongate compressed form, dark brown colour, wrinkled apices, and coarse incremental lines. It is the only species as yet recorded from the Solomon Islands.

ADDITIONAL NOTE.   (H. B. GUPPY.)

A species of the *Litoritinidæ* (*Littorina scabra*) is commonly found in this group on the leaves and trunks of mangroves, Barringtonias, and other littoral trees, the branches of which overspread the rising tide. These molluses occur at heights varying from one or two feet to eight or nine feet above the high-water level; and they possess an unusually delicate operculum as compared with those of other species of the same family. They do not seem to be able to withstand immersion in salt water for any length of time, since out of six individuals kept submerged for twenty-four hours, three died. When first placed in the water, they were evidently very much out of their element, and tried in vain to creep out of the vessel. The delicate character of the operculum indicates a transitional stage between marine and terrestrial molluses ; and the experiment above referred to, throws a little light on this subject, since only the younger of the six individuals survived. One would have expected that the younger individuals would have been less able to withstand immersion in sea-water, but such was not the case, since they recovered from an immersion which killed the older individuals. In explanation of this unexpected result, I would infer that, on the theory of the inheritance of peculiarities at corresponding ages, the younger individuals would retain more of the marine habits of the original parent of the species, because in the first place only the adults of this parent species would have been modified to suit the new condition.

CHAPTER XVII

A MONGST the matters to which I devoted some attention in this group of islands, was the annual rainfall. As far as I know, there have been no continuous observations previously made there ; and the only record of rain-measurement, which I have been able to find referring to this region, was an observation made on board the Austrian frigate "Novara" in the middle of October, 1858, whilst to the northward of St. Christoval, when three inches of rain were registered in five hours.[1] I therefore set myself to work to do what I could in this matter, making rain-guage stations at Santa Anna and Ugi and keeping a register myself on board. Mr. Fred Howard undertook to make these observations at Ugi, and I supplied him with a rain-guage for this purpose. His register, which extended over a period of fifteen months from October, 1882, to the end of the following year, was kept with great regularity ; and as I was able to compare his observations with my own on board for a few days, I have every confidence in the accuracy of his observations. At Santa Anna, Mr. William Henghan, to whom I had supplied a guage, undertook at first to keep the record, beginning in the last week of October, 1882 ; but he left the island two months after, when Mr. Charles Sproul voluntarily undertook to measure the rainfall, which he did with great regularity until the end of the following year. I regret to learn that Mr. Sproul has recently died at Sydney. He was one of those men who in a quiet inoffensive way have done much towards preparing the way for future settlers in this group. I have the greatest confidence in his observations, since for a few days at Santa Anna we were able to compare our daily measurements.

Before proceeding to consider the results of these rain-measure-

[1] Scherzer's " Voyage of the 'Novara,'" Eng. edit., 1861.

ments, I will endeavour to convey to the mental eye of my readers
a general idea of the most striking atmospheric phenomenon in
connection with the rainfall of these regions. I refer to the oncom-
ing of the *black squall.*

A clear and serene sky at first gives no token of the sudden
change that is to quickly follow; but the stillness of the air and its
increased dryness, together with the consequent greater scorching
power of the sun's rays and the apparent nearness of surrounding
shores, give sufficient warning of the onset of the rain squall to those
acquainted with these seas. In a short time a low black arch
appears above the horizon, often in an unexpected quarter, and
rising rapidly it sweeps majestically with great swiftness until it
appears to span the heavens. Onward it rushes, quicker far than
one imagines; and now must the navigator beware. Under yonder
advancing arch a white line of foam marks its van. There, away
towards one of its corners, a waterspout rises in fantastic shape; sea
and cloud meet in mid-air and become intermingled in the whirling
column. Lightning plays about beneath the arch and within its
black mass, illuming for the moment its dark recesses and leaving
it in the next far blacker than before. Peals of thunder herald on
the advance of the black squall.

"Clear lower deck!" "Hands aloft!" "Shorten sail!"
Such were the words of command which were almost daily
issued during our cruises in these islands. In a few brief
minutes, the ship is prepared to meet the squall. The temperature falls very perceptibly, and the officer of the watch gives
a slight shiver as he dons his oilskins. The wind is freshening,
a few large drops of rain fall, the men crouch under the bulwarks, and now the arch is overhead and we are in the thick of the
squall. Down comes a deluge of rain which in less than a minute
wets all who are unprotected through and through. The ship heels
well over, even with her scanty canvas. There is nothing more to
be done. We listen to the whistling of the wind in the rigging
and patiently wait until the weather clears. In half-an-hour the
arch has swept over us, and is pursuing its rapid course towards the
neighbouring mountain-peaks, perhaps of Bougainville or it may be
of Guadalcanar. The blue sky begins to show itself; and in less
than an hour all is as before. With reefs shaken out and more sail
made, the ship proceeds, plunging cheerily on under a fresh breeze
as though glad to shake herself clear of the squall. The sea losing its

z

murky colour reflects the bright hue of the sky now serene; and its white-topped waves sparkle in the sun. The wizard of the storm has shaken his wand, and the scene is changed, as though by magic.

All nature seems invigorated by this short battle of the elements and to be indebted to the bounty of the black squall. Whilst everything before was depressed and lowering, all is now bright and cheerful. Nature has in truth had its accustomed shower-bath, and the reaction that ensues does good to all; makes men the happier and the stronger, elicits a loud chorus from the lower creation in which bird, reptile, and insect, before hushed in the depressing gloom, now combine in strange medley; and the inanimate world shares in the bright change which has followed the storm.

If it be night, the increased luminosity of the sea may be the warning of the arched squall. The ship throws off a bright wave of phosphorescence on either side of the bow, and leaves a luminous track in her wake. Overhead the cloudless star-lit sky conveys its warning; for the stars shine with increased brilliancy, those of less magnitude usually invisible with the naked eye are now distinctly seen; and if the navigator, who has often tried in vain to count the six stars in the Pleiades, can do so now, let him look out for the black squall. Such are the warnings. Then sweeps along the lowering arched mass with its rain and its waterspouts, its wind and its thunder and lightning. On it comes, looking all the blacker as it spreads athwart the heavens and turns the star-lit night into a lightless gloom. Overtaken in the night by such a squall, unable to see more than half a cable's length on either side, and perhaps in the vicinity of sunken reefs the position of which is uncertain, a sailor has need of all his wits. On one occasion, when in this situation, we came unexpectedly in soundings, whilst, as we thought, a hundred good fathoms and more lay beneath our keel. The time was anxious, but nothing could be done until the squall was over. When the arch has passed, the stars begin to show themselves, and in a short time they shine out with all their lustre.

With this description of the rain-squall, or black-squall, or arched-squall, as it may be also conveniently termed, I return to the consideration of the rainfall of this region; and first with regard to the observations at the east end of the Solomon Group. During 1883, 125·03 inches of rain were measured at Santa Anna, a small island lying at the extreme eastern limit of these islands. Two-thirds of the total amount fell in the five months between the beginning of April and the end of August. At Ugi, which lies nearly 60 miles north-east of Santa Anna, 146·24 inches of rain were registered during the same year. About one-third of the total rain for the year fell in the two months of April and July. On comparing the totals for each month at these two localities, there will be found to be but little agreement, which is due to the circumstance that the daily rainfalls of these two places have little relation one with the other, a heavy fall at one island being often only indicated by a slight fall of rain at the other. It is thus evident that locality has a great influence on the rainfall in this part of the group; and probably Ugi owes its greater rainfall to the proximity of the high land of St. Christoval. Here, as in other parts of this group, I often had opportunities of observing how the contiguity of land affected the rainfall in a single shower. I might have been in the interior of an island exposed to a deluge of rain for a couple of hours, and have found, as I did once in the Shortland Islands, that there had been very little rain on board. Another time, when in my Rob Roy canoe on the south side of Treasury harbour and not more than a mile from the ship, a rain-squall passed over me leaving scarcely a drop behind; but as it swept over the ship and was approaching the steep slopes of the island, a smart shower of $\frac{20}{100}$ of an inch fell on the deck.

I cannot gather from the observations made in this eastern part of the group, that one season of the year has a heavier rainfall than another. On comparing the two records for 1883 of Ugi and Santa Anna, it might be thought that the closing months of the year would usually prove to be the driest; but on referring to the register kept on board the ship in this locality in the latter part of 1882 (page 365), which is one of the heaviest records we had in the Solomon Group, such an inference would be negatived. Nor do I find from these registers of rainfall that there appears to be any relation between the amount of rain and the prevalence or non-prevalence of the south-easterly trade, which usually becomes well established in May and lasts till the end of November or the beginning of December, when the north-westerly and westerly winds set in. These observations point towards the inference, therefore, that the distribution of rain through the seasons in this part of the group is capricious; and they do not warrant the conclusion that one season is wetter than another.

Perhaps a comparison of the number of rainy days, or days on which not less than $\frac{2}{100}$ of an inch of rain were measured, may help us to form a more definite conclusion. It will be seen that at Santa Anna and Ugi there were much the same number of rainy days, 182 in the former island and 178 in the latter, or in round numbers about half the total number of days in the year were rainy.[1] At Santa Anna, during the prevalence of the trade wind, there were on the average 15 rainy days per month, and at Ugi 13 per month; whilst during the months from December to April inclusive, when westerly and variable winds prevailed, there were 18 rainy days per month at Santa Anna, and 19 per month at Ugi; so that we may infer that in this year of 1883 there were fewer rainy days per month during the prevalence of the south-east trade, i.e., from May to November, than during the period of westerly and variable winds, i.e., from December to April.

I come now to the subject of the greatest daily fall of rain in this eastern end of the group. On the 13th of June, 1883, 7·73 inches were registered at Santa Anna; whilst at Ugi on the same day only an inch and a half of rain fell, a circumstance showing how confined in their areas some heavy rainfalls may be. At Ugi the heaviest daily fall of 5·75 inches was recorded on the 28th of January of this same year; whilst at Santa Anna only a little more than two inches ell on this day; and here is another proof of the restricted locality of heavy rainfalls. On the 20th of November, 1882, when H.M.S. "Lark" was off the east end of St. Christoval, 5·74 inches of rain fell on the ship; whilst only a small amount of rain was measured at Santa Anna and Ugi. . . . . . With reference to the character of the rain in this part of the Solomon Group, I may remark that as in other tropical regions it is very heavy. A fall of an inch in an hour is very frequent during a rain-squall; but not uncommonly the rain falls far more heavily. Thus, on one occasion on board H.M.S. "Lark," when in this part of the group, 2·00 inches fell in an hour; and at another time 1·03 inches fell in 25 minutes, and on another occasion an inch fell in half-an-hour.

But inasmuch as heavy falls of rain are not peculiar to the tropics, since far greater falls than those above named have occurred in temperate Europe, we can only judge of the character of the

---

[1] From the record of the rainy days during the six months from June to November of the previous year (1882), it appears that at least 110 days were rainy. During the same months of the following year, only 84 days were rainy.

rainfall in this region by the total annual fall and by the frequency of heavy falls. Thus we find that at Ugi, in 1883, on 56 days the fall exceeded an inch ; and that at Santa Anna, more than an inch of rain fell on 41 days. At Ugi, the daily records on eighteen occasions exceeded two inches ; at Santa there was a lesser number of falls of over two inches, viz. 11.

If I were to estimate the probable annual rainfall at the *coast* in this part of the Solomon Group, I should place it at not far under 150 inches. Although only possessing the rain-register for a small portion of 1882, I am of the opinion, from having spent a large part of the year in this eastern end of the group, that the fall for 1882 was heavier than the rainfall actually registered for 1883;[1] although this is but a conjecture, it enables me to estimate the probable annual fall with some confidence at about 150 inches at the *coast* in this eastern end of the group.

The observations made on board the ship amongst the islands of Bougainville Straits (Treasury, Shortlands, Faro, etc.) during portions of the year 1883 and 1884 now claim our notice. As shown on page 365, 60·43 inches of rain fell in the five months from June to October of 1883, this amount being a little under that which fell at Ugi (65·70 inches) and at Santa Anna (67·72 inches) in the same period, the two regions lying towards the opposite ends of the group. During the same period of the following year, we measured 67·66 inches of rain in Bougainville Straits, an amount a little in excess of that of the previous year. During the same periods, *i.e.*, from June to October inclusive, in 1883 and 1884, there were the following number of rainy days, 120 in the one year and 118 in the other. At Santa Anna and Ugi, at the opposite end of the group, the total of rainy days for the same period in 1883, numbered only two-thirds of the amount in Bougainville Straits. During these five months in 1883 there were 16 daily records of over an inch of rain in Bougainville Straits ; at Santa Anna and Ugi, in the same period, there were 23 and 26 daily records exceeding an inch. In the same period of 1884, in Bougainville Straits, there were 22 such daily records, but the total fall was about 7 inches greater than in the previous year.

I may now draw some inferences from the above observations. In the first place, it is probable that the annual coast rainfall of Bougainville Straits and that of the eastern end of the Solomon

[1] *Vide* footnote referring to number of rainy days in 1882 on p. 356.

Group are much about the same, viz., about 150 inches : the chief difference between the two regions being, that in the former region, there are a greater number of rainy days and fewer heavy falls. The heavy falls, when they do occur, are not easily forgotten ; thus, at Treasury we measured, in July, 1884, 11 inches of rain in 10 successive hours ; but the daily record was only 8·09 inches, since the rain began in the evening of one day and lasted well into the following morning.

During the heavy rainfalls in these regions the streams swell in an astonishingly quick manner. Rivulets become turbid streams, the whole hill-slope discharges a continuous sheet of water, and the water rushes down the permanent stream-courses with the roar of a mountain-torrent. Large blocks of stone are swept some distance along the lower courses of the streams ; and the trunks of trees are carried by each successive flood further and further towards the mouth of the stream.

It should be now remarked that the average rainfall for the year, which I have estimated from observations made in different parts of the Solomon Group at about 150 inches, only applies to the *coast*. It is probable that this estimate is generally applicable to the coasts of these islands, except on the lee sides of the loftier islands.[1]

This brings me to the question of the rainfall in the higher regions. The rainfall will increase with elevation until a certain height is reached, where the clouds attain their maximum density ; at such a level the greatest rainfall will occur. I learn from an interesting paper by Mr. Bateman on this subject,[2] that it may be inferred that in the Lake District of England the greatest rainfall occurs at an elevation of 2,000 feet, which is the level of maximum cloud density. In India, an elevation of 4,500 feet represents the level at which the greatest rainfall occurs. In the Solomon Islands, a greater height will have to be attained before the level of maximum cloud density or that of the greatest rainfall will be attained. Probably I shall not greatly err if I assume it to be between 5,000 and 6,000 feet. I have already observed that the south-east trade, subject to its usual variations, is the prevailing wind in the eastern part of the group for nearly two-thirds of the year. Coming laden with its watery burden, it first strikes the eastern slopes of St.

[1] By the lee sides, I mean those sheltered from the prevailing S.E. trade.
[2] Journal of the Victoria Institute. Vol. XV. No. 59.

Christoval ; but although the higher regions of this island must cause the rain-clouds to precipitate a large amount of their moisture, the higher peaks do not rise in sufficient mass to a height that would receive the greatest rainfall, the extreme height being 4,100 feet. The rain-clouds, with the bulk of their moisture, would therefore be driven over the higher regions of this island, and would deposit the greater part of their burden on the higher slopes of the mountainous eastern portion of Guadalcanar. Since this island, in its eastern portion, rises in mass to a height of some 5,000 feet and attains a maximum elevation of 8,000 feet, it does not seem probable that, during the prevalence of the trade for nearly two-thirds of the year, a considerable quantity of rain would be deposited on the western side of the island ; and, that such is the case, is shown in the fact that the dense forest-growth that clothes the steep eastern and southern slopes of the island gives place, on the lee or west side of the mountains, to a vegetation which gives to the western portion of Guadalcanar, when viewed from seaward, the appearance of a savannah or a prairie.

The lofty mountain-masses of the east end of Guadalcanar, which forms one of the finest specimens of coast-scenery in the world, are usually enveloped in rain-clouds at their summits. But occasionally one of the peaks is visible above the thick cloud-covering, marking by its elevation, as it were, the line of greatest rainfall lying below. In the same manner the high peaks at the east end of Bougainville, which have an elevation of between 7,000 and 8,000 feet, may be seen occasionally to project above the rain-clouds ; but there is, probably, a smaller quantity of rain deposited on the higher slopes of this island than on those of Guadalcanar, because the mountains are more isolated, possess for the most part the tapering volcanic profile, and do not rise "en masse," as in the case of the high lands of Guadalcanar. The greatest rainfall in the Solomon Group takes place on the steep southern and eastern slopes of this island of Guadalcanar. Huge mountain-masses appear to rise directly from the sea to a height of some 5,000 feet, ultimately attaining a height of 8,000 feet. The fall there must be tremendous, especially when, as is frequently the case, the land of St. Christoval does not interpose itself in the path of the moisture-laden trade-wind. Then, loaded with vapours after its passage across a wide expanse of ocean, and with but a thin tract of intervening lowland to rob it of its moisture, the trade strikes at once upon the precipitous mountain-slopes as against some Cyclopean rampart. There is no ravine or breach in the mountain-mass to ease the tension. There, on those mountain-slopes, a terrific precipitation must occur, which, if the annual rainfall of the coast is 150 inches, will here be three or four times that amount. This is no exaggerated language, but is the opinion I have formed, after having carefully considered the physical geography of these regions.

The subjoined rainfalls of a few localities in other parts of the world may be interesting to compare with that of the Solomon Group :[1]

```
England......................................32  inches.
Singapore....................................97     „
Atlantic Doldrums...........................225     „
Western Ghats...............................302     „
Cherraponjee.........................v......610     „
```

SOLOMON ISLANDS.

```
(a.) at the coast...............................150     „
(b.) on the higher slopes of Guadalcanar 400 to 500 inches probably.
```

Comparing the rainfall of the Solomon Islands with some results obtained in other parts of the Pacific, I would draw attention to the small rainfall of Port Moresby on the south-east coast of New Guinea, where 34·44 inches were registered at the Mission Station in 1875.[2] In Fiji the rainfall appears to vary between 60 and 250 inches per annum, according to the degree of elevation above the sea, and to the position of the station on the lee or weather sides of the islands, the greatest annual falls occuring in the interior of the large islands.[3] In Oahu, one of the Sandwich Islands, during 1873, the rainfall at the coast was 37·85 inches; whilst at a distance of $2\frac{3}{4}$ miles in the interior, it was 134·06 inches, the elevation being only 550 feet above the sea.[4]

I will now make a few remarks on the barometric pressure, temperature, and other features of the meteorology of this group. They are based on the results of the observations made by Lieutenant Leeper on board the ship, and by Mr. F. Howard at Ugi. (Tables appended.)

---

[1] Somerville's "Physical Geography," 7th edit. pp. 331-334.

[2] Stone's "A Few Months in New Guinea," p. 143.

[3] Rain-guagers have been numerous in this colony, and their list would extend beyond the limits of a foot-note. (Vide Horne's "Year in Fiji," &c., &c.)

[4] Mosely's "Naturalist on the 'Challenger,'" p. 497.

As is usual in these regions of the Pacific, the fluctuation of the barometer, whether daily, yearly, or monthly, is very small. Thus, the range during the 22 months we passed in the group, was from 29·83 to 30·18 inches, or about a third of an inch ; whilst the average monthly range was rather under a quarter of an inch, and the usual diurnal variation about ·04 of an inch.

Whilst endeavouring to compare the temperatures of the different seasons, I have mainly used the Ugi register, since it gives a continuous record for more than a year. At Ugi in 1883, the portion of the year from June to September inclusive was slightly the coolest, but the difference in the means was not 2° ; and, in truth, taking all the thermometric observations into consideration, the seasons are scarcely distinguished by their temperatures. As Lieutenant Leeper[1] remarks in his report, the temperature varies but little all the year round, the monthly mean varying between 80° and 85°. The annual mean temperature may be placed at 82° to 83°, and the range from 75° to 95°. The daily variation is considerably affected by the exposed or protected position of any locality at the coast. Judging, however, from the data at my disposal, it is usually less than 10°, e.g., 79° at night, and 88° at mid-day.

From the hygrometrical observations, it may be inferred that the climate of these islands is generally very moist. The *relative humidity*, taking 100 as saturation, ranged at Ugi in 1883 from 54 to 100 ; but the monthly range was usually from 72 to 95, the mean for the year being 83.[2] This mean degree of relative humidity is much greater than that of Levuka in Fiji which would seem to average about 70 ;[3] but in truth there is little necessity for me to remark further on this well-known feature of the climate of these islands. Yet, I should add that this proportion of aqueous vapour would not necessarily be oppressive in a temperate latitude. In a tropical climate, however, any influence that retards the evaporation from the skin of the normally excessive perspiration, is a cause of personal discomfort, such as would not be experienced in a drier

[1] *Vide* Quart. Journ. Roy. Met. Soc. vol. XI., p. 309. The instruments used on board were previously verified at Kew. From want of leisure, Lieut. Leeper was unable to do much more than tabulate his observations. I have therefore extracted from them such general facts and inferences as they sustain.

[2] There are no observations for January, but since the mean relative humidity varies with the rainfall, I have approximately estimated that for January to be 83.

[3] Lieut. Lake's observations for 1876 and 1877. (Quart. Journ. Met. Soc.)

locality lying in the same latitude. The effects of this combination of heat and moisture are to be seen in the rankness of the vegetation, and in the rapid rusting of steel. Although the foregoing remarks may be taken as generally applicable to the group, it should be stated that on the lee side of a mountainous island, such as the western end of Guadalcanar, there is a comparatively dry atmosphere, and the difference is also shown in the character of the vegetation.

The moderate intensity of the sun's rays in these islands is to be ascribed to the presence of aqueous vapour in quantity in the atmosphere. When, however, a thunderstorm and its accompanying rain-squall are portending, the air is unusually dry, and the sun's rays are very fierce. At such times it often happens that the sky is overcast; and thus it comes about that the unwary traveller, by rashly baring his legs and arms, suffers severe sun-burns when he least expects it. Waterton and other travellers have, through ignorance of this fact, been laid up for several days, and even weeks. I was unable to walk any distance for about ten days, after experiencing a severe sun-burn of the legs as the result of baring them during an overcast day. The affection is peculiarly painful, though it often excites but little sympathy.

My remarks on the meteorology of this group will not be complete without a short reference to the prevailing winds. The South-east Trade Wind and the North-west Monsoon carry on a continual struggle for the mastery in these islands. However, for two-thirds of the year the Trade prevails, viz., from April to November. The appended record of winds, which extends over a considerable period, I have prepared from the observations made on board H.M.S. "Lark" in different parts of the group, and from the registers kept by Mr. Sproul and Mr. Howard at Santa Anna and Ugi. It will be there seen that at the eastern extremity of these islands, viz., in the vicinity of St. Christoval, the Trade announces its onset in April by unsettled weather, and frequent thunderstorms. In May, it becomes established, but, as Lieutenant Leeper remarks, it blows in fits and starts, is interrupted by calms, variable winds, and heavy rain-squalls, and does not blow home as in Fiji and the groups to the eastward. At the opposite end of the group, in Bougainville Straits, the Trade appears a month later, and does not become established until June. In this locality, however, it is more fitful than in the eastern islands, blows lighter, and is less to be depended on by the navigator.

It may be generally stated that the north-west and west winds set in about the end of November or the beginning of December, and prevail until the end of March. Although heavy gales accompany the frequent shiftings of the wind, especially when it is from the S.W., these islands are beyond the sweep of the hurricanes which in this season of the year occasionally devastate the groups to the eastward. The period of the westerly winds in the Solomon Islands is also characterised by calms and variable winds. The exhilarating freshness of the Trade then gives place to the enervating influence of the Monsoon ; and, in consequence, the period of westerly winds is the sickly season.

RAIN-REGISTER AT SANTA ANNA.

(Kept by Mr. Charles Sproul [1] between October 25th, 1882, and December 31st, 1883.)

The rain-guage used was of the common round funnel pattern (5·7 inches). The observations were made at Port Mary on the west side of the island. The elevation of the guage was some four or five feet (or less) above the high tide level.

MONTH.	Total in inches and hundredths.	Number of rainy days.[2]	Greatest daily fall.
1882.			
October, 25th—31st..........	3·06	5	1·70
November.	7·60	15	1·97
December.....................	13·96	24	2·24
	Total, 24·62	Total, 44	
1883.			
January.	5·23	12	2·03
February.....................	9·63	20	2·00
March.........................	4·40	13	·84
April..........................	14·96	24	3·22
May...........................	11·28	16	3·33
June.	26·88	19	7·73
July...........................	18·61	23	3·45
August.........................	11·74	15	2·02
September.....................	4·81	12	2·52
October........................	5·68	9	1·67
November.	6·57	11	1·20
December.....................	5·24	8	1·68
	Total, 125·03	Total, 182	

[1] I am indebted to Mr. William Heughan for commencing this register.

[2] By *rainy days* are meant those days on which not less $\frac{1}{100}$ of an inch of rain were measured.

Results for 1883.—*Total rainfall* for 1883 ; 125·03 inches. Two-thirds of the total fall, *i.e.*, 83·47 inches, were recorded during the five months from April to August. *Greatest daily fall,* 7·73 inches. *Total number of rainy days* 182, *i.e.*, one half of the year. On 41 days, more than an inch of rain fell.

RAIN-REGISTER AT UGI.

(Kept by Mr. Fred Howard between October 1st, 1882, and December 31st, 1883.)

The rain-guage used was of the round funnel pattern (about 5¼ inches). The observations were made at the residence of Mr. John Stephens at Selwyn Bay on the west side of the island. The elevation of the guage was from four to six feet above the high-tide level.

MONTH.	Total in inches and hundredths.	Number of rainy days.	Greatest daily fall.	Relative humidity taking 100 as saturation (see table, p. 367)
1882.				
October...............	10·68	18	2·45	
November..........	10·16	16	4·60	
December............	9·57	21	1·36	
	Total, 30·41	55		
1883.				
January...............	13·46	16	5·75	(83)
February.............	13·89	17	4·00	82
March...............	10·02	16	3·00	83
April.................	23·28	26	3·00	88
May.................	6·39	9	1·65	83
June	12·83	12	3·70	84
July.................	24·60	25	2·85	89
August...............	15·76	15	4·75	83
September..........	7·36	14	1·50	81
October.............	5·15	7	1·75	76
November..........	5·30	11	1·10	79
December............	8·20	10	1·30	83
	Total, 146·24	178	.	

Results.—During the last quarter of 1882, the rainfall was 30·41 inches ; and the number of rainy days was 55.

During 1883, the *total rainfall* was 146·24 inches. The greatest monthly records were those of April and July : during these two months 47·88 inches fell, or about one-third of the total fall for the year. The *greatest daily fall* was 5·75 inches. The *total number of rainy days* was 178, or about one half of the number of days in the year. On 56 days more than an inch of rain fell ; and in 18 days more than two inches fell.

RAIN-REGISTER KEPT ON BOARD H.M.S. "LARK."

(I am indebted to Lieutenant Leeper for assistance in keeping this register.)

The rain-guage was raised about eleven feet above the water-level. I did not commence these observations until towards the close of the first season; and since, during the two following years, we spent about two-thirds of each year in this region, the record is, in consequence, not continuous.

(A) OFF THE NORTH COAST OF ST. CHRISTOVAL AND THE NEIGHBOURING ISLANDS IN 1882.

1882.	Total in inches and hundredths.	Number of rainy days.	Greatest daily' fall.
Sept. (from the 9th),	18·40	15	3·32
October,	10·84	21	2·38
Nov. (to the 21st),	18·31	12	5·74
Total,	47·55	48	

Results.—Total Rainfall for this interval of 74 days from Sept. 9th to Nov. 21st, 1882, was 47·55 inches. The *greatest daily fall* was 5·74 inches. The *number of rainy days* was 48, or about two-thirds of the whole. On 17 days, more than an inch of rain fell; and on 8 days, more than two inches fell.

(B) OFF THE NORTH COAST OF ST. CHRISTOVAL AND THE NEIGHBOURING ISLANDS IN 1883.

1883.	Total in inches and hundredths.	Number of rainy days.	Greatest daily fall.
April 13th—30th,	10·43	15	1·62

(C) BOUGAINVILLE STRAITS IN 1883.

1883.	Total in inches and hundredths.	Number of rainy days.	Greatest daily fall.
June,	16·32	26	2·23
July,	10·25	24	2·12
August,	7·78	23	1·10
September,	15·07	22	2·20
October,	11·01	25	2·10
Total,	60·43	120	

Results.—During these 153 days, there fell 60·43 inches of rain. The greatest fall in one day was 2·23 inches. The total number of rainy days was 120, or about four-fifths of the whole. On 14 days, more than an inch of rain fell; and on 7 days, more than two inches fell.

(D) BOUGAINVILLE STRAITS IN 1884.

1884.	Total in inches and hundredths.	Number of rainy days.	Greatest daily fall.
April (from the 8th),	7·82	12	4·32
May,	4·02	17	1·02
June,	9·22	22	1·58
July,	18·16	19	8·09
August,	11·87	21	2·58
September,	17·46	23	3·76
October,	10·95	23	1·84
Total,	79·50	137	

Results.—During these 207 days, there fell 79·50 inches of rain. The greatest daily fall was 8·09 inches. The total number of rainy days was 137, or about two-thirds of the whole. On 24 days, more than an inch of rain fell; and on 7 days, more than two inches fell.

OBSERVATIONS[1] OF THE BAROMETER AND THERMOMETER IN
THE SOLOMON GROUP, BY LIEUT. LEEPER, R.N.

(Taken on board H.M.S. "Lark.")

MONTH.	THERMOMETER.			BAROMETER.		
	Highest.	Lowest,	Daily Mean.	Highest.	Lowest.	Daily Mean.
1882.	o	o	o	In.	In.	In.
April, ...	94	74	84·4	30·09	29·88	30·041
May, ...	94	78	84·5	30·09	29·89	29·994
June, ...	92	77	83·7	30·18	29·86	30·013
July, ...	90	75	81·8	30·14	29·92	30·05
August, ...	94	75	81·1	30·16	29·96	30·067
September, ...	92	76	80·9	30·14	29·93	30·041
October, ...	89	77	81·4	30·18	29·88	30·021
Nov. 1st to 22d, ...	88	78	81·5	30·13	29·84	29·981
1883.						
April 14th to 30th,	92	75	82.1	30·08	29·86	29·974
May, ...	...	...	...	...	29·91	29·99
June, ...	93	78	81·8	30·08	29·91	29·99
July, ...	94	75	82·3	30·12	29·88	29·96
August, ...·...	92	78	83·5	30·08	29·92	29·992
September, ...	95	76	82·6	30·10	29·91	29·992
October, ...	95	75	83·3	30·12	29·86	29·993
Nov. 1st to 12th,	90	76	81·5	30·08	29·91	29·982
1884.						
April 5th to 30th,	90	76	82·2	30·15	29·83	29·984
May, ...	95	78	84·5	30·13	29·86	29·992
June, ...	94	77	82·2	30·14	29·93	30·023
July, ...	87	76	81·5	30·10	29·87	29·985
August, ...	87	76	81·0	30·15	29·85	30·009
September, ...	90	75	82·3	30·15	29·92 .	30·025
October, ...	96	75	81·1	30·12	29·85	30·007

[1] The observations were taken at 4 a.m., 8 a.m., 4 p.m., and 8 p.m.

Results calculated from observations of the temperature in the shade, and of the wet and dry bulb thermometers taken at Ugi at 9 a.m., by Mr. F. Howard.[1]

THERMOMETER IN SHADE.				HYGROMETER.[2]				
MONTH.	Highest.	Lowest.	Mean.	Mean Dry Bulb.	Mean Wet Bulb.	Mean Dew Point.	Mean Elastic Force of Aqueous Vapour.	Mean Relative Humidity, Saturation 100.
1882.								
October.....	87	76	81·7	...	...	...	...	...
November..	84	78	80·5	...	..	...	..	...
December..	84	80	81·4	...	...	...	...	...
1883.								
January....	86	79	82·0	...	...	...	...	...
February...	85	79	81·5	81·6	78·0	75·6	·885	82
March.......	86	78	81·8	81·7	78·3	76·0	·898	83
April........	83	76	80·0	80·1	77·8	76·2	·904	88
May........	85	78	81·6	81·6	78·2	75·9	·895	83
June........	84	77	80·6	80·6	77·5	75·4	·880	84
July........	83	77	80·2	80·2	78·0	76·4	·912	89
August......	84	77	80·3	80·3	76·9	74·6	·857	83
September .	84	77	80·9	80·9	76·9	74·2	·846	81
October.....	85	76	82·0	82·0	77·0	73·6	·830	76
November..	86	77	82·0	82·0	77·8	74·9	·867	79
December..	84	79	81·3	81·4	78·0	75·7	·891	83

81·2—Mean for 1883.

WIND-RECORD FOR EACH MONTH.

Prepared from the observations taken on board H.M.S. "Lark," and by Messrs. Sproul and Howard, at Santa Anna and Ugi.

January.

1883. At Ugi, S.W. to W. in first half; variable in latter half; S.E. 1 day. At Santa Anna, N.W. and W.; S.E. 5 days; occasional squalls.

February.

1883. At Ugi and Santa Anna, N.W. to S.W.; no S.E.; latter part, fresh winds and squalls

March.

1883. At Ugi and Santa Anna, N.W. to W. in first half, with strong winds and thunderstorms; latter part variable; S.E. 4 days at Ugi, none at Santa Anna.

[1] The instruments were supplied by me. The Thermometer was by Negretti and Zambra: and the wet and dry bulbs were good reliable instruments. They were a'l first compared with the ship's instruments, which were supplied by the Meteorological Office after being verified at Kew.

[2] Calculated from Glaisher's Tables.

April.

1882. Amongst the eastern islands (east of Florida) ; first part, calms and light northerly winds; latter part, calms and light S.E. winds; thunderstorms frequent.

1883. At Ugi and Santa Anna, first part, N.W. and S.E. ; latter part, calms and E. to S.E. ; S.E. for 7 days at Ugi; heavy rain ; squalls in middle of month.

1884. In Bougainville Straits, light northerly and westerly winds, with calms ; easterly during the last few days.

May.

1882. Between Bougainville Straits and west end of Guadalcanar, numerous calms and light winds from N.W. through S. to S.E. ; thunderstorms frequent.

1883 At Ugi and Santa Anna, E. to S.E. ; usually strong.

1884 In Bougainville Straits, light N.E. and easterly winds, with a great deal of calm weather.

June.

1882. At the north coast of St. Christoval, Ugi, and Santa Anna ; calms, N.N.E. and easterly winds ; average force 2.

1883. At Ugi and Santa Anna. S.E. often strong, with variable winds. In Bougainville Straits; first part light E. and S.E. winds; latter part, S.E. ; very squally ; frequent thunderstorms.

1884. In Bougainville Straits ; first half, light E. and E.S.E. winds ; latter half, light S.E. and S.S.E.

July.

1882. At the north coast of St. Christoval and Ugi, first part S.E., with frequent heavy squalls ; latter part, light S.E. and S.W. winds, though squally.

1883. At Ugi and Santa Anna, E.S.E. to S.E. ; fresh and squally, sometimes blowing hard, interrupted by calms and varying winds. In Bougainville Straits, light varying winds from N.E. to S.E.

1884. In Bougainville Straits, first part light S.E. winds and calms ; latter part fresh easterly winds and bad weather.

August.

1882. At the north coast of St. Christoval and Ugi, E.N.E. to S. ; average force, 3 to 4 ; frequent rain-squalls.

1883. At Ugi and Santa Anna, S.E. strong ; in latter part heavy squalls, interrupted by calms. In Bougainville Straits, E.N.E. to S.E. ; force 2 to 3.

1884. In Bougainville Straits, S.S.E. to S. ; thick weather with rain-squalls in first part.

September.

1882. At Ugi and the Three Sisters, S.E. and S.S.E. ; in latter part of month heavy, and accompanied by thick weather and violent squalls.

1883. At Ugi and Santa Anna, E.S.E. to S.E. strong.
In Bougainville Straits, calms, and light E. to S.E. winds.
1884. In Bougainville Straits, first part light S.E. winds and heavy rain-
squalls from N.E. ; latter part fresh S.S.E. and dirty weather,
followed by light N. to E. winds.

October.

1882. At Ugi, Santa Anna, and off the north coast of Guadalcanar; in first
part, strong S.E. ; in latter part, easterly winds with calms.
At Ugi, S.E. in first half, variable with calms in latter half.
1883. At Ugi and Santa Anna, S.E., fresh.
In Bougainville Straits, first part S.E. to S. ; latter part N.E. to
S.E., squalls and thunderstorms.
1884. In Bougainville Straits; first week, light N.E. to S.E. winds ; second
week, S.S.E. to S., force 2 to 4 ; third week, N.W. to N.N.E., force
3 to 8, rain-squalls and thunderstorms; last part, variable and
E.S.E. winds.

November.

1882. At Ugi and Santa Anna; first half, N.W. and S.E. ; latter half, S.E.
and variable.
1883. At Ugi and Santa Anna, fresh E.S.E. to S.E; northerly towards end
of month with squalls and thunderstorms.

December.

1882. At Ugi and Santa Anna, westerly and variable; S.E. for 6 days:
latter part, squally.
1883. At Ugi and Santa Anna; in first half, E. to S.E.; in latter half,
N.W. to S.W. and squally.

THE EFFECTS OF THE CLIMATE ON THE WEIGHT
OF THE BODY.

During the last two surveying-seasons in these islands, the officers and
crew were weighed with the object of determining the effect of service in
this climate on the body-weight. The period spent in this region during
each year extended from April to November.

After eliminating various sources of error, such as sickness, immaturity,
etc., I find that during the surveying-season of 1883, which occupied between 6½ and 7 months, eighteen out of twenty persons lost weight, the
average loss being 6¾ lbs., and the range of the loss 1 to 12 lbs. Of the
two exceptions, one gained 3 lbs. and the other experienced no change. On
returning to the colonies, we spent between 3 and 4 months in the genial
climate of northern New Zealand, at the end of which period I find that
the average gain of weight was about 6½ lbs. In other words, the loss was
regained.

During the season of 1884, which lasted 7 months, eleven out of the
twenty persons weighed in the previous year were alone available for these
observations. All of them lost weight, the average loss being 5¾ lbs., and
the range 1 to 8 lbs. This diminution in the average loss of weight dur-

ing this season should be noted. . . . . I should add that five individuals, who had not been on board in the previous year, lost during this season on the average 5 lbs. per man.

I may therefore conclude that the effect of seven months' service in this region on the body-weight is, on the average, a loss of from 6 to 7 lbs. Although this loss of weight is mainly attributable to the climate, it is evident that the character of the diet has an important influence in the matter. For the greater part of the time spent in these islands, the crew were on preserved and salt rations, a diet which reduces the weight of the body. One of the results of an elaborate series of observations made by Dr. A. Rattray of H.M.S. "Salamander," whilst serving in the Western Pacific from 1864-67, was to show that salt diet in a tropical climate is an important factor in reducing weight, and that other influences, such as that of hard work, increase the loss. During various cruises in the tropics, usually lasting about three months, he weighed between 70 and 100 men with the following results. The effect of a tropical climate alone was to reduce the weight of 64 per cent., the average loss being 5 lbs. When the unfavourable conditions of a wet season and salt diet were added, 76 per cent. lost weight, the average loss being 7 lbs. By the further addition of hard work, 91 per cent. lost weight, the average loss being about the same. The loss of weight after each cruise was regained in 7 or 8 weeks during the stay in Sydney.[1]

[1] Proc. Roy. Soc., vol. XIX., p. 295 (1870-71). In this paper Dr. Rattray treats at length of the effects of a tropical climate on the various organs and functions of the body.

GENERAL INDEX.

A.

B.

C.

D.

E.

F.

G.

K.

L.

M.

N.

O.

P.

Q.

R.

S.

T.

Y

Z

THE END.

S. Cowan & Co., Strathmore Printing Works, Perth.

www.ingramcontent.com/pod-product-compliance
Lightning Source LLC
Chambersburg PA
CBHW030811110726
47900CB00006B/1592